AUSTRALIA'S NATIONAL PARKS

AUSTRALIA'S NATIONAL PARKS

M. K. MORCOMBE

With a foreword by
John Gorton, PRIME MINISTER OF AUSTRALIA

Introduction by Osmar White

LANSDOWNE

LANSDOWNE PRESS PTY LTD
346 St Kilda Road, Melbourne 3004

First published 1969
© Michael Morcombe 1969

Library of Congress Catalog Card Number 72-79356
SBN 70180050 X

Jacket
Front
Cradle Mountain and picturesque Lake Dove, Tasmania
Back
Ormiston Gorge

Frontispiece
Ormiston Gorge
Over
Across the continent much superb scenery, like this in
Windjana Gorge, has yet to receive national park
protection; preservation is justified by tourist potential
alone

Designed by Derrick I. Stone

Type set by Dudley E. King, Linotypers, Melbourne 3000.   Printed and bound by Lee Fung, Hong Kong

"AUSTRALIA'S NATIONAL PARKS"

Foreword by the Prime Minister

This book outlines the great natural wealth of the Australian continent in landscape and in flora and fauna.

This wealth is part of our heritage. It belongs to the Australian people and it is a source of wonder and interest to all who visit us. We must protect it for future generations, for it is a legacy man cannot replace and must not destroy.

"Australia's National Parks" makes a valuable contribution to conservation, to the efforts of our conservationists and to the sum of our knowledge of the unique features of our environment. It will help towards a greater understanding and enjoyment of the land in which we are privileged to live.

JOHN GORTON

14 July 1969

CONTENTS

Beyond the delicate tracery of a mallee thicket rise the fascinating blue domes of the Stirling Range

INTRODUCTION

It seems to me that God made this region for all the people and all the world to see and enjoy forever. It is impossible that any individual should think that he can own any of this country for his own in fee. This great wilderness does not belong to us. It belongs to the nation. Let us make a public park of it and set it aside . . . never to be changed but to be kept sacred always.

These words were used by Cornelius Hedges, the great American conservationist, in a plea to Congress for legislation to reserve Yellowstone National Park, Wyoming, in its natural state for the inspiration, education and recreation of present and future generations. They were written in 1872, almost 100 years ago. In their broadest connotation they have become a prime article in the creed of conservationists all over the world.

The swarming family of man has made a great and permanent change on the face of the earth since it emerged as the dominant species in the animal kingdom about 40,000 years ago. To preserve that dominance and increase it, men have demolished mountains, linked oceans, turned rivers from their courses, felled forests for crop lands and pastures, made deserts bloom—and created vast wastelands where there was once abundance. In no part of the planet where man proliferates has the old order of nature remained unaltered.

The speed at which alteration is being made seems constantly to accelerate. Human ingenuity in manipulating physical forces is creating a new terrestrial environment and every new technique of manipulation is described as progress. But is the definition really true? How does one distinguish between the changes which increase the stature and security of humanity and those which diminish them?

The scientific conservationist gives an unequivocal answer: It is possible to determine the direction of change only by preserving points of reference. If parts of the natural earth are set aside and as far as possible protected from human interference, then man-made change can be measured and evaluated with accuracy, and progress can be distinguished from retrogression.

This book records the visible realities of Australian wildernesses which have been set aside with this basic idea in mind. Michael Morcombe's photographs portray with accuracy and sensitivity the unique character of regions of the Australian continent which have remained relatively unaffected by the works of men. They embrace not only the salient topography and climatic spectrum, but also a wide and representative range of the remarkable plants, animals and birds which have evolved and survive naturally only in the Australian environment. In a sense they are a composite likeness of primitive Australia itself—a land of great beauty, terrifying austerity, and dramatically violent moods.

No one could look at these pictures and doubt that the nation possesses assets of incalculable value in its great nature reserves or remain indifferent to the plea, implicit in such a record, that the pride of Australians in such an inheritance should assure their perpetual protection.

The desirability of reserving land for public pleasure and recreation was recognised by colonial Governments in the middle of the 19th century. The first laws to protect scenic areas were passed in Tasmania as early as 1863. In 1872 King's Park, Perth—today one of the most beautiful and skilfully managed areas of native bush in the Commonwealth—was dedicated for public use under amended Crown Land regulations. In 1879, New South Wales established Royal National Park at Port Hacking, south of Sydney. South Australia reserved Belair in the Mount Lofty Ranges in 1891. Victoria declared Wilson's Promontory a sanctuary in 1896.

Over the years the amount of land reserved or resumed for protection against forms of economic exploitation likely to change its character has grown to about 25 million acres in six States and Federal territories. This may seem an impressive total, but it is only a little more than 1·5 per cent of the

4

continental area and it includes millions of acres of desert in which plant and animal communities are sparse and the landscape and climate forbidding. In only two States, New South Wales and Tasmania, and in the Northern Territory, does the land reserved as park amount to more than one per cent of the whole area. In South Australia the figure is only 0·3 per cent and in Queensland and Western Australia it is only 0·5 per cent.

Government spending on management and active protection of the reserves is equally modest. Per capita expenditure on national parks and reserves in Victoria is only 14 cents a year. Other State figures are: Queensland 17 cents, N.S.W. 23 cents, Tasmania 37 cents, South Australia 28 cents, and Western Australia 29 cents. However, in the very sparsely settled Northern Territory, the annual expenditure is $6.71 a head—a reflection, one feels, less of an enlightened attitude on the part of the Commonwealth Government than of the fact that the States no longer exercise effective taxing powers.

Only in recent years have Australian legislators accepted the idea that conservation of national parklands involves more than the preservation of scenically attractive areas for public recreation. There is now a general, if somewhat diffuse, recognition that down-to-earth economic advantages can accrue from systematic protection of fauna and flora. Apart from the ever-growing revenues derived from tourism, the ecologist is assuming his rightful place in national planning and his science is aided by the protection of his 'controls'. This is particularly true in Australia, where the balance of nature is often delicate. Enormous areas of land, the productivity of which could have been increased had it been scientifically managed, have been ruined, probably beyond reclamation, by the ignorance or indifference of pastoralists. Nature reserves accessible to the public are of great value in creating a climate of public opinion—and, therefore, a political force—opposed to such reckless destruction of national assets for the profit of a few.

A growing awareness of the wisdom of both general and selective conservation has been reflected in the amendments to the old Crown Lands Acts and in new laws brought down in both State and Federal Parliaments during the last two or three decades. Unfortunately, however, national consistency has not been achieved. A general principle has been acknowledged, but precise objectives have neither been perceived nor defined by the legislators. The stated purpose of declaring reserves varies widely between State and State—from vague generalization indicating that the aim is to maintain natural environment for public recreation, education and enjoyment to the enumeration of such specifics as the prevention of soil erosion and preservation of catchment areas.

New South Wales, Tasmania and the Northern Territory provide for the protection of sites of historic interest. Queensland and Victoria give priority to maintenance of natural conditions. Uniformity has not been achieved even in the definition of what constitutes a national park. In some categories of reserve, limited economic exploitation is permitted; selective logging in forests or seasonal grazing. In others, scheduled as 'primitive areas', there is a blanket prohibition on the introduction of exotic species.

In all probability complete uniformity in regulations covering all types of reserve is neither practicable nor desirable. But what is practicable and desirable is nation-wide legislation which puts the permanence of public ownership beyond all doubt, and the compilation of lists of priorities in work to be done and funds to be expended for the protection of this public property.

Some progress has been made towards achieving secure tenure. In Victoria, New South Wales and South Australia, a national park can be declared or revoked only by Act of Parliament. This at least assures that when sectional interests advocate other forms of land use the merits of their case are publicly debated and that the weight of informed public opinion has due influence on legislative action.

The machinery of national park administration also varies in design and efficiency between State and State. Executive control of the nation's most important nature reserves is vested in no fewer than 16

separate agencies. Seven of these are part-time bodies, membership of which often includes a majority of
public servants representing departments with a vested interest in promoting other forms of land use.
Only in New South Wales is control and management rationally centralized in a full scale department
headed by the Director of National Parks and Wild Life. Park trusts still exist and do useful work, but
they are subservient to departmental policy. No formal system of professional training for the service
has yet been established.

In other parts of Australia park management is the province of officers detailed for the work by
Government agencies with loosely related interests, such as primary industry, fisheries and forestry.
Often supervision and enforcement of regulations is desultory and heavily dependent on the co-operation
of the overburdened police force or on the enthusiasm of honorary rangers.

A fair summation of the situation is that Australian governments have embraced a principle but as yet
have fallen far short of practising it with vigour and efficiency.

Nevertheless established parks and reserves are fairly representative of the continental topography and
ecology although there are still important gaps to be filled, particularly in northern and north-western
Australia. The scenic spectrum is excitingly wide.

Holidaymakers in the dreaming green valleys of Tasmania where oaks, elms and poplars have been
harmoniously established in the landscape for more than a century are often heard to exclaim, 'How
English!' American tourists, making a fast coach tour through the grim but colourful flat lands flanking
the Flinders Ranges declare to goodness that they could well be in New Mexico or Arizona. Indian
businessmen flying from Sydney to Broken Hill are reminded of the plains of the Deccan. Indonesian
Colombo Plan students see in the sugarlands south of Cairns a startling likeness to the plains of West Java.
Much of the Pilbara Plateau in north-western Australia is nostalgic country for South Africans who have
made a safari on the fringes of the Kalahari. Oil drillers sweating it out between the sand ridges of the
Gibson desert comment sourly that they might just as well be in the Rub' al Khali of Saudi Arabia.

But these judgements are superficial. They are based on first impressions rather than genuine
observation. The remarkable thing about Australia is that, for all its diversity in climate, terrain and
coloration, the differences between its parts are always outweighed by the similarities. The sombre,
sun-scorched Pilliga Scrub of New South Wales, the stony rises of the King Leopold Ranges in the
Kimberley country, the heathlands of the Australian Alps, the rocky islands studding the Great Barrier
Reef, the jungles of Cape York Peninsula are all unmistakably part of the same land mass.

The unique entity of Australia is due to the geological antiquity of its soils and to its long separation
from other continents. Its fauna and flora have evolved in isolation and in some cases are a continuum into
the present of forms of life which were established on earth before the first coal measures were laid down
300 million years ago. An overriding aim of national parks policy must surely be to insure that these species
are not exterminated by gross human interference with their habitat and to devise ways of making them
accessible for both scientific study and aesthetic enjoyment.

Yet in practice it is extremely difficult to achieve compatibility between complete protection and ready
accessibility. A classical and tragic instance of failure to do so is the condition of the great Blue Mountains
National Park in New South Wales. Disastrous bushfires, attributable in almost all instances to human
agencies, and soil erosion caused by uncontrolled grazing and of badly routed, unsightly walking tracks,
have reduced magnificent forest and heathlands to stunted caricatures of what they originally were.
Mountain streams have dried up and become mere muddy, watercourses whose headwaters drain the
sprawling settlements of holiday shacks and boarding houses which split the great reserve in half. A
colourful bird population has been diminished beyond belief. Marsupial animals which once abounded

6

both on the tops and in the deep gorges are now rarely seen. The breathtaking sandstone precipices and the weathered rock towers are still there, but they frown on a scene of muted desolation. There is probably no more admonitory example in all Australia of how quickly a great national asset can be whittled away by a combination of ignorance and the greed of 'developers' who, in the vernacular, know how to make a quick quid out of Nature.

On the other side of the ledger, the Kosciusko State Park—with the exception of the areas near the lamentably hideous winter sports settlements which are inoffensive only when veiled by snow—is a heartening example of what scientific management can achieve to regenerate land mutilated by misuse as well as preserve that which has escaped depredation. That part of the 1,322,000 acre reserve which was for many years administered by the Snowy Mountains Hydro Electric Authority is proof that strict conservation, ready accessibility and high utilization are not inimical, provided money and know-how are available. Tens of thousands of sightseers use the reserve every year without appreciably damaging it. Their enjoyment is not lessened by the controls imposed on them.

Another instance of intelligent regeneration and effective conservation—this time without the backing of formidable technical and financial resources—is to be found in the comparatively small Warrumbungles National Park in north-western New South Wales. Here about 22,000 acres of reserve, all reclaimed from pastoral misuse, encompass the spectacular remains of Tertiary volcanoes and one of the most fascinating aggregations of plant species in the Commonwealth. The soil and climate of the region are so harsh and variable that the survival of any community of plants and animals is a matter of knife-edge balance, yet naturalists have listed 122 kinds of native birds and any walker can observe specimens of snow-gums, pygmy palms, rainforest figs, ancient Xanthorrea grass-trees, orchids, alpine heaths and a dozen varieties of eucalypts and acacias within an hour of setting out from the base camp on Wombelong Creek. A rough but passable road gives access to the heart of the park and walking tracks, skilfully engineered to minimize both erosion and defacement of the landscape, make it possible for anyone in reasonable physical condition to enjoy the weird botanical cocktail as well as some of the State's most spectacular mountain scenery.

Perhaps it is fortunate that a high proportion of Australia's great national parks are still somewhat difficult to reach. Most are accessible by motor car from nearby centres of population, but many are far distant from the cities. People who feel that they can afford the time, money and energy to visit, let us say, the Murchison Gorge or the Stirlings and Porongorups in the far west, the Geikie Gorge in the West Kimberleys, the Carnarvons of central Queensland or the Windsor Tablelands north of Cairns are genuine nature lovers. They do not resent the discomforts of what some conservationists rather floridly describe as 'the wilderness experience'—and their behaviour creates few problems. But the security afforded by this accidentally selective usage cannot be expected to last. The tourist industry in Australia is growing rapidly. By the mid 1970s half a million holidaymakers from America, Asia and Europe will be coming into the country every year. Domestic tourism is growing even more rapidly. Affluence has made Australians the most air-minded people in the world and four out of five families own their own motor-car and use it for long journeys. It is no longer a hazardous adventure to cross the continent from east to west or north to south—or drive around it on a network of peripheral highways. Every beauty spot illustrated in this book can be reached by ordinarily enterprising travellers with time to spare. As road and air transport is still further improved, traffic to and from the more remote reserves will increase vastly and heavy pressure will be brought to bear on the controlling authorities to establish or increase accommodation in or near the parks and 'open them up' with vehicular and walking tracks.

Since the nature areas are public property it is entirely reasonable that the public should be given the

8

opportunity to enjoy them—provided the qualities and conditions which make them attractive in the first place are not destroyed by ignorance of the techniques of conservation or by rapacious commercialism which all too often exercises powerful political influence. The failure of the Queensland Government to prevent the destruction of some of the finest coral gardens in the world by sewage effluent from tawdry tourist hotels on the islands of the Great Barrier Reef—and the decimation of the reef's mollusc population by unregulated shell collectors—is a national tragedy the magnitude of which is still unrealised. The boarding-house barons have already done as much damage as the oil oligarchs threatened to do until public outcry resulted in a Commonwealth Government promise not to grant drilling permits in reef waters.

If moral and aesthetic arguments advanced by conservationists fail to convince legislators that the protection and expansion of national parks and reserves are good business for the nation, then a little simple accountancy may do so.

The money spent by tourists in the Northern Territory every winter, to marvel at the flaming beauty of Ayers Rock at sunset, the harsh grandeur of the MacDonnell peaks, the galaxies of flowers which cover the desert after rain, the green jungles of the Top End, the crimson canyons of Katherine Gorge, now exceeds the value of production from all other industries in the region—including mining and beef-cattle raising.

The scenery and the quaint and beautiful creatures recorded by Michael Morcombe's cameras could be money-makers for the nation—and big money-makers—long after Kambalda's nickel ore has been worked out and Mount Tom Price has been exported to Japan. Whether or not the promise is realised will depend on the zeal and vigilance of ordinary Australians in protecting from spoilers the assets of the great concern in which they *all* own shares.

OSMAR WHITE
1969

PREFACE

The national parks are more than scenic beauty. They are an escape from the cities' concrete jungles, they are national recreation areas and valuable tourist attractions—yet they are even more than this. National parks preserve, intact, segments of the natural environment. The land as it was when the first pioneers fought inland, the coasts and the deserts as they were when first discovered, and the wildlife as it was before the coming of European Man.

The national parks aim to preserve land, plant and animal life in the balanced relationship which has been established over thousands of years of slow evolution. A delicate balance, between prey and predator, between resources and populations.

This natural world is one from which mankind has a great deal yet to learn, for his own population is out of control, destroying vital natural resources at an unprecedented rate, and upsetting the ancient balance of nature on a massive scale. No-one knows what the ultimate consequence will be, but some predictions can be made, perhaps solutions found, by scientific study of the ecology of the natural world, or what remains of it.

It is not only a matter of protecting the remnants of nature from mankind, but of enabling man to continue to use and benefit without exhausting all of nature's resources; of saving something of the raw materials of science, for the future.

Far from being useless bush, valued only by sentimental naturalists, national parks and wildlife sanctuaries are vital outdoor laboratories for experiments that can be performed in no other place. A great deal of study is carried out in the open air and in direct contact with nature; the results are practical benefits. But as the wild and undamaged places of the earth become more and more exploited for commercial purposes, facilities for this kind of research become less and less.

Tomorrow, our need will be greater; by the end of the century such wilderness that remains undamaged will be priceless. Yet the foresight of Australian politicians is such that less than one

IO   *Whisky Bay, Wilson's Promontory, where a smooth sweep of beach is enclosed between piles of tumbled boulders*

Stormy seas surge against the cliffs of a coastal scenic reserve near Eaglehawk Neck, Tasman Peninsula

per cent of this continent is reserved in national parks and wildlife sanctuaries! Five per cent is regarded as an absolute minimum; ten per cent is most desirable as the portion of the continent to set aside as national parks and wildlife sanctuaries.

Although 'a national park is a place where people may reflect, study and enjoy the benefits of the earth', it is vital that the pressure of human visitors does not destroy the wilderness and wildlife which are the essential qualities of national parks. This is a dilemma of national park management: to provide for visitors, tourists, by the thousand, yet to prevent the gradual degradation of the park's land, fauna and flora. People, wandering unrestricted, may in time destroy the very things that they would come to see. Here is a conflict in national park purpose and use: whether they are to serve as holiday playgrounds, or give inspiration and instruction to those who would like to wander more deeply into the bushland wilderness, or be reserved for scientists who, for the benefit of mankind, seek to interpret the secrets of nature.

Year by year, at a rapidly accelerating rate, Australia's scenic treasures are being destroyed until we shall be able to leave to our children a legacy of million-dollar roads going only to places as congested or as unattractive as those they left behind.

Tremendous damage has been done by men who gave no thought to the long-term effect of the heedless cutting of the forests, the over-stocking of the arid interior, or the senseless killing of unique birds and marsupials.

In 1950 the Tasmanian Government sold, to a paper-pulp company, a great tract of lofty Mountain Ash trees in the Mt Field National Park, altering by act of parliament the park boundaries to make the 'vandalism' legal. In this national park, these magnificent trees were the property of all Australians, held in trust by that Government.

Today, the wood chip, paper pulp business looms as an unprecedented threat to Australian forests. Proposals are to take every tree in some areas, every standing sapling, no matter how small or stunted, reduce all to chips, and sell to Japan. This will bare vast tracts in New South Wales, Tasmania, Western Australia and the Northern Territory, including areas where re-growth will be very slow. The damage will probably be permanent, bringing this semi-arid continent a step closer to becoming total desert almost out to its coastal fringes. The chip-wood price is so low that Australians will not benefit, except those few who are directly responsible for this devastation.

But as the pioneering struggle to conquer the land draws to a close, and the city-dwelling majority of the population becomes restless for its share of the outdoors, the outback, the bush, there seems to be growing among new-generation Australians an increasing awareness of the need to preserve some of the land and the wildlife; an immense tourist potential is now recognized.

In recent years more land has been dedicated to national parks than ever before. But Australia's national parks remain pitifully small compared with the great parks of Africa, the United States and the U.S.S.R.

The late Professor Alan Marshall suggested the way that must be taken:

'The key to the survival of wild animals and plants is the preservation of their habitats. This undeniable fact cannot be stressed too thoroughly. Lyrebird, Koala, Mallee-fowl, Platypus and Pademelon—these will continue to live only if large tracts of the sort of country in which they evolved, and to which they are irrevocably adapted, are set aside for their use.'

In many instances, it is already too late. The next few years will see the destruction of habitat and of fauna accelerate, and unless urgent steps are taken soon Australia could find that it has lost its heritage for all time.

MICHAEL MORCOMBE
JUNE, 1969

NATIONAL PARK REGIONS

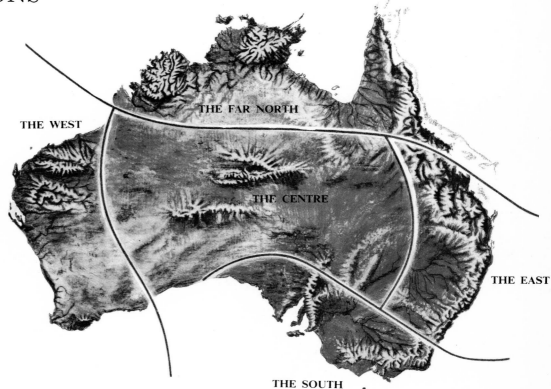

THE WEST

THE FAR NORTH

THE CENTRE

THE EAST

THE SOUTH

Australia's national parks constitute a wonderland that is scattered far and wide across a vast, largely desolate continent. On the eastern coast are many of the best-known parks—Royal National and Ku-ring-gai Chase near Sydney, the Blue Mountains National Park, Lamington south of Brisbane. Most are on the Great Divide, or not far inland. Their densely forested green ranges hide a great number and variety of birds, and unique marsupials. Almost any of the eastern national parks can be reached and explored within the two or three weeks annual holidays available to a Sydney, Brisbane or Melbourne family.

Totally different are the national parks of central Australia. This is well known as a region of immense tourist potential; its scenic attractions are mostly within a day's drive of 'the Alice'. It is an area whose national parks can be visited, if not fully explored, during the week or two that most visitors can stay. The centre is a tremendous contrast to the soft green landscapes of the east coast. Barren, red-rock gorges, harsh spinifex and stunted mulga scrub replace the blue-green valleys, the dim forests and silvery cascades of eastern parks. The centre's national parks are red earth masked by wide drifts of papery ever-lastings; red sandhills and stony ranges, and gorge walls which rise in unbelievable colour against skies of deep pure azure blue.

Australia's far-northern national parks are scattered from the Kimberleys to the Barrier Reef; most are in tropical Queensland, clustered along a relatively short stretch of coast from Mackay north to Cooktown. Almost every island along Queensland's northern coast, and the coral cays of the reef are national parks, and portions of the coastal tropical rainforests—the damp, gloomy world of the jungle, home of some fantastic birds, and marsupials closely related to those of nearby New Guinea.

Westwards, still in the tropical north, is famed Katherine Gorge National Park, which despite its distance from the southern cities attracts some forty thousand visitors each year. Further west again, in tropical Western Australia, are national parks with river gorges equally attractive but entirely different—Geikie Gorge, and Windjana's deep gash through an ancient coral reef.

From the tropics we move southwards to the western parks. First the iron-red ranges and gorges of the Hamersleys, the chasms of Cape Range, then down to the wildflower-studded plains of Kalbarri, and Yanchep near Perth. In Western Australia's extreme south-western corner are national parks which preserve the soaring giants of the Karri forest, the jagged, wildflower-covered peaks of the Stirling Range, the granite headlands and the cliffs of the Albany coast.

Finally, Australia's southern parks. The huge Kosciusko National Park, with the continent's highest mountains; the superb scenery of Tasmania's Cradle Mountain—Lake St. Clair National Park; South Australia's Wilpena Pound with cliffs of purple-blue, magenta and red in the distance. In the south are parks as remote as Frenchman's Cap and Lake Pedder, or as welcoming as the sweeping beaches of Victoria's popular Wilson's Promontory National Park.

13

The ringing, whip-crack calls of Eastern Whipbirds sound often through the rainforests of east coast national parks

Only in the wild bush of our largest national parks will such creatures as the marsupial 'cat' (Dasyurinus) survive the onslaught of civilization

Part One: THE EAST COAST

Most of the eastern national parks are on the high plateaus, mountainous ridges, precipitous slopes or gorge-like valleys of the Great Dividing Range, or on ranges which branch towards the coast as high spurs from the main line of the Great Divide. There are very few parks on the western plains of New South Wales or southern Queensland—among these few are the Warrumbungles and Mount Kaputar, both of volcanic origin. But almost universally, the dominant theme of the east-coastal national parks is of blue-green mountain ranges, and luxuriant forests; the rich wilderness within these parks shelters a tremendous variety of bird and marsupial wildlife.

Almost all these national parks are easily accessible, and few would be more than a day's drive from either Sydney or Brisbane.

Christmas Bells push up from the damp heathlands and
swamps of Ku-ring-gai Chase and northwards,
Gibraltar Range National Park
Right
Beyond a banksia tree flowering on the clifftop at Governor
Game lookout lies the Pacific, and one of the beaches of
Royal National Park

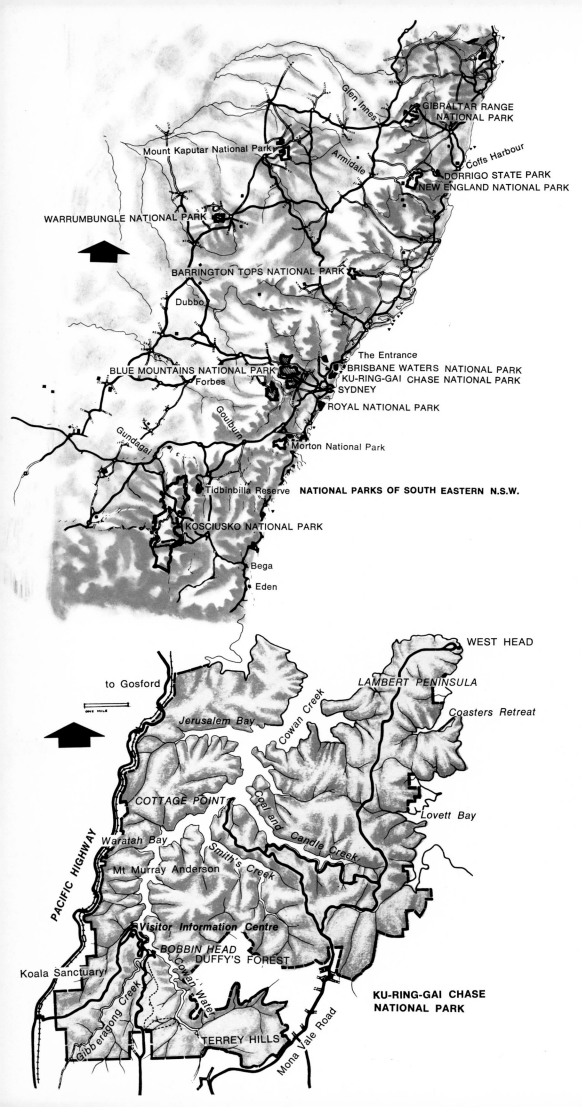

THE EAST
NEW SOUTH WALES

ROYAL NATIONAL PARK

Two great national parks, Ku-ring-gai Chase and the Royal National Park, border Sydney to the north and south and are within twenty miles of the heart of the city. Together these have preserved more than 70,000 acres of bushland, a scenically magnificent coastline of cliffs, and sheltered inlets where the sea has penetrated between steep forested hills.

Royal National Park was Australia's first, and probably the second national park in the world, becoming a public reserve in 1879 and being dedicated a public park in 1886. Known at first simply as the National Park, it was proclaimed the Royal National Park in 1955 after being visited by Her Majesty Queen Elizabeth II in 1954.

This is a great tract of natural forest, a sanctuary for more than seven hundred species of Australian flowers, plants and trees, nearly two hundred and fifty species of birds and many kinds of marsupials. Its eastern boundary, the Pacific coast, is along ten miles of dramatic headlands and high cliffs, broken here and there by fine surf beaches.

With these attractions, Royal National is extremely popular with Sydney residents and visitors alike, though the vast majority make no closer acquaintance than to drive along its scenic roads, picnic on one of the grassed clearings, or use its beaches.

Rising in the hills south of Royal National and running almost the length of the park, the Hacking River flows into a seemingly landlocked harbour known as Port Hacking, which forms the northern boundary of the park. It is easy to hire a boat at the little park village of Audley, and row upstream into some of the most beautiful river scenery, where lush rainforests crowd the banks as the waterway winds beneath high, forested hills. The smooth waters mirror the great boulders, low cliffs, wooded heights and overhanging greenery of tree ferns, bangalow palms, vines and other semi-tropical vegetation.

Roads radiate from Audley to various coastal and scenic attractions. The Lady Carrington

20

Drive tunnels for six miles through the rainforest, following the Hacking River's twisting course through a deep valley, below the green canopy of giant Coachwoods and figs whose branches may carry Elkhorn and Staghorn ferns, and down into the dim world of fern-gullies, vines and palms. Other roads lead to the coastal resorts Garie Beach and Wattamolla, while walking tracks wind through the bushland to other beaches in the park, Era, Burning Palms and Werrong.

Rainforest along the creeks and rivers of Royal National Park grow on rich, chocolate-coloured Narrabeen shale, which was formed almost 200,000 years ago. This shale is exposed where gullies have been cut through the overlying hard sandstone. The lush vegetation is typical of the lush forest areas which follow Australia's eastern coast northwards to tropical Queensland. The area also shows open eucalypt forests and heathlands which are more typical of the Sydney region.

In the rainforest thickets amidst ferns and vines is the home of many birds of beautiful plumage and song—Satin Bowerbird (*Ptilonorhynchus violaceus*), Rufous Fantail (*Rhipidura rufifrons*), Black-faced Flycatchers (*Monarcha melanopsis*), Lewin Honeyeater (*Meliphaga lewini*), Wonga Pigeon (*Leucosarcia melanoleuca*), Brush Cuckoo (*Cacomantis variolosus*) and the Superb Lyrebird (*Menura superba*).

The Satin Bowerbird has been the subject of much study at Royal National Park which is a most accessible place for frequent observations. The bowerbirds are peculiar to Australia and New Guinea and are of great interest to ornithologists owing to their departure from usual bird behaviour. The male bowerbird of each species (there are eight in Australia) builds a bower or playground where he sings and displays during the breeding season. This bower is gaily decorated and is the focal point of each bird's territory; it seems to be an object of attraction for females in the vicinity.

But the densely forested gullies are only one small part of the Royal National Park. There are

high hills of soaring eucalypts, and the sheltered inlets along Port Hacking so popular with the owners of small boats. Sandstone, heath-clad heights meet the Pacific in precipitous headlands, where to walk the clifftops with a strong breeze blowing and the ocean surging far below is a most exhilarating experience.

Though the extensive sandstone belt of the Sydney region is too infertile to permit much agriculture it is one of the most prolific wildflower regions in eastern Australia. This park's wildflowers include the tall red and orange spikes of *Banksia ericifolia* flowering in profusion in autumn, Red Bottlebrushes (*Callistemon*), Pink Boronia (*B. latifolia*), Native Rose (*B. serrulata*), many heaths (species of *Epacris*), Christmas Bells (*Blandfordia nobilis*) and the famed crimson-flowered Waratah (*Telopea speciosissima*) which is the floral emblem of New South Wales.

KU-RING-GAI CHASE NATIONAL PARK
Ku-ring-gai Chase, similar in many respects to Royal National, is situated twenty miles north of Sydney, on the southern shores of beautiful Broken Bay, where the high sandstone hills drop steeply to sheltered creeks and inlets along seventy-four miles of national park protected coastline.

Preserving 35,000 acres of Hawkesbury sandstone bushland, Ku-ring-gai Chase was originally reserved and dedicated as national parkland in 1894. Its popular centre is at Bobbin Head, a boating and picnic centre on the sheltered upper reaches of Cowan Creek. A new information building provides an excellent park interpretation service for visitors while park rangers (as in every national park where a ranger is stationed) are always willing to assist visitors.

The extensive sandstones of the Sydney region, upon which both Ku-ring-gai and Royal National Parks are situated, were laid down as sediments during the Triassic period about 150,000,000 years ago. About 10,000,000 years ago, the whole of the east coast of Australia was uplifted, causing

21

Pleasure craft moored at Bobbin Head, Ku-ring-gai Chase National Park

The Satin Bowerbird, whose walled nuptial chamber on the jungle floor is 'painted', and decorated with flowers, golden leaves, blue feathers and bleached shells

22

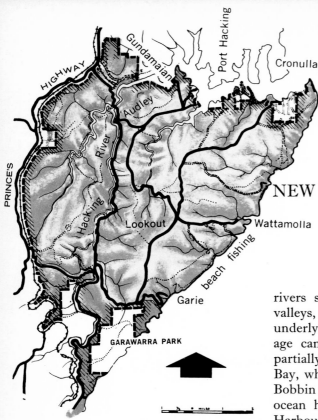

ROYAL NATIONAL PARK

NEW SOUTH WALES

rivers such as the Hawkesbury to carve deep valleys, often right through this sandstone into the underlying shale. Later again, when the last ice age came to an end, these deep valleys were partially flooded, forming the harbours of Broken Bay, where the sea has penetrated upstream past Bobbin Head. Between the two parks, the rising ocean has filled other valleys to make Sydney Harbour and Botany Bay.

The magnificent Ku-ring-gai coastline is best seen from the lookout on Commodore Heights, above West Head—a panorama across forested hills to the west; over the landlocked waters of Broken Bay with the coastline reaching away to south and north; and eastward over the wide Pacific.

Extensive walking tracks traverse the foreshores of Cowan Water, or strike inland over creeks and hills through the natural bushland. It is on these tracks rather than from roads that wildlife will be seen—perhaps a black-tailed Swamp Wallaby and certainly many of the birds of the park.

Along the streams may be glimpsed the little Azure Kingfisher (*Alcyone azurea*); in the dense fern gullies the Eastern Whip-bird (*Psophodes olivaceus*), Yellow-throated Scrub-Wren (*Sericornis lathami*), Yellow Robin (*Eopsaltria australis*) and the red King Parrot (*Aprosmictus erythropterus*). In open forests of the slopes may be found Blue Wrens (*Malurus cyaneus*), the Golden Whistler (*Pachycephala pectoralis*), Rufous Whistler (*P. rufiventris*), Sacred Kingfisher (*Halcyon sanctus*), Dollar-bird (*Eurystomus orientalis*), Mistletoe-brid (*Dicaeum hirundinaceum*), Kookaburra (*Dacelo gigas*) and numerous parrots and lorikeets.

The heathlands, especially when banksias or bottlebrush shrubs are in flower, will be noisy with the calls of the New Holland Honeyeaters (*Meliornis novae-hollandiae*), the Tawny-crowned Honeyeaters (*Gliciphila melanops*), and possibly also Brown-headed Honeyeaters (*Melithreptus brevirostris*), Noisy Miner (*Myzantha melanocephala*), Red Wattle-bird (*Anthochaera carunculata*)

and Eastern Spinebill (*Acanthorhynchus tenuirostris*).

These two great national parks, Ku-ring-gai and the Royal, have come to us by accidents of the past; they were reserved only because nobody wanted these rugged sandstone escarpments and valleys for any other purpose. It was 'useless' land unsuited to agriculture, and far-sighted men were able to have the land made into national parks unequalled in the neighbourhood of any other great city.

The combined area of Ku-ring-gai Chase and Royal National, 74,000 acres, represents most of the land set aside for bushland recreation and for preservation of fauna and flora within easy reach of Sydney's two million inhabitants—one acre for every twenty-seven people.

BRISBANE WATERS NATIONAL PARK

Across Broken Bay northwards from Ku-ring-gai Chase lies some of Sydney's most beautiful scenery. Broken Bay is the mouth of the Hawkesbury River, the lower reaches of which contain some of the most delightful river views to be found anywhere on the Australian continent. Within Broken Bay the river's estuary divides into three long narrow branches, Pittwater, Cowan Creek (in Ku-ring-gai) and Brisbane Water; within these are hundreds of miles of sheltered water beneath steep, sometimes precipitous banks.

Brisbane Waters National Park (16,000 acres) is a region of exposed sandstone heights dissected by deep gullies where there is the dense vegetation of rainforest remnants—ferns, figs and vines. The forests are dominated by tall eucalypts, and areas of heathland where, as in similar country in Ku-ring-gai and Royal National Park, the wildflowers are at their best between July and October.

Similar to Brisbane Waters in topography, vegetation and fauna is Dharug, a national park created late in 1967, covering 29,000 acres of dissected sandstone plateaus.

When the *Endeavour* anchored in Botany Bay in 1770, the eastern coast had a considerable

Aboriginal rock engravings, Brisbane Waters
National Park, near Sydney

population of Aborigines. Great piles of bleached shells, clams, mussels, whelks and crabs still indicate the feasting places favoured by generation after generation of the native inhabitants.

Another reminder of the vanished Australoid people of the Sydney coast is in extensive rock etchings on the flat, bare sandstone coastal plateau tops. More than six hundred galleries of their art have been found within fifty miles of Sydney, many within national park boundaries, though a greater number elsewhere are in danger of destruction.

The Aborigines engraved huge figures, up to sixty feet in length, of men, birds, fish and other creatures. These engravings, common only from the Hunter River valley in the north to the Royal National Park in the south, are not exceeded in size, range of subject and imaginative concept by any series of outline rock engravings elsewhere in the world.

These engravings were made by chipping into the flat sandstone a line of shallow holes, later connected by grooves, or worn into a continuous outline as they were followed, traced and re-traced by generations of tribesmen chanting the legends and ceremonies which the drawings depicted. Human and huge spirit beings dominate many of the engraved galleries of this region. With them are to be found mammals, birds, many kinds of fish, whales, sharks and dolphins. The hunting and catching of these creatures is shown by groupings of engravings in many galleries, and the outlines are often linked by the footprints of the animals and their hunters.

MUOGAMARRA SANCTUARY
In the Muogamarra Sanctuary (a wildlife refuge west of the Pacific Highway between Cowan and the Hawkesbury River) there is an engraving of the whale feast, and of a fishing party returning to camp. Another, in Brisbane Waters National Park, depicts the coming of animals to Australia, and numerous engravings within the Ku-ring-gai Chase can easily be reached along the trails.

The four thousand known figures which they have left in six or seven hundred galleries are (at present protected within park boundaries at Brisbane Waters, Dharug, Ku-ring-gai, and Royal) an enduring record of their religious and economic life, and an interesting reminder of the vanished inhabitants of the Sydney region.

BOUDDI NATURAL PARK
Overlooking Maitland Bay, on the Pacific shore a few miles east of Brisbane Waters, is the little Bouddi Natural Park (1,200 acres) where high coastal hills slope steeply to one of the prettiest bays along the coast.

The heights are covered with huge old red gums, and its Bombi Moors put forth a most interesting display of spring wildflowers which in turn attract many nectar-eating birds. Trails follow the coast from Kilcare Beach around Gerrin Head to Maitland Bay, and past Bouddi Head, across Bombi Moor to Little Beach; others climb to lookouts at Point Panorama, Bullimar Outlook, and Mt Bouddi.

HALLSTROM NATURE RESERVE
The Sir Edward Hallstrom Nature Reserve, on heights overlooking Berowra Creek, just west of Ku-ring-gai Chase, has been established for the purpose of breeding koalas under simulated natural conditions. Koalas in the wild have become alarmingly rare, owing mainly to loss of natural habitat. With the generous assistance of Sir Edward Hallstrom this reserve has been established and equipped with necessary buildings, water supply, tree plantations for koala food, and provided with some visitor facilities. It is also valuable in preserving an area of almost two thousand acres of the Hawkesbury sandstone country. Many similar projects will be needed in other parts of Australia if the endangered, rare wildlife species are to survive.

BLUE MOUNTAINS NATIONAL PARK AND RESERVES
The Blue Mountains look to be not more than a

The Blue Mountains, where a large national park covers the deep, blue-misted valley of the Grose River, northwards of Katoomba

Rufous Fantail (Rhipidura rufifrons), *an inhabitant of many densely forested east coast national parks*

NEW SOUTH WALES

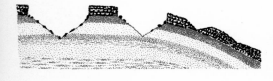

When the Blue Mountains region was elevated, its rejuvenated rivers cut slowly into the hard sandstone capping, then having broken through, rapidly into underlying softer rock.

Gradually the valleys widened, blocks falling as cliffs were undermined, but always there remained a precipitous edge of resistant sandstone.

Today the Blue Mountains around Katoomba are a hollow shell of the original plateau—more has been carved away than remains. The Great Western Highway follows a ridge bounded on either side by sheer cliffs and enormous valleys. Th Blue Mountains National Park occupies the Grose River Valley, which is enclosed on almost all sides by high cliffs, and other smaller areas are also national parkland.

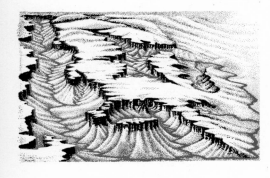

low range of hills when approached from Sydney by the Western Highway. The so-called mountains really form a plateau, or at least the eroded remnant of a plateau, rising to about 3,600 feet in the west and sloping gently in the east.

For many years the Blue Mountains were an impassable barrier to westward expansion of settlement until, in 1813, Blaxland, Lawson and Wentworth successfully planned their route along the flat-topped ridges. The Western Highway and the railway follow closely along this old route.

The Blue Mountains are part of the Great Dividing Range where the presence of a hard sandstone capping has led to the shaping of some tremendous precipices. From lookouts and other vantage points along the central ridge panoramic views unfold across the broad valleys hemmed in by stark, perpendicular cliffs. In the immense valley depths the forest canopy slopes down to rivers walled by high vertical sandstone and steep slopes. From the valley floors giant masses of sandstone in pink, grey and pale gold, tower upwards, some bearing light scrub. These valleys present an ever-changing pattern of colour—green, mauve, blue, purple.

Some spectacular mountain scenery is to be seen at Katoomba, Leura and Blackheath and particularly when viewed from the five-mile Cliff Drive. An extension of the drive goes to Cahill's Lookout and, where the Drive emerges at Narrow Neck Plateau, the vast blue Megalong and Jamieson Valleys appear, walled by sheer rust-coloured cliffs. The Drive reaches its peak at Cyclorama Lookout, the highest point in Katoomba.

Although the high vantage points are easily reached by road, the terrain of the deep, forested valleys and the narrower gorges of the tributary streams is so rugged that considerable areas are rarely visited except by skilled bushwalkers and rock climbers. The valley of the Grose River, within the Blue Mountain National Park, is accessible only to walkers, though clifftop lookouts give a panoramic view.

This valley is the major part of the national park's 243,000 acres; its borders follow closely the top of the immense sandstone cliffs, with the roadless park occupying the broad valley far below. Another large sector of this park lies on the Western Highway, with an access road through from Glenbrook to Woodford. In addition there are several small Blue Mountains reserves, totalling 11,000 acres, protecting sites of outstanding scenic beauty.

Govett's Leap and Echo Point, popular high lookout points, are on the brink of enormous cliffs of whitish sandstone, streaked with yellow and reddish tones. They are marked by tilted and curved rock strata which reveal the deep compressions which originally elevated the Blue Mountain's plateau. Here and there, headlands jut out over the precipice, and pillars of rock including the famed 'Three Sisters' stand as isolated tall spires. Deep gaps in the level line of the cliff rim indicate other gorges joining the main broad canyon, and in places glistening white streaks down a cliff mark a waterfall.

This region is famed for its distant views which become more blue at each succeeding ridge until away across the broad valleys the mountain precipices are an intense cobalt blue. The appearance of so much blue is possibly due to extremely small droplets of oil in the atmosphere, rising from the extensive eucalyptus forests within enclosed valleys. Concentrated between high walls this intensifies the light refraction phenomenon known as 'Rayleigh scattering' which causes distant objects to look blue.

Down in the glens and gorges the valley floors are completely hidden beneath dense foliage. It is necessary to descend one of the cliff trails to appreciate the luxuriance of the forests, the size of the trees and the thickness of the undergrowth. Here in the rich valley soil grow tall gums, treeferns, maiden-hair ferns, wattles and mint bushes. In the Grose River Valley there remains one of the best stands of the huge Blue Gums (*Eucalyptus deanei*).

Hundreds of miles of bush trails have been constructed through the Blue Mountains opening up many parts of the bushland which abounds in native flowers, shrubs, towering gums and other trees and wildlife. Platypus are still common in the clear streams, wallabies and grey kangaroos may occasionally be seen, and various possums and gliders are present.

It is along the valley trails that many of the most interesting birds will be seen. A species unique to the sandstone and limestone areas of this region is the Rock-Warbler (*Origma solitaria*) which frequents rocky ravines and usually keeping near streams. Other birds of these forests include the Golden Whistler, Wonga Pigeon, Crimson Rosella and Yellow Robins. From September or October until March there is an abundance of little Rufous Fantails, with their long tails spreading every now and then to a fan of bright orange-red, they flutter and dance along the rainforest and fern-gully tracks. On the heathlands there are many honeyeaters, attracted to the wildflowers which bloom there.

JENOLAN CAVES

Jenolan Caves are one hundred and thirteen miles west of Sydney, situated in rugged country of the western Blue Mountains and surrounded by the natural bushland of a 6,000 acre wildlife reserve. They are one of the best known and most spectacular series of underground limestone caverns in Australia.

There are two types of caves: great natural archways of Grand Arch, Devil's Coachhouse and Carlotta Arch which can be explored independently, and eight underground or 'dark' caves which may be explored only with a guide. The caves are lit with electricity to display the superb colours and intricate formation of the stalactites, shawls, stalagmites, pillars, canopies, and nodules. These caves probably began to form around half a million years ago as water from rivers and streams dissolved and eroded the elevated lime-stone and marble strata of the region; this process continues today.

The first white man to stumble upon the caves was the bushranger James McKeown who terrorized travellers and settlers along the Great Western Road. One of his victims, James Whalan, eventually tracked him to one of the great arches caves at Jenolan. The next day Whalan returned with his brother and two troopers and they captured the bushranger in a large cave now known as McKeown's Hole.

For many years the Whalan brothers guided visitors to the area. The caves and their environs were declared a reserve in 1866 and a regular 'keeper' was appointed.

The whole system of caves has not yet been completely explored by speleologists. Eight sections of the maze of known caverns and tunnels have been opened to the public—the Imperial Cave, Chifley, Lucas, Orient, Skeleton, Temple of Baal, Ribbon and River caves.

Well-made tracks and nature trails give access to the flora and fauna sanctuary. Colourful bird-life abounds in the reserve. A glimpse may be caught of the Spiny Anteater or Echidna, as he crosses the McKeown's Valley track—or close by there may be a Waterdragon, one of our largest lizards or amongst the limestone rocks the Cunningham Skink.

At night time many other animals are in evidence: Ring-tailed Possums, Brush-tailed Possums, the Sugar Glider and Greater Glider. The Boobook Owl may be heard far away, while deep in the reserve the Grey Kangaroo, the Red-necked Wallaby, the Black-tailed Wallaby and the Walla-roo graze on the open spaces. Sometimes a Wombat will be seen rambling along the road.

Over
The volcanic spires and high ridges of Warrumbungle National Park: from left, Belougery Spire, Crater Bluff and the narrow wall known as the Breadknife

The Warrumbungles are the remains of volcanic eruptions of about 13,000,000 years ago. The volcanic cones and craters are gone, their softer ash cut away by streams which now flow through the gorges and valleys of the park

WARRUMBUNGLE NATIONAL PARK

Some of Australia's most spectacular scenery is in the Warrumbungle National Park (14,000 acres), twenty miles west of Coonabarabran and three hundred miles north-west of Sydney.

Before white settlement swept across the plains this was the home of the Kamilaroi people; 'now the Aborigine has gone from this place of sheltered gorges, permanent springs and prolific wildlife, leaving only some patterned lines of stones marking out his sacred bora ground. These people lived as part of nature; their killing was never extermination, nor did they make a desert of the land. Today, bare paddocks almost surround the Warrumbungle Range. As the wave of denudation spreads, these rough hills become more and more vital as a last refuge for wildlife—one of the few remaining places of natural beauty on the western plains.

The Warrumbungles, a jagged knot of spires, domes and mesas, are the remains of volcanic eruptions of about 13,000,000 years ago; they are among the world's rarest extinct volcanoes. High, vertical pinnacles mark the throats of volcanoes which were plugged by solidifying trachyte (a viscous lava) and where magma poured through a great crack in the volcano's cone now stands the slender, jagged wall of the 'breadknife'. The cones and craters are gone, their softer ash cut away by the streams which now flow through the deep gorges and valleys of the park.

Trails lead to the major scenic features of the Warrumbungles. Belougery Split Rock is an easy two-hour walk. Others may be tackled as two or three-day hikes with climbs to the high summits of Mt Exmouth (4,000 feet), to Bluff Mountain and to Belougery Spire. At several points along the track, for those who use the cut trails only as a starting point for rough treks through the more rugged parts of the range, or for those who wish to witness the 'once in a lifetime' spectacle of a sunrise from the summit of Mt Exmouth, there are small huts which can serve as a 'base camp', or for overnight shelter. The colouring of any of the peaks particularly at sunrise or sunset is one of the most beautiful features of this park.

From the heights of the Pincham Trail, the park's main, six-mile track which climbs and follows the ridge of ancient volcanic peaks, the 'Grand High Top', at 3,500 feet, gives a sweeping view of all the major peaks, with the sheer, slender walls of the Breadknife immediately below. Here we are on the eroded rim of the volcano whose centre is the mammoth column of Crater Bluff.

Described as 'the place where east meets west', the Warrumbungles feature fauna, and some flora, of both the moist east coast and the dry western plains. In damp gorges and on the shaded slopes of the high peaks conditions similar to the moist coastal regions have been created. On the high peaks there are Snowgums (*Eucalyptus pauciflora*); tough Blackboys (*Xanthorroea*) find a footing on the rocky summits, and the Kurrajong (*Brachychiton populneum*) with its bright, shiny leaves, lends a splash of greenery to the red-brown scree slopes. Wherever there is permanent dampness, a deep canopy of figs can be seen as well as ferns, including the Necklace Fern and the common Maiden-hair Fern. During spring, the Warrumbungles exhibit a wealth of wildflowers and become fragrant with the scent of flowering trees and native shrubs.

Birdlife is prolific here; the most conspicuous are the brightly-plumaged parrots, the eastern Rainbow Lorikeets, Scaly-breasted Lorikeets, King Parrots, Crimson Rosellas and Eastern Rosellas. Western parrots include Galahs, Crimson-wing Parrots, Cockatiels, Blue Bonnets, Red-backed and Ringneck Parrots and Major Mitchell Cockatoos. Living in the forested valleys are birds which are usually inhabitants of the wet forests hundreds of miles nearer the coast—the Leaden Flycatcher, Dollar-bird, Southern Yellow Robin, Golden Whistler, Spotted Pardalote, Blue Wren, Eastern Spinebill Honeyeater, and Eastern Shrike-tit. Yet, intermingling with these birds are such dry-country inhabitants as the Red-backed

NEW SOUTH WALES

Kingfisher, Red-capped Robin, White-winged Triller and Spotted Quail-thrush.

Wallabies and kangaroos are plentiful and koalas were once part of the park fauna. No koalas had been seen for several decades, but quite recently several were sighted on the spurs of Mt Exmouth. A fenced plantation of suitable koala food trees has now been established and it is hoped that koalas may be bred here for release in the Warrumbungles bushland.

MOUNT KAPUTAR NATIONAL PARK

Similar in many ways to the Warrumbungles is the majestic Nandewar Range in which the Mount Kaputar National Park (15,000 acres) is situated. This park lies fifteen miles east of Narrabri which is three hundred and fifty-five miles from Sydney.

This is magnificent mountain parkland with many jagged peaks of volcanic origin rising more than 4,000 feet from the extensive plains of north-western New South Wales. In winter, light snow occasionally covers their summits. Superb panoramic views are obtainable from the heights of Mt Kaputar (5,000 feet) or from Mt Coryah (4,800 feet), down into Yulladunidah Crater and from many lookouts. The park also has other peaks of rugged grandeur, plateau tops, deep gorges and precipitous cliffs.

The wildflowers are at their best in November and December while shrubs, ferns, trees and vines all add to the park's beauty.

At an altitude of 4,500 feet, in the centre of the national park, there is a permanent spring, Dawson's Spring, which is the source of a creek flowing down over small waterfalls into a deep gorge. Here pools and banks of ferns create a setting of considerable beauty. Near Dawson's Spring is the camping area, where cabins and amenities are available. At this altitude the winter climate is bracing and summer temperatures are a pleasant twenty degrees lower than on the surrounding plains.

NEW ENGLAND NATIONAL PARK

One of the largest remaining areas of virgin rain-

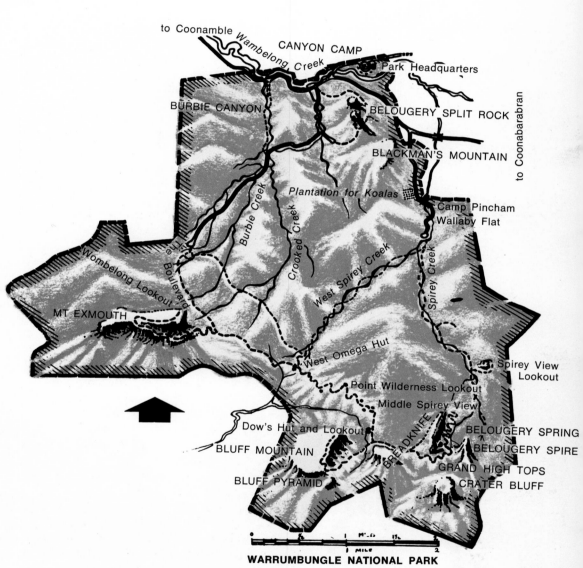

WARRUMBUNGLE NATIONAL PARK

Top
From the heights of Lamington National Park are many panoramas across lush jungles and high ridges of eucalpyt forest

Below
Misty valleys of lush rainforest, ancient mossy forests of Antarctic Beech—this scene typifies New England National Park, Lamington or Dorrigo
Right
Rock pinnacles rising high above the jungle-clad eastern slopes of the New England Tableland, at Gibraltar Range

NEW SOUTH WALES

forest in New South Wales this park is a jungle-clad escarpment, rising more than four thousand feet from the lowlands of the Bellinger River to the cliff rim at Point Lookout, 5,250 feet above sea level.

From its heights a breathtaking panorama unfolds eastwards, away across forested ridges and darker green gullies, deep river valleys, past the heights of the Dorrigo Plateau and over lowland towns to the Pacific coastline more than eighty miles away. Among its most moving spectacles must be the first light of a sunrise gilding the serried ridges far below, or the view down upon a silent sea of misty cloud blanketing the lowland world, or the magnificence of a full moon rising over the rim of the Pacific Ocean.

Three and a half miles north around the rim from Point Lookout is the great craggy bluff of Darkie Point (5,100 feet).

The rugged grandeur of this region results from the uplifting of the New England Tableland—these precipices are the eastern brink—and the eroding, by the Bellinger River and its tributaries, of lava flows from volcanoes which were active twenty to forty million years ago. On the towering sides of the scarp can be seen the layering where flows of lava have covered beds of scoria or ash, the lava now showing as bare rock faces or tree-covered ledges; in many places seeping water has washed out the softer ash beds to form large caves.

The great range of altitude, from near sea level to heights well above five thousand feet, together with varied soils, some of rich volcanic derivation, and an annual rainfall of about one hundred inches has resulted in an exceptionally diverse flora. There are three separate zones within a few miles: sub-alpine on the windswept heights, temperate forests on the steep eastern slopes down to about 3,500 feet, and sub-tropical rainforest below.

The high tops, Lookout Point around to Darkie Point and Wright's Lookout, receive occasional heavy snowfalls and are subject to winter frosts

with temperatures as low as 10°F. Snowgums, Silvertop and other small eucalypts are to be found here, with snowgrass the predominant ground cover except where pockets of soil, especially on Barren Mountain and Wright's Lookout, allow the growth of many profusely flowering shrubs and heaths.

Temperate rainforests clothe the high eastern slopes, overflowing in places into creek valleys of the plateau top—the road passes through such a forest half a mile before Point Lookout. Tall Antarctic Beeches are dominant, with an under-storey of Mountain Blueberry, Mountain Laurel, Sassafras and Possumwood.

Extending down the steep slopes to about 3,500 feet altitude, the temperate rainforest has a mysterious air, its ancient trees shrouded with pendant moss and lichen and with enormous tree ferns covering the forest floor. Some of the largest trees are estimated to be three thousand years old.

The Antarctic Beech (*Nothofagus moorei*) which occurs also in Tasmania, New Zealand and Terra del Fuego, is considered by some authorities to be evidence of a great continent once extending from the Antarctic to these places. They are not a relic from an ice-age but a normal forest for high cloudy mountain tops.

Below 3,500 feet altitude a gradual change becomes apparent: Coachwood takes the place of Beech and different hardwoods are seen, enormous trees of Tallow-wood, Blue Gum, Brush-box and Blackbutt. Finally at 2,500 feet the true sub-tropical rainforest is reached. Trees here are covered in huge Staghorn, Elkhorn and Birds-nest ferns, liana vines and many orchids.

This great variety of habitat permits an exceptional number of different birds within the park—birds of heaths, open eucalypt forests and of the big scrubs; altogether about ninety species.

More difficult to find are the shy marsupials, the Red-necked Wallaby (*Wallabia rufogrisea*), Swamp Wallaby (*W. bicolor*), Pademelon (*Thylogale*), Wallaroo (*Macropus robustus*) and Grey Kangaroo (*M. major*); in the trees, the Tiger Cat

(*Dasyurops maculatus*), Greater Glider (*Schoinobates volans*), Sugar Glider (*Petaurus breviceps*), Squirrel Glider (*P. norfolcensis*) and various possums and marsupial mice.

Nearly all of the New England National Park is a trackless wilderness; any bushwalkers descending from the scarp must be prepared for really rough conditions and slow progress. Summer months are wet, so the best walking weather is from May to November though temperatures may drop below freezing at high altitudes. Many interesting routes can be planned, and the park rangers are well qualified to advise.

For most visitors, not wishing to tackle a wilderness trek, there is a limited track system, mainly linking high lookouts—the Point Lookout circular walk (one and a half miles), the Banksia Point round trip (one mile), Wright's Lookout and return (five miles), to the derelict antimony mine (fourteen miles). There are longer tracks of eighteen or twenty miles, or along parts of the fifty-two miles of fire trails.

DORRIGO STATE PARK

Where the Dorrigo Mountain drops steeply to a deep valley cut by the Little North Arm of the Bellinger River there is a patch of virgin subtropical rainforest. It is a small remnant of the huge forests of valuable cabinet woods which once covered this plateau—forests which would now be far more valuable to Australia than are the small and poor, bracken-infested dairy farms for which those magnificent rainforests were felled.

The lower ridges of the park's deep valley are covered with hardwood forests where Blackbutt (*Eucalyptus pilularis*), Tallow-wood (*E. microcorys*), Mahogany (*E. resinifera*) and a variety of gums predominate. The higher slopes, gullies and plateau rim carry rainforest which forms a closed canopy overhead. At ground level trailing lianas, which are often several hundred feet in length, and barbed lawyer-vine tendrils grow.

The park protects a rich variety of bird and marsupial life; a valuable sample of the former

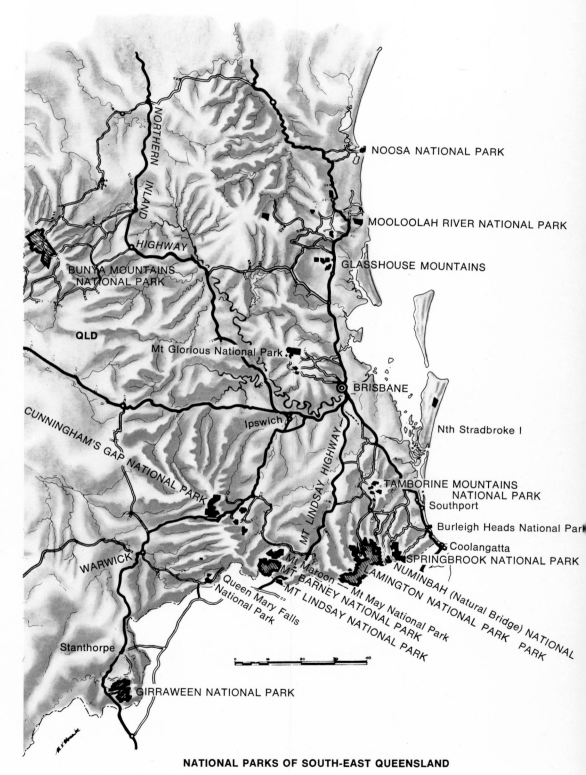

NATIONAL PARKS OF SOUTH-EAST QUEENSLAND

37

38

Regent Bowerbird (Sericulus chrysocephalus)

wildlife population of the denuded Dorrigo heights.

From the 'glade', a delightful small clearing and lookout area with camping amenities, there are several short trails through adjacent rainforest—two or three miles altogether. One trail leads past a rather beautiful little waterfall to 'Weeping Jenny', the old watering-place for bullock teams coming up the mountain.

GIBRALTAR RANGE NATIONAL PARK
Back in the dreamtime of the Kumbainggiri people—goes an old Aboriginal legend from the Clarence River—a warrior, Balugan, was chosen to lead his tribesmen in a vengeance raid to recapture the beautiful women of the tribe, stolen by marauders from over the mountains.

As the warriors set out they were accompanied to the edge of the tribal lands, the top of the range, by the beautiful young lubra Guangan, promised in marriage to Balugan.

In the evening Balugan killed a wallaby and a crimson-plumaged mountain lowry. As the men slept he made for Guangan a cloak of wallaby skin, and as they spoke of their love he decorated her hair with the brilliant feathers of the mountain parrot; late into the night they made love, then slept. In the morning Balugan led the warriors over the range while Guangan waited on a great rounded boulder.

At the end of the day the survivors returned. Balugan was not among them. Guangan watched and waited, and longed for her lover, sobbing out her grief through the night.

Her tears cut rivulets into the side of the granite boulder, and, dropping to the ground, formed two creeks, known today as the Dandahra and the Coonbadja. For seven days Guangan wept, refusing all comfort from her people. Her slim body slipped slowly from the rock, and she sank feet first into the earth.

Through the cold, sad winter months that followed, nothing grew around Guangan's rock. Not until the sun was warm and the first spring

storms rolled over the mountains did the spirit of Guangan stir beneath the ground—a tender shoot, pushing from the earth near the great boulder. Watered by the Dandahra and the Coonbadja it grew swiftly to a slender, supple tree, leaves pointed like the hunting spears of Balugan, and flowers glowing like the hot sun, red as the mountain lowry's feathers in Guangan's hair.

Nine thousand acres of Waratahs now bloom around Guangan's rock, which still bears testimony to the story. Long white streaks of tearmarks, and the rivulets, are still easy to distinguish. Nothing grows in the coarse granite soil at the foot of the rock through the winter, until the New England spring storms awaken the scarlet Waratahs, drawing them from the coarse granite earth to rival the brilliant plumage of the parrots nesting in the tall gums overhead.

Gibraltar Range National Park now covers part of the Kumbainggiri tribal lands. Of the Park's 38,000 acres, nine thousand are profusely covered with Waratahs through October and November. Their scarlet blooms, moving endlessly in the mountain breeze (say the few remaining tribesmen) are symbolic of Guangan's restless love; their pointed leaves are Balugan's spears.

Though the Waratahs are the most spectacular of the wildflowers, there seems almost unending variety of smaller flowers. In swamps—and easily visible from the Gwydir Highway which cuts through the park—are Christmas Bells (*Blandifordia grandiflora*) in profusion during December. A little earlier, in October, the Golden Glory Pea (*Gompholebium laitfolium*) holds huge dusky yellow flowers on slender swaying stems, among the granite boulder outcroppings along the highway, and elsewhere in the park. About this time, too, orchids are in flower—the pink *Dendrobium kingianum* on damp, shaded sides of boulders, blue Sun Orchids (*Thelymitra venosa*) on the forest floor and, in November, the tall, strangely shaped Slipper Orchid (*Cryptostylis subulata*). Already several hundred species of flowering plants have been found in this comparatively new park.

On the steep eastern scarp, where the land drops three thousand feet into deep gorges, there are waterfalls, such as the Dandahra Falls, 800 feet high. Here the vegetation is subtropical rainforest, with massive tall trees of Cedar, Rosewood, and Native Ash. There are Stinging Trees, Strangler Figs, Coachwoods and Corkwoods. On the comparatively flat plateau top, the granite region, forested hills are interspersed with swamps—the Christmas Bell habitat. Further westward, in the 'rain shadow' of the range, are the great forest eucalypts, the Mountain Ash, Manna Gum and Bloodwood.

Such a wide variety of habitats has given this park a wealth of fauna, including the rare Rufous Scrub-bird in the high rainforest. Other birds of the 'big scrubs' of Gibraltar Range include the Noisy Pitta, the Spine-tailed Log-runner, the Paradise Rifle-bird, the Superb and the Prince Albert Lyrebirds, the Whipbird and the Satin Bower-bird. Nearby, in the lower forests and their swamps and heaths, is a different world of wildlife. The brilliant Crimson Rosella or Mountain Lowry, Blue, and Red-backed Wrens, Southern Emu-wrens, and at least eight species of honeyeater. Though far from complete, the Gibraltar Range bird list exceeds eighty species.

Gibraltar Range contains a great area of magnificent scenery, but much is accessible only to experienced bushwalkers who are prepared to fight through the trackless scrubs into the deep gorges, and to camp out. However, there are easy trails to Dandahra Falls, the Pinnacles, and Raspberry Lookout. A good road leads five miles in to Mulligan's Hut on the Dandahra Creek, near the falls and the edge of the scarp, a pleasant picnic or camping area.

LAMINGTON NATIONAL PARK
High above the Queensland-New South Wales border rise the three thousand foot-high escarpments of the Lamington plateau, where Queensland's best-known national park covers 48,510 acres of mountain peaks, cliffs and gorges, and dense rainforest.

Along its southern precipices some peaks rise almost to four thousand feet before dropping abruptly in huge cliffs and bluffs to the river valleys; lookouts on these heights command a view across the whole of north-eastern New South Wales—over valleys, ranges and plains which on a clear day, can be seen reaching away to the coast like a gigantic relief map.

At other times the valleys are blanketed in low-lying mist, an equally fascinating spectacle.

The northern slopes of Lamington are less precipitous, though steep. Several roads wind up the range, climbing steadily above deep valleys until the plateau heights are reached.

Most of the plateau and the ranges and valleys are very densely vegetated; in the semi-tropical rainforest grow giant trees, some with widespread buttresses and green trunks and branches where mosses and ferns grow. Also growing here are the huge Tristania (*Tristania conferta*) trees, the Rough-barked Hoop-pine (*Araucaria cunninghamii*), and a giant stinging tree (*Laportea gigas*) as well as Cedar, Bloodwood, Beefwood and Carribean trees.

In November the Flame trees (*Brachychiton acerifolius*) bring brilliant splashes of vermilion to the dark green slopes, and the Moreton Bay Chestnut comes into bloom. Through January and February the wheel-like arrangements of deep-crimson flowers of the Firewheel (*Stenocarpus sinuatus*) are a feature of these forests.

Orchids adorn many of the trees and mossy boulders in spring. There are more than twenty species, ranging in colour from pure white to deep mauve—the Orange Blossom Orchid (*Sarchochilus falcatus*) which resembles the flowers of the orange both in colour and scent, the Spider Orchid (*Dendrobium tetragonum*), the yellow-green Olive Orchid (*Sarchochilus olivei*) and the Ravine Orchid (*S. fitzgeraldii*). But most spectacular is the October display of the golden King Orchids (*Dendrobium speciosum*) when orchid clumps a

The Rufous Scrub-bird (Atrichornis rufescens), *an elusive inhabitant of mountainous eastern rainforests, accomplished mimic and ventriloquist, whose resonant calls burst out with deafening volume*

Right
Coomera Falls, Lamington National Park, in the magnificent Gold Coast hinterland

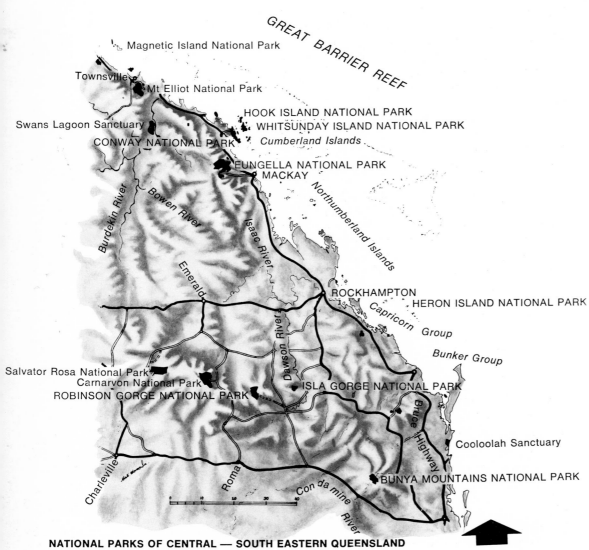

NATIONAL PARKS OF CENTRAL — SOUTH EASTERN QUEENSLAND

yard across, or larger, form brilliant yellow wreaths around the branches of many of the rainforest giants.

Less conspicuous, but of equal beauty, is the orchid *Dendrobium kingianium*, whose pink and red-suffused flowers appear on damp, mossy boulder surfaces, often on the brink of the perilous high cliffs. In many places there are magnificent orchid grottos where large numbers of orchids of various species may be found together among the boulders and on the trees overhead.

One of the best known of the botanical features of Lamington is its forest of ancient Antarctic Beech (*Nothofagus moorei*) trees flourishing in the higher parts of the park. These gnarled and mossy giants are of tremendous age, many carrying upon their limbs great clumps of flourishing Staghorn, Elkhorn and Crows Nest ferns, and aerial orchids. These forests on Mt Bithongabel and Mt Hobwee can be reached by well graded and signposted walking tracks which cover more than ninety miles through this park.

Amid this jungle lushness of Lamington many of the coastal rivers, the Coomera, Nerang, Albert and Logan have their headwaters and these streams form innumerable waterfalls. There are said to be more than five hundred waterfalls of exquisite beauty—tributary creeks tumble from the high plateau in ribbons of white, down fern-covered cliffs to disappear far below in the lush vegetation of inaccessible ravines. Many of these falls bear the liquid-sounding aboriginal names from the Nerangbullum and Wangerriberra tribes whose territory this once was.

The roads which wind up to Lamington from Beechmont and from Canungra terminate at two mountain lodges, Binna Burra and O'Reilly's, one at either end of the plateau. Both overlook many miles of mountain ridges and deep valleys: from Binna Burra there are vistas, in clear weather, as far as the Pacific and the Gold Coast, while O'Reilly's looks inland over the blue valleys and peaks of the McPherson Ranges.

From these centres the trails radiate outwards,

tunnelling through the rainforest to cliff-edge lookouts, waterfalls, wildflowers and tropical birds.

It is not a long walk from Binna Burra to where the waters of the Coomera plunge into an immense, fern-clad gorge, set between hills covered with dense rainforest, or to the high Ship's Stern Range. A longer trail with many magnificent views, is the Binna Burra—O'Reilly's (or vice versa) and return walk, a total distance of about twenty-eight miles. From O'Reilly's, tracks lead to heights overlooking the New South Wales border, to Canungra Creek and its Blue Pool, to the Lost World Plateau, to the Stairway Falls, and to Echo Point. Short walks go to the western cliffs where Pat's Bluff overhangs the Albert Valley, to the Moonlight Crag, and to Raining Cliffs.

Birdlife is numerous and varied. Distinctive bird voices to be heard are the resounding whip-crack call of the Eastern Whipbird (*Bophodes olivaceus*), the harsh, drawn-out 'Meow' of the Cat-bird (*Ailuraedus crassirostris*) and the calls of the Albert Lyrebird (*Menura alberti*). Other magnificent birds include the gold-and-black Regent Bowerbird (*Sericulus chrysocephalus*), the Satin Bowerbird, and some of the brilliantly plumaged King Parrots (*Aprosmictus scapularis*) and Rainbow Lorikeets (*Trichoglossus moluccanus*). At O'Reilly's guesthouse many birds come each day to be fed, affording memorable close-up views.

Less easily found is the Buff-breasted Pitta (*Pitta versicolor*) which keeps to the floor of the rainforest, feeding upon land-snails and insects; its nest may be found quite by chance, tucked between the root buttresses of one of the trees.

In Lamington's forest is the 'mystery bird' of the east-coast jungles, the Rufous Scrub-bird (*Atrichornis rufescens*). Certainly it is one of the most elusive, rarely showing itself but running among and beneath the low dense entanglements of vines, logs and fallen debris. Its call is so powerful that it is almost deafening at close range, and it is an accomplished mimic and ventriloquist,

which makes the owner of the voice all the harder to locate; its nest is seldom found. This bird is of particular interest to scientists in that, lacking furcula or wishbone, it belongs to the same primitive group as the Lyrebird.

SPRINGBROOK NATIONAL PARK

Springbrook National Park is a composite of three small areas: Warrie ('rushing') and Border Park—together 1,540 acres and Gwongorella ('dancing water')—1,318 acres. The Nerangballum Aboriginals once lived in this territory and these early associations are preserved in the naming of the parks and their natural features. These reserves may be reached by road from Brisbane—a distance of seventy-five miles.

This region derives its name from its many springs, gushing brooks and waterfalls arising from the very heavy rainfall of the region. The water cascades from the plateau, spurs and ridges of the McPherson Range where Springbrook lies between the watersheds of the Nerang River and Tallebudgera Creek, overlooking the Tweed River Valley in New South Wales. Its most famous falls are Purlingbrook at Gwongorella and the Twin and Blackfellow Falls at Warrie.

Within a comparatively small area there is scenery comprising sheer cliffs and crags, water-falls, and caves, set in gorges green with luxuriant tropical vegetation. Large trees form a canopy above tree-fern glades and palm groves carry arboreal ferns and orchid clumps on their trunks and branches. Bird life is abundant and similar to that at Lamington.

NATURAL BRIDGE NATIONAL PARK

Nearby, and about seventy miles from Brisbane, is a small national park, Natural Bridge (491 acres), located in the Nerang (Numinbah) River Valley between Springbrook and Lamington National Parks. A rock bridge with a glow worm cave beneath and Cave Creek Falls are its main scenic features. Most of the reserve is high rain-forest with some impressive views of distant high escarpments and silvery ribbons of waterfalls.

Top
Sixty feet above ground, golden orchids (Dendrobium) cling among mosses, ferns and vines on a jungle tree

Centre
The spires and cones of the Glasshouse Mountains rise suddenly above flat coastal plains of southern Queensland

Right
Bushwalkers descend a rough granite peak in Wyberba National Park

Below
Cunningham's Gap, a pass in the mountain chain of the Great Divide, southern Queensland.

CUNNINGHAM'S GAP NATIONAL PARK

Cunningham's Gap is a deep saddle between the four thousand-foot peaks of Mt Cordeaux and Mt Mitchell. This pass in the chain of mountains of the Great Dividing Range is the route which Alan Cunningham travelled in 1828 on his expedition to find an access to the fertile plains of the Darling Downs which he discovered in 1827; the Cunningham Highway now winds over the Divide at this point. Cunningham's Gap National Park covers 7,470 acres in the Gap and on the surrounding mountain slopes, and is situated seventy miles from Brisbane.

In the vicinity of the Gap the mountain slopes are clad in dense rainforest, with more open forest towards the summits. Graded walking tracks zigzag up the slopes to heights overlooking the Fassifern Plains far below, and to views along the chain of peaks of the Great Dividing Range which recedes into the distance.

Where the trails penetrate the rainforest, giant Spear Lilies, ground and arboreal orchids, Staghorns, Elkhorns and groves of Piccabeen Palms (*Archontophoenix cunninghamiana*) are to be seen; even from the highway, in October, the huge golden masses of the King Orchids (*Dendrobium speciosum*) can be glimpsed high on the trunks and limbs of the rainforest giants.

GLASSHOUSE MOUNTAINS NATIONAL PARKS

A familiar landmark from many parts of south Queensland, the Glasshouse Mountains rise as sudden, isolated spires, domes and conical pillars of rock, and consist of eight principal peaks with numerous surrounding low outcrops and foothills. The mountains received their name from Captain Cook who sighted them in 1770 and so named them because of their resemblance to the glass furnaces of his native Yorkshire.

Four of the 'mountains' have been set aside as small national park areas—Mt Beerwah (1,823 feet) in 320 acres of park; Mt Tibrogargan (925 feet), 720 acres; Mt Coonowrin (1,231 feet),

46

QUEENSLAND

280 acres; Mt Ngungun (775 feet), 120 acres. Others are well protected in forestry reserves—Mt Tunbubudla (1,025 feet), Beerburrum (906 feet) and Tibberoowuccum (675 feet).

The Glasshouse Mountains were within the territory of the Kabi tribe of Aborigines, and the names from their legends are perpetuated in the present naming—some of the word meanings are: Coonowrin—'crookneck'; Ngungun—'charcoal'; Tibberoowuccum—'squirrel i.e. glider or possum coming out'; Tibrogargan—'squirrel eating'; Beerwah—'up in the sky'.

TAMBORINE MOUNTAIN NATIONAL PARK

The Tamborine Mountain Parks are less than fifty miles from Brisbane. At Tamborine is the first national park proclaimed in Queensland—Witches Falls (324 acres) established in 1908 and embracing a jungle-clad ledge and forested hillside where, tumbling over a cliff, is the silvery cascade of spray which gives the park its name. The vegetation varies from jungle to open forest and features arboreal ferns and rock gardens, fig trees and rainforest trees.

Tamborine is now a composite of small scenic reserves, totalling 1,374 acres, located at points of attraction around the mountain which is part of the Darlington Range, a long spur of the McPherson Range. The mountain is famed for its bird life, which includes the Regent Bower-bird, lyrebirds, brush turkeys, whipbirds, pigeons and parrots.

The reserves on Tamborine include, in addition to Witches Falls, the Cedar Creek Falls (412 acres) where the falls, which are in three sections, are regarded as one of the finest scenic attractions in southern Queensland; Palm Grove (288 acres) containing large groves of Piccabeen Palms under Black Bean and Yellow Carbeen trees of immense size; Henderson's Knob (or, The Knoll, 185 acres) with high views, cascades, falls and dense rainforest; Joalah (89 acres) of heavy rainforest with fine examples of treetop Elkhorns, Staghorns and orchids; MacDonald Park (30 acres) where a circuit track winds through luxuriant forests of hardwood and jungle species; and Macrozamia Grove (18 acres) containing an extensive grove of these cycads, some of great size and age.

BUNYA MOUNTAINS NATIONAL PARK

The summits of the Bunya Mountains command extensive views of the Darling Downs and eastern plateau. The mountains are part of the Great Dividing Range where the Bunya Mountains National Park (24,000 acres) has been set aside to preserve a magnificent forest of Bunya Pine (*Araucaria bidwillii*) a tall, coniferous tree endemic to south-eastern Queensland. Also in this area are rainforest and open hardwood forests, and some unusual species of vegetation which include backhausia scrub, yellow stringybark, native cypress, bottle trees and grass trees of great antiquity.

The Bunya Mountains were a rendezvous for Aboriginal tribes from hundreds of miles around when, every third year, the time came for a heavy crop of the large milky white bunya nuts. These were roasted and long feasts held, with tribal boundaries suspended and all hostilities forgotten. 'Bunya' is derived from Aboriginal 'Bon-yi', the local name for the tree; the names of the highest peaks, Mt Mowbullan (3,610 feet)—'bald head' and Mt Kiangarow (3,725 feet)—a species of ant, are also reminders of the tribe whose territory this once was.

Good roads climb to the mountain tops, and fifteen miles of walking trails wind through the forests to the most spectacular waterfalls and lookouts.

NOOSA NATIONAL PARK

A rugged high headland forms the main part of the tract of coastal country of Noosa National Park (825 acres) situated near the popular seaside resort of Noosa Heads, 100 miles from Brisbane.

From the park entrance where there are excellent picnic facilities, seven miles of graded

walking tracks follow around the rocky headland shores, above rocky points and past sheltered beaches framed by Pandanus Palms and banksias. Pockets of rainforest cling to some of the heights and gullies in the northern section and wildflower heaths cover the southern slopes and coast. The tracks lead to many seascape outlooks, passing such features as the Boiling Pot, Stairway, Granite Bay, Fairy Pool and Hell's Gates.

A road winds up the slopes to Tingarana Lookout from which an encircling view sweeps from inland mountains, coastal plains, the river estuary, the long beach northward to coloured sands, around to glimpses of the open Pacific Ocean in the east.

CARNARVON NATIONAL PARK

Gouged from the white sandstone of the Great Dividing Range four hundred and seventy miles north-west of Brisbane is the fantastic world of the Carnarvons. The Gorge, twenty miles long with white, yellow-tinted and occasionally rust-stained white walls six hundred feet high, is the main feature of the Carnarvon National Park. At its entrance this chasm is more than a mile wide, narrowing upstream and in the many deep tributary canyons to a few feet in width.

Beyond the confines of the gorge, to either side, are higher sandstone bluffs, the edges of basalt-capped plateaus which have resisted erosion and remain at elevations of well over three thousand feet. To the north, looming above the rim of the gorge, are the Bulkanoo Cliffs—while to the south this outer canyon is enclosed by Battleship Spur (the best place for an overall view) and other massive rock walls. Between the Bulkanoo Cliffs and Battleship Spur has been carved the maze of narrow, twisting ravines of the Carnarvon Creek and its tributaries.

The basic walking route follows the main gorge, but it is worthwhile to explore the fascinating narrow side ravines where there may be waterfalls, lush vegetation, and ferns of many descriptions in the damp shaded recesses between overhanging cliffs. Provided you keep below the line of cliffs you will not get lost; all streams flow down to the main gorge and to the camp.

Carnarvon Gorge breaks from the range between two huge white walls of cliffs, a mile apart, Boolimba Bluff to the north and Warrumbah Bluff southwards. Between lie the Kooramindangie Plains, where the camping area and ranger's residence are situated. From here all exploration must be done on foot, following a rough trail beside the creek, which is crossed and re-crossed many times.

For the first two miles the main gorge's trend is west-north-west, with the distant cliffs on either side gradually closing in from at first a mile apart, to twenty chains, and steadily narrowing further upstream. Tributary creeks, some dry, break in from right and left; their narrow and often crevice-like ravines, many hundreds of feet deep, are often densely vegetated. First, from the north, enters Wagooroo Creek, then Koolaroo Creek from the south, and, some two miles into the gorge, Kamoodangie Creek cutting down from the massive heights of Bulkanoo Cliffs.

A short distance upstream from the opening of Kamoodangie is Angiopteris Ravine—its entrance, behind dense vegetation, is signposted. This is the only place where the rare *Angiopteris* ferns grow, their fronds reaching fifteen feet long. Altogether there are more than twenty species of ferns in the Carnarvons, ranging from the delicate filmy ferns, to tree ferns forty feet tall.

A further half mile upstream the side gorge of the Kongaboola and Kamoloo creeks breaks in from the left; here a short track leads to a long gallery of Aboriginal paintings on the face of an overhanging cliff wall.

Queensland possesses a unique inheritance from the Australian Aborigines in the 'art galleries' in many caves of the Carnarvons. They contain huge numbers of rock carvings and paintings, most being simple hand stencils, or the stencils of common objects such as boomerangs, clubs, stone axes and shields. There are occasional geometrical

Carnarvon Gorge Aboriginal Paintings

49

Pandanus characterizes the tropical coasts. These palms in silhouette at sunrise frame a scene along beaches and headlands of Noosa National Park

Pandanus characterizes the tropical coasts. These palms in silhouette at sunrise frame a scene along beaches and headlands of Noosa National Park

Right
Carnarvon Gorge, a twisting, twenty-mile canyon between massive white sandstone cliffs

motifs—large red, black or white crosses and circles. Some drawings may be interpreted as local objects which were important in the daily life of these people, the fruits of Zamia and Cuppa, Kurrajong seed pods, and the Bottle Tree.

Beyond this 'art gallery' the main gorge loops around enormous, square-cut sandstone 'castles' as high as the main walls; this section, the Parrabooya, like many other parts, is scenically magnificent.

About two miles upstream from the 'art gallery' is the Cathedral Cave, where an even larger frieze of paintings and engravings can be seen. The paintings which decorate the long back wall form one of the most extensive frescoes of Aboriginal art in the region, extending for approximately two hundred feet.

Very close to the Cathedral Cave, emerging from the southern side, is the narrow ravine of the Boowinda Creek, which begins on the heights of Battleship Spur, and is well worth a quick look. The Boowinda's ravine narrows to a crevice whose smooth walls overhang to hide the sky in places, the air is cold, and ferns grow on many ledges above flood level.

The main Carnarvon Gorge, still many hundreds of feet deep, twists into the ranges below the overshadowing heights of the Consuelo Tableland for another fifteen miles beyond Cathedral Cave, but the ten mile return walk to this cave is usually enough to satisfy most visitors; certainly they will see some of the most spectacular scenery. For those who enjoy rough walking the Carnarvon's twenty mile gorge, tributary ravines and rugged tableland heights will be a great attraction.

Though many other gorges can be found in sandstone country elsewhere in Queensland, the permanent dampness of the Carnarvon supports a rich flora that may well be unique, with an impressive wildflower display in the early spring. Cabbage tree palms grow profusely whilst tree ferns, maiden-hair, Elkhorns and orchids grow in the more sheltered areas. The gorge's lush greenery is a striking contrast to the surrounding sparsely-timbered, dry plains.

Platypus are found in the deeper pools and catfish, eels, perch and crayfish can be seen in the creek. Many coastal bird species occur here.

Part Two: THE CENTRE

The vast central desert region touches upon all states except Tasmania, and takes in the greater part of the Northern Territory. All of Western Australia is desert or very dry except some coastal areas and the Kimberleys; most of South Australia north of Port Augusta is desert or semi-arid; the dry country touches Victoria's north-western corner, bites deep into western New South Wales, and takes much of western Queensland.

The centre is a region of red plains and red sand dunes, distant purple ranges, fiery red gorges, extensive dry claypans and glaring white dry salt lakes—and of unexpected contrasts provided by the lush greenery of river gums, and even palms, around river pools and waterholes. But, although these desert and semi-arid lands cover the major part of this continent, the centre has but a small proportion of the national parks. Most are small reserves clustered close around Alice Springs, in or near the Macdonnell Ranges, at Ayers Rock, and a few other places of obvious tourist interest. Recently, however, two very large areas (land useless to pastoralists) have been set aside as the Simpson Desert national parks, one in the south-western corner of Queensland, the other along South Australia's northern border. The creation of additional parks and sanctuaries has become an urgent necessity now that grazing cattle and sheep are causing so much serious and probably permanent damage. Grazing will eventually make the entire centre a vast lifeless dustbowl of shifting sands and bare rock, incapable of supporting much plant or animal life.

Further spectacular areas should be declared national parks while they are still worth having as parks; other areas, especially parts of the interior of Western Australia, should become flora and fauna reserves or sanctuaries while they are still scientifically useful. Purely from the commercial point of view, governments should recognize the value of national parks—tourists now contribute more to the economy of the Northern Territory than all other industries, including the cattle and mining industries. Tourism is a permanent, ever-growing industry which does not, like mining and grazing, destroy natural resources. Protected within national parks, these natural resources of scenery, wildflowers and wildlife will never be 'worked out'.

Wedge-tailed Eagle (Aquila audax)

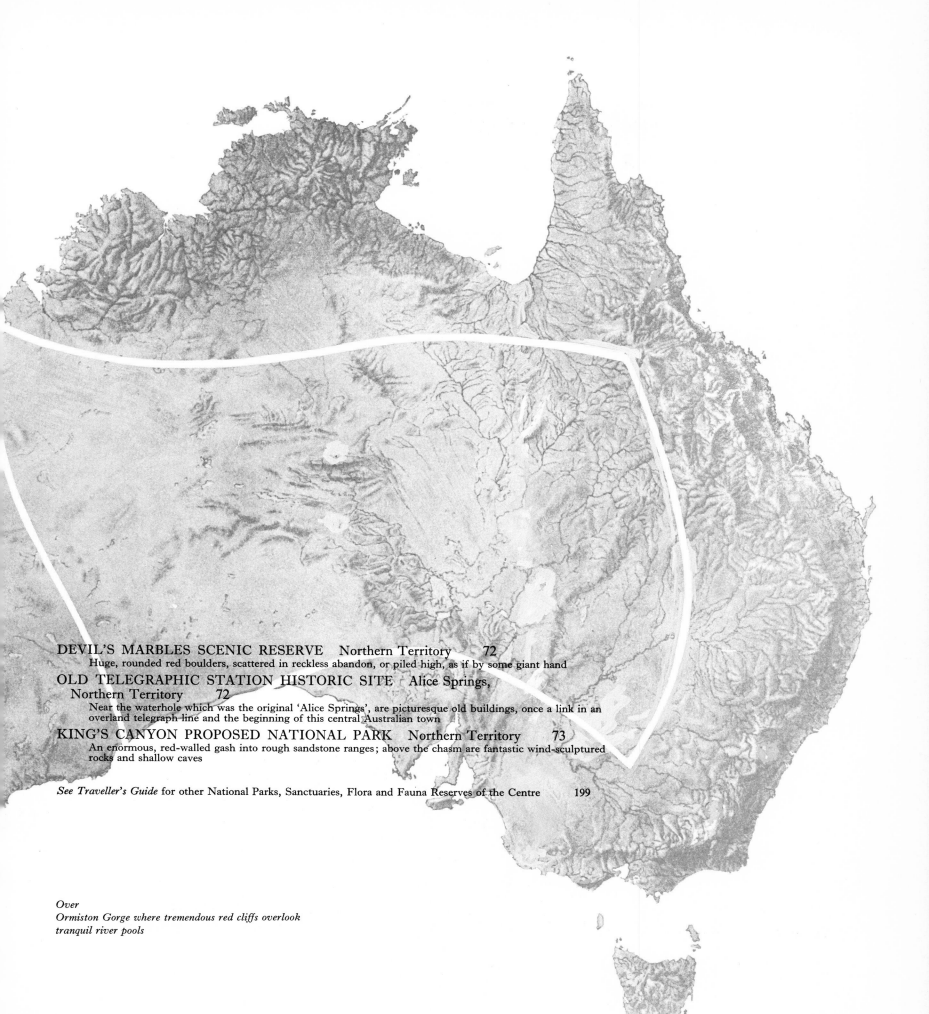

DEVIL'S MARBLES SCENIC RESERVE Northern Territory 72

Huge, rounded red boulders, scattered in reckless abandon, or piled high, as if by some giant hand

OLD TELEGRAPHIC STATION HISTORIC SITE Alice Springs,
Northern Territory 72

Near the waterhole which was the original 'Alice Springs', are picturesque old buildings, once a link in an overland telegraph line and the beginning of this central Australian town

KING'S CANYON PROPOSED NATIONAL PARK Northern Territory 73

An enormous, red-walled gash into rough sandstone ranges; above the chasm are fantastic wind-sculptured rocks and shallow caves

See Traveller's Guide for other National Parks, Sanctuaries, Flora and Fauna Reserves of the Centre 199

Over
Ormiston Gorge where tremendous red cliffs overlook
tranquil river pools

THE CENTRE
NORTHERN TERRITORY

THE MACDONNELL RANGES

In this sunwashed, fiery land, this 'desert' of red plains, red sand dunes, ochre and rust-tinted canyons, golden spinifex and haze blue distance, where there is no voice but the dry whisper of desert winds, there are vast tracts where it seems as if no man ever intruded. Yet for thousands of years men have come, lived and hunted here, and left unmarked the face of the land except by painted ochre-pigment patterns on cave and cliff walls telling of their legends of creation, animals, and the spirit world.

Today this wrinkled skin of the continent's centre is still unchanged in the rough, broken ranges—these at least appear to have escaped the relentless, desert-making deterioration of vegetation which drought, coupled with overgrazing, has caused across millions of acres of the surrounding mulga-plains country.

Sweeping east and west of Alice Springs in a two hundred mile boomerang arc the Macdonnells are the major central Australian range. From the air the pattern of their saw-toothed ridges—the eroded remnants of a much greater range—can be seen in all its rugged detail, bare of vegetation except for a smudge of yellow spinifex on the stony heights and the scattered green of Ghost Gums on the intervening flats.

Since their original elevation to heights of ten or fifteen thousand feet these ranges have been worn down over a period of almost five hundred million years. The numerous deep gorges which dissect the Macdonnells are the work of rivers which, when these regions were much better watered, carved away the heights leaving only the most resistant rock as an occasional massive peak or isolated tor. As evidence of the original folded rock strata which was the backbone of that ancient mountain, are the parallel lines of jagged ridges which form the Macdonnells today. Among the highest peaks are Mt Ziel (5,022 feet), Mt Sonder (4,526 feet) and Mt Conroy (4,100 feet).

Probably the most spectacular of all central Australian scenery is that along the gorges of the Finke River. Flowing southwards it has cut through each of the east-west ridges of the Macdonnells in turn, a series of red-walled gorges and gaps, before breaking out onto the plains and eventually vanishing into the desert sands to the north-west of Lake Eyre.

Along its course Ormiston Gorge, Glen Helen Gorge, and especially the long, twisting gorge through the Palm Valley Fauna and Flora Reserve provide some of the most colourful scenery to be found in Australia.

ORMISTON NATIONAL PARK

At Ormiston a tributary of the Finke has cut through the range almost at the foot of Mt Sonder, whose misty blue bluffs dominate the horizon for many miles. Ormiston is the gateway to a huge rock-rimmed basin known as Ormiston Pound; the national park includes both gorge and pound within its 19,000 acres.

This is a world of naked hills whose broken rock escarpments reflect innumerable hues of fiery colour, from rich burnt umber tones to bright yellow tints, dazzling white, vermilion and rust, with here and there, grey and coal black veins.

To see Ormiston it is necessary to walk through the gorge which involves scrambling over the boulders in places. On each side the dark red rock rises vertically to considerable heights—but most impressive of all is the enormous wall of cliffs which must rise almost a thousand feet on the north-west side, towering over the gorge, and building up towards the heights of Mt Sonder.

GLEN HELEN NATIONAL PARK

Just a few miles south-west of Ormiston the Finke River has broken through another of the Macdonnell's long red-rock ridges to form Glen Helen Gorge, eighty-one miles west of Alice Springs. This wide gap of vivid rock between high red cliffs is filled from wall to wall by a clear, still and permanent pool which reflects the beautiful

colours of the gorge walls and the bright blue of the inland sky. Glen Helen is a small national park, with an area of 954 acres.

PALM VALLEY FAUNA AND FLORA RESERVE

The third of the Finke's colourful gorges is in many ways the most interesting. This is the large Palm Valley Fauna and Flora Reserve, a very small section of which is known to tourists as Palm Valley, an oasis of relic palms and certainly the loveliest valley in the Centre.

A good road leads seventy-six miles westwards from Alice Springs to Hermannsburg Aboriginal mission, and for a short distance south of the mission, but low gears and four-wheel traction are essential once the road enters the sandy bed of the Finke River. The area most visited by tourists is a wide canyon which breaks into the main river gorge from the west; sheltered below high cliffs the tall palms grow in great numbers beside rock pools, their lush foliage, suggestive of the tropics, contrasting strangely with the inland scenery of bare cliffs and barren-looking ranges.

The Palms (*Livistona mariae*) were discovered in 1872 by the explorer Ernest Giles and grow nowhere else; except for these relics sheltered in the damp gorges along the Finke River, palms have a strictly peripheral distribution in Australia, being found on eastern, northern and north-west coasts. Other plant life relics lingering in the Macdonnell Ranges include a cycad (*Macrozamia*) and a number of species of ferns and mosses which grow only on the damp walls of narrow, shaded gorges. The waterholes have been found to shelter animal life which is no longer widely distributed in central Australia—there are freshwater fish now found only in northern rivers or in the Murray-Darling river system, and earthworms and snails found elsewhere only near the coast.

The palms, cycads, and these forms of animal life have survived here since central Australia had a much wetter climate than today; the aridity is in fact thought to be comparatively recent. Indicators of the past climate are the many dry river beds which seldom or never carry water, and the fossil remains of crocodiles (which must have had a lush tropical environment) found in the arid Lake Eyre region.

The Palm Valley Fauna and Flora Reserve is one of the largest areas obtained in central Australia for the preservation of scenery, animal and plant life. Its 113,280 acres cover not only the small tourist area known as Palm Valley, but also a hundred miles of twisting gorges where the meandering Finke River has cut deep into the James and the Krichauff Ranges.

The only road is through the deep sand of the river bed which may or may not be negotiated in jeep or landrover, depending upon the depths of sand piled up, and the driver's skill or luck in choosing his route among the channels gouged out in the last floods. But if time permits it is well worthwhile to leave the vehicle and, as I did, walk five or six miles down the gorge, camping on the soft dry sand overnight to see the sunset and sunrise on the vivid red walls of the gorge.

Towering overhead, the cliffs catch the full force of morning and late afternoon sunlight. Their incandescent colours darken the sky to a depth of blue which must be seen to be believed. The incredible blues which are a feature of photographs taken in central Australia can be experienced here by the human eye, unlikely though this may seem to the city dwellers accustomed to hazy pastel skies.

The palms are not confined to the small Palm Valley of the tourist, but are to be found in isolated patches further down the Fink's long gorge. Many miles downstream, near a deep, mile-long pool of permanent water known as Boggy Hole, is the Glen of Palms, named by Ernest Giles on his exploratory trip almost a hundred years ago; here there are many hundreds of these palms.

Top l to r
Finke River pools at Glen Helen
Tall relic palms in Palm Valley's rugged gorges
This small gecko is well able to cope with desert heat and drought

Below l to r
Beyond the Ghost Gums rise the dark red cliff walls of Trephina Gorge
Jessie Gap near Alice Springs
A tree-lined river pool at the entrance to Ormiston Gorge

Right
Mt Sonder dominates the landscape near Ormiston and Glen Helen national parks

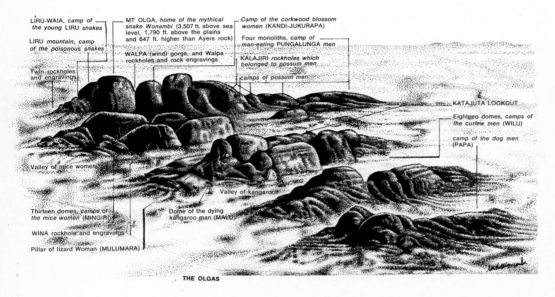

LIRU-WAIA, *camp of the young LIRU snakes*

LIRU *mountain, camp of the poisonous snakes*

Twin rockholes and engravings

MT OLGA, *home of the mythical snake Wonambi (3,507 ft. above sea level, 1,790 ft. above the plains and 647 ft. higher than Ayers rock)*

WALPA (wind) *gorge, and Walpa rockholes and rock engravings*

Camp of the corkwood blossom women (KANDI-JUKURAPA)

Four monoliths, *camp of man-eating PUNGALUNGA men*

KALAJIRI *rockholes which belonged to possum men*

camps of possum men

KATAJUTA LOOKOUT

Eighteen domes, *camps of the curlew men (WILU)*

camp of the dog men (PAPA)

Valley of mice women

Valley of kangaroo

Thirteen domes, *camps of the mice women (MINGRI)*

Dome of the dying kangaroo man (MALU)

WINA rockhole and engravings

Pillar of lizard Woman (MULUMARA)

THE OLGAS

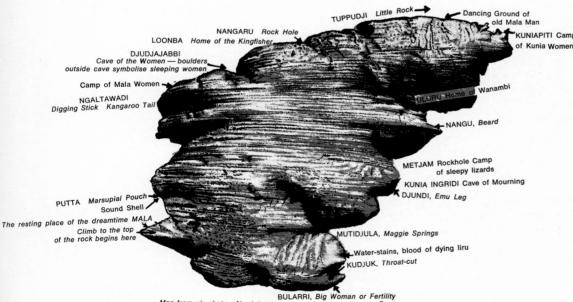

TUPPUDJI *Little Rock*

Dancing Ground of old Mala Man

NANGARU *Rock Hole*

LOONBA *Home of the Kingfisher*

KUNIAPITI *Camp of Kunia Women*

DJUDJAJABBI *Cave of the Women — boulders outside cave symbolise sleeping women*

Camp of Mala Women

NGALTAWADI *Digging Stick Kangaroo Tail*

ULURU *Home of Wanambi*

NANGU, *Beard*

METJAM *Rockhole Camp of sleepy lizards*

KUNIA INGRIDI *Cave of Mourning*

PUTTA *Marsupial Pouch Sound Shell*

DJUNDI, *Emu Leg*

The resting place of the dreamtime MALA

Climb to the top of the rock begins here

MUTIDJULA, *Maggie Springs*

Water-stains, blood of dying liru

KUDJUK, *Throat-cut*

BULARRI, *Big Woman or Fertility Cave*

Map from air photo. Aboriginal names from data gathered by W. E. Harney, first Ranger at Ayers Rock.

1,143 ft above ground level 5½ miles around the base
2,870 ft above sea level
AYERS ROCK [ULURU]

AYERS ROCK—MT OLGA NATIONAL PARK

The Rock or 'Uluru' as the Aborigines called it, was the symbol of the Uluritdja people and it played an important part in the legends of their 'dreamtime'. Its caves, boulders, springs and water-streaked cliffs were the totems marking out, throughout centuries of tribal lore, the chants of the Uluritdja ritual . . . chants given by dreamtime heroes who came at the beginning, and remain sleeping within the mountain.

Here, above the waterhole we call Maggie Springs, was their *kapi agulu wanambadjara*, place of the sacred water-python which rules over the mountain. On the rock's red cliffs was their place of the *Ningeri*, the black water-goanna whose symbol is the ravine down the mountain face, where the tribesmen chanted 'The storm water like the *Ningeri* digs a path down the mountain.'

Woriaki, an initiation cave forbidden to women, has walls stained by the blood of the first ritual heroes. Chanting the Mala ritual the elders of the tribe would cut veins in their arms to renew the blood stains on the old paintings. In the caves there are paintings which represent an ancient cult of *Edjaradjaredja*, (the marsupial mole) and there is a place near the base of the rock which is the totem of *Titjearra*, the Bristle-cheeked Honey-eater calling from the *Owidyeru* tree a chant of the gathering of fruit.

On a slender, tall vertical slab of rock (the 'kangaroo-tail') which was the Aborigines' sacred *wana*, digging stick, there is the outline of *Loondba*, the Red-backed Kingfisher who gave the first warning of danger during the Mala ritual.

The *Kunia* totem of a deadly chant which destroys by the singing is the *Kumbundura*, a water-streaked stain down a cliff of the rock; a small spear made of the wood of the Uredjunba tree and rubbed with blood was pointed in the direction of those being 'sung', and they were believed as good as dead.

Today these places of sacred ritual are abandoned by the Aborigines. Only the oldest of the

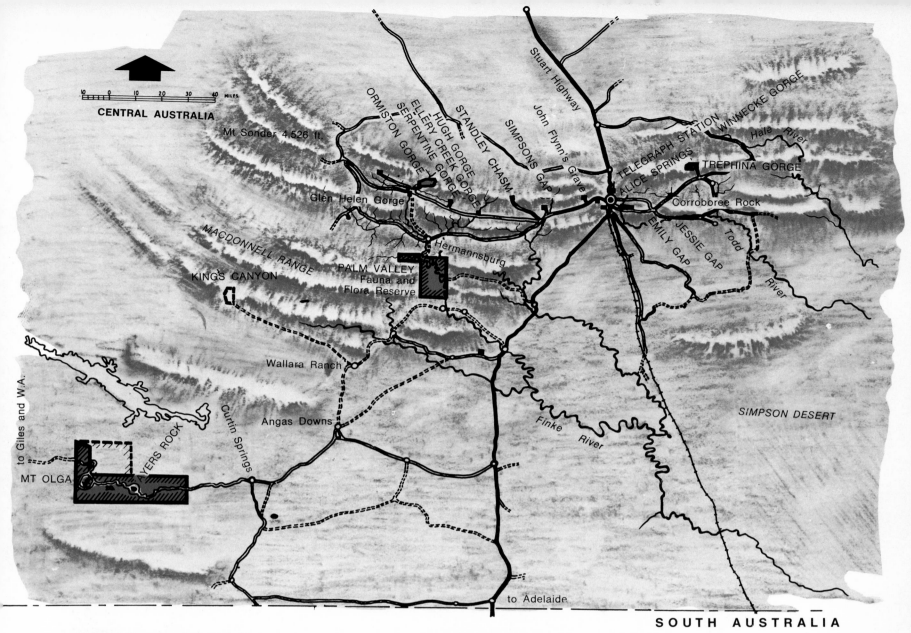

Mt Sonder 4,526 ft.

Glen Helen Gorge

ORMISTON GORGE
SERPENTINE GORGE
ELLERY CREEK GORGE
HUGH GORGE
STANDLEY CHASM
SIMPSONS GAP
John Flynn's Grave
Stuart Highway

TELEGRAPH STATION
WINNECKE GORGE
Hale River
ALICE SPRINGS
TREPHINA GORGE
Corroboree Rock

MACDONNELL RANGE

KINGS CANYON

PALM VALLEY
Fauna and
Flora Reserve

Hermannsburg

EMILY GAP
JESSIE GAP
Todd River

to Giles and W.A.

MT OLGA
AYERS ROCK

Curtin Springs

Wallara Ranch

Angas Downs

Finke River

SIMPSON DESERT

to Adelaide

men remember the chants of the ancient rituals. Fortunately, the late Bill Harney, the first ranger at Ayers Rock, recorded the ritual of the rock as given to him by old men of the Mala (Desert Kangaroo-rat) totem, and the caves remain at the base of the rock, decorated with paintings telling stories of great events in their lives.

Ayers Rock is not a huge boulder lying on the plains, but the summit of a buried sandstone hill; a protruding tip of a vastly greater rock mass which underlies the plains. Sandstone was deposited during the Cambrian period and, in some subsequent earth movement tipped on end. This accounts for the near-vertical bands across its surface—these bands of stone were originally laid down as horizontal layers. The Rock's famous shape—the smooth, rounded, giant 'monolith'—is the result of erosion upon its almost jointless sandstone. By the erosion process known as spalling, rock flakes large and small are split from the surface of the main rock mass by the alternating heat and cold of desert days and nights

and the penetrating of water. One of the largest of these now visible is the *Wana* of the Aborigines, a 500 foot strip of stone, which today is known as the 'Kangaroo-tail'.

Ayers Rock is a photographer's delight—its colour changes from pink to flaming red in the rays of the rising and setting sun and during the day the colour varies from brown to many shades of purple.

It measures more than five miles around the base and is encircled by seven miles of road. The surrounding countryside is inhospitable and yet after a rare thunderstorm this wasteland can be transformed into a sea of flowers and green vegetation.

The summit of the rock is a wide expanse of stone where a few scraggy bushes manage to survive and a cairn marks the highest point. A climb to the summit (1,140 feet) is most rewarding for the panorama of vast plains and distant mountain ranges which unfolds across the horizon.

Over left
Vivid cliffs of the Finke's long meandering gorge through Palm Valley Fauna and Flora Reserve

Over right
The Red-backed Kingfisher called 'Loondba' by the Aborigines of Ayers Rock

61

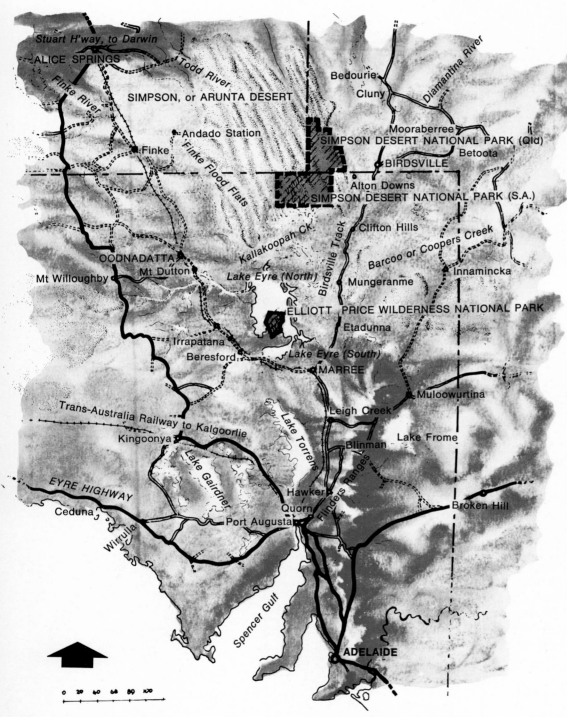

Map labels (reading across the image):

Stuart H'way, to Darwin
ALICE SPRINGS
Todd River
Finke River
SIMPSON, or ARUNTA DESERT
Bedourie
Cluny
Diamantina River
Andado Station
Mooraberree
Finke
SIMPSON DESERT NATIONAL PARK (Qld)
Finke Flood Flats
BIRDSVILLE
Betoota
Alton Downs
SIMPSON DESERT NATIONAL PARK (S.A.)
Kallakoopah Ck.
Clifton Hills
Barcoo or Coopers Creek
OODNADATTA
Mt Dutton
Lake Eyre (North)
Mungeranme
Innamincka
Mt Willoughby
Birdsville Track
ELLIOTT PRICE WILDERNESS NATIONAL PARK
Etadunna
Irrapatana
Beresford
Lake Eyre (South)
MARREE
Muloowurtina
Leigh Creek
Trans-Australia Railway to Kalgoorlie
Lake Torrens
Lake Frome
Kingoonya
Blinman
Lake Gairdner
EYRE HIGHWAY
Hawker
Flinders Ranges
Broken Hill
Ceduna
Quorn
Wirrulla
Port Augusta
Spencer Gulf
ADELAIDE
0 20 40 60 80 100

Twenty miles towards the western boundary of
this national park rises the fantastic silhouette of
the Olgas. Mount Olga was a sacred place to the

Aboriginal tribes of the area and they called it
'Katajuta', meaning 'mountain of many heads'.

Blue in the far distance, then tinted violet, the
high rounded domes become a magenta hue as
the miles between diminish, until, when the
domes soar above, the Olgas show their vivid red
colour.

The Olgas were first sighted by Ernest Giles on
14 October 1872, but, blocked by Lake Amadeus,
he was unable to reach the range until 12 September 1873. It was he who named the highest dome
Mt Olga after the Queen of Spain. Giles wrote in
his journal, ' . . . it displayed to our astonished
eyes, rounded minarets, giant copules and
monstrous domes. There they have stood as huge
memorials from the ancient times of earth, for
ages, countless eons of ages since creation first had
birth. Time, the old, the dim magician, has
ineffectively laboured here, although all the
powers of oceans at his command: Mt Olga
remained as it was born.'

This incredible range is about four and a half
miles long and three miles wide; it rises abruptly
and spectacularly 1,790 feet above the surrounding
spinifex plains. The highest dome is 3,500 feet
above sea level, and it is surrounded by some
thirty smaller rocks which are separated by
narrow ravines.

Here is more scope for exploration than the
simple shape of Ayers Rock allows and although
Ayers Rock has become better known, the Olgas
are equally spectacular. This is a place which
would prove rewarding to the active hiker and
rock-climber (and some of the smooth-sided
domes would test the skill of a mountaineer) while
its variety of vista, ever-changing with time of day
and angle of sun, creates innumerable oppor-
tunities for photography or painting.

If you visit the park in early spring, as I did, or
between July and mid-September, or in a year
when good winter rains have penetrated into the
arid heart, you will find the dry red earth of
surrounding flat mulga-scrub plain and the red

sandridges covered by wildflowers, with other plant species flowering on the slopes, the creek-beds and the ravines of the Olgas.

MACDONNELL RANGES
SMALL PARKS AND RESERVES

In the Macdonnell Ranges east and west of Alice Springs there are several small national parks, each centred upon gorges and rugged red-rock range scenery. Largest of these is the Trephina Gorge Scenic Reserve of 4,378 acres forty-six miles east of Alice Springs, while much closer to Alice Springs is the Emily and Jessie Gap Scenic Reserve of 1,046 acres. A dirt road, usually in good condition, leads from Alice Springs to Trephina Gorge via Corroboree Rock. Another slightly longer route is through beautiful scenery via Ross River, Green Valley, Jessie Gap and Emily Gap.

These gaps and gorges, together with many similar natural features of the Macdonnells—some being small scenic reserves and others well-known tourist attractions which will eventually become scenic reserves—are all the result of erosion. Over the ages the rivers have cut away all soft stone to leave the hardest quartzite standing in jagged ridges whose vivid colour is due to varying amounts of iron oxide staining the rock. Where the rivers have crossed the hard bands of quartzite, only this part has yielded, becoming the gorge through wide quartzite, or a gap through a narrow band of quartzite.

Some beautiful areas to be visited are Standley Chasm, 2,735 acres, forty-three miles west of Alice Springs. The cliff walls are 250 feet high, only twelve to eighteen feet apart and brilliantly coloured. This is a photographer's joy as the walls change to brilliant red at noon. Simpson's Gap National Park, 640 acres, is a permanent watering place surrounded by river gums and steeped in Aboriginal legend. Other interesting areas are Redbank Gorge 3,200 acres, Serpentine Gorge, 1,920 acres, Corroboree Rock, 18 acres and Green Valley Scenic Reserve, 1,239 acres.

DESERT NATIONAL PARKS

The heart of Australia is a vast expanse of arid and semi-arid terrain stretching from the Great Sandy Desert's Eighty Mile Beach (far north-western Australia) across the scrub and spinifex Tanami Desert, and the wrinkled red-brown ridges of the Macdonnells, to the forbidding sand dunes of the Simpson Desert.

The Great Sandy Desert's dunes slope into the surf of the Indian Ocean more than twelve hundred miles from the eastern fringe of the Arunta (or Simpson Desert). Altogether, a distance of over one thousand miles extends from the precipitous cliffs of the Nullarbor's meeting with the Great Australian Bight, northwards over the plain's featureless monotony, the gibber-stone deserts, the sparse scrub of the Great Victoria Desert, the ancient Archaeozoic gneiss domes and ramparts of the Musgrave Ranges, and across the Tanami to the woodlands of the tropical north.

Within this enormous area of arid and semi-arid land are situated not only the scenically spectacular reserves and national parks which tourists visit close around Alice Springs, but also a few enormous desert wildlife sanctuaries and parks.

ELLIOTT PRICE WILDERNESS
TANAMI SANCTUARY

The Tanami Sanctuary (9,000,000 acres) is three hundred and sixty miles north-west of Alice Springs; the Simpson Desert National Parks join across the Queensland-South Australian border, and on the shores of Lake Eyre, almost surrounded by saltpan and dry mudflat, is the Elliott Price Wilderness National Park (160,000 acres).

Many other desert regions have national park or sanctuary potential as they contain flora and fauna whose preservation is of national importance. These regions include the Petermann Ranges, the northern Nullarbor, and the Lake Disappointment area in the far interior of Western Australia.

SIMPSON DESERT

The Simpson Desert is an expanse of arid

Top
Katajuta, 'mountain of many heads'—the Olgas rise from the red dunes of the desert

Right
A watercourse between the tremendous red domes of the Olgas

Below
Ayers Rock is the best-known feature of a desert national park which reaches westwards to the Olgas

country about 30,000 square miles in area in which both Queensland and South Australia have large national parks. It is a region of consolidated sand dunes, running in long parallel south-west to south-east lines following the direction of the prevailing winds, and sparsely covered with spinifex. Every dune is a barrier, difficult even for a four-wheel-drive vehicle, so the desert has been crossed against the trend of its hundreds of high sand ridges on very few occasions.

Like the Tanami Desert, or the Nullarbor, or almost any of the dry interior, this is not true desert in the sense of an arid area totally devoid of life. Everywhere there is vegetation—stunted, gnarled Mulga (*Acacia*) shrubs, twisted Corkwood (*Hakea*) trees and Desert Oaks (*Casuarina decaisneana*), with needle-pointed Porcupine Grass (*Triodia*) growing in clumps beneath the sparse trees and among the boulders of the ranges. After good rains—rare though this may be—a luxuriant spread of ephemeral plants bursts forth and the bare earth is carpeted with transient wildflowers including Wild Orange (*Capparis mitchellii*), Pussy Tails (*Ptilotus atriplicifolius*) and White Paper Daisies; the red plains and sandhills are transformed with their white, gold, pink and purple colours. The seeds of these bright everlastings can lie dormant for years, surviving drought and heat, only to burst into flower in a few short weeks after rain. Others spring to life from dormant underground roots or tubers; among the perennials are the succulent, magenta-flowered Parakeelya (*Calandrina balonensis*) which holds enough moisture to keep cattle alive during long dry spells, and the fiery red Sturt Desert Pea (*Clianthus formosus*) which carpets the bare plains.

In all Australian deserts there is a great number of birds, especially during a good season. Conspicuous are the birds of prey ranging from tiny Kestrels (*Falco cenchroides*) to the mighty Wedge-tailed Eagle (*Aquila audax*). The Forktailed Kites (*Milvus migrans*) are the commonest and will be seen by the dozen soaring above station homesteads.

Today the Wedge-tailed Eagle, one of the world's most majestic birds, is more a creature of the vast interior than of the settled southern fringes of the continent. Even in those remote parts it is persecuted by the pastoralist, poisoned and blasted from the skies by men who cannot admit to the value of this bird and who are blind to its powerful majesty. Preying principally upon rabbits and very rarely upon any but dead or dying sheep, the Wedgetail is indisputably more beneficial than damaging; in belated recognition of this, Western Australia has recently lifted the bounty which was paid for eagles killed.

Master of the skies, perfectionist in flight, the Wedge-tailed Eagle is one of the creatures symbolic of the Australian outback, of the clear inland skies and the ranges; an awe-inspring bird, denizen of the great open spaces of our land.

I have watched these eagles above the ridge of a steep rocky hill, rising high in effortless, soaring flight until their mighty span was a near-invisible speck in the sky. Or with indiscernible twist of wingtips one would turn, to sweep low across the bare flank of the rock and spinifex-studded ridge, so that its sudden rush might panic some small creature to expose itself, for a fatal instant, to the eagle's swoop and outstretched talons.

In a tree overhanging a ravine part way down the hill's steep slope the Wedgetail pair had constructed a huge eyrie of branches and sticks. As I watched from a distance of about a quarter of a mile, one of the soaring eagles, on half-closed wings, suddenly dived, following the hill's steep slope at tremendous speed, uttering a wild clear cry, then, with six-foot span of wings fully outthrust, lifted almost vertically until the momentum of its dive was spent. For an instant the eagle's black shape hung almost motionless, then again dropped earthwards in another fantastic dive down the slope, skimming on back-swept wings between the stunted mulga trees, gaining speed for a second upward rush . . . again its thrilling cry rang out. This display flight of the Wedgetail seemed to crystallize all my vague feelings for the

*The Bilby, or Rabbit-eared Bandicoot
(Thylacomys lagotis), a vanishing marsupial, now
confined to the arid interior of W.A. and the
Simpson Desert*

untamed. Not only the Wedgetail, but also many other creatures of the interior will need protection in years to come. For some it is probably already too late.

When the rains penetrate into the arid lands (either from the north, under the summer monsoonal weather pattern, or from the south under the influence of the Antarctic system) the bird population seems to explode. Many species are highly nomadic, following the erratic rains across the interior and breeding wherever, and whenever, conditions are favourable. Only in this way can the birds make good the enormous losses which occur whenever the long droughts strike.

Among the most colourful of small desert birds are the Orange Chat (*Epthianura aurifrons*) and the Crimson Chat (*E. tricolor*), the little Zebra Finches (*Taeniopygia castanotis*) which are to be seen in flocks throughout the inland, and the rather rare Painted Finch (*Emblema picta*), an inhabitant of the ranges and gorges. My visit to the Macdonnell Ranges and Ayers Rock, in September 1968, followed widespread rains and chats were common. Their conspicuous display flights above the low shrubs (in which their nests would be hidden) indicated that they were breeding; but commonest of all nests, as usual, were the bulky structures built by the Zebra Finches.

Unexpected in central Australia is the presence of a kingfisher, the Red-backed (*Halcyon pyrrhopygius*) as these birds are usually inhabitants of streams and lakes; however, this species, which I came upon, dives upon small reptiles and large insects, and may often be found many miles from any water.

One of Australia's most beautiful little parrots, the Scarlet-chested (*Neophema splendida*), is an inhabitant of the semi-arid lands of the Nullarbor and eastwards, but trapping for the aviary trade has made the species very rare in the wild. However, another rare species, the little Bourke Parrot (*N. bourki*) seems to be growing more plentiful in parts of the far interior.

The Australian deserts abound in animal life,

with mammals ranging in size from the giant Red Kangaroo to the small insectivorous Jerboa marsupial mouse (*Antechinomys speceri*) and the little, hopping rodent kangaroo-mice (*Notomys* and *Pseudomys*).

But over a vast area the defenceless native animals are disappearing. While the introduced cat and fox are partly responsible, grazing animals, sheep, cattle and rabbits, have probably caused the most damage, destroying the low vegetation which sheltered the little native creatures, and competing for food which is often scarce. It has been said that sheep in the inland grow wool entirely at the expense of the natural vegetation.

After a long study of prevailing conditions through the centre, biologist Sir Francis Ratcliffe concluded that the inland is in danger of conversion to true desert. In many places we have such deserts in the making--where the sparse native scrub has been eaten out; where, when the wind blows hard, the skies across hundreds of miles are red with dust. Without doubt, overgrazing of semi-arid Australia will in time bring a vast man-made Sahara of drifting sands, barren stony plains, and huge dust storms.

The Australian semi-arid regions have life also in their many furred creatures. The Tanami Sanctuary is an important refuge for many of these creatures, while others occur in the more southerly Simpson Desert National Parks, and in the proposed northern Nullarbor reserve.

One of the most beautiful of the desert mammals is the Rabbit-eared Bandicoot (*Macrotis lagotis*), which is about the size of a small rabbit, but has a long snout and very long ears. Though once widespread over the southern half of Australia, this bandicoot now survives only in a few remote places. Sheep and cattle, trampling the bandicoots' burrows and compacting the soil (into which it tunnels for insect food) have contributed to its decrease; this bandicoot may continue to survive only in parks and sanctuaries where stock is not permitted.

But the most remarkable of desert creatures

69

Top
At dusk the desert hopping-mice (Notomys) emerge from *their burrows in the sandhills*

Right
Wind-whipped dunes create a scene of savage beauty in the Great Sandy Desert

Below
A thunderstorm breaks over parched mulga-scrub plains in the vast arid interior

must surely be the Marsupial Mole (*Notoryctes typhlops*), which lives beneath the sand of the more arid deserts from the Nullarbor northwards to the far side of the Great Sandy Desert, at the Eighty Mile Beach near Broome. Very few have been seen alive, which is hardly surprising, for it is said to emerge from beneath the desert soil only after rain, or in overcast weather. Its body shape resembles the true moles of the northern hemisphere, mouse-sized and with silken fur. As a result of thousands of years of subterranean life, the eyes have completely degenerated and only at the embryo stage can they be detected, as pigmented spots. The snout is protected for pushing through the soil, by a horny shield, and the mole is well equipped for tunnelling with enormous claws, especially on the third and fourth digits of the forelimbs.

Even the most insignificant and uninteresting of creatures merits protection, for each is a living part of the natural community of life; part of the natural environment which has been, and will increasingly become, a source of scientific information, vital for the well-being and advancement of mankind and, perhaps, in the final analysis, vital to his continued existence. We cannot, with our present inadequate knowledge of life, assume any species of animal or plant to be so useless or so detrimental to our interests that it must be exterminated, or simply conveniently forgotten until extinct. Samples of all unchanged 'wilderness' environments need to be preserved for scientific study—and this includes tracts of the arid lands of the interior.

Although at a casual glance the sparsely settled heart of Australia seems the last area in need of wildlife sanctuaries or national parks, the wide spread of the pastoral industry into all regions capable of carrying stock has meant that few inland parts have not been degraded. To study the damage caused by sheep or cattle grazing on semi-desert lands which exist in precarious balance achieved after millions of years of evolution, scientists must be able to make comparisons with the original, unspoiled conditions, where the soil, climate, plants and animals are in equilibrium. Here, then, is commercial justification for national parks and sanctuaries, quite apart from tourist and aesthetic considerations.

DEVIL'S MARBLES SCENIC RESERVE

Situated on both sides of the Stuart Highway, approximately sixty miles south of Tennant Creek, the Devil's Marbles are well known to all who have travelled by road from Alice Springs to Darwin. The 'Marbles' are a collection of gigantic rounded granite boulders, some the size of a house, balanced precariously one on top of another, in scattered heaps across a wide shallow valley. The Aborigines believed that these huge boulders were eggs laid by the mythical rainbow snake.

The original granite mass from which the marbles were fashioned had three main sets of joint planes at right angles to each other, breaking the granite mass into rectangular blocks ten to twenty feet square. Erosion along the joints, together with the flaking away of thin slabs from surfaces has gradually rounded the corners to the extent that most blocks are now egg-shaped or spherical; where the surrounding granite has been worn right away these boulders are left one upon another in great heaps. The Devil's Marbles area is a scenic reserve of 4,500 acres.

OLD TELEGRAPH STATION HISTORIC SITE

This park area of more than 1,000 acres is situated on the Stuart Highway, two miles north of Alice Springs. It preserves the historic buildings, equipment and other relics of the first settlement of Alice Springs, established in 1872, and built where water was available from springs on the bed of the Todd River. Serving as a telegraph repeater station, this was the main link in the overland telegraph line to Darwin. Restoration work has been undertaken to prevent further deterioration of the very old buildings, and hundreds of trees, principally native species, have been planted. As many visitors to Central Australia wish to see local fauna such as emus and kangaroos, which they may not be lucky enough to encounter in the wild, a fenced fauna park has been established to house such creatures.

KING'S CANYON

King's Canyon is an enormous gash in the red sandstone at the western edge of the George Gill Range, 230 miles south-west from Alice Springs.

Beyond the wide entrance to the canyon, past an oasis of deep rock pools, the towering walls close in to form a high crevice from which a waterfall tumbles after rain. Here the canyon walls are smooth and are several hundred feet high; below is a small creek flowing among white ghost gums and obstructed in places by fallen blocks of sandstone to form still pools. Around these deep rock pools eucalypts, palms and primitive cycad plants grow. The smooth walls of the canyon result from stone slabs breaking away along vertical joints, the line of the joint through the sandstone mass becoming the smooth rockface. Along the top of these cliffs is a remarkable variety of rounded and undercut sculptured shapes and shallow caves, resulting from the differential erosion of soft and hard layers of sandstone.

King's Canyon is one of many places of spectacular scenery not yet included in the national parks system of Australia, however, it probably will become a park in the near future. With many places of considerable scenic interest, or value in conservation, it has been difficult to persuade governments to place the land under control of the national parks authorities. When, as in the case of King's Canyon, the region is already a well-known tourist attraction, it is an urgent necessity that proper control be established to preserve its beauty.

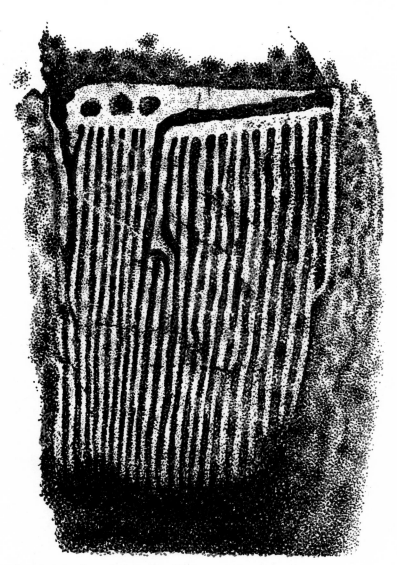

Aranda tribe, Central Australia; Witchetty Grub totem design, showing three eggs, and a curved line representing a woman with one hand to her head, watching a totemic ceremony

Top
The desert national parks are the home of many beautiful birds. Orange Chats nest in low shrubs, often near claypans or dry salt lakes

Right
Although the rock itself is red its hues change by the hour

Below
Scattered casually across the barren plains, or piled high one upon another, astride the Stuart Highway, are enormous rounded granite boulders known as the 'Devil's Marbles'

Part Three: THE FAR NORTH

The national parks of the tropical north contain a great diversity of scenery, ranging from red gorges of the Kimberleys and the Northern Territory's 'top end', to gloomy jungles and forested mountain ranges, and coral islands of the great barrier reef. The unifying features of this whole wide region are its tropical climate and its remoteness from the southern cities.

The westernmost part of Australia's tropical north, the Kimberleys of Western Australia, contain some of this continent's most spectacular scenery, but set deep in country that is often inaccessible even with 4-wheel-drive vehicles.

The Northern Territory has some wonderful scenery at Katherine Gorge, and in western Arnhem Land. National parks should be declared in the huge Arnhem Land Aboriginal Reserve, to preserve not only the landscape and wildlife but also Aboriginal paintings and artefacts, and to protect the Aboriginal sacred sites.

There are many national parks in far northern Queensland, but very few in one of the most interesting parts which has great national park potential—Cape York Peninsula. This is a region of great importance for its tropical birds and marsupials, many of which do not occur further south.

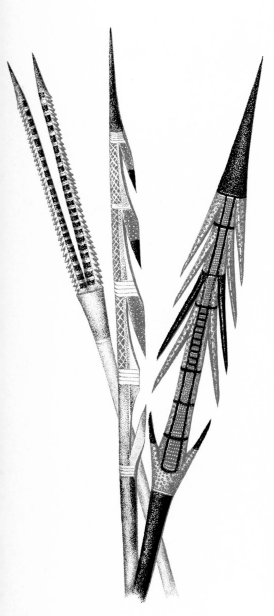

Aborigine's spear-heads from Arnhem Land, N.T.

See Traveller's Guide for other National Parks, Sanctuaries, Flora and Fauna Reserves of the Far North 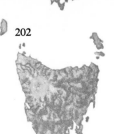 202

Like a huge castle wall the Napier Range divides the West Kimberley plains

Right
Brooking Gorge near Fitzroy Crossing, with attractive scenery and easy access, has national park potential

78

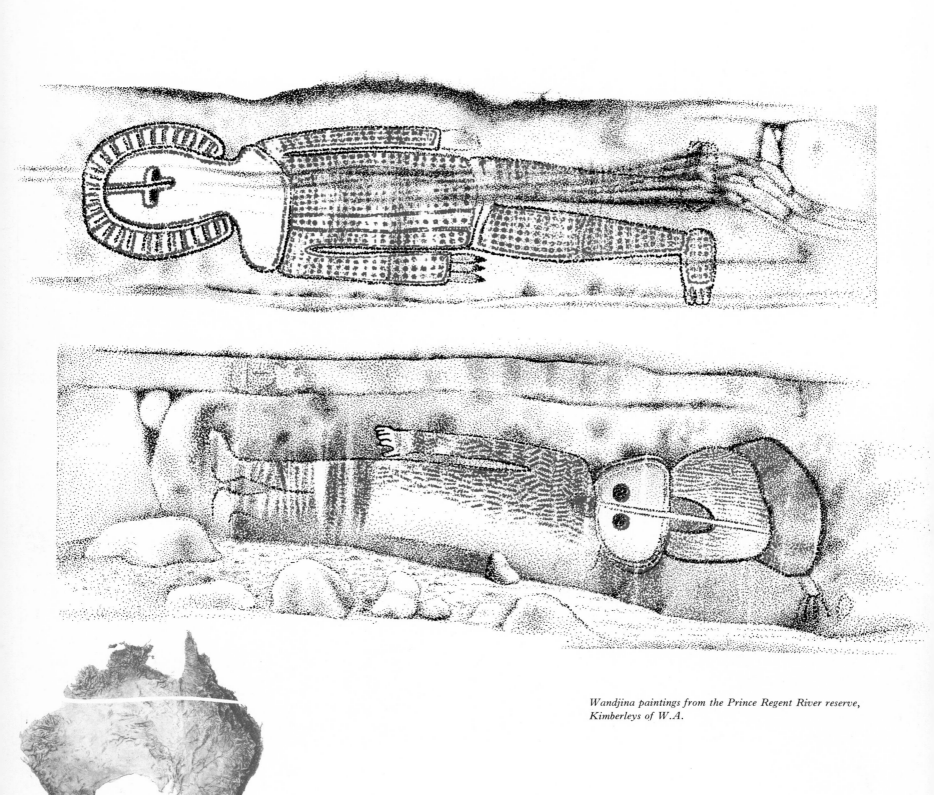

Wandjina paintings from the Prince Regent River reserve, Kimberleys of W.A.

THE FAR NORTH
WESTERN AUSTRALIA

WINDJANA GORGE PROPOSED NATIONAL PARK

About seventy miles east of Derby, the narrow, three-mile Windjana Gorge has been cut through the Napier Range by the Lennard River. The rock walls of Windjana stand like jagged battlements three hundred feet above the long, still pools of the river. When the late sun shines into the western entrance of the gorge, it accentuates the ochre stains, the rust and brown-streaked walls of rock; it highlights great white boulders which seem to balance upon their own reflections in the river pools, where they fell during the raging floods of 'the wet', years ago.

At other times these forbidding walls of rock, blackened and stained by ages of weathering, become lost in the distant, misty blue veils of their own shadows. When the moving lines of sunlight strike across these soaring cliffs they highlight a rugged, massive texture, showing the grey colours of weathered stone, and revealing as inky black shadows the entrances to caves and grottoes where Aboriginal paintings and burials still remain as evidence of an almost-vanished culture.

The Lennard River runs in the wet weather but in the dry season only large pools remain in the gorge. Zebra fishes and harmless freshwater crocodiles inhabit the waterholes. Trees lean from the darkness of overhanging, shadowed cliffs, lining the river's banks.

Down by the gloomy bank the sunlight picks out the tall, alert shape of an egret. This graceful bird seems to stalk its own reflection in the dark water . . . a sudden, spearing plunge for a fish shatters the mirrored image; ripples radiate outwards the length of the glassy pool, sending the reflected colours of rock and sky wavering and blending in crazy patterns of distorted trees and canyon walls.

In few other places have I been so aware of the wildlife around me. Between the sheer walls of this narrow river canyon the ceaseless calls of birds are echoed and amplified—the bustling songs of honeyeaters, the soft murmuring of tiny Peaceful Doves, the screeching of white Corellas, the piping whistle of an eagle, the metallic calls of bright little finches at their nest, and a noisy commotion as a flock of Babblers arrive and the birds go through their circus-clown antics.

The riverside trees in parts of Windjana Gorge are festooned with flying foxes. If disturbed, these foxes fall in thousands from the branches, to fill the narrow space with fluttering black bat shapes and an indescribable din—the incessant screechings of a hundred thousand giant bats shut between echoing walls.

This range's massive ramparts lift suddenly, vertically, from flat plains; it seems to march across the west Kimberley landscape like a mighty barrier, always a ragged, jagged skyline of dark grey rock. Once this was a coral reef comparable to Queensland's Great Barrier Reef. The rock is extremely hard, grey at the surface, but white or coloured where polished by floods, or broken, where boulders have fallen. Geologists put the age of its Devonian limestone at three hundred million years.

When man, the Stone Age Aborigine, first set foot on this continent some twenty or thirty thousand years ago he painted vivid, decorative, yet very important images representing his complex tribal and religious practices. In the caves of these ranges remain his representations of the animals so important in his way of life—water python, emu, crocodile, kangaroo, goanna. Some show the mythical beings of his rituals; among these the main figure is that of Wandjana, the rain god.

These galleries of Aboriginal paintings, daubed on the rock in red, yellow, white and black, are valuable relics of a vanishing culture; they remain as witness to thousands of years of ritual and ceremony of Stone Age man in Australia, and should be preserved for future study.

Beautiful Windjana Gorge witnessed death on more than one occasion in the early days when white settlers were struggling for a foothold in the north—sudden shots reverberating from its cliffs,

The Napier and Oscar ranges of the Kimberleys, where Geikie Gorge National Park, Windjana and Tunnel Creek are situated, were once coral reefs comparable to Queensland's Great Barrier Reef. This was some three hundred million years ago. Uplifting of the land mass has exposed these ancient reefs, which are remarkably intact, and rise suddenly with vertical walls from the flat plains. Northwards are the mountainous King Leopold Ranges which long ago formed the coastline.

Very similar, though smaller, are the jagged limestone outcrops and ranges at Chillagoe, north Queensland.

A flock of Brolgas (Grus rubicunda) *on swampy tropical
grassland plains*

Right
A Darter, or Snake-bird (Anhinga novae-hollandiae)
beside a tropical lily lagoon holds its wings to the sun to dry

82

silencing the soft calls of birds; bullets and spears cutting stockmen from their horses and stampeding the wild-eyed bullocks from its placid river pools. Murderous shots from a heavy rifle to signal the start of a cattle-killing rampage; excited warriors rushing from behind rocks and trees to help cut down the stricken white men, then to hurl deadly shovel-nosed spears into the flanks of bullocks trapped between narrow canyon walls.

The murder of the stockmen in Windjana Gorge was one of the first acts of terror by Sadamara, former police black-tracker Pigeon. This rugged range and particularly this river gorge was, for a time, a secure refuge for 'Pigeon's mob'—the horde of wild blacks and renegade cattle spearers that gathered for a promised massacre of all white men.

Windjana saw dancing and revelry that night, its towering walls lit by leaping flames where the exuberant warriors and their lubras feasted on the bullocks. And when the crates of gin from the drovers' supply waggon were broken open the orgy of feast and dance changed. Simmering jealousies, rivalries and tribal feuds became uncontrollable, frenzied men and women fought and killed along the dark river banks; the long canyon must have echoed to their wild, primitive cries.

In Windjana Gorge the first battle occurred between the rebellious Kimberley natives and the police patrols. Though surprised just before dawn, and apparently trapped, Pigeon, with Captain, Ellemara and others of his gang, dived for the caves beneath the cliffs and fought back, using their stolen rifles with skill enough to make the patrol abandon any hope of taking the caves by a sudden rush. Then, when he'd had enough of the fight—when twice wounded by police bullets—Pigeon, with his warriors and lubras, vanished into the depths of the caves.

Many times, when closely pursued, Pigeon disappeared into the caves of the Oscar and Napier Ranges. The 'cave of bats' (where, through ages

past the bones of his tribe had been placed) was his hiding place while he recovered from the deep wounds of the Windjana fight. Always he chose caves he knew to have an outlet through crevice or pothole somewhere along the jagged crest or even away on the far side of the range; in these caves he could not be trapped.

The Kimberley tribesmen regarded this land as their own, their birthright. White men and their beasts fouled the clean, clear waterholes, destroyed the vegetation of river banks, drove away the wild game. They desecrated the places sacred to the tribes since the dreamtime—hills, trees, rocks and springs revered in legend, ritual and corroboree; they had stolen the tribal hunting grounds, and had disrupted a vital way of life. So it is hardly surprising that the Aborigine should regard the cattle on his tribal lands as his to kill in place of vanishing native game.

The renegade black-tracker Pigeon was one of the few of his race to really try to rid his land of those who pillaged, desecrated and destroyed these tribal lands. These ranges, river gorges and caves were a last stronghold of the Australian Aborigine. They are linked with some of the most exciting episodes in the settlement of the Australian continent, hardly more than seventy years ago.

Now that the cultural identity of these original Australians is all but lost and they are for the most part a demoralized, often-despised minority without the pride and purpose of the wild native, these places should be preserved and protected. As well as scenic grandeur the Kimberley ranges and river gorges are of considerable historical interest, being a reminder of early times when there was excitement and real danger in pioneering the north, and of Stone Age man's fight to continue undisturbed his ancient way of life.

Although the Australian Academy of Science, in a report compiled in 1962, recommended that an area of 123,000 acres in the Napier-Oscar ranges, including Windjana Gorge, Tunnel Creek, Geikie Gorge and Brooking Gorge be fully

reserved, the Western Australian Government has acted only in the case of Geikie, which is now a small national park. This is hard to understand in view of the tremendous tourist potential of these fascinating ranges and gorges. At present the river pools serve a relatively minor purpose as watering places for cattle, and this is causing their steady deterioration. It is noticeable that the lush greenery of river banks—pandanus palms, shrubs and creepers—is best in Geikie Gorge now that cattle are kept out of the national park.

Whatever the tourist potential of Windjana Gorge, its richness of wildlife (which accentuates, and makes one *feel* the visual beauty of this place) must be preserved: a part must be set aside as a refuge for wildlife.

For scenic grandeur, the first half-mile in from the south-west entrance is certainly impressive, and easy of access. Here the canyon carved by the Lennard River sweeps around a bend, and cliffs three hundred feet high reflect in the long pools of still water. A little less spectacular are some inner reaches of Windjana Gorge, where cliffs are lower and there are wide sandbars in the river bed—yet this is equally rich in wildlife, and could be left undisturbed as a sanctuary for the many wild creatures which help set the character of Windjana Gorge.

WANDJINA PAINTINGS

In 1837, when Sir George Grey first penetrated the rugged ranges of the West Kimberleys in Australia's far north-west, he found paintings unlike any seen elsewhere—these were the Wandjina figures.

These figures were tall, with heads painted to a striking pattern, eyes and nose combined in one unit encircled by long radiating red eyelashes, and always mouthless. An oval band of red, yellow or white colour, representing a headband, surrounds the face, and from it radiate long lines of red; the body and limbs are decorated with lines which represent falling rain.

Many theories were advanced to account for the

Over
Geikie National Park, where the Fitzroy River has cut a winding gorge through the Oscar Range

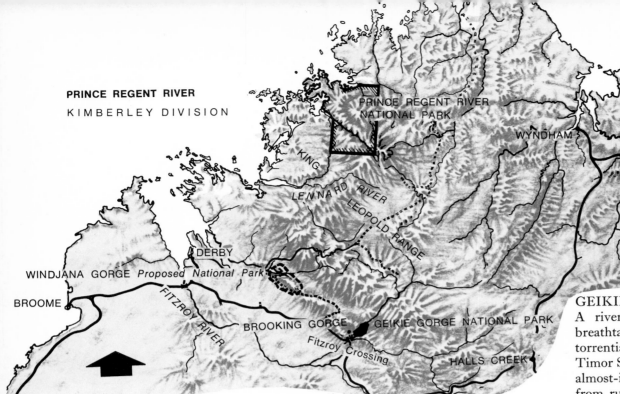

origin of the Wandjina paintings, so different were they from all previously known Aboriginal art. Not until ninety years after their discovery did anthropologists show that the Wandjinas were the work of the Aborigines, and that the ritual of the retouching of these paintings was a vital part of their ancient culture. Unless the paintings were retouched, by the ritual leaders of the tribe, before the onset of 'the wet', there would be drought and hunger.

Wandjinas were mythical dreamtime heroes who created the land. At the end of their travels and exploits they left their shades upon the walls of the caves and entered the rock waterholes. The sacred ritual of repainting their images will bring the monsoon rains, and relations between the sexes will be normal; the retouching of the many totemic animal paintings—of wallaby, echidna, eagle, dingo, goanna, crocodile, brolga and barramundi—will ensure their increase in due season. Fused with the Wandjina paintings are those of giant rainbow serpents which live in the sacred waterholes (which are stocked with the spirits of babies) near the Wandjina caves.

It is fortunate that these places are in almost inaccessible regions north and north-west of the rugged King Leopolds where they have been safe from human damage. The straight, fiord-like gorge of the Prince Regent River is one such region sheltering this Aboriginal art in a setting of spectacular beauty. In recognition of this, and perhaps with an eye to the eventual tourist development of the region's magnificent coastline, the West Australian government has set aside a reserve of 1,500,000 acres, on the Prince Regent River, for the preservation of the fauna, flora and anthropological treasures of the region.

GEIKIE GORGE NATIONAL PARK

A river born of tropical thunderstorms and breathtaking cloud-burst deluges and built of torrential cyclonic rains sweeping in from the Timor Sea; a river with headwaters in the rugged, almost-impassable King Leopold Ranges, fed from rushing waterfalls in ravines of the ranges and from floodwaters escaping the swamps and the vast inundated plains. A river growing, gathering strength—in places it reaches miles wide either side of its deep main channels . . . then a thundering torrent, racing between high rock walls to escape the banked-up pressure of swollen tributaries and of hundreds of square miles of flooded river flats and billabongs. This is the Fitzroy, one of Australia's greatest rivers.

Its course to the sea is not unobstructed—jagged ranges bar the way with walls of flint-hard limestone. At the junction of Oscar and Geikie Ranges the Fitzroy has carved a wide, deep, twelve-mile canyon through which its floods race in maelstrom fury towards lowland plains and distant sea.

When the river rises in the gorge, only treetops thrashing in the strong current mark the position of dry-season sandbars. Muddy watermarks high on treetrunks, logs caught among the branches, and white-polished rock walls are dry-season reminders of this river's mood in 'the wet'. This is Geikie Gorge, Western Australia's first national park for the far north.

The Fitzroy River in its savage flood-time spate is a sight seen by few—the wet season is not the time for tourists to attempt a visit. Winter months in the Kimberleys are dry and pleasant, but their coolness is short lived. By October the mercury is again climbing above the century.

Through November and into December the sun beats upon hard-dried, deep-cracked earth which has not felt the touch of rain for eight months or more. Distant hills, their bare rock too hot to touch, are reflected in shimmering heat mirage; the dry wind is like a furnace blast. Some time in December the air becomes oppressive.

Cumulo-nimbus thunderheads build threatening black fortresses in the sky . . . heavy raindrops signal the breaking of a storm and, perhaps, the beginning of the wet season.

Soon steady rain is softening the cracked blacksoil plains, and roads are becoming water channels or impassable quagmires. The swamps and billabongs fill as the deluge continues; the creeks all run a banker, and the rivers rise. By now the Aborigines, with age-old wisdom, have shifted their camps from shady creekbeds to higher ground. The birds—those that nest in 'the wet'—are noisily active in courtship and nest-building. Star Finches, Crimson Finches, Banded Finches and Pictorellas build nests as the rain falls.

In the swamps and on flooded grasslands the Nankeen Night-Herons, the Magpie-Geese and the Brolgas display and mate. The Jabiru, White Ibis, Reed-Warbler, and Golden-headed Fantail-Warbler nest in autumn as the rains fade out and lush grass shoots up. Later, in dry winter months, when the tall rank grasses seed, bright parrots select hollows in the picturesque ghost gums—there are Corellas, innumerable Budgerigars, rainbow-plumaged Red-collared Lorikeets, and brilliantly coloured Red-winged Parrots. Rainbow Birds, Red-backed Kingfishers, Sacred King-fishers, Mistletoe Birds and Blue-winged Kooka-burras wait, nesting in the hot dry months of spring or early summer.

The visitor to Geikie in the cool dry winter months does not see its floods, but instead, a river with long pools of still dark water. Standing on its tree-lined bank he may look up and see, wedged among the branches, the logs and debris of past floods and the muddy stain of high water levels on the white gums. Where the river has undercut the limestone cliffs and where the still waters lap lazily into small caves, the rockface is polished white for twenty feet or more above the pool, showing the level of summer's rushing torrent. Higher, the stone is stained rusty red and, towards the jagged crest, is grey from weathering.

I was in Geikie at the end of September; still,

hot days, when the water of the river's long pool was glassy smooth. We sat in the shade on a sandbar, and watched the changing shadows and colours on the cliffs across the water. As the sun dipped lower through the afternoon the rockface shadows lifted and shrank; the rock colours brightened under the full force of its light, and reddened as the sun settled towards the horizon, seeming alive with luminescent heat and forming a glowing band between the cool blue tones of sky and water.

A small tree leaning out over the water from a crevice on the opposite cliff-face supported a thousand or so flying foxes, all noisily, incessantly squabbling among themselves, and just visible as limp, leathery black shapes hanging from the branches. Once, for a moment, a Johnson's Crocodile—a small, inoffensive fresh-water species—showed on the surface of the pool's dark water.

Bird life, as always along Kimberley rivers, was conspicuous. Tiny Diamond Doves and Peaceful Doves fluttering down from the dense riverbank shrubbery to drink at a small pool in the wet sand, accompanied by Yellow-tinted Honeyeaters, maintained a soft murmuring of bird sounds through the long hot afternoons. In nearby bushes Star Finches had eggs in their large, football-shaped nest. White Cockatoos, in twos and threes, winged their way along the gorge from roosting places or nests, to feeding grounds out on the plains, and a pair of Whistling Eagles floated high over the clifftop's rocky spires.

Occasionally, a breath of wind would ruffle the water's surface—slow smooth ripples, spreading out to the most sheltered reaches of the long pool, lapping into the caves and throwing the reflections into broken patterns of stone, sky and water. It was like a giant abstract painting, in which warm rusts, ochres and burnt-earth colours intermingle with white, grey, and with the cool blues and greens of reflected sky and of lush riverbank vegetation. Not frozen, however, as on painter's canvas, but forever moving, creating endless variations of the same living scene with the lazy

89

Victoria Settlement, Port Essington

ripples of each faint breath of air. How different must be 'the wet'-season mood of the Fitzroy River floods.

Geikie Gorge has great beauty—of detail, of colour and reflection—rather than large scale grandeur or scenic vista. It has neither the awe-inspiring height of cliffs nor the canyon architecture of Windjana. Geikie is wide and long, but not of enormous depth. This is a relatively small national park, its seven thousand acres being a narrow strip enclosing the river's course through the ranges.

PRINCE REGENT RIVER RESERVE

Much further north, in the Kimberley Division in the north-west of Western Australia, locked between the sea and rough, trackless, almost-impassable country, is the 1,500,000 acre Prince Regent River flora and fauna reserve . . . a wildlife sanctuary of the greatest importance.

This must be some of the most rugged, and most difficult country to penetrate on the Australian continent. The jagged coastline on the map suggests a fiordland coast, with hills falling steeply to the sea, and many islands and land-locked sounds. But this is a tropical area, with rainfall estimated at well over fifty inches per annum, supporting vegetation almost equatorial rainforest in character, and with many plant species not found in other parts of Western Australia.

The Prince Regent River has its headwaters at a height of two thousand feet between Mt Hann and Mt Agnes, and falls to sea level in less than thirty miles through an enormous, precipitous gorge. At present most of this region is inaccessible even to four-wheel-drive vehicles, but could eventually become a valuable tourist attraction.

The fauna is not yet well known, but is thought to be typical of high rainfall areas of the Kimberleys: rock wallabies of several species, Sugar Gliders, and many small marsupials. The very rare Scaly-tailed Possum (*Wyulda squamicaudata*), occurs only in this part of the Kimberleys,

WESTERN AUSTRALIA

Totemic goanna emerging from totem well through the water lilies. Artist: Mutitupuy, Yirrala (Gove, Arnhem) area.

and has been found on the southern side of the Prince Regent estuary.

Aboriginal cave paintings and rock carvings are numerous, making this district important for anthropological studies.

With its magnificent scenery the Prince Regent River could be one of the world's outstanding national parks—a tourist attraction as well as an extremely valuable wildlife sanctuary. One and a half million acres of this rough terrain assures that many places will remain undisturbed—well away from the points of greatest tourist interest. It is hardly surprising that the Australian Academy of Science has declared the Prince Regent River area to be of 'outstanding value as a biological reserve and a national park of great scenic beauty . . . a priceless national asset.'

TUNNEL CREEK
A few miles east of Windjana Gorge a stream known as Tunnel Creek flows beneath the Napier Range. The cavernous tunnel eroded by the stream is about half a mile long. In the middle the ceiling has collapsed forming a shaft to the top of the range.

This is the place known as the Cave of Bats, where the outlawed Aboriginal Sadamara hid while recovering from his wounds. Its walls and ceilings are covered with flying foxes in great numbers, and it is possible to walk right through from one side of the range to the other—if you do not mind the risk of stepping on one of the small freshwater crocodiles which inhabit the creek. It has been proposed that Tunnel Creek be included with Windjana Gorge in national parkland.

BROOKING GORGE
With a deep permanent pool bordered by lush vegetation of eucalypts, pandanus, and Leichardt Pine, Brooking Gorge could be a national park of great tourist potential. It is only ten miles from Fitzroy Crossing, and therefore almost on the route of every around-Australia traveller.

The Australian Academy of Science has recom-

mended that 'the ranges and gorges (i.e. the Napier and Oscar ranges, Windjana, Brooking and Geikie gorges, Tunnel Creek) should be excised from the pastoral leases which at present contain them and should be set aside as Class A reserves; an expert committee should survey the area and recommend that certain parts be selected and gazetted for public recreation, and others for the preservation of Aboriginal and archaeological sites, for flora and fauna, and for geological purposes.'

That recommendation was in 1962. By 1969 the Western Australian Government has given only a small area at Geikie Gorge the necessary national park status and protection.

WOOLWONGA WILDLIFE SANCTUARY
Situated on the lower reaches of the South Alligator River and covering more than 193,000 acres of paperbark swamps and lagoons, Woolwonga waterfowl sanctuary is the breeding ground for huge numbers of Magpie Geese, together with Pigmy Geese, Jabiru, Brolga and many other birds.

The sanctuary may be reached from Darwin through Humpty Doo (where it is well worthwhile spending a day at the small Fog Dam bird sanctuary) then towards Mt Bundy—to this point the road is good. Shortly before Mt Bundy a left turn marks the beginning of the long rough dirt track to Jim Jim, and on to Oenpelli, western Arnhem Land. The presence of colourful and abundant wildlife make this dry and dusty journey, with rock and muddy river crossings, well worthwhile.

On the wide grassland plains will be seen herds of introduced Asian buffalo and an occasional wallaby, and numerous water birds in every billabong. This road, across deeply cracked black-soil plains, is passable only in the winter, for it becomes a quagmire during the summer wet season. Jim Jim, a tiny tourist settlement, is almost on the threshold of the sanctuary.

The great paperbark (*Melaleuca leucadendron*)

swamps, which cover tens of thousands of acres in the Woolwonga sanctuary, are at the confluence of three rivers or creeks. The South Alligator River, Deaf-adder Creek and Jim Jim Creek rise in the rugged escarpment of western Arnhem Land, and spill the monsoon floods into a maze of channels, billabongs, lagoons and swamps where they converge on the coastal lowlands.

One of the most interesting and certainly the most numerous of the bird species in this area, is the Magpie Goose (*Anseranas semipalmata*) which has been the centre of some conflict and research. With the establishment of experimental ricefields along the Adelaide River, the great flocks of Magpie Geese became a problem—the rice was planted in one of the breeding areas of the geese, the birds naturally tended to concentrate in great numbers on the flooded ricefields, damaging the new plantings.

Magpie Geese still occur in flocks of up to thirty thousand in the breeding area, a narrow coastal strip in the Northern Territory. The establishment of the large Woolwonga sanctuary to protect one of this bird's main breeding swamps would seem to have ensured the survival of the species.

Another bird of these far northern swamps and billabongs is the Jabiru (*Xenorhynchus asiaticus*), a tall, dignified and strikingly-coloured bird with a huge bill. Frequently on the large water-lily leaves may be seen the Jacana, or Lotus-bird (*Irediparra gallinacea*) which has long slender toes that enable it to walk on floating vegetation.

Birds are not the only wildlife here. On one occasion I hid by a grassy clearing at the edge of a paperbark swamp, where a tiny stream flowed through a series of shallow pools before disappearing into the morass of the great swamp. In this moist hollow the grass was close-cropped like a lawn, and green, though this was well into the dry season; impressed into the soft clay in a great many places were the tracks of wallabies.

With camera and telephoto lens set up behind a dense screen of paperbark foliage I filled-in time,

while waiting for the wallabies, by watching the many birds which came to drink as the sun broke into the clearing and the day grew warmer.

Several Egrets, their plumage snowy white, flew into the clearing to stalk slowly along the little creek, and a White Ibis (*Threskiornis molucca*) wandered out from the gloomy shadows of the swamp. A Black-fronted Dotterel (*Charadrius melanops*) shepherded its two tiny fluffy chicks from tall grass down to the waters edge, and from a low branch an Azure Kingfisher (*Alcyone azurea*) every now and then plunged into the shallow water for some small fish or crustacean. A female Shining Flycatcher (*Piezorhynchus alecto*) spent a full hour bathing, splashing in the shallows, preening on a twig, then frolicking in the water.

It was almost eleven before the first of the Agile Wallabies appeared. Bounding leisurely down to the pool it paused for a moment, then splashed across through the shallows to lie in the shade, where it stayed until afternoon. Before long several others appeared. Small, cinnamon-red wallabies, quite unafraid and unsuspecting, springing lightly down from the dry forest to drink at the pool. One, with a heavy pouch, carried a large joey. At the slightest sound—as the click of the camera shutter—the nearest wallaby, barely twelve feet away, would sit upright, long ears twitching and turning. If suddenly alarmed, the wallaby would leap away with a great bound, thumping the ground to send its fellows racing for the bush.

The little Agile Wallaby (*Wallabia agilis*) is still common in some parts of the far north. It may often be spotted in the headlights' beams at night along the back tracks, or be heard crashing away through the bush well beyond the campfire.

COBOURG PENINSULA, MURGANELLA AND DALY RIVER WILDLIFE SANCTUARIES

Although the Woolwonga waterfowl sanctuary is large, it is far surpassed in area by three great tropical wildlife sanctuaries: the Cobourg Peninsula, 505,000 acres, the Murganella wildlife

Perulba tribe drawings; flying possums (Sugar Gliders) at Prince Regent River

93

NORTHERN TERRITORY

sanctuary at the extreme north-west corner of Arnhem Land adjoining Cobourg Peninsula, 677,000 acres, and Daly River wildlife sanctuary, west and south-west of the mouth of the Daly River, 444,900 acres.

All are coastal sanctuaries. Their vegetation is principally tropical monsoon forest, *Eucalyptus* woodlands, and extensive mangroves or, at Daly River, tropical tussock grassland. Unfortunately, the natural state of much of these north-coastal sanctuaries has been damaged by great numbers of introduced Asian buffaloes which, in particular, destroy the beauty of the lily lagoons by their wallowing in the mud, and they probably make the swamps uninhabitable for many native creatures.

Most of the far northern coast from Daly River eastward around Arnhem Land is low, or with rather low cliffs, but broken by numerous bays and extensive estuaries, silted river mouths and tidal mudflats, all of which support extensive mangrove forests. The mangroves, of which there are many species (altogether fourteen genera in tropical Australia), are trees adapted for growth in waterlogged soils of high and fluctuating salinity. They are able to flourish though the tides here rise and fall as much as forty feet.

The mangroves shelter a diversity of wildlife, their most notorious denizen being the large salt-water crocodile, which reaches a length of about twenty-five feet; when the rivers are in flood it may be found many miles inland. But the crocodile has been consistently hunted, and has suffered a tremendous population decline.

A strange creature housed in these mudflats and mangrove swamps of the far north is the Goggle-eyed Mudskipper (*Periophthalmus expeditionum*), a fish which can leave the water to walk across the mudflats, and 'it can even climb trees. It is surprisingly fast out of the water, paddling along on its large, elbow-like pectoral fins, or 'skipping' away from a pursuer by a powerful flicking of body and tail. The five Australian mudskipper species, all confined to the tropics, are able to breathe out

of the marine environment by extracting oxygen from a supply of water held in their pouch-like gill chambers, and perhaps also through the skin.

These extensive tropical-coast mangroves have a rich bird life, with many birds found only among mangroves. Among those endemic to mangroves are the White-breasted Whistler, Mangrove Bittern, Mangrove Kingfisher, and Mangrove Robin. Others may also be found at times in adjacent open forest or scrub, or in freshwater swamps.

The Mangrove Bittern (*Butorides striata*) inhabits the muddy foreshores of inlets and rivers, and builds a loose platform of sticks for a nest, in a tree in the water. Like other bitterns, it adopts an upright, frozen-stick posture if disturbed.

The Mangrove Kingfisher (*Halcyon chloris*) is coloured blue-green above and white beneath, with a white collar and black streak through the eye. It is confined to the mangroves and drills into an arboreal termite's nest to construct its own nest.

One of the most colourful of the mangrove birds is the Red-headed Honeyeater (*Myzomela erythrocephala*). The male is unmistakeable, having an intense crimson head and lower back, while its wings and most of its body are dull brown; the female has only a tinge of red on her forehead. These little honeyeaters are very active, fluttering among flowers and chasing insects. Their nest is well hidden, usually near the top of a tall mangrove tree. Also nesting in the mangroves is the White-breasted Whistler (*Pachycephala lanioides*) a species found only in mangroves. The Mangrove Robin (*Peneoenanthe pulverulentus*), coloured a rich brown above and white beneath, nests in the fork of a mangrove, up to fourteen feet above the water.

The small (five-inch) Rufous-banded Honeyeater (*Conopophila albogularis*), also called Red-breasted Honeyeater, is a brownish colour, with grey about the head and darker grey through the eye, white throat, and a red-brown band across the breast. It is an active bird, constantly chasing

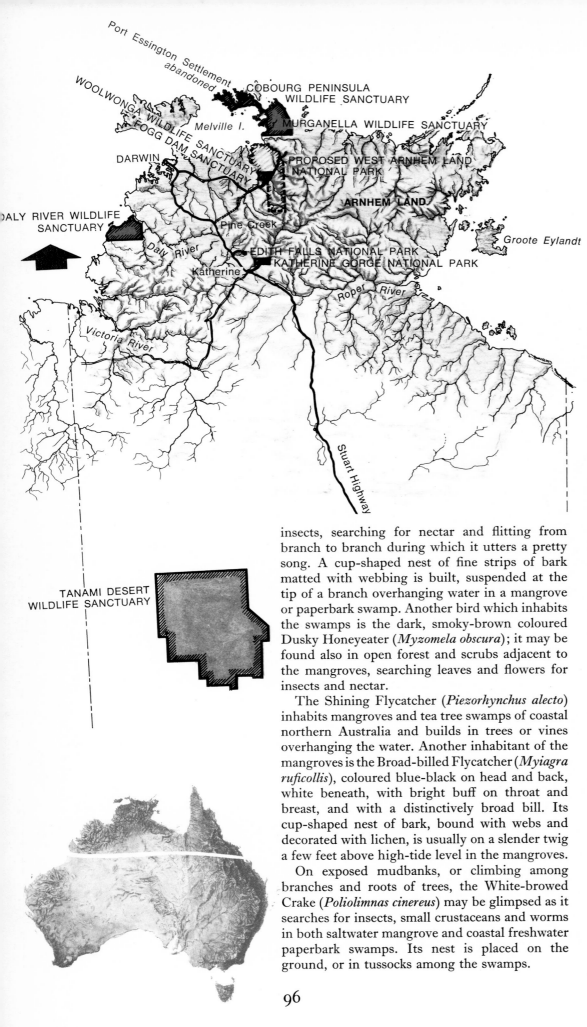

insects, searching for nectar and flitting from branch to branch during which it utters a pretty song. A cup-shaped nest of fine strips of bark matted with webbing is built, suspended at the tip of a branch overhanging water in a mangrove or paperbark swamp. Another bird which inhabits the swamps is the dark, smoky-brown coloured Dusky Honeyeater (*Myzomela obscura*); it may be found also in open forest and scrubs adjacent to the mangroves, searching leaves and flowers for insects and nectar.

The Shining Flycatcher (*Piezorhynchus alecto*) inhabits mangroves and tea tree swamps of coastal northern Australia and builds in trees or vines overhanging the water. Another inhabitant of the mangroves is the Broad-billed Flycatcher (*Myiagra ruficollis*), coloured blue-black on head and back, white beneath, with bright buff on throat and breast, and with a distinctively broad bill. Its cup-shaped nest of bark, bound with webs and decorated with lichen, is usually on a slender twig a few feet above high-tide level in the mangroves.

On exposed mudbanks, or climbing among branches and roots of trees, the White-browed Crake (*Poliolimnas cinereus*) may be glimpsed as it searches for insects, small crustaceans and worms in both saltwater mangrove and coastal freshwater paperbark swamps. Its nest is placed on the ground, or in tussocks among the swamps.

ARNHEM LAND

Arnhem Land is an area of about 31,200 square miles, in northern Australia. A national park is now being sought for a part of the rugged western escarpment of Arnhem Land, where caves and rock shelters hold magnificent galleries of Aboriginal art.

It was in this region that the 'X-ray' style of painting reached a higher level of development than in any other part of Australia. These artists painted not only what they saw, but also that which they knew to exist: within the outlines of human beings, animals, birds, fish, they showed the internal organs and bones, depicted in decorative patterns of fine lines and of solid colour. Anthropologist Charles Mountford has expressed the opinion that in no other part of the world has this type of art reached such perfection.

In friezes up to a hundred feet long, in some parts of western Arnhem Land, the paintings cover the walls and ceilings of caves and rock shelters. Natural ochres of red and yellow, of white clay, black manganese or charcoal, were used, as in other parts of the continent. Occasionally, human blood was used, and in some instances the use of brown, blue and purple has been recorded in the far north. However, red is the predominant colour, with yellow and white in widespread use.

Not only do these rock art paintings cover all available surfaces, but often figures were painted over each other; the important thing was always the act of painting, rather than the contemplation of the completed work of art. Painting according to the conventions of tribal culture, the artist did not bother to try to recapture the real world of nature which was constantly about him, but was concerned with deeper, more important meanings. His art was not often play, nor a pastime, but, in his belief, vital to his survival; behind every figure, pattern and decorative design was meaning —perhaps of ritual significance, perhaps of the exploits of dreamtime heroes, or perhaps of his power over the animals he would kill.

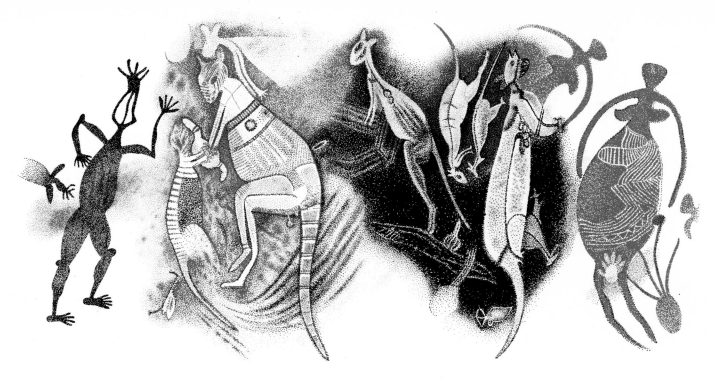

Miailli tribe drawings; Western Arnhem Land
L to r—Spirit rocks; kangaroos; birds and kangaroos

It was also in far northern Australia, particularly in Arnhem Land and nearby islands, that the art of painting upon large sheets of bark reached its finest development. These paintings were the expression of a rich mythology and the result of long tradition, and need to be viewed with some knowledge of the story, myth or ritual they depict if they are to be fully appreciated. Yet, appraised purely for artistic or decorative qualities—which is their appeal to the uninformed viewer—many of these paintings remain as fine works of art. Some have a great deal to contribute to world art as works in their own right, and as a source of decorative motifs and patterns, or as examples of storytelling through symbolic expression. With the recent increased interest in Aboriginal art, bark paintings are becoming available for sale in large numbers, often at quite high prices. Though all are painted by age-old techniques, most are now produced solely for the tourist trade, and are no more than a repetition of the most popular of the traditional motifs and patterns, rather than individual works of art painted with a purpose and meaning vital to the artist.

However, whether the paintings were produced for some age-old ritual or whether made for sale, the techniques are much the same, and to this extent at least, all are authentic.

On a large sheet of bark, prepared by the removal of rough outer layers and treated with a fixative (the sap of a tree-orchid bulb) the painter works with natural pigments of red and yellow ochre, white, and black manganese or charcoal. These are ground with water to a creamy con-sistency on flat stones and applied with brushes made of stringy-bark, or with a frayed or chewed stick, or, for fine lines, with a small feather or palm-leaf fibres.

Bark paintings which are not influenced by European man are being produced in fewer numbers as the old Aborigines, who participated in the tribal rituals and were initiated into the tribal secrets, die. Those examples of their bark and rock art which have been preserved, together with their weapons and artefacts, will become the last record of their ancient culture, and of the early history of man in Australia. When these far northern national parks are established and developed to the extent that visitor information centres are constructed, some of these art works and other objects could be displayed at a site within the region where the tribesmen once hunted, rather than all be hidden in southern museums.

The Northern Territory Reserves Board has for many years been trying to have established, on the western edge of Arnhem Land (just west of the huge Aboriginal reserve), a national park worthy of the name, and large enough to compare with those of Africa, America or Asia. The proposed national park would be mostly of extremely rough, broken ranges where there is much magnificent scenery including the Jim Jim falls, abundant wildlife, and many fine examples of Aboriginal rock art. The park would extend northwards to the coastal swamplands which are rich in birdlife, and would preferably link with the Woolwonga waterfowl sanctuary.

Gunwinggu tribe, Central Arnhem Land; pregnant woman

97

EDITH FALLS NATIONAL PARK

A chain of waterfalls, cascading over cliffs of
yellow, rust-red, brown or white rock, to deep
pools of incredibly clear water fringed with the
lush tropical greenery of massed pandanus palms:
this is Edith Falls National Park in the Northern
Territory, a place of great scenic beauty not yet
well known to the tourist throng.

A rough dirt road leads to the first and lowest of
the falls, where the river drops to a large pool on
the plains at the foot of the range—this is the area
most visited. But higher, in the rough, broken
terrain of the hills, are waterfalls and pools which,
though perhaps smaller, are of greater beauty;
these upper falls are accessible via a stony track
which usually requires a four-wheel-drive vehicle,
then walking trails lead to the river gorge, pools,
and falls.

During the dry season the sheltered pools are
mirror-smooth, or with slow, glassy ripple reflect
rock, sky, pandanus and eucalypt greenery in an
ever-changing mosaic of intermingling colours—
a contrast to the floods which thunder down these
cataracts in 'the wet', leaving record of their
heights as polished rock and broken trees, up the
sides of the gorge. From July to August, the
fiery-orange blossom of vermilion gums (*Eucalyptus miniata*) makes a spectacular display, attracting
honeyeaters and Red-collared Lorikeets to feed
noisily among the blossoms.

Deep rock-pools beneath each waterfall are
inhabited by freshwater crocodiles which are fully
protected here. Occasionally, one may be seen
sunning itself on a ledge or, where the water is
shallow over a rock bar, glimpsed on the bottom.

At various places in these rugged ranges are
galleries of Aboriginal art. One of these, faded and
streaked by years of seeping water, can easily be
seen on a rockface near the lowest, most readily
accessible waterfall.

Edith Falls is not scenery on a grand scale, but
in many ways, it is more beautiful than some huge
geological features which are well-known tourist
attractions. And because its beauty lies in detail—

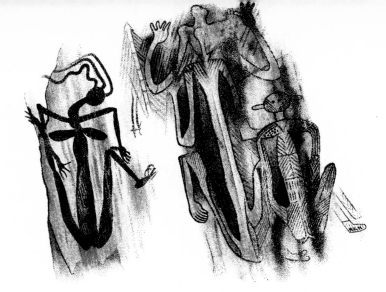

Aboriginal rock paintings, Edith Falls Reserve, N.T.

in clear, clean pools and lush tropical vegetation —it is a place which will easily become degraded by careless over-use.

KATHERINE GORGE

On the Katherine, a river running south-west from western Arnhem Land for almost 150 miles, lies spectacular Katherine Gorge. Great square-sided walls, broken by narrow canyons and blazing with colour under the tropical sun, guard the Katherine River's zig-zag course. At Katherine Gorge the river fills from wall to wall the huge gorge whose sides plunge vertically, from heights of three hundred feet, to depths of more than one hundred feet. In very few places in the main gorge is it possible to walk along the river banks near water level—from a boat the rockface can be seen to continue steeply far down into the clear water.

Throughout each day the colours, the shadows and the sunlight constantly change; morning light outlines one wall of the gorge, while afternoon light strikes the opposite rockface so that the rock glows as if lit within by fire.

The water, too, has many moods. Often the wind through the long chasm whips the surface to choppy little waves; or the breathless calm of a still, hot day mirrors the orange-red cliffs, with only a slow glassy ripple breaking the image.

But these are the dry season moods of the gorge. Through 'the wet' it is often a far more savage mood, but one seen by very few people; the twenty mile road from Katherine township to the gorge is impassable when the river is in flood. The gorge becomes a torrent of thundering, brown water, bearing tree-trunks and debris, imprisoned between immovable walls. It was this raging water which carved into the ranges, cutting deep along the rectangular fault lines which have determined the shape of the gorge.

Where tourists in the dry season change boats between first and second gorges, the shallows disappear beneath huge rapids marked by twelve-foot high waves. Mudbanks and shores disappear as their trees thrash about in the current. When the floods have subsided, there remains evidence of their height in the debris wedged into branches and rock crevices twenty feet, and more, above the level of the placid dry-season pools.

The only satisfactory way to see this gorge is by boat. Tours through the gorge are available during the cooler months. Starting at the camping area downstream, the boats follow the wide, lower or first gorge; here the sides are very steep but not always vertical, and trees line the banks.

A little way into the gorge several huge boulders well out in the river are a favourite sunbasking place for Freshwater Crocodiles (*Crocodilus johnstoni*) which often do not move as the boats pass by. Other crocodiles may occasionally be seen on treetrunks sloping from the water. Some must be near the eight-foot maximum length for this species. Within the protected waters of this park, freshwater crocodiles seem to have remained quite numerous despite the slaughter which has wiped them out in many other places.

Several miles into the gorge the walls become vertical, broken here and there by narrow canyons which have resulted from erosion along faults breaking into the main gorge. A rock bar marks the end of the lower gorge; here it is necessary to leave the boat to walk several hundred yards around wide shallow pools and very low, wide waterfalls or rapids. In this area there are extensive galleries of Aboriginal rock art. One of the paintings, depicting a crocodile, is more than ten feet long; other paintings feature human figures larger than life size, together with many small drawings. From here a second boat is needed for the exploration of the main gorge.

It is in this second gorge that the Katherine is most spectacular, with very high vertical and overhanging cliffs dropping sheer to deep water. This is not a straight gorge; it follows a series of sudden right-angled corners, with a straight course in between—this is the pattern of erosion along faulting in the rock mass.

In places the floods, rushing constantly against the foot of a cliff, have undercut to form caves whose floors are far below even the dry-season waterlevel. Some caves are frequented by colonies of Fairy Martins (*Hylochelidon ariel*); their bottle-shaped mud nests cling by the hundred to the ceilings of the overhanging cliffs.

Most boat tours go no further than a rock barrier in the water at the end of this 'second gorge'. However, with a boat light enough to carry across the shallows and rapids, it is possible to explore many miles further into the depths of Katherine Gorge.

In June and July on the rough plateau above the gorge are tall flowering gums (*Eucalyptus miniata*), bearing masses of brilliant orange flowers which attract many birds. Pairs or flocks of Red-collared Lorikeets (*Trichoglossus rubritorquatus*) are conspicuous by their high-pitched chattering and screeching as they feed among the nectar-laden blossoms, together with many honey-eaters. Equally spectacular of plumage are the Crimson-winged Parrots (*Aprosmictus erythropterus*) and many bright little finches including the Crimson Finches (*Neochmia phaeton*) which live in this area.

The camping area is frequented by a group of Great Bower-birds (*Chlamydera nuchalis*) which have a bower among some big boulders on the hillside. This bower is decorated with many colourful items 'borrowed' from campers. These birds are renowned as vocal mimics.

The rough ranges are the habitat of Rock Wallabies (*Petrogale brachyotis*) and occasionally one may be seen on a ledge in the gorges. On the spinifex-covered rocky plateau Euros (*Macropus robustus*) are still quite common.

KATHERINE GORGE ABORIGINAL PAINTINGS

The sandstone ranges of the Katherine River headwaters have long been an Aborigines' stronghold. In the Katherine Gorge area there are many examples of their art.

On smooth-cleft rock surfaces at the base of the gorge's huge walls, protected from rain and running water, the tribesmen have painted tall figures of their ritual or dreamtime heroes, and of the animals of their world. The figures are life-size and often larger—men, six or nine feet tall; crocodiles, ten or fifteen feet long—in keeping with the stature and exploits of the great spirit beings of the dreamtime who, in Aboriginal belief, are still alive today, in spirit. Behind every painting lies a story, without which we cannot fully appreciate the work; most Aboriginal art is sacred art, conveying through its symbolic representations, myths of their creative era, the dreamtime. But as fast as our interest and appreciation of Aboriginal art increases, the traditional Aboriginal way of life disappears, and with it, the works which reflect their complex traditions—often thoughtlessly destroyed, or fading with time.

Aboriginal paintings from the walls of Katherine Gorge, N.T.

PALMERSTON NATIONAL PARK

Situated along the Palmerston Highway, over-looking the Johnstone River twenty miles from Innisfail, is the Palmerston National Park with an area of 6,315 acres. This park was established primarily to preserve the jungle and rainforest vegetation growing near the Highway as a scenic drive through typical north Queensland jungle.

The luminous world of the rainforest is one of soft green light filtered through translucent leaves of tree canopy, ferns and mosses. The highway, tunnelling through lush green rainforest and tortuously twisting around the steep-flanked spurs of the range, climbs three thousand feet from the coast at Innisfail to the heights of the Atherton Tableland. The road is often wet from the constant seepage from the forest floor. Roadside cuttings become banks of delicate ferns; and where there is a break in the overhanging foliage, clusters of tall tree ferns glow brilliant green in the sunlight against a dark backdrop of jungle walls. This is a road to take slowly, for the beauty of this scenic journey through the high tropical rainforest is unsurpassed in Australia.

Bird life is abundant in this park. You may find a Cassowary stalking across the highway, impressive as no other bird, with his powerful thick legs and heavily clawed, dangerous feet, wire-like black plumage, sharp eyes beneath heavy casque, and exotic colours of brilliant blue, red and yellow splashed down his neck and breast. Other birds to be seen include Rifle-birds, Buff-breasted Pittas, Regent Bower-birds, Brush Turkeys and Scrub Hens.

Marsupials live here also, but they emerge from their hiding-places only at night. There are Tree Kangaroos, Green Possums looking like faded mossy tree branches, strange chocolate-brown Lemur-like Possums, and the Striped Possum.

From the highway, signposted walking tracks lead to the waterfalls which are the real scenic features of the park. Winding aisles between huge, buttressed trees lead down among moss-covered boulders and luxuriant growths of delicate ferns,

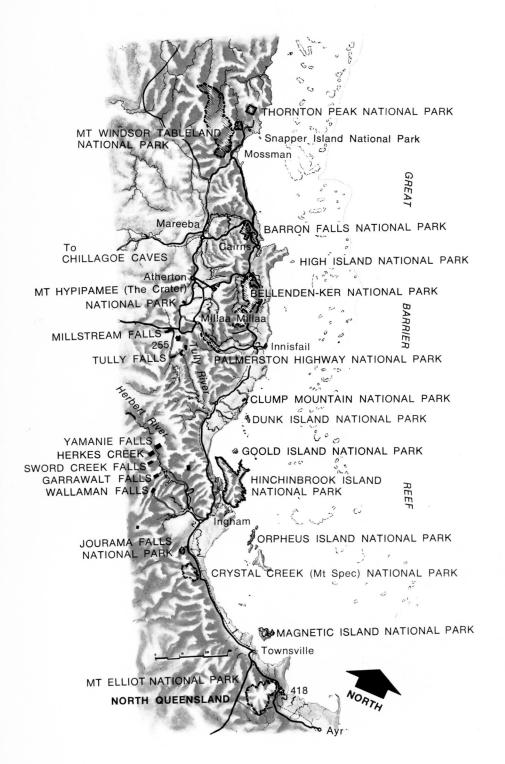

MT WINDSOR TABLELAND
NATIONAL PARK

THORNTON PEAK NATIONAL PARK

Snapper Island National Park

Mossman

Mareeba

To
CHILLAGOE CAVES

Atherton

MT HYPIPAMEE (The Crater)
NATIONAL PARK

Millaa Millaa

MILLSTREAM FALLS

255

TULLY FALLS

Cairns

BARRON FALLS NATIONAL PARK

HIGH ISLAND NATIONAL PARK

BELLENDEN-KER NATIONAL PARK

Innisfail

PALMERSTON HIGHWAY NATIONAL PARK

CLUMP MOUNTAIN NATIONAL PARK

DUNK ISLAND NATIONAL PARK

GOOLD ISLAND NATIONAL PARK

HINCHINBROOK ISLAND
NATIONAL PARK

Ingham

ORPHEUS ISLAND NATIONAL PARK

CRYSTAL CREEK (Mt Spec) NATIONAL PARK

MAGNETIC ISLAND NATIONAL PARK

Townsville

MT ELLIOT NATIONAL PARK

NORTH QUEENSLAND

418

NORTH

Ayr

Herbert River

Tully River

YAMANIE FALLS
HERKES CREEK
SWORD CREEK FALLS
GARRAWALT FALLS
WALLAMAN FALLS

JOURAMA FALLS
NATIONAL PARK

GREAT

BARRIER

REEF

to a dim moist world of soft green light. Tall trees soar to a dense canopy which shuts out almost all sunlight. Some are smooth-trunked but with widespread buttresses.

There is little undergrowth in the half-darkness near the forest floor, but on tree trunks and branches the epiphytic ferns and arboreal orchids flourish; mosses give a green-velvet texture to old logs and to spreading buttresses, and the ground is thickly matted with an ancient accumulation of moist, rotting leaves. Fallen trees, devoured by fungi, are soon soft and rotten in the constant humid warmth of the rainforest.

Here there is unexpected beauty, highlights of vivid colour against the green gloom of the jungle. A huge orchid clump in the crotch of a lofty tree catching the sunlight, golden against the blue-sky gap in the forest canopy. Or a shaft of light striking down from some opening in the foliage to high-light the new red fronds of a fern, or to set aflame the vivid leaves of the 'bleeding heart' tree, or to catch in brilliant white the spray and foaming white water of cataract and waterfall. Nandroya, Tchupella, and Wallacha Falls—each is worth a visit; none is any great distance from the road along tracks which are well maintained.

This magnificent Palmerston National Park exists today because someone had the foresight to preserve a narrow strip of rainforest along the Palmerston Highway at a time when the valuable forests of the Atherton Tableland were (as they still are) being destroyed to provide cow paddocks.

Our forests were regarded by the early settlers as a nuisance and a hindrance; popular but inaccurate belief being that the tallest trees and biggest scrubs grew on the best land, so that the sooner it was cleared the better. Along Australia's eastern highlands, where steep slopes were once protected by forests, there are many eroded slopes and abandoned farms overgrown with tangled lantana: the result of clearing lands of limited soil fertility. Dr Leonard Webb wrote in *The Great Extermination*, 'even on the favourable basaltic red loams of the Atherton Tableland the alienation of

Sunbird

forests was followed by needless tree destruction . . . and the general failure of farming.'

The forests should be preserved, both in forestry reserves and in National Parks, rather than needlessly destroyed. Yet even today there are cries for the destruction of more of our forest remnants for agricultural 'development'. It is to be hoped that a proposed enlargement of the narrow Palmerston National Park will be approved by the Queensland Government.

BARRON AND TULLY FALLS NATIONAL PARKS

Formerly among the most spectacular in Australia, the famed Barron and Tully waterfalls are no longer the scenic highlights they once were. Hydro-electric schemes have taken water from both falls, so that the visitor has little chance, except perhaps in the wet season, of seeing the falls as they were before the dams robbed them of their thundering white water.

Queensland has economised on the price of electric power, but has cut into the value of its tourist industry. It is to be hoped that the surviving waterfalls of Queensland will not be sacrificed to any such short-sighted 'economy' measures. These irreplaceable natural assets will bring an ever-growing hoard of visitors, and thus represent a tremendous natural resource if they can be protected within national parklands and wisely safeguarded against destructive 'developmental' works. There can then be an ever-increasing exploitation of their tourist potential without sacrifice of the qualities which attract visitors. This requires development compatible with preservation of natural scenic beauty.

Barron Falls park area is 7,000 acres and Tully Falls park is 1,240 acres. Although the falls have lost their grandeur, the rugged grandeur of the gorges remains. At Tully walking tracks lead to pools near the falls.

MT WINDSOR TABLELAND NATIONAL PARK

Fifteen miles inland from the coast to the north-west of Mossman, it covers the slopes and heights of the most northerly high plateau between the Atherton Tableland and Cape York, and is the northern limit of the great areas of rainforest in Queensland.

Mt Windsor National Park covers a magnificent, and largely inaccessible wilderness region at the headwaters of the Upper Daintree River, and includes the rugged Upper Daintree and Adeline Creek gorges, and the Adeline Creek Falls. The tableland has an average elevation of about 3,500 feet, with some peaks exceeding 4,000 feet; to the east these heights drop precipitously to the coast.

Because it preserves so large an area of virgin rainforest the Mt Windsor Tableland National Park is of tremendous importance as a wildlife sanctuary. Among the creatures which live only in these far northern jungles are the Bennett's Tree Kangaroo (*Dendrolagus bennettianus*) which is confined to a small area of mountainous forests between Cooktown and the Daintree River, and the Musk Rat-kangaroo (*Hypsiprymnodon moschatus*).

Tree kangaroos are of New Guinea origin, the two species in Australia having come via Cape York. The Musk Rat-kangaroo is small; rat-sized as its name indicates. It is the most primitive member of its family, forming a connecting link between the possums and the kangaroos—it is the only kangaroo which retains an opposable first toe on the hindfoot (such as the possums use greatly for climbing), the fore and hind limbs are still approximately equal in length, and the tail is naked of fur, and scaly. It runs on all feet instead of leaping, and lives upon insects, tubers and other vegetable matter which it obtains by scratching among the litter of the rainforest floor. As the Musk Rat-kangaroo appears to be uncommon over much of its limited range, the Mt Windsor Tableland and the Bellenden-Ker National Park further south will provide a living place for this interesting, primitive marsupial, as well as for the many other creatures of the rainforests.

MILLSTREAM FALLS

A wide waterfall set in a broad valley, Millstream Falls carries a good flow of water throughout the year. In contrast to most north Queensland waterfalls it is not surrounded by dense jungle, but is in open eucalypt forest. Though it is easiest to view the falls from above, they are probably most attractive from below, when the long crest of white water against the sky and black rock is most impressive.

Millstream Falls are two hundred feet wide, probably the widest in Queensland, and drop sixty feet to a shallow but attractive gorge where the river flows away among boulders and trees.

This open eucalypt forest country has its own wildlife. One of the most startling creatures that is likely to be encountered by the visitor is Australia's largest lizard, the Perentie (*Varanus giganteus*), which can grow to a length of eight or even nine feet, and is quite common through grasslands and open forests of the far north.

Another northern reptile, the Frill-necked Lizard (*Chlamydosaurus kingii*) is well able to utilize the element of surprise at any encounter— suddenly expanding a great flap of brightly-coloured skin around its neck and with a loud hiss opening a bright pink mouth; an effective bluff which gives the lizard an instant to streak for cover.

CHILLAGOE CAVES NATIONAL PARKS

The old mining town of Chillagoe is situated about 140 miles west of Cairns and ninety miles from Mareeba, in a huge band of limestone which stretches from Alma-Den, fifteen miles to the south-east to the Walsh River twenty-five miles to the north-west, with a width of about two miles.

Rising to about 150 feet above the plains in countless places across this limestone belt are spectacular, vertical-walled towers of hard, dark-grey limestone, deeply dissected by fissures and knife-edged ridges which give their high walls the appearance of ancient castle battlements. It is an extraordinarily rugged and weird topography.

In these jagged limestone outcrops many caves have formed, penetrating as far as seventy feet below the level of the surrounding plains and extending beyond the borders of the surface limestone massif. Many caves have been found, scattered over a wide area, and it is certain that many more, perhaps larger than those already known, remain to be discovered.

The best of the known caves are protected within national park areas, and closed against unauthorized entry. Guided tours are conducted through these caves; intending visitors to Chillagoe should first check with the Forestry Department or Tourist Bureau for the times when cave inspections are available.

Altogether 4,732 acres in nine reservations have been set aside as National Park. Among the caves included in these reserves are the Royal Arch Caves, the Donor (or Madonna) Cave, in which a rock profile is said to bear a likeness to the Madonna, the Tower of London Caves, Jubilee and Piano Caves, Cathedral Caves, Eclipse Caves, Ryan Imperial Cave, Markham Cave, Royal Archway Cave, Geck and Spring Caves.

Many of these caves are of considerable size. One chamber of the Royal Arch Cave has a length of 170 feet, a breadth of more than one hundred feet, and a height of forty feet. Some have attractive stalactite and stalagmite decorations, with colours ranging from pure white to deep rich red-brown, with tones of light brown, grey-brown and grey, while in one cave a greenish coloration is dominant. Aboriginal paintings have been found on the walls of some of the shallow caves.

BELLENDEN-KER NATIONAL PARK

A mountain of moods, now capped in billowing white, then lost in lowering grey, or hidden in tropical storm-clouds which can dump feet of rain upon the coastal slopes within a few days; a blue outline above the eastern horizon, sharply defined in the clear morning air, high above the mist-filled valleys of the tableland, or a black silhouette against an evening sky reddened by the

Left
Massed ferns overhang the Palmerston Highway where it winds through the national park

Above and Right
Castle-like towers of hard coloured limestone dominate the landscape around Chillago, north Queensland; beneath are extensive caves

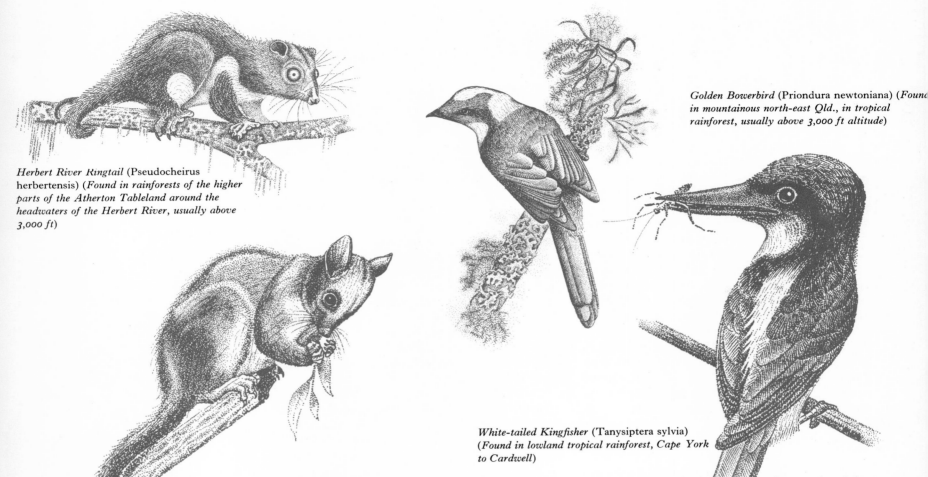

Herbert River Ringtail (Pseudocheirus herbertensis) (*Found in rainforests of the higher parts of the Atherton Tableland around the headwaters of the Herbert River, usually above 3,000 ft*)

Golden Bowerbird (Priondura newtoniana) (*Found in mountainous north-east Qld., in tropical rainforest, usually above 3,000 ft altitude*)

White-tailed Kingfisher (Tanysiptera sylvia) (*Found in lowland tropical rainforest, Cape York to Cardwell*)

Coppery Brush-tail Possum (Trichosurus vulpecula johnstonii) (*Confined to mountain rainforests of the Atherton Tableland northwards to Cooktown*)

haze of lowland cane fires. This is Mt Bartle Frere (5,000 feet), the highest peak in Queensland and a magnificent climax to Bellenden-Ker National Park's 80,000 acres of towering peaks, rough river gorges and tropical rainforest. The park lies between Gordonvale and Innisfail to the west of the Bruce Highway.

Originally reserved in 1885 for the protection of native fauna, this twenty-four mile strip of mountainous terrain along the Bellenden-Ker range was dedicated as national parkland in 1921. It is rich, tropical rainforest with distinctive flora and fauna. The extreme ruggedness of the terrain has safeguarded its natural beauty; this area should long continue to be a refuge for jungle creatures which have vanished from other areas cleared of their tall timber and scrub.

From lookouts on Mt Bartle Frere (reached only after a long climb through dense scrub) are magnificent views: on one side are canefields and rich river flats, and on the other side, the green patchwork design of the Atherton Tableland. But the climb to the summit is not to be taken lightly—

it is a long trail, rising many thousands of feet through damp, dense scrub where the pathway is not always clear and clouds or rain may close in suddenly.

The high gorges of the Bellenden-Ker range are the headwaters of the Mulgrave and Russell Rivers which almost encircle the mountain to flow finally across the flat canefields below. To clear dense vegetation from even the lower slopes would bring massive erosion under the heavy rainfall which totals two hundred inches a year, and would bring devastating floods to the fertile flats below as well as making the beautiful rivers mere muddy channels.

On the heights of Bellenden-Ker the visitor can find the Golden Bower-bird, the Prince Albert Rifle-bird, and the Tooth-billed Bower-bird, while on the lower coastal slopes live the Yellow-breasted Sunbird and the incredibly beautiful White-tailed Kingfisher.

The Bellenden-Ker range has its origin as a horst—a gigantic block pushed upwards where the earth's crust, between parallel faults, was subjected to some tremendous pressure. Since its elevation to heights considerably greater than today's 5,000 feet the story of Bellenden-Ker and of the Atherton Tableland has been of unceasing erosion. Innumerable waterfalls tumbling from the high cliffs of the escarpments have gradually cut back the land to form the steep-sided valleys and gorges of rapids and cataracts to be seen today. Here and there where hard rock strata is undercut by soft stone many rivers still tumble over high falls to deep gorges of dense jungle.

These high ranges of Bellenden-Ker National Park, together with other national park areas along the north Queensland coast, and some forestry areas, are the greatest belts of tropical rainforest to be found on this dry continent. As such they are unique within the Australian scene. This rainforest is among the richest and most fascinating of Australia's natural wonders; a world of luminous half-light filters down through depths of leaves, ferns and mosses, amid huge buttressed trees and luxuriant undergrowth. Hidden in this green twilight are such creatures as the Tree Kangaroo, the twenty-foot Scrub Python, the Cassowary, Cuscus, huge bright butterflies and tropical orchids.

JOURAMA FALLS NATIONAL PARK
A few miles south-west of Ingham is the little-known Jourama Falls National Park, a small and comparatively recent addition to Queensland's national parks.

This is not a single waterfall, but a series, none very high yet attractively situated among huge boulders and tropical greenery. As well as the falls there are many rapids, and deep, clear rock pools. The surrounding hills are of open eucalypt forest, with greater luxuriance of vegetation along the river. and around the falls.

Though this is not as spectacular as some of the high waterfalls it is in every way a most attractive place, showing not the slightest sign of human activity. At present it is necessary to walk a mile or two before reaching the falls.

MT HYPIPAMEE NATIONAL PARK
Fifteen miles south of Atherton, on the Atherton Tableland at an altitude of 3,250 feet is Mt Hypipamee, commonly called 'The Crater', which is something of a geological oddity, for near its summit is an enormous vertical shaft which suggests an extinct volcano, but as it has granite walls, it is not a volcanic crater. Surrounding the shaft are 900 acres of tropical rainforest, and the upper reaches of the Barron River pass through the park.

From the lookout on one edge of 'The Crater' it is possible to look down the vertical walls to the dark green water of the lake 180 feet below; this water is about 250 feet deep.

'The Crater' is well known to naturalists for its Golden Bower-birds (*Prionodura newtoniana*), and there are bowers within the park. The marsupials here are of great interest, for some are confined to high altitudes, and are found in few other places: the Coppery Brushtail (*Trichosurus vulpecula johnstoni*) and the Lemur-like Ring-tailed Possum (*Hemibelideus lemuroides*), the Green Possum (*Pseudocheirus archeri*) and the Herbert River Ringtail (*P. herbertensis*).

Above the graded walking track to the crater shaft some magnificent great Staghorn Ferns may be seen high in the huge rainforest trees. This is one of the most beautiful walks in north Queensland. A longer return track goes down to the Barron River; it is possible to barbecue by the pretty Dinner Falls where Black Pine and Kauri Pine grow.

EUNGELLA NATIONAL PARK
Eungella, 'Land of Cloud', could equally be called 'land of ferns', for in this glorious rainforest country of the Clarke Range there is a prolific growth of ferns of every description. Huge epiphytic Staghorns (*Platycerium grande*) and Elkhorns (*P. alcicorne*) cling to tree-trunks and branches, along with innumerable other smaller ferns of the eternally damp rainforest. But most fern species are on the forest floor where beds of

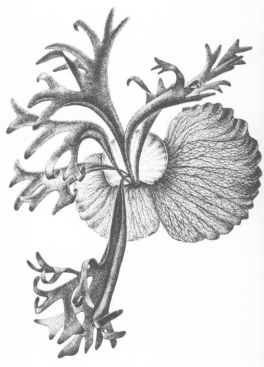

Elkhorn Fern (Platycerium alcicorne)

Far left
Wallaman Falls, where a sheet of spray plunges a thousand feet down an enormous jungle-filled canyon

Below
In Jourama Falls National Park, near Ingham, a river drops to a valley of huge boulders and tropical vegetation

Right
Bellenden-Ker National Park looms above misty tableland valleys and the gorges of the Johnstone River; its summit, Mt Bartle Frere, is Queensland's highest mountain

'fishbone' fronds unfurl their new, delicate growth, opening out red, shading to pink and then turning to green. Other ferns have a fragile lacework pattern—trailside clumps of Maidenhair ferns (*Adiantum cunninghamii*) and the Giant Maidenhair Fern (*A. formosum*).

Tall tree-ferns build, inch by inch over many years, trunks up to ten feet tall to hold aloft lacy fronds eight or ten feet long. But most impressive are the aerial fern-gardens, populated by many species of fern, which build into wide platforms in the treetops sixty or eighty feet above the ground, and occasionally low enough to see in detail. Sometimes these heavy fern masses fall.

The principal fern forming the mass is a huge Stag or Elkhorn, or a massive, ancient cluster of these, or crow's nest ferns. Year by year, the erect and basin-like shapes of these epiphytic ferns have accumulated falling leaves which have rotted in the dampness, and together with countless layers of old and decaying leaves of the fern itself, form the 'soil' of a 'garden' in the treetops. Other fern species become rooted in the rich mass, with orchid clumps and other plants, until leaves of half a dozen species can be distinguished around the perimeter of the massive fern-clusters on tree-trunk and branch.

The rainforest animals are not slow to take advantage of the giant ferns. In mature rainforest, vegetation at ground level is scarce; the dim light, so far beneath that dense foliage canopy at treetop level, does not allow much active growth except where a fallen tree admits a shaft of light and undergrowth flourishes in a tangled mass. So most of the arboreal marsupials find daytime refuge in the high foliage and the ferns. The Aborigines knew this—a collector seeking marsupials in the far northern rainforests long ago wrote:

'The Aborigines select a likely spot in the thick scrub, and some ascend different trees in the vicinity with the aid of a climbing cane. They then diligently search the staghorn, fern and orchid clumps and the tops of the bangalow

Diplazium dilatatum (*Eungella*)

Hare's Foot Fern (Davallia dubia) (*Eungella*)

Fragrant Fern (Microsorium scandens) (*Eungella*)

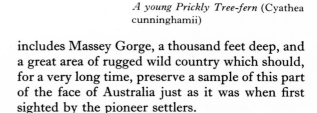

A young Prickly Tree-fern (Cyathea cunninghamii)

Prickly Tree-fern (Cyathea cunninghamii)

Fishbone Fern (Nephrolepis cordifolia) (*Eungella*)

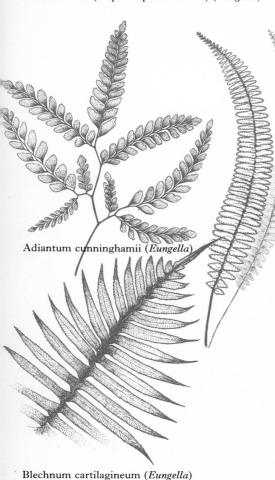

Adiantum cunninghamii (*Eungella*)

Blechnum cartilagineum (*Eungella*)

palms, and as soon as they have driven the animals from their sleeping quarters they catch them alive, tap them on the head and throw them down.'

The Sugar Gliders also favour the ferns as a hiding place, perhaps when hollows are scarce; a shaking or probing of a large Crows-nest Fern may cause an explosion of life as a phalanger family awakens, and each parachutes away to safer refuge elsewhere.

Eungella is one of Queensland's largest national parks, containing 122,600 acres. It straddles the mountainous Clarke Range west of Mackay and overlooks the central Queensland coast, and it forms the high watershed between the Broken River, a tributary of the Burdekin, and the Pioneer River. From the heights and ramparts of Mt Dalrymple (4,190 feet), Mt William (4,082 feet) and Mt David (3,900 feet) the park terrain drops, in steep jungle-clad slopes and gorges, to the flat, fertile lowlands of the Pioneer Valley.

Most of Eungella National Park is inaccessible, except to experienced bushwalkers. Its rugged terrain ensures the preservation of unique rainforest fauna and flora. But a section of the park has been developed sufficiently to show visitors the rainforest and the scenery: fourteen miles of circuit tracks lead to walks along the pools of the Broken River's course through the rainforest, and to high vantage points overlooking the Pioneer Valley 3,000 feet below.

This section of the park most visited by tourists lies about fifty miles inland from Mackay, though at its northern extremity, at St Helens, the park is only seven miles from the coast. From a camping and picnic area by the Broken River (where the platypus may occasionally be seen) tracks radiate to rainforest trails and to the high escarpment. Features of the park include prolific growths of Alexandrina palms, tree-fern and Cabbage Palm groves, and waterfalls and cascades on Finch Hatton Creek at the lower level of the park. It

includes Massey Gorge, a thousand feet deep, and a great area of rugged wild country which should, for a very long time, preserve a sample of this part of the face of Australia just as it was when first sighted by the pioneer settlers.

WALLAMAN FALLS NATIONAL PARK

On Stony Creek in north-eastern Queensland are the Wallaman Falls, in an awe-inspiring chasm, with a sheer drop of a thousand feet to rocks and rainforest far below. From one side of the abyss water falls more than 980 feet to disintegrate in spray on the boulders of the gorge. Pouring out over the rim of the void the river remains, for the first few hundred feet, a column of foaming white water; six hundred feet down it races past the blackened rock walls in bursts of spray; nine hundred feet down it is lost in a cloud of mist through which its remaining barrage comes in surges, spattering across the deep dark pool below.

Eventually a walking trail may be constructed to the foot of the falls. At present it is a half-day struggle—a thousand-foot climb, down and back up again over very steep, loose-surfaced slopes through tangled rainforest. Ingham District Forester, Norm Clough, offered to accompany me on a climb to the bottom of the gorge to photograph the falls from below. Laden with camera gear, we scrambled down the steep scree slopes, following a route we hoped would avoid the cliffs which enclose the falls on almost all sides towards the bottom.

An hour's climbing, slashing away with a cane knife at the barbed tendrils of the lawyer cane, and stinging trees which can inflict a burning shock, brought us to the floor of the gorge. Jumbled boulders, which seemed pebbles from the lookout a thousand feet above, were now house-sized, and slippery with moss, spray and seeping water. If the view from above was spectacular, then to stand at the bottom of a thousand feet of crashing water was spellbinding: from the rim of the huge cliff above the river jetted into space, white against the blue sky and red-brown rock, before

A species of Lastreopis

thundering into the shadowed depths of the gorge.

THE CRATER LAKES

Situated at an altitude of 2,400 feet, near the top of the Atherton Tableland, where numerous conical hills and old lava flows remain as remnants of past volcanic activity, the Crater Lakes are two of Queensland's smaller, but best-known national parks. Lake Barrine National Park is 1,213 acres in area and Lake Eacham is 1,200 acres. Each park—they are only a few miles apart—centres upon its deep, placid and picturesque lake, but also preserves a surrounding strip of magnificent tableland rainforest. The lakes each lie within, and almost completely fill, a deep crater whose ridges of coarse volcanic ash testify to an explosive origin.

Soundings have revealed an average depth of 480 feet for the deep blue waters of Lake Eacham, and 360 feet to the bottom of Lake Barrine; these waters are cool even in the hottest weather which is a great attraction for swimmers. Tropical jungle grows right to the water's edge but there is a great depth of clear water even beneath the overhanging trees, vines and ferns.

LAKE BARRINE NATIONAL PARK

The Gillies Highway runs through this park which is situated thirty-eight miles from Cairns. Picnic facilities have been provided for visitors. Four miles of walking tracks have been made; encircling the lake is the main track cut into slopes where extensive fern-banks flourish, and which also passes by the famous twin kauri pines.

Lake Barrine is a bird-watcher's paradise, in fact, the entire Atherton Tableland is exceptionally rich in variety of bird life, with 215 species recorded. In the vicinity of Lake Barrine in just one week, observers from the Royal Australian Ornithologists' Union recorded ninety-five species, many being tropical birds which only inhabit the dense rainforests of North Queensland. The Prince Albert Rifle-bird(*Ptiloris magnificus*),

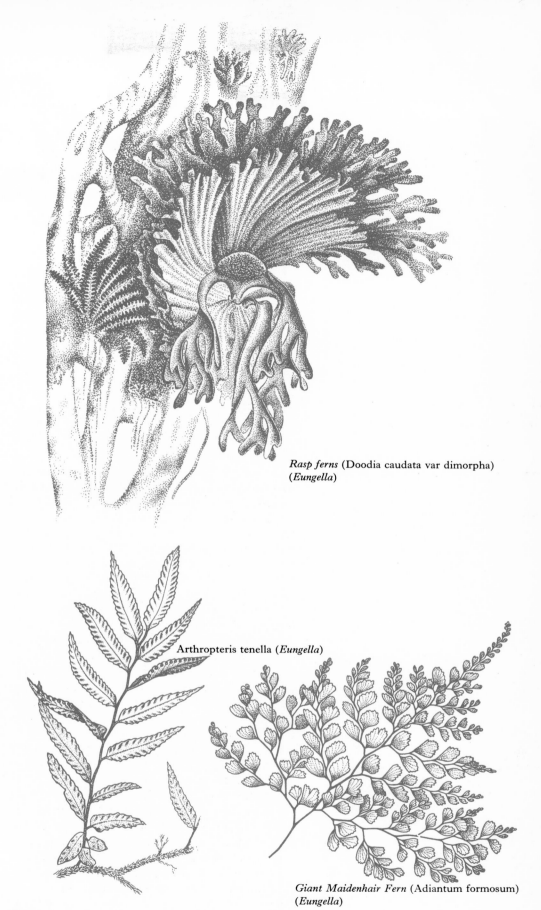

Rasp ferns (Doodia caudata var dimorpha) (*Eungella*)

Arthropteris tenella (*Eungella*)

Giant Maidenhair Fern (Adiantum formosum) (*Eungella*)

Over
Eungella, 'land of cloud', a large national park of jungles, gorges, and eucalypt forests on the 4,000 ft ramparts of the Clarke Range, near Mackay

113

Buff-breasted Scrub-wren (Sericornis laevigaster) (*Found in rainforests from north-east Qld. to north-east N.S.W.*)

Black Treecreeper (Climacteris melanota) (*Found in north Qld. forests*)

the Whipbird and the Tooth-billed Bower-bird (*Scenopaeetes dentirostris*), are quite common.

Platypuses are at times found near the edge of the lake and marsupials, Brush Turkeys and an occasional Cassowary can be seen in the rainforest.

LAKE EACHAM NATIONAL PARK

Lake Eacham is forty-seven miles from Cairns via the Gillies Highway which winds through lush rainforest as it approaches the lake.

More than four miles of walking tracks go through the park and the visitor can get to the Wishing Well, Vision Falls and Goddard Falls in addition to the main track which circles the lake. Maidenhair ferns, Staghorns, Elkhorns and Tassle Ferns are common.

This park is also considered to be a bird-watchers' paradise.

MAGNETIC ISLAND NATIONAL PARK

A large, mountainous, forested island within sight of Townsville, Magnetic Island is a favourite resort for visitors. Launch services operate from Townsville and gives access to the island. Magnetic Island was named by Captain Cook in 1770 in the belief that it contained magnetic ores which affected his compass.

A major part of the island—an area of 6,260 acres—was proclaimed a national park in 1956. This area includes mainly the steep and rugged parts of the island. Mt Cook rises to 1,628 feet, and its spurs reach the seas as high, boulder-strewn headlands, between which are protected bays and beaches behind the coral reefs. In several of these bays tourist resorts have been established.

There are more than five miles of walking tracks within the national park area, leading to heights and crags from which panoramic views embrace the island coastline, the ocean and the distant mainland.

DUNK ISLAND NATIONAL PARK

Dunk Island, six miles from the Queensland

coast near Tully, is clad with luxuriant rainforest and open eucalypt forest of which 1,805 acres are national parkland.

Its coastline on the seaward side is rough, but on the mainland side there are stretches of sandy beaches. More than five miles of walking tracks lead to places of interest from the tourist resort area which is just outside the park section of the island. Charter air services and a launch provide access to Dunk Island.

HERON ISLAND NATIONAL PARK

In the Capricorn Group lies Heron Island, a flat coral cay of about forty-two acres in area. Thirty acres are national parkland and the other twelve acres are well-established as a tourist resort.

Built of coral reefs, broken coral debris and sand, the island rises no more than eight feet above the sea. However, it is covered by Pisonia forest which has grown to a height of forty or fifty feet, and by groves of Pandanus and Casuarina near the beaches.

This island is noted for its abundant bird life. The Wedge-tailed Mutton-birds (*Puffinus pacificus*) nest here in great numbers in October each year, burrowing into the ground beneath the trees, and they later migrate to the Northern Hemisphere. Among the branches are nesting colonies of White-capped Noddies (*Anous minutus*) and a pair of White-breasted Sea-eagles (*Haliaeetus leucogaster*) often nests on the islands. Other sea birds common to this island are Cormorants, Sea-curlews, Sandpipers, Oyster-birds, Terns, Seagulls and Herons. Thousands of turtles each year come ashore to lay their eggs in the warm sand.

Prolific marine life surrounds this island and for this reason Queensland's first Marine Biological Research Station has been established here. Scientists come from all parts of the world to study the coral and its creatures.

It is usual for marine life to be richest near the open sea, so the further from the coast, the more luxuriant the reef is likely to be. Heron Island is

Lake Eacham and Lake Barrine, both on the Atherton Tableland at an altitude of about 2,400 ft, occupy craters of great depth. Each is surrounded by ridges of volcanic ash (now covered by jungle). It is believed that these craters were formed by volcanic explosions, or a series of violent explosive eruptions; an alternative explanation is that the volcanoes collapsed inwards when their subterranean reservoirs of lava subsided, leaving deep calderas which later filled with water. Lake Eacham's water surface is 131 acres, its depth almost 500 feet; Lake Barrine covers 256 acres and is 360 feet deep.

Golden Bowerbird (Priondura newtoniana)

approximately fifty miles out from Gladstone on the Queensland coast.

Twelve miles further into the Pacific is One Tree Island, well on the outer edge of the reefs. Among the reefs of this little cay the coral takes every shape and colour—the delicate, branching staghorn coral (*Acropora*), the mushroom corals (*Tungia*), the dark brown brain coral (*Symphyllia*), and the flat table corals (*Porites*).

When low tide exposes the reef and the sea remains only in still pools, some of the reef's inhabitants may be seen. The nudibranch mollusks, with flower-like exposed gills, are among the most colourful of the reef creatures; as well there are darting reef fish, golden Demoiselles (*Pseudopomacentrus apicalis*), vermilion and turquoise Venus Tusk-fish, bright orange and blue Anemone fish (*Amphiprions papuensis*) and many others.

HINCHINBROOK ISLAND NATIONAL PARK

Cut from the mainland by a mosaic of tidal channels and mangrove islets, Hinchinbrook lifts an abrupt, massive mountain wall rent by deep, ravine-like valleys. A tiny settlement clings between ocean and mountain; the rest is wilderness, dense rainforest, rarely penetrated, nor damaged yet by man. For its visitors, Hinchinbrook provides picturesque mountain and waterfall scenery and is a centre for marine attractions, boating, fishing and reef exploring, to which the mountain massif is a background of spectacular beauty.

It rises as a jagged mountain wall beyond miles of jigsaw-patterned mangrove islets, where tides intersect green flats with silver channels of sea then ebb to reveal orange and brown sand and mudflats. My first glimpse of the island was from Highway One, between Ingham and Cardwell. Away across the main deep channel it appears as a huge, forbidding fortress, its spectacular parks such as Mt Bowen (3,650 feet) brooding beneath cumulo-nimbus storm clouds hiding the highest summits and pouring through the high gorges to cast blue shadows on the dark green slopes.

Except for reef resorts at the northern tip of the island, this remains a wilderness area which will long continue as a wildlife sanctuary. It is a place for the most adventurous bushwalker, and an unchanging reminder of the original scenic grandeur of Australia's eastern seaboard.

GREEN ISLAND NATIONAL PARK

A coral atoll of thirty acres, Green Island, eighteen miles north-east of Cairns, is one of the most popular of the island national parks.

As usual with coral cays, Green Island is flat, and only a few feet above sea level. It is surrounded by a great expanse of coral reefs which are the main attraction for visitors who are able to see the coral and marine life through the portholes of an underwater observatory or from glass-bottomed boats.

Unfortunately, some change in the balance of nature in the underwater world has led to a build-up of the Crown-of-Thorns Starfish (*Acanthaster*) population. This starfish feeds upon the coral polyps, leaving in its wake large areas of dead, colourless coral. The reasons for this invasion of starfish are not known, nor has any means of preventing the damage to the reefs been found.

Green Island has an area of only thirty acres, of which the national park preserves seventeen, while the remainder is occupied by tourist accommodation and facilities. Within its encircling ring of dazzling white beach the island has a dense green tree cover, the tallest species including Coral, Damson, White Cedar and Pandanus. A great variety of birds may be seen among the trees, on the beaches, and over the reefs.

CONWAY AND THE WHITSUNDAY ISLANDS NATIONAL PARKS

Here is a truly magnificent coastline of jungle-clad mountain peaks, an island-studded bay, and coral reefs. Conway National Park lies at the

Top l to r
Lake Eacham, with azure-blue waters 480 feet deep, lies cupped in a volcano's crater and surrounded by dense tropical rainforest

Protected by poisonous spines in their dorsal fins, Butterfly Cod (Pterois volitans) *drift casually through Barrier Reef waters*

Right
Heron Island, a low coral cay surrounded by reefs extending northwards twelve hundred miles to New Guinea; almost every islet is a national park

Below
From Highway One near Ingham there is an impressive panorama across tidal flats, mangrove swamps and channels to mountainous Hinchinbrook, Australia's largest island national park

QUEENSLAND

The tiny flat coral cays of the Great Barrier Reef, such as Green Island and Heron Island, are formed of coral debris thrown up on the reefs, and are never higher than a few feet above high tide line. They are surrounded by reefs far more extensive than their area of dry land. The Great Barrier Reef stands in water too deep for the growth of coral; it appears that the coral polyps have built up the reef top while the Queensland coast was slowly sinking.

The high mountainous islands along the Queensland coast were formed when slow subsidence of the land flooded coastal valleys, and left former mountain ranges protruding above the sea as islands. Coral reefs have formed in places around these offshore islands, but are not extensive by comparison with those of the Great Barrier Reef further to the east. The beautiful Whitsunday group of islands, and mountainous Hinchinbrook Island, are among many formed in this way.

southern gateway to the offshore islands and the Barrier Reef; a region of superb scenery where the steep hills of the coast and the islands, blue-green with luxuriant tropical vegetation, plunge abruptly to blue and emerald coral seas. Here and there, the smooth white sweep of a beach breaks the dominance of blues and greens.

Beyond the sheltered, small inlets of Shute Harbour, tall peaks of islands lift from the sea, their mountainous profiles betraying the rugged character of their terrain; one beyond another, they extend as far as the eye can see, hiding completely the ocean horizon.

Viewed in a panoramic sweep from lookouts on the mainland hills the nearest islands can be seen in some detail. Long Island, South Molle Island, and North Molle are the largest, rising steeply from the sea to five or six hundred feet, and covered with dense vegetation.

The Conway Range, forming Conway National Park, rises to 1,850 feet in its south-eastern heights, then plunges abruptly to the depths of Whitsunday Passage. The passage is a twenty mile-long channel which lies between the islands fringing the coast north of Cape Conway on the west, and the Cumberland islands on the east. Beyond the Whitsunday Passage there is a long chain of large islands—Shaw Island, Lindeman Island, Hamilton and Dent Islands, Whitsunday Island, Hook Island and Hayman Island.

Whitsunday Island is the largest, twelve miles by ten and rising to a peak of 1,438 feet above sea level. Deep inaccessible gorges have formed on the mountain slopes, with lush tropical vegetation clinging wherever it can find foothold on the cliffs. Around its coastline these gorges meet the sea in numerous bays of sheltered waters and pure white beaches. On this island 27,000 acres are national parkland, though there are tourist resorts at several points along its coast.

East of Proserpine lies Lindeman Island where there is a tourist resort and an airstrip and 1,767 acres of national park. Its highest point is Mt Oldfield (700 feet) and it is claimed that seventy-

two islands may be seen from here. Like other islands in the Cumberland group, it is fringed by coral reefs. Its vegetation is mainly open eucalypt forest and some teatree. Eight miles of graded tracks give access to scenic places such as Coconut Bay, Boat Port and Mt Oldfield.

The true Great Barrier Reef, however, is thirty miles further seaward. Rugged and picturesque Brampton Island has an area of 1,280 acres of national parkland, with walking tracks to scenic parts and to the peaks. Deeply indented Hook Island has much of its scenic beauty protected within a national park of 12,800 acres. Long Island, separated from the mainland by a beautiful, narrow waterway, has 2,066 acres of national park. Molle Island, nearest to Shute Harbour, has 1,016 acres of park and is a grassy island with small areas of scrub and light forest country.

Regular launch services, from Shute Harbour and Airlie Bay, from Bowen forty-two miles northwards, and from Mackay sixty-three miles south, call at the tourist resorts on these islands. As well there are many launch cruises through the scenic passages between the islands, and out to the Great Barrier Reef.

The greater part of the coastal Conway Range, and parts of these scenic islands, remain an almost inaccessible wilderness which can be penetrated only by those willing to carry a pack and 'rough it' in a spirit of adventure. But for the hundreds of thousands of tourists who visit the island resorts and cruise the waterways, the virgin forests of the ranges create a magnificent scenic setting for the enjoyment of leisure-time.

The forests of the mountainous ranges and islands are a refuge for bird and animal life, thus constituting a vital outdoor laboratory for research, and contributing to conservation. Brush turkeys may often be encountered along trails through the forests, and scrub fowl fly up from beside the pathway to perch on branches and eye the intruder suspiciously for a moment before flying ponderously through the forest to quieter parts.

Our national parks exist today through the

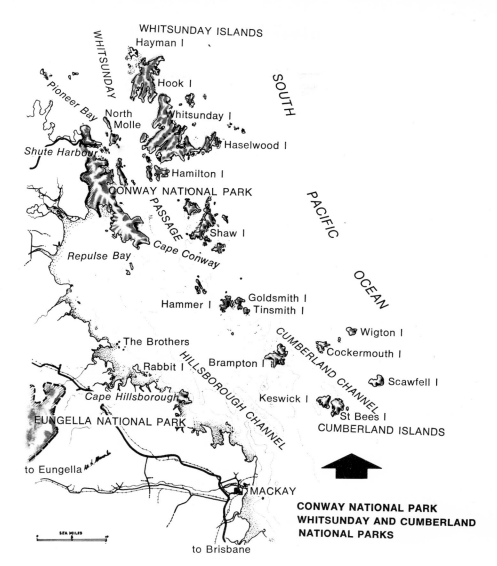

WHITSUNDAY ISLANDS
WHITSUNDAY
Hayman I
Hook I
Pioneer Bay
North Molle
Whitsunday I
Haselwood I
Shute Harbour
Hamilton I
CONWAY NATIONAL PARK
PASSAGE
Cape Conway
Shaw I
Repulse Bay
SOUTH
PACIFIC
OCEAN
Goldsmith I
Hammer I
Tinsmith I
Wigton I
The Brothers
CUMBERLAND CHANNEL
Cockermouth I
Rabbit I
Brampton I
Scawfell I
HILLSBOROUGH CHANNEL
Cape Hillsborough
Keswick I
St Bees I
EUNGELLA NATIONAL PARK
CUMBERLAND ISLANDS
to Eungella
MACKAY
CONWAY NATIONAL PARK
WHITSUNDAY AND CUMBERLAND
NATIONAL PARKS
SEA MILES
to Brisbane

efforts of men, with some thought for the future, who have worked and fought unselfishly for the dedication of the land for the benefit of all Australians. Once parliamentary approval is given, one would suppose the national parks to be safe from destruction, at least by those whose only interest is the quick profit gained from 'land development'!

At Shute Harbour, superb scenery, which attracts thousands, has been sacrificed in order that a privileged few may live with a view; the magnificent panorama of islands and oceans is for all time disfigured by roads, service stations and the jumbled roofs of holiday shacks.

THE GREAT BARRIER REEF

The Great Barrier Reef is the most massive structure erected by living creatures on the face of this planet and yet it was built by a most primitive creature—small marine organisms called coral polyps. These coral animals have built a rampart, 1,200 miles in length, rising two hundred feet above the ocean bed to the seaward side. Each of these soft-bodied creatures, Anthozoans, or 'flower animals' (resembling blossoms and displaying colours which brighten the reefs) secretes limestone to build a protective tubular stone shelter. In their countless millions these corals build, according to their species, a variety of beautiful corals: massive boulder-like shapes, or delicate branching staghorns, to form reefs, cays and islands. Their limestone walls can withstand the pounding of storms from the South Pacific; the thousand-mile barrier of the reef protects Queensland's shores and shelters the coastal waters.

The Great Barrier reef carries an incredible population of living creatures, quite apart from the countless millions of reef-builders. The marine fauna includes fish in tremendous numbers and variety—the triggerfish, the vividly-coloured wrasse, the huge groper, the stonefish armed with deadly venom. As well there are colourful starfish, sea urchins, crabs, and shellfish which include the

Giant Clam growing to four feet long and weighing several hundredweight.

On the beaches of the reef's coral islands the female Green Turtle, driven by instinct which may have brought her a hundred miles, struggles above high-water mark to dig, lay her eggs and return to the sea before sunrise.

The reef's geographic location makes it a favoured breeding ground for birds as well as for the vast array of marine life. Michaelmas Cay, out from Cairns, is a nesting place for terns and gulls by the thousand. Six species of tern nest on the islands of the Capricorn group: the Crested Tern (*Sterna bergii*), the Lesser Crested (*S. bengalensis*), the Black-Naped (*S. sumatrana*), the Bridled (*S. anaetheta*), the Roseate (*S. dougalli*) and the Little (*S. albifrons*) Tern. These island colonies may number thousands of birds, especially crested terns whose eggs, placed several feet apart, cover all suitable ground. The bulky nest of the Osprey (*Pandion haliaetus*) may be seen on many reef islets, and on some, the White-breasted Sea Eagle

121

Sunrise over a tropical wonderland; here, in the Whitsunday and Cumberland groups near Mackay, are more than a hundred island national parks

Right
From the heights above Shute Harbour, Conway National Park, spreads a panorama of islands, each clad in dense jungle and set in coral seas

(*Haliaeetus leucogaster*) also nests.

Any account of the Great Barrier Reef must include the story of the battle for its preservation. There is every possibility that this coral wonderland, the world's longest coral reef and a major part of Australia's attraction to international visitors, may gradually deteriorate until it is no more than a lifeless mass of grey-white limestone crumbling beneath the breakers of the South Pacific. There is every chance that the story of the reef, like many other segments of Australia's recent history, will be one of the destruction of great natural assets in a greedy grab for short-term commercial profits. And, inevitably, such destructive episodes in the past have occurred against a background of government apathy or (amazing as it seems in retrospect) even approval. In the not-too-distant future we could see parts of the reef blasted apart for limestone, and oil-drilling rigs in its azure sea; oil pollution would certainly have a disastrous effect on the reef. On adjacent shores we will see massive destruction of coastal scenery to haphazard, shanty-town beach resort development, and the cancerous devastation wrought by beach mining for mineral sands.

No other nation which calls itself progressive would hesitate so long before declaring the *entire* reef, together with significant portions of the adjacent coastline, a national park. There is no doubt that such a move would have the support of all Australians, excepting only those who would 'develop' the continent—at any cost. In September, 1968, 13,000 Queenslanders signed a petition urging that the whole reef be declared a national park.

At present, many of the islands of the reef (approximately 160) have national park status and protection, but this does not protect the reefs. The declaration of underwater reefs as national park would not be entirely new—the United States has Key Largo, and the Virgin Islands National Park, 'preserving multi-coloured marine "gardens" of corals, sponges, sea fans and fishes, for exploration by snorkel-geared swimmers'.

Part Four: THE WEST

*A Western Spinebill taking nectar from
Red-and-Green Kangaroo-paw*

The western region is very clearly defined. It is cut from the rest of Australia's well-watered coastal lands by a huge expanse of desert, which stretches unbroken from the Great Australian Bight to the far north-west coast. For the traveller there can be no mistaking the isolation of the west. To reach this fascinating region it is necessary to cross either the treeless expanses of the Nullarbor, or, coming from the north, to skirt the western edge of the Great Sandy Desert where Highway One follows the eighty mile beach from Broome to Port Headland. It is not difficult, when negotiating these hundreds of miles of bare, barren-looking country, to appreciate what a barrier these deserts have been, and still remain, to the spread of plant and animal life. During thousands of years of isolation the birds, furred animals and wildflowers of the west have assumed forms distinctly different to those of the rest of the continent—only in the west are found the Honey Possum, Red-capped Parrot or, among wildflowers, the golden and bronzed flowers known as dryandras, the many species of kangaroo-paw, or the Christmas Tree, famed for its fiery mass of cadmium yellow or orange flowers.

Although there is much in the west which is scenically beautiful—the iron-red Hamersley gorges, the Kalbarri coast and multi-coloured river gorge, the jagged peaks of the Stirlings, or the giant Karri Trees and lush undergrowth of Nornalup—it is the distinctiveness of the western fauna, and, much more, of the flora that makes the western parks different to those of any other region.

THE WEST
WESTERN AUSTRALIA

HAMERSLEY RANGE

The Hamersley Range, more than 200 miles long, is situated in a dry and thirsty land, yet water has sculptured its iron-hard rock, gouged its canyons and fashioned its square-cut bluffs. Dissected by water over countless ages the Hamersley massif appears as a mauve monolith in the far distance, but becomes at close range a tortuous landscape of chasms, rock ribs and terraced summits vibrant with raw-oxide hues of red, streaked with black and dark rust-brown. Among the peaks in the Hamersley Ranges are Mt Bruce (4,024 feet), Mt Brockman (3,654 feet) and Mt Margaret (2,798 feet).

The sheer walls of the gorges, rising up to 300 feet high, are horizontally banded in rock layers of red, brown, blue and mauve. They are composed of near-flat strata lying almost undisturbed where they were formed at the beginning of time; an ancient mass that may have been one of the first solid sections of the earth's crust when it began to cool from the molten state, aeons ago. These rock walls rise in steps and ledges where harder layers have resisted erosion. At other places they rise sheer and smooth from creek bed to tableland far above. In the direct rays of the sun these cliffs can glow like red-hot coals against the sky's dark blue. Photographs show vivid hues which will be accepted as true only by those who have seen this land. Streaked with the gold of dry spinifex, or smudged with a hint of green after rain, and accentuated by the lush green foliage hanging from the white branches of Ghost Gums twisting from crevice and plateau rim, these gorges form a landscape of incredible colour.

The main gorges are Dale, Wittenoom, Hamersley and Yanpire, which vary in character. From Wittenoom Gorge the road follows a gum-lined

Left
The Hamersley Range, a 4,120 ft high massif of iron-red rock banded in gold wherever the spinifex has found a footing

Right
Dale's Gorge, a painted chasm in ranges famed for colour; in strong contrast to dark red rock are Ghost Gums, golden spinifex, poolside greenery

Osprey

WESTERN AUSTRALIA

creek into a long wide canyon, steadily climbing all the time until the comparatively flat plateau top is reached, and the tracks divide, branching out to various gorges or other features of this part of the Hamersleys. We will sample famed Dale's Gorge situated within a flora and fauna reserve.

The road winds easily between white-trunked Ghost Gums, over jagged little ridges, and across stony spinifex flats until, suddenly the ground drops away in front, falling to reveal a long, narrow slash, a gorge cool and green in depths far below.

From above, looking down through the crowns of trees that cling to rock crevices and ledges, we can glimpse the reflections of water. Streams rarely flow in this arid area but pools are found in the deepest gorges where ferns and river gums grow. Red walls cut vertically to a world of waterfalls, still pools and lush greenery. A path zig-zags down the near side, to the top of the falls; this is another world, after the heat, dust and red glare above. Beds of ferns cover shaded banks wet with seepage below the cliffs, and the pools are fringed with rushes which hide a Reed-warbler, whose ringing notes reverberate between the close walls of the gorge.

This is magnificent scenery which has attracted visitors from all parts of Australia, and it will bring an ever-growing throng of visitors as roads improve. It is a national asset deserving the protection of national park status. At present some parts of the Hamersleys are fauna reserves, with no amenities, and with no real guarantee of protection if threatened by destructive forces of mineral exploitation.

The Australian Academy of Science has recommended a large national park here. The Hamersleys cover a vast area, and though parts of the range will provide mineral riches, there is room also to preserve the best of the scenery.

CAPE RANGE NATIONAL PARK
North West Cape projects like a beckoning finger where the nor-nor-west trend of Australia's western coastline turns abruptly north-east. This is a semi-arid region subject to sudden but infrequent cyclonic storms. The dominant feature of the cape peninsula is the rugged mountainous spine formed by the Cape and Rough Ranges. The eastern escarpments overlooking Exmouth Gulf are deeply dissected by rocky ravines whose walls rise as sheer cliffs. The scenery is spectacular at close range. In some of the big canyons and caves there are examples of early Aboriginal art.

In 1964 a national park of 33,171 acres was established to include the rugged scenery of Cape Range. The Cape Range National Park is situated along the range top between Learmonth and the new United States naval radio base which is at the tip of North West Cape. Roads which were built by oil exploration companies in the Cape Range are still negotiable by four-wheel-drive vehicles, and recent improvements permit access with ordinary cars.

KALBARRI NATIONAL PARK
Not far north of Geraldton, on the western coast, the Murchison River cuts a magnificent, tortuous course to the Indian Ocean. With headwaters in the dry mulga of the north-west it flows infrequently, but after floods in the wake of a summer cyclone its long still pools vanish and the gorges are filled with the sound of raging torrents. Its lower reaches have carved canyons through coloured rock, to meet the sea where the cliffs of Red Bluff rise hundreds of feet in great steps and overhanging ledges.

Here the bright striations of layered sandstone are most vivid. Alternating lines of hard brown rock, and softer sandstones of yellow and red and white, form blurred streaks on each overhanging cliff.

On the harder rocks are intricate textures engraved by wind and spray, and through the ages, seeping water has festooned the rock cavities with stalactites which are exposed where wind and sea have cut the hills, and where the undermined rocks have slipped leaving great scars of vivid new rockface.

Gullies and headlands break the line of the coast; each headland a massif streaked and striped by its composite rock layers. Against these cliffs, where they are underpinned by sheer walls of dark rock and immense boulders blackened by the sea, the westerly swell surges and breaks with thunderous sound in long lines of white foam and explosive bursts of spray.

In the red-rich light of late afternoon the western cliffs are rugged bands of luminous orange, rust and red, standing between the cool tones of azure sky, dark green scrub, and the turquoise depths of sea.

These coastal gorges include the banded red, yellow and white coastal cliffs at Wittecarra Gully, where it is believed the Dutch captain Pelsart marooned three crew members for their part in the mutiny and massacre which came after the wreck of the *Batavia* on the Abrolhos Islands in 1629.

Inland, the greater part of this National Park is sandplain, where occasional small trees grow bearing orange or yellow cones of banksia or tall white plumes of grevillea. In places the plain disappears beneath the smaller flowers which include massed stands of golden verticordia. From these wildflower plains one comes suddenly upon the gorges. The river can be seen winding far below, curving away in great loops which in ten miles of gorges bring it but a few hundred yards nearer the sea.

Kestrels lift in the wind along the rock precipices of the canyon rim, pinions spread and fanned tail twisting for balance; then they dive, till far below, yet still high above the green line of gums which fringe the river, they remain conspicuous by their fast smooth flight. Though but specks in the void these falcons lend depth and dimension to the river gorges.

Their soaring flight past red rock walls makes the sheer drop of rockface real, and there is something fascinating in their level glide out from high

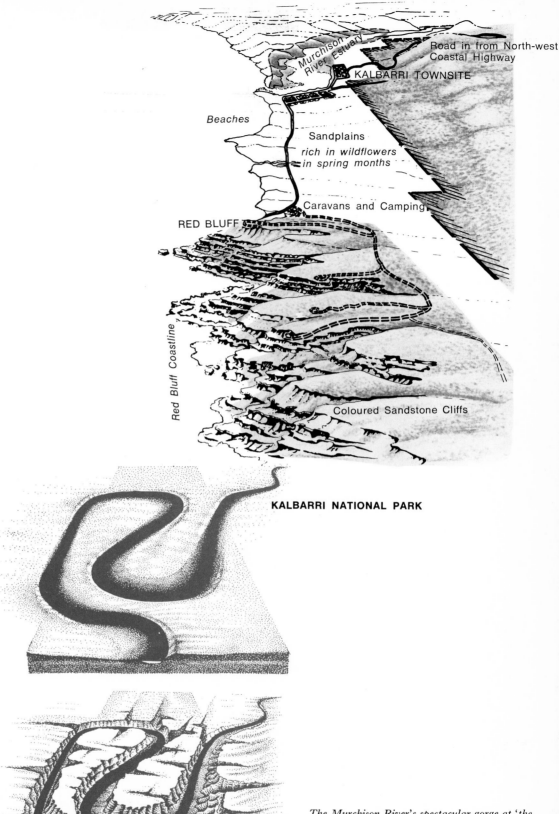

KALBARRI NATIONAL PARK

The Murchison River's spectacular gorge at 'the loop', in Kalbarri National Park, is cut into red sandstone almost five hundred feet thick. In late Tertiary, or perhaps early Pleistocene times the Murchison River meandered over flat plains close to sea level. Abrupt uplifting of the whole region, amounting to about 600 feet, then caused the river to cut deeply into its old winding bed until, today, it is again near sea level— but five or six hundred feet below the plains in a tremendous fifty-mile gorge.

129

Right
The Ground Cuckoo-Shrike (Pteropodocys maxima) *is
commonly seen among the rough ironstone ranges of the
north-west*

Below
*Stony ranges, white-trunked trees and needle-sharp
porcupine grass typify the North-West Cape, Barlee Range
and Dale's Gorge parks and reserves*

WESTERN AUSTRALIA

rock walls with the earth dropping away suddenly till far beneath. Though now far below, a falcon is still visible from the rim of the canyon as a rust-red shape moving over the green depths . . . until it vanishes beneath overhanging red-rock walls. These Kestrels nest in the gorges, on projecting ledges of cliffs fantastic in shape and colour.

Birds may be the only sign of life here. This is where one can see what the land once was; here the wild beauty of the gorges remains as a magnificent example of the primeval landscape. These rocks show all the colours of the heart of Australia. Corroboree colours of red and brown, white and rich ochre-yellow in layered strata of Silurian sandstone, glowing against dark blue skies when lit by the low sun of early morning, or late in the day. Probably the most spectacular scenery of the park is at 'The Loop', where the gorge twists and turns for five miles.

Once, in late Tertiary of early Pleistocene times these plains were close to sea level. Sudden uplifting caused the river to flow with increased vigour, cutting a deep gash along the old meandering course and thus exposing red and striated sandstones of weird and beautiful patterns.

At present the only access to The Loop is across twenty miles of sand tracks which generally require a four-wheel-drive vehicle. Intending visitors should enquire at the Kalbarri township as regular tours are conducted into this part of the gorge.

ABROLHOS ISLANDS SANCTUARY

The Abrolhos Islands, sometimes called the Houtman Abrolhos, lie in the Indian Ocean, about forty miles west of Geraldton; they are a cluster of low sandhills surrounded by extensive coral reefs. The largest, West Wallabi Island, has an area of· about fifteen hundred acres, and like the other islands, it is clad only in low scrub with a fringe of mangroves.

The Houtman Abrolhos were discovered by Dutch marines in 1619. Some of their ships, after crossing the Indian Ocean, were wrecked on these reefs. One of these was the *Batavia*; after the ship foundered on the Abrolhos in 1629 some of the crew mutinied and massacred many of the castaways on these islands. Some of the old wrecks have been located in recent years, and objects such as cannons have been brought up from the reef channels.

The Abrolhos is the main refuge and breeding place for thousands of sea birds on the Western Australian coast. There are several species of shearwater and many terns. The Lesser Noddy (*Anous tenuirostris melanops*) and the Shag (*Phalacrocorax varius nitidus*) breed only on the Abrolhos, in the west.

A few species of land birds occur on the Abrolhos but these appear very sensitive to human interference and several are in danger of extinction. One is an endemic form of scrub wren, the other a form of the painted quail.

The Abrolhos Tammar Wallaby (*Protemnodon eugenii binoe*) occurs on West and East Wallabi Islands, and there are numerous reptiles. The Osprey (*Pandion haliaetus*) and the White-breasted Sea-eagle (*Halioeetus leucogaster*) are the main predators, and nest on rocks and small islets scattered across the reefs. Fishing is good here, but because the islands are the centre of a crayfishing region there is considerable damage at times to the fauna, with the unique wallabies being used occasionally as cray bait.

Launch excursions can be arranged from Geraldton to the Abrolhos Islands.

YANCHEP NATIONAL PARK

Situated on the coastal plains thirty-two miles north of Perth, Yanchep National Park is best known for its numerous and beautiful underground caves. Set in limestone hills which rise to heights of 270 feet above Loch McNess the caves have been developed as its principal tourist attraction. In these caves water and limestone have produced some beautiful formations and caverns. The decoration of ceilings and floor by stalactites and stalagmites is extensive; in the

Crystal Cave massed stalactites hang low over a wide pool of an underground stream, with perfect reflections in the mirror-smooth water forming the 'Jewelled City'.

But there is also much of interest in Yanchep's six thousand acres of bushland reserve, established to preserve wildlife and flora, which is dominated by massive Tuarts (*Eucalyptus gomphocephala*). The sandy soils of the coastal plains support dense undergrowth beneath these trees, and low heathy scrub, in parts, rich in wildflowers. The Red-and-green Kangaroo-paw (*Anigosanthos manglesii*) will be seen here in August and September when the *Banksia menziesii* trees carry pink and orange flowers, and the Orange Banksia (*Banksia prionotes*) is covered with flowers of orange and white. Late in November the Christmas Tree (*Nuytsia floribunda*) bursts out in a massed display of cadmium yellow and fiery orange.

Near an attractive natural lake are grouped the various tourist facilities—swimming pool, golf course, boating facilities, hotel and guest house, and a small zoo of Australian animals.

DARLING RANGES

Barely fifteen miles to the east of Perth the long line of the Darling Scarp forms a blue-green backdrop to the city. Among the forested hills and valleys, thousands of people find recreation, following the winding bush tracks to picnic places in sunny clearings.

They enjoy a national treasure in this great green belt of forest, yet very little has been dedicated as national parkland. Most is for commercial timber. The hardwood, jarrah, is the principal timber tree in Western Australia, but large areas are also being put in private hands for mineral and agricultural exploitation. These forest areas provide attractive drives and scenic views and we must ensure that an adequate part is preserved in national parks, to belong to everyone.

At winter's end these hills turn gold, as myriad fluffy yellow flowers of wattle scrub burst out,

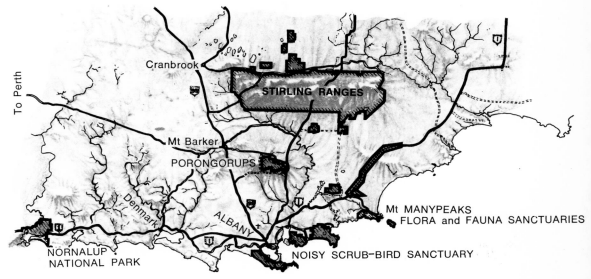

painting the undergrowth in sunlit colour. Kangaroo-paws appear on the sandy flats. Small but fascinating orchids begin to push through the carpet of fallen casuarina and banksia leaves. Thickets of prickly dryandra bushes become studded with yellow and orange. New Holland Honeyeaters (*Meliornis novae-hollandiae*) plunge long beaks into flower after flower, and stop only to burst into strident song, or to dash away in aggressive pursuit of a trespassing Spinebill, or to flee before the pugnacious attacks of a larger Red Wattle-bird (*Anthochaera carunculata*), that wants the flowers.

Once in a while the fast tempo of honeyeater activity misses a beat. A rapid trill of alarm from one bird is quickly echoed and amplified by all. The ripple of fright and warning runs through the bush . . . and there is a sudden hush, as every small bird freezes or dives for cover while the swift silent shape of a hawk slips through the treetops.

The honeyeaters nest in the prickly dryandra bushes. After their young have flown, these well-knit nests of grass, bark and spiders' web, hang in the bushes a year or more, and the rains swell the soft fluffy lining where the bird once put her eggs. Small creatures find cosy homes in the old nests. In the two-inch cups built by Spinebills I have found Pygmy Possums with droopy ears (which spread wide and alert at night) folded over big sleepy eyes; tiny hands clinging fearfully, and clockwork-spring tail curled tight.

In these forests the 'Chudich', or Native Cat,

Top
High above the river, above ledges and huge boulders, are Kalbarri's coloured cliffs, wind-eroded caves and narrow side ravines

Left
In Kalbarri National Park the Murchison River has carved a tremendous fifty-mile gorge, most spectacular here in the sweeping curve of 'The Loop'

Right
Surrounding the river gorge and reaching inland behind the coastal cliffs are three hundred thousand acres of sandplains and wildflowers

hides in hollows of logs and trees, and steals out to hunt as daylight fades. On the leafy forest floor it hunts in sudden short rushes, uttering a 'chuck, chuck' sound, and an occasional soft low growl. In the treetops it moves with lithe, feline grace with a smooth, low gliding walk and effortless leaps; its heavy tail flicks up to help the jump and streams behind in a long bushy arch.

Though not a true cat, but a carnivore of marsupial stock, it is superb in teeth and muscle—alert, quick, strong, and often fearless in its attack. In most states it is very rare, or even extinct; the forests of the south-west may be one of its last strongholds.

The forests of the Darling Ranges, reserved for timber and water catchment, shelter a large part of the fauna and flora of Western Australia, yet within this area there is no extensive biological reserve to provide for scientific study of the ecology of the jarrah forest community. The Australian Academy of Science has recommended that an area should be selected in one of the major water catchment areas of the Darling Range, possibly the Serpentine River portion. If ever this area is relinquished by the Forests Department it should be made a permanent reserve for the scientific study of flora and fauna, so that changes wrought by man in his exploitation of the jarrah can be measured by comparison with the undisturbed bush of the reserve, and the results applied in the long-term conservation of the forest's natural resources.

There is also need for a large national park in the ranges. Near Perth there are several minor parks, but these are much too small to be national in importance, and are entitled to the term 'national park' only by long-standing public custom. They have been developed principally as public recreation areas. Best-known is John Forrest National Park (3,647 acres) of which part remains as semi-natural bushland. Serpentine National Park (1,571 acres) includes Serpentine Falls; Walyunga (4,000 acres) is where the Swan River cuts through the Darling Ranges, and there

are small national parks at Kalamunda (919 acres) and Lesmurdie Falls (80 acres).

But these so-called 'national parks' do not compare with the great areas of heavy forest further south where the Wungong and Serpentine rivers flow through deep valleys of big timber and tall, tangled undergrowth. Here is potential for a large and worthwhile national park, including a large part of the water catchment area. Tourist facilities have been developed already around the major reservoirs, and particularly at Serpentine Dam. The whole area is accessible by narrow forestry tracks which wind for countless miles through wildflower scrub beneath the tall trees.

Within an hour's drive of the city suburbs these quiet, shaded tracks give glimpses of birdlife including Splendid Wrens (*Malurus splendens*) unmistakable in vivid blue, and the Red-winged Wrens (*M. elegans*) of rust-and-blue plumage, which forage timidly in the creekside thickets. In many parts the Western Yellow Robin (*Eopsaltria griseogularis*) is common, and in spring the whip-crack challenge of the Golden Whistler (*Pachycephala pectoralis*) shatters the forest quiet again and again.

Often, Black-gloved Wallabies (Brush) (*Wallabia irma*) bound across the track—the forests are the main refuge of these beautiful creatures; and the Grey Kangaroo (*Macropus major*) also, is quite common in the Darling Ranges.

DRYANDRA, AND TUTTANING RESERVES

White trees, some with trunks splashed and streaked by lines of cinnamon and rust, stand against a sky which takes a darker, stronger hue when backdrop to bleached limbs and sunlit branches of Wandoos. Beneath these trees the ground is patterned with shadows, littered with fallen branches; open spaces are broken here and there, by a fallen tree, a clump of bushes, and ringed with low dense scrub or laterite ridges clad in sharp-leaved, golden-flowered Dryandra bushes. Here, with its red back arched, a Numbat

sends sticks and dirt flying with short impatient jerks of a paw, and claws rasp the side of a half-buried log . . . it pauses, with long flickering tongue and pulsating throat, to sweep the termites from their galleries.

This is wandoo woodland in virgin state, and here at Dryandra it remains sanctuary for one of Australia's most beautiful marsupials, the Numbat or Banded Anteater (*Myrmecobius fasciatus*). Here an almost defenceless creature survives because it has safe refuge in hollows of logs and limbs scattered beneath the trees. Unlike most marsupials, which venture forth only under cover of darkness, the Numbat is abroad during daylight hours. Extensive clearing of south-western wandoo forests and excessive burning off (which destroys the hollow logs which are its only refuge) have made this extremely attractive Australian rare in most parts of the west.

I once spent six days photographing birds at Dryandra, and several at Pingelly but did not see a Numbat until I deliberately set out to find one. I spent a full day walking quietly through the forest and driving slowly along the narrow tracks which wind among the trees. Late in the afternoon I glimpsed a Numbat loping across the track a hundred yards ahead, distant but unmistakable with that long bushy tail arching high over its back. Within seconds I had reached the spot but the Numbat had vanished though there was little scrub for concealment. A closer search revealed its refuge—a small hole in the trunk of a fallen tree.

These forests also shelter a wealth of birdlife. Brightly plumaged parrots which nest in the highest hollow branches. In thickets and scrub on sandy soil are the wide mounds where Mallee Fowls' eggs are incubated by the heat of buried leaf-mould. Trees and undergrowth support wrens, honeyeaters, tree-creepers and sittellas.

Dryandra is a forestry reserve, yet it contains much wandoo woodland in almost natural state. Tuttaning is a reserve for flora and fauna, and here the plant life is rich and varied, including wildflowers of sandplain, granite, laterite and woodland soils. Among these is *Dryandra proteoides*, at one time thought to be extremely rare, but it is abundant in parts of this reserve if in few other places.

Though islands in a sea of bare, barb-fenced farmlands, and meagre remnants of the Australian bush, fauna and flora reserves have preserved some samples of this land as man found it, and protected the indigenous plants and animals which have evolved here over aeons of time. When the land is changed—developed—its creatures must adapt to new conditions or vanish, or linger only in isolated pockets of bush where a little of their world has been spared.

When these patches of virgin bush are too small, their flora and fauna must always be vulnerable. Not only do they suffer to a greater extent the creeping menace of weeds and grass from surrounding farmland, and fires that can easily cover their whole area, but they also suffer the isolation of an island. Any bushland reserve surrounded by barbed wire and denuded paddocks becomes subject to changes in the composition of its wildlife population, losing the original balance between its many creatures—the fine balance between hunter and hunted. The result is a loss of many of its wildlife inhabitants and most of its flora.

Some creatures are more vulnerable to new predators such as the cat and fox; some recover too slowly, rear too few young at a time or cannot vary breeding times to take advantage of good seasons. They are able neither to build their numbers quickly after fire or natural disaster, nor repopulate with newcomers from distant areas— unless the national park or nature reserve is large.

However, small reserves serve a valuable purpose in saving some rare plants and animals from quick extinction and provide a haven for many creatures still common. If these wildlife reserves are to continue to shelter this rich and diverse flora and fauna it is important that no development be undertaken which would lead to

destruction of the natural bush cover. The visitor to these reserves can see birds and wildflowers along existing tracks and firebreaks, and may glimpse animals which are rare elsewhere simply by driving slowly along the access roads after dark.

Although Dryandra is at present a State Forest, the Numbat is as well protected here as in most national Parks. The Western Australian Government has been requested to make this a fauna reserve or national park as soon as it is no longer useful for forestry. As it is one of the last strongholds of such a beautiful creature as the Numbat, and of Mallee Fowl and other wildlife, the creation of a fauna reserve here will have the support of most Australians and, hopefully, local farmers and the Western Australian Government.

YALLINGUP CAVES AND MARGARET RIVER

The country west of the Bussel Highway (between Margaret River and Augusta) contains some of the most outstanding scenic attractions of southwest Australia. Its preservation and careful development will play a great part in attracting tourists to the district.

The numerous large caves of the region are its main attraction. There are over one hundred known caves on the sixty mile coastal strip between Yallingup and Augusta and four are open to the public: Yallingup Cave, Mammoth and Lake Caves at Margaret River and the Jewel Cave at Augusta. Fragile stalactites of every possible shape, stalagmites over thirty feet in circumference and beautiful water pools decorate the caves.

These caves have long been of great scientific value containing (particularly the Mammoth Cave) the richest Quaternary deposits of fossil mammals yet found in Western Australia. The fossils, at least 37,000 years old, include creatures long extinct in the west—the Tasmanian Wolf or Thylacine, the Tasmanian Devil, and the prehistoric *Nototherium* and *Sthenurus*. Other fossils are of animals such as the Grey Kangaroo

Top
Western Ringtail (Pseudocheirus occidentalis)

Centre l to r
From the heights of Mt Manypeaks extend views of spectacular coastlines, rich in wildflowers, birds and small marsupials now rare, or extinct, elsewhere

Beyond this sheltered beach the granite hills of Mt Gardner rise above Two People Bay.

This native rat is a nocturnal visitor to the large south-western wild flowers during dry summer months

Below l to r
A Numbat breaks into a termite's mound to lick out the mass of white 'ants'

Western Shrike-tits (Falcunculus frontatus) inhabit south-western Wandoo and Salmon Gum woodlands

The richly plumaged Red-capped Parrot is common in the bushland of south-western parks

Far right
The Karri forest, where massive smooth-trunked giants in places grow to 300 feet. Small areas are preserved in national parks at Nornalup and near Pemberton

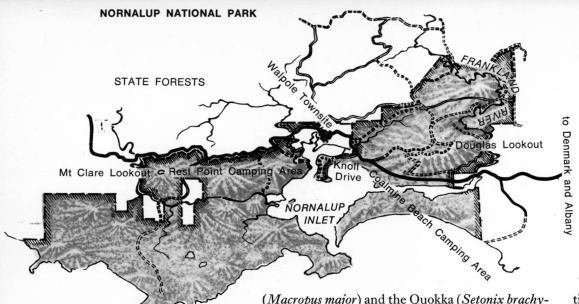

STATE FORESTS

Walpole Townsite

FRANKLAND RIVER

Douglas Lookout

Mt Clare Lookout — Rest Point Camping Area

Knoll Drive

Coalmine Beach

NORNALUP INLET

Coalmine Beach Camping Area

to Denmark and Albany

(*Macropus major*) and the Quokka (*Setonix brachyurus*) still living in the bushland above.

The jarrah forest of the area has great variety, growing in sandy soil, limestone outcrops and extensive swampy depressions. The bush shelters the Marsupial or Native Cat (*Dasyurinus geoffroyi*), the Brush-tailed Phascogale (*Phascogale tapoatafa*) —its popular name is the Aboriginal word 'Wambenger', and various smaller marsupials.

Among the many birds, some of the most brilliantly plumaged are the Red-capped Parrot (*Purpureicephalus spurius*), the Red-eared Firetail Finch (*Zonaeginthus oculatus*), the Banded (or Splendid) Blue Wren (*Malurus splendens*) and the Red-winged Wren (*M. elegans*).

NORNALUP NATIONAL PARK

In the rain-soaked region of the lower south-west of Western Australia the 33,000 acre Nornalup National Park is located. Here vast Karri (*Eucalyptus diversicolor*) forests grow; trees up to 286 feet in height with girths of twenty-four feet have been measured. White and salmon-yellow splashed columns of karri soar straight and branchless through the crowns of the banksias and peppermints and rise a hundred feet or more to where the lowest limbs spread; then lift their smooth, slender lines still higher, branching again and again, white against the sky, until they are lost in their high canopy of leaves. Below, in a cool, shaded world, dappled and green-filtered where long rays of sunlight break through the forest canopy, are flowering shrubs and creepers; and the luxuriant undergrowth shelters shy, secretive birds.

High thin notes and bursts of reeling song trace the passage of a small family party of wrens. In the south-western forests they could be Red-winged Wrens, whose song begins with several high squeaks; or the Splendid Wrens, clad entirely in rich iridescent blue banded with black, that launch straight into the strong, reeling trills of their song. If you stand quietly and imitate their squeaks they will often steal close, inquisi-

tively, keeping low and almost always screened by the thick undergrowth. They may even bounce across the ground at your feet—but never stay. They hop from beneath the skirts of grass-tree or blackboy with tails jauntily erect, pausing here and there to stab at some small insect in the damp leaf-litter of the forest floor . . . then fly, with long tail streaming behind, to catch the others of their party that have moved ahead. Soon all are lost in the forest thickets, though calls and bursts of song trace their hidden path beneath wattle and bracken and blackboy.

At Nornalup the karri forest stands at the edge of the sea. The heavy timber of the hills comes almost to the water's edge along the shores of Walpole and Nornalup inlets and along the Frankland River. An Osprey, or Fish-hawk (*Pandion haliaetus*), is often seen patrolling the narrow, steep beaches as it perches on the dead limb of a karri leaning far out over the sea.

Bright parrots fly beneath the tree-tops and Purple-crowned Lorikeets nest here in summer when the karri trees are flowering. The vermilion and blue of the Western Rosella, and the rich red, purple and green of the Red-capped Parrot bring glimpses of colour to this forest world of gentle greens and blues. White-tailed Black Cockatoos roam in flocks, stripping the flaking bark from the branches for grubs, and shattering the forest quiet with their raucous voices.

The fauna of Nornalup National Park is typical of the south-western karri country. Among the most attractive of the mammals is the Western Ring-tail Possum (*Pseudocheirus occidentalis*) which differs from its grey eastern relatives in its dark, often almost black coloration.

Perhaps, in the dense thickets and rank undergrowth bordering the swamps and streams of the extreme south-west of Western Australia, there may still survive a remnant population of the Potoroo. There were two south-western species, but now, both seem to be extinct. *Potorous gilberti* has not been recorded alive since it was first collected by John Gilbert in 1840. Equally

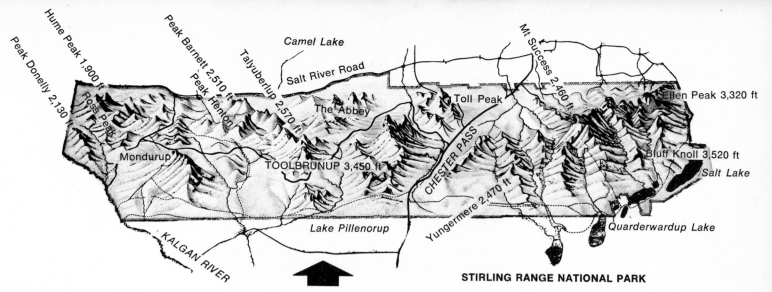

rare is the Broad-faced Potoroo (*Potorous platyops*) which is one of the smallest members of the kangaroo family.

Nornalup National Park is not really large. Its beauty lies where massive trees rise from tangled greenery, where white Clematis and purple-blue *Hardenbergia* creepers, with red-splashed Coral Vines, festoon the thickets, and where orchids bloom in the spring and summer months. Only the clear calls of birds and the murmuring of creeks break the quiet.

Its wilderness should be cherished. We should not permit any development which would destroy these very qualities which make this national park so popular with the tourist, and so valuable to all who are capable of any appreciation of nature.

The hushed green wilderness of Nornalup is accessible by narrow tracks which wind through the forest. This is a place to let the car creep along in low gear where the tracks tunnel through the thickets and wind beneath colonnades of living trees which have stood for centuries; or to stand at the foot of a karri and look up to its awe-inspiring heights, or watch for a glimpse of a Golden Whistler (*Pachycephala pectoralis*) whose loud clear calls ring from the scrub.

STIRLING RANGES NATIONAL PARK

This remarkable range of rugged peaks, preserved by the Stirling Ranges National Park, is situated about forty miles inland from the south coast of Western Australia. Because the range is near the coast and rises so suddenly from the flat plains, the taller peaks carry caps of cloud for at least a few hours most days of the year.

My first experience with the Stirlings was impressive. It was an Easter visit, a day when low clouds swirled around the peaks and in misty wraiths streamed with the wind through chasms and fissures edging the high rock walls.

Clouds banked up from the south against the steep slopes of the Stirlings, and pushed by the strong southerlies poured eerily down the sheer walls of the leeward rockface, following the swirls

and eddies of wind currents obstructed, baffled and deflected by the solid jagged masses of quartzite and sandstone projecting into the high air currents—streaming lines of vapour that revealed the strength of high winds unfelt in the sheltered valleys. We climbed a little way towards the foot of the cliffs until the clouds lowered and misty rain made photography futile; until the scrub was wet and the panorama of distant views had been hidden. Here and there among wind-lashed foliage we glimpsed impressive wildflowers, a hint of the floral wealth which can be found here in spring and early summer months.

Now and then a break in the enveloping cloud revealed dark walls of rock streaked by the shine of seeping water . . . a menacing, primeval fortress taking shape two thousand feet above as the tenuous veils of mist were drawn aside.

Almost a year later when we drove slowly up the steep winding gravel to the foot of Bluff Knoll the sky was a hard light blue, whitened away to the north by summer's smoke and heat haze. Just in from the roadside a brilliant mass of cadmium-flowered *Nuytsia*, the western Christmas Tree, stood in spectacular contrast with its fiery gold against the blue shadows of this peak's rough-walled bastions.

The constant cloud coverage has created a cool, humid environment which has permitted the evolution or survival of plants now found only on the summits of the peaks. Some, like the Mountain Bells (*Darwinias*), are confined to a few acres of the highest parts of the Stirlings, and grow nowhere else in the world.

Many free-flowering shrubs grow among the heaths and low scrub covers the sandplains, slopes and high ridges, and in the spring and summer months impressive wildflowers bloom in great profusion.

These ranges support a large and varied honey-eater population—a constant vociferous reminder of the immense floral wealth of the area. In few other places are there such concentrations of nectar-eating birds as on the higher slopes of the

The Cranbrook Bell (Darwinia meeboldii) *is one of many 'mountain bells' which grow in no other place but the Stirling Ranges*

Right

Bare granite domes of the Porongorups; Karri forests, with tall graceful trees, cover the slopes

Stirlings in spring. Here the honeyeaters by far outnumber all other birds though there are but fourteen honeyeater species and one lorikeet, the Purple-crowned, among a hundred and seven species recorded in this national park.

On the lower slopes of the ranges and out in the sandplain heath and mallee there is a greater diversity of birds. In the valleys the Scarlet Banksias (*Banksia coccinea*) are the most conspicuous of many large wildflowers which flower all year round and support perhaps seven or eight species of honeyeater.

Purple-crowned Lorikeets (*Glossopsitta porphyrocephala*) always seem to be encountered in the Stirlings. These nectar-eating parrots have an interest in the masses of wind-dwarfed mallees, and feed among the large golden flowers of the Bell-fruited Mallee (*Eucalyptus preissiana*) which blooms along the razor-back ridge of Mondurup's summit in October when the lorikeets are common. In flight they seem incredibly swift, appearing as noisy clusters of dots or small, crimson-splashed forms rushing across the sky. At rest, these leaf-sized parrots melt into the foliage, hard to detect though incessantly noisy; small shrill screechings enliven the bush where they feed among the blossoms of flowering gums.

PORONGORUP RANGE NATIONAL PARK

Rising abruptly from flat plains, the Porongorups is a small range in the south-west of Western Australia, twenty miles south of the Stirling Range. It has a grandeur of scenery far greater than its comparatively low, 2,080 feet altitude would suggest. The range is about ten miles long and its highest point Twin Peak rises to more than 2,080 feet. Constant weathering of its magmatic granite has formed steep-sided peaks capped by rounded domes and massive boulders from which views across the flat plains encompass the jagged silhouette of the Stirling Range on the northern horizon, around to the southern coastline at Albany.

This is a small national park of 5,384 acres, with very attractive scenery. The soaring white, grey and salmon-tinted trunks of the giant karri trees which cover the western half of the range are one of its most beautiful features. The undergrowth, typical of karri forest, displays many colourful wildflowers from September through October.

Late spring, summer, and early autumn months are the best times for visiting this area. The Porongorup Range is accessible by good roads from Albany and Mt Barker.

MOUNT MANYPEAKS, AND TWO PEOPLE BAY FLORA AND FAUNA RESERVE

On the south coast of Western Australia is land rich in natural beauty. High hills slope steeply to the sea, their grey granite flanks bared by the surging ocean, or spread with low dense shrubbery which holds a hidden wealth in wildflowers. Backing these hills are sand-heath plains and pockets of forest. Here, in many places, man's disruptive exploitation of the land has not intruded, and this dense bush still shelters a rich flora, colourful birds and many unique and rare marsupials.

At Two People Bay on the western side of Mt Manypeaks, in December 1961, the Noisy Scrub-bird (*Atrichornis clamosus*) was rediscovered—the last had been seen in 1889. Interest in this rediscovery was worldwide and caused the Western Australian Government to create a fauna reserve of 11,460 acres in this area.

In January 1967, a rare species of carnivorous marsupial, the Dibbler, made its unexpected reappearance, after being 'lost' for eighty-three years. I had been searching for Honey Possums among the golden flowers of banksias along the coastal slopes of Mt Manypeaks when I captured a pair of Dibblers. Instead of a minute, almost toothless, nectar-eating possum, I caught two nine-inch, speckle-furred carnivores, well equipped with needle-pointed incisors. No one

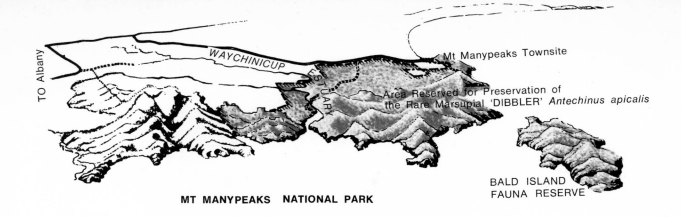

had suspected that this marsupial would be arboreal in habits; its feet and tail seemed appropriate for a terrestrial life. The survival of this interesting and most attractive little marsupial will depend upon the preservation of the dense wildflower scrubs and heaths which clothe the slopes of the hills and headlands at Mt Manypeaks.

In summer, when the bush is dry, the Dibbler and other bush creatures find the abundant nectar of these large wildflowers most attractive. In the tangled mass of the banksia's flowers are countless tiny insects far too small to pollinate the flowers; they are food for other creatures such as birds, Pygmy Possums and Honey Possums which frequent this area.

When the misty rains retreat from the south coast in December, and when warm days predominate through January and February, the coastal hills and heathlands put forth their greatest wealth. I was able to count eleven species of banksia where I found the Dibblers, and most of them bear their cones or long spikes of gold, crimson or bronze, through the summer months. In spring, summer and well into autumn, the Mt Manypeaks area has many wildflowers (and is exceptionally rich in wildlife) displayed in a setting of magnificent coastal scenery.

CAPE LE GRAND NATIONAL PARK

Along Western Australia's southern coast, steep hills jut into the ocean and wide smooth sweeps of white beach curve between rocky headlands. Beneath their bare granite slopes the ceaseless swell of the ocean thunders against the cliffs, breaking and boiling over great blocks of blackened stone. Sheets of spray lifted by the southerlies form mist on the higher slopes and wet the stunted scrub. This is a spectacular coast, particularly picturesque at Albany's ocean cliffs, and from hills overlooking King George's Sound. Further eastwards, and more precipitous, are the granite domes of Mt Gardner, Mt Manypeaks, and the triple peaks of the Barren Range. Further yet, just east of Esperance, rise the slopes of Cape le

Grand, named in 1792 by the French explorer D'Entrecasteaux.

Cape le Grand flanks Esperance Bay on the east and its ocean views encompass the multitude of small islands known as the Recherche Archipelago which are fauna sanctuaries. As well as protecting a wealth of flowering plants, Cape le Grande National Park also protects unique marsupials and many birds. Found here is a form of rock wallaby (*Petrogale lateralis hacketti*) which differs from those found elsewhere on the mainland, but is identical to the rock wallabies of the Recherche.

One of the most remarkable of all the strange creatures of Australia, certainly one of the smallest, and one which is an object of international scientific interest, is also found here. This is the Honey Possum (*Tarsipes spenserae*), a furred counterpart of the avian honeyeaters, whose way of life it imitates by night in search of nectar in the south-coast wildflowers. Only in this region has sufficient wealth and diversity of bushland flowers permitted the evolution of a marsupial so dependent upon nectar or so extensively adapted to this way of feeding. The Honey Possum has found an exclusive niche—with beak-like snout, and fine, darting brush-tipped tongue it has an advantage over any other mammal which, from time to time, may visit the large banksia and bottlebrush spikes.

This delightful creature may be found—by lucky chance or at times of scrub-clearing or fencing—right along the sand-heath plains of Western Australia's south coast, but its bushland haunts are being destroyed at an ever-increasing rate. It is most fortunate that land has been set aside here, at Cape le Grand, and in other south-coast sanctuaries; a valuable contribution to conservation by the Western Australian Government.

Though the chance of the casual visitor ever catching a glimpse of the nocturnal Honey Possum is remote, the knowledge that the south-western wonderland of wildflowers and superb coastal scenery also shelters one of this country's most fascinating creatures can only make this southern coast the richer, lending greater lustre to its more conspicuous attractions, its birds, flowers, and its coastal scenery.

Cape le Grand National Park was established mainly to preserve and to provide controlled access to the coast's scenic beauty, with tourist development in mind. It is to be hoped that roads and other facilities will be placed where they will neither spoil natural beauty nor endanger the valuable plant and animal life of the park. All tourist facilities are within easy distance at Esperance, where sheltered beaches are an attraction. South-coast summers are mild, making this a popular region through late spring, summer and early autumn months when the wildflowers are at their magnificent best.

FITZGERALD RIVER

To the west of Cape le Grand, but east of Albany, and encompassing the Mt Barren range, is a flora and fauna reserve of 604,000 acres where many of the best of the western wildflowers are protected across wide tracts of sand-heath plains and upon the slopes of the coastal ranges.

Breaking through this line of hills at the foot of Mt Barren, the Fitzgerald River joins the ocean in a setting of impressive coastal scenery. Along its upper reaches is the richest flora of the reserve, which in its wide tracts preserves many plant species found in no other part of the world. It is possible, too, that marsupials rare elsewhere may still be sheltering in this large, relatively unknown sanctuary, for little has yet been done to investigate the animal life of this region. Almost certainly its low wildflower heaths would shelter Honey Possums, possibly the rare Dibbler still survives here as at Mt Manypeaks, and, though it must be considered most unlikely, there may even be a small surviving population of the Broad-faced Rat-Kangaroo, which has long since vanished from its only known haunts in other parts of the south-west.

But it was principally for the preservation of the unique western wildflowers that this large reserve was established in 1954. Across its wide sand-

heath plains and on the slopes of its coastal ranges there are innumerable forms of plant life, among the strangest of which is the Royal Hakea (*Hakea victoriae*), whose foliage is of colour unequalled by any other Australian shrub or tree.

Small, rather insignificant flowers are all but hidden in the curved shells of great stiff leaves of yellow, orange and purple. Its new foliage is green, becoming bright yellow, intricately veined and patterned in lines and patches of green. Older leaves lower on the thin, upright stems show richer hues as age brings forth markings of orange, red and purple.

There are many wildflowers of equally spectacular beauty, but with colour in flowers rather than foliage. Among the best of this region is the Scarlet Regelia (*Regelia velutina*), a tall, soft-foliaged shrub, native to the slopes of the Mt Barren Range.

LAKE MAGENTA

The Lake Magenta fauna and flora reserve (Class A) of 232,700 acres of mallee eucalypt country in southern Western Australia, was created as a sanctuary for the Mallee Fowl and other mallee wildlife, and for the flora of the region.

Among the bird species recorded during a brief survey (1953) were the Southern Scrub Robin (*Drymodes brunneopygia*) and the Shy Ground-wren (*Hylacola cauta*) which are almost always confined to mallee country, and are fast disappearing where huge areas are being cleared. Other birds include the Blue-breasted Wren (*Malurus pulcherrimus*), Rufous Tree-creeper (*Climacteris rufa*) and Purple-gaped Honeyeater (*Meliphaga cratitia*).

The Red-tailed Wambenger (*Phascogale calura*) and the Honey Possum (*Tarsipes spenserae*) are among the more interesting of the region's marsupials.

Below
The 'Dibbler' (Antechinus apicalis), *a small marsupial rediscovered by the author at Mt Manypeaks*

Right
Western Australia's southern parks protect a wealth of wildflowers, and such delightful creatures as this mouse-sized Honey Possum, here feeding at Banksia sphaerocarpa *flowers*

Part Five: THE SOUTH

This is Australia's region of mountains; yet it contains, also, scenery of coasts, forests and even of desert landscape. Here are to be found Australia's highest mountain ranges, reaching their climax in the 7,000 ft peaks of Kosciusko National Park. But there is more of interest in the southern parks than mountains alone. There are many national parks protecting magnificent coastal scenery—Victoria's Port Campbell National Park, Wilson's Promontory, and Mallacoota; Tasmania's Freycinet Peninsula, Tasman Peninsula, Port Davey, Rocky Cape and Bruny Island; South Australia's Lincoln National Park.

Surprisingly, too, among the national parks of southern Australia there are tracts of semi-desert land. Victoria's largest park, Wyperfeld, contains desert dunes, sandplain, and a chain of dry lakes, and South Australia has preserved a large area of mallee and low scrublands in semi-arid regions, thereby providing a permanent home for wildlife. The national parks of the south provide this great variety of scenery—snow-capped mountain ranges that are without equal in any other part of Australia, desert scenery, and parks containing luxuriant forests, soaring trees and lush fern gullies. Yet very few of these national parks are really remote, or difficult to reach; few are more than a day's drive from either Melbourne, Adelaide or Hobart.

Lyrebird singing and displaying at mound

Over
Impressive grandeur of the Snowy Mountains.

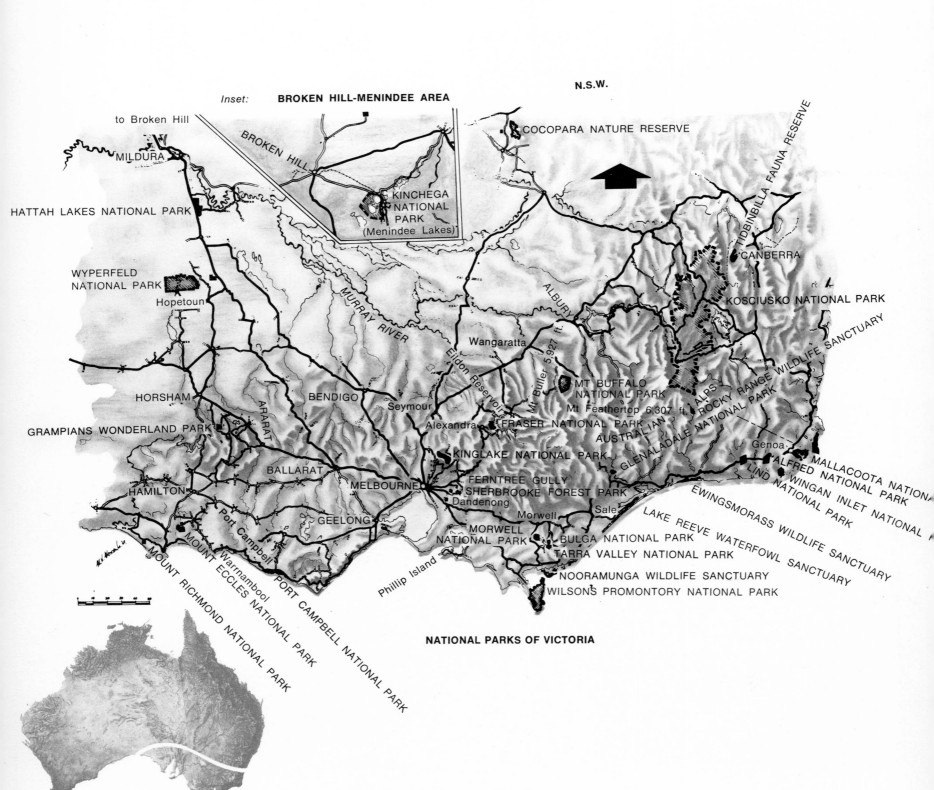

Inset: **BROKEN HILL-MENINDEE AREA**

to Broken Hill

MILDURA

BROKEN HILL

KINCHEGA NATIONAL PARK
(Menindee Lakes)

HATTAH LAKES NATIONAL PARK

WYPERFELD NATIONAL PARK

Hopetoun

N.S.W.

COCOPARA NATURE RESERVE

TIDBINBILLA FAUNA RESERVE

CANBERRA

KOSCIUSKO NATIONAL PARK

MURRAY RIVER

ALBURY

Wangaratta

Eildon Reservoir

HORSHAM

ARARAT

BENDIGO

Seymour

Mt Buller 5,927 ft.

MT BUFFALO NATIONAL PARK

Mt Feathertop 6,307 ft.

ALPS

ROCKY RANGE WILDLIFE SANCTUARY

GRAMPIANS WONDERLAND PARK

Alexandra

FRASER NATIONAL PARK

AUSTRALIAN

GLENALADALE NATIONAL PARK

Genoa

MALLACOOTA NATIONAL

ALFRED NATIONAL PARK

KINGLAKE NATIONAL PARK

BALLARAT

HAMILTON

MELBOURNE

FERNTREE GULLY
SHERBROOKE FOREST PARK

Dandenong

Morwell

Sale

WINGAN INLET NATIONAL

LIND NATIONAL PARK

EWINGSMORASS WILDLIFE SANCTUARY

LAKE REEVE WATERFOWL SANCTUARY

Port Campbell

GEELONG

MORWELL NATIONAL PARK

BULGA NATIONAL PARK

TARRA VALLEY NATIONAL PARK

Warrnambool

MOUNT ECCLES NATIONAL PARK

PORT CAMPBELL NATIONAL PARK

Phillip Island

NOORAMUNGA WILDLIFE SANCTUARY

WILSON'S PROMONTORY NATIONAL PARK

MOUNT RICHMOND NATIONAL PARK

NATIONAL PARKS OF VICTORIA

THE SOUTH
VICTORIA

KOSCIUSKO NATIONAL PARK

In the south-eastern corner of New South Wales lies the Kosciusko National Park, one of Australia's largest national parks with an area of 1,322,000 acres. This great mountain fastness of weathered snow-bound granite outcrops, alpine plateau and steep, forested ridges is best known as a winter playground, having some of the finest and most extensive snowfields in Australia. The region is just as fascinating in summer when thousands of visitors tour the alpine roads, drive almost up to the highest peaks, fish for trout in the cold, clear streams, hike or ride horseback across the high plains.

Kosciusko possesses the only mountains in Australia which top 7,000 feet. Its most spectacular scenic feature is an enormous, steep-sided gorge where the western edge of the Kosciusko plateau drops abruptly from a wall of summits— Mt Kosciusko (7,314 feet), Townsend (7,251 feet), Carruthers (7,047 feet) and Twynam (7,207 feet) —to the gorge of the Geehi River 4,500 feet below. West of the river rise the steep Geehi Walls, and from Scammel's Spur Lookout, on the Alpine Way, magnificent views unfold of the whole western escarpment of Kosciusko.

On the slopes of Kosciusko from June to October miles of smooth deep snow attract the skiing enthusiasts. These long downhill slopes, sparkling white in the brilliant sunshine of this crisp, heady climate, are an irresistible challenge to the skier. During the short winter there is more snow country in these Australian Alps than in Switzerland—several thousand square miles, from the Snowy Mountains to the Victorian Alps and down to altitudes of 4,500 feet.

The Australian alpine regions are quite distinctive. There are no conifers on these heights, but instead, there are eucalypts. Most common are the Snow Gums (*Eucalyptus coriacea*), which have become specialized for life in the snow. Stunted and twisted with smooth bark streaked red, brown and creamy-white, these trees cover large areas at altitudes between 4,500 and 6,000 feet.

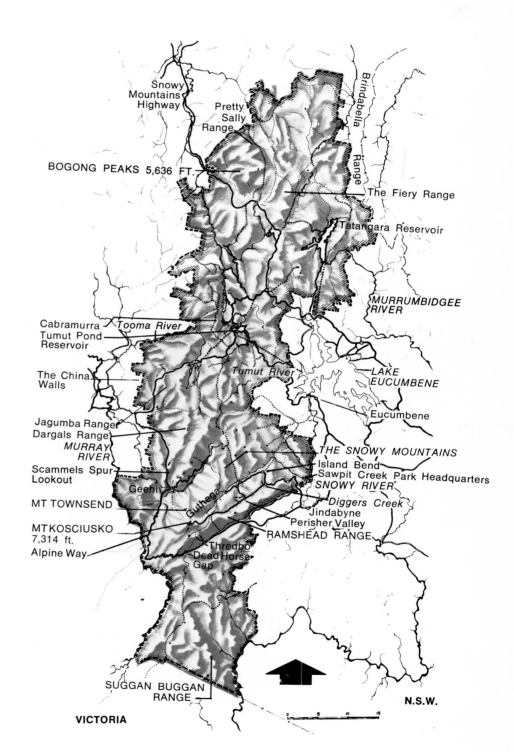

KOSCIUSKO NATIONAL PARK

The finest and most extensive snowfields in Australia are in the Kosciusko National Park

As the last of winter's snowdrifts melt away, alpine wild-flowers appear, a few at first, then in mass array

Right · Below
Lake Albina, almost at Kosciusko's summit, lies at the brink of a tremendous river gorge; beyond rise the blue ridges of the Geehi Walls

154

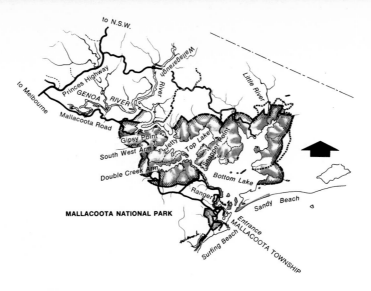

MALLACOOTA NATIONAL PARK

The timbered ranges and high plains of the park form the largest permanent refuge in all south-eastern Australia for native birds, mammals and plants. The great range of altitude produces a wide variety of vegetation following well-defined zones. Below 4,000 feet, giant Mountain Ash, Candlebark and Stringybark trees; at 4,500 feet these forests give way to stunted Snow Gums, while above 5,700 feet are treeless alpine plains, heaths, sphagnum bogs and massive bare granite summit outcrops.

As the snows melt for another summer the streams become rushing torrents, green slopes and ridges appear and the snowdrifts shrink to small patches of dazzling white. In January the alpine flowers appear in glorious massed arrays unequalled in few other mountain areas in the world—Snow Daisies (*Celmisia longifolia*), Alpine Podolepis (*Podolepis robusta*), Orange Everlastings (*Helichrysum acuminatum*), Alpine Sundews (*Drosera arcturi*), Mountain Gentians (*Gentianella diemensis*), Alpine Groundsels (*Senecio pectinatus*), Grass trigger-plants (*Stylidium graminifolium*) and many others adding beauty and colour to the display.

The sphagnum bogs are home for beautiful black-and-yellow banded Corroboree Frogs (*Pseudophryne corroboree*) which are confined to these mountain heights.

Birdlife is abundant—brilliantly plumaged Crimson Rosellas, Gang-gang Cockatoos, birds of prey including Wedgetail Eagles, and many small birds such as Flame Robins which nest in summer among the Snow Gums and Mountain Ash forests.

Kosciusko National Park possesses two remarkable series of limestone caves, one on the Yarrangobilly River, adorned with magnificent stalactites and stalagmites, canopies and glittering limestone, the other at Cooleman, north-east of Yarrangobilly.

MT BUFFALO NATIONAL PARK

Another alpine area with magnificent scenery is the Mt Buffalo National Park (27,280 acres) in the Victorian Alps, 200 miles north-east of Melbourne. It is a popular winter resort area but is also an attraction in summer when many alpine wildflowers bloom. Mt Buffalo National Park, 5,000 feet above sea level, stands in isolated grandeur above the Ovens River valley. From the distance it resembles a huge hump-backed bison standing guard over the distant Australian Alps.

Visitors will be impressed with the magnificent views of green valleys and mountain streams, and the peaks, often snow-capped, of Mts Bogong, Feathertop, Painter, Hotham and in the far distance Mt Kosciusko. Trails, popular with horseback riders in summer, lead to various points such as the southern rim of the plateau to view the Black Wall cliff-face and far below, the Buffalo River Valley. Shorter trails follow around Lake Catani. Scenic walks are to be enjoyed through the bush, in quietness broken only by the calling of birds and running streams.

TIDBINBILLA FAUNA RESERVE
Located in the Australian Capital Territory, Tidbinbilla Fauna Reserve consists of 11,500 acres. Rough granite ranges up to 5,000 feet rise between the Cotter and Murrumbidgee Rivers. Part of the reserve has been developed for visitors while the remainder is a valuable wildlife sanctuary.

MALLACOOTA INLET NATIONAL PARK
A belt of wooded hills sloping to the water's edge along the shores of Mallacoota Inlet was reserved in 1909 to form this beautiful national park near the far-eastern tip of Victoria. Set in some of Victoria's most beautiful lakeland, against a background of forests and distant mountain ranges, this park offers perfect peace and solitude in a perfect setting.

The national park preserves the great natural beauty of the Mallacoota Inlet—a deeply indented

156

shoreline of more than a hundred miles, and an area of 11,225 acres of forest. It includes a number of islands, and surrounding hills.

Mallacoota Inlet was formed by the drowning of the valley of the Genoa River, possibly by a rising sea level at the close of the ice age. The national park is best seen from the water, and boats may be hired. This is recognized as one of the best fishing resorts in Victoria, and fishing is permitted from the jetties and shores.

Mallacoota birdlife is varied, with the ocean, the beaches, lakes, islands, mud-flats, heathlands, open forest and jungle all having their own type of birdlife; a total of more than 200 species has been recorded for the area.

Plant life is interesting and an attractive floral association includes the Bloodwood, whose magnificent, creamy-coloured blossoms attract hundreds of Rainbow Lorikeets in the autumn, and the Rough-barked Apple-box. The national park and parts of surrounding districts are rich in wildflowers, with wildflowers of the heathlands, open forest and of the jungles in the gullies.

In some of the picturesque places around the inlet, jetties, with picnicking facilities nearby, have been constructed. Boating services are available at Mallacoota and Gipsy Point. Camping is not permitted in the park, but in extensive camping-areas on the shores by the township of Mallacoota, near beaches, golf links and boating facilities.

WILSON'S PROMONTORY NATIONAL PARK

One of the most popular of Victoria's national parks (sharing with Mt Buffalo the greatest popularity for people on extended visits) is Wilson's Promontory, 150 miles south-east of Melbourne. With an area of 102,379 acres, it is also one of Victoria's largest national parks.

The promontory projects into Bass Strait as a mountainous peninsula, connected to the mainland by a low strip of sand. At one period it must have been an island, until a fall in sea level and

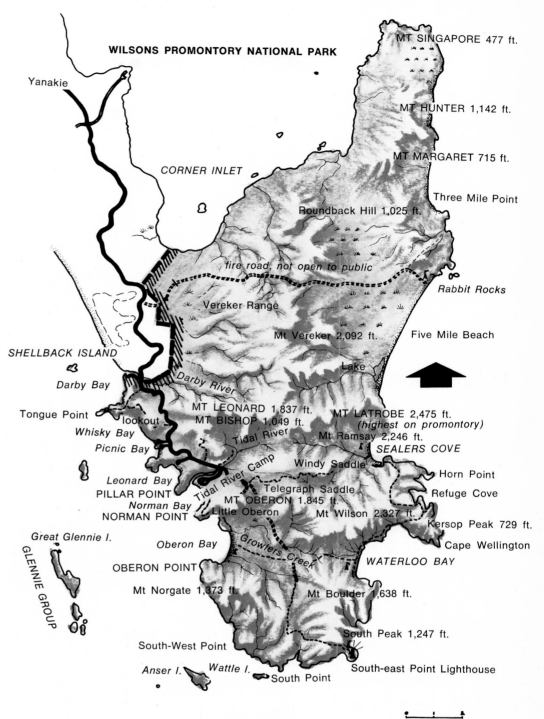

an accumulation of dune sand connected its northernmost hills to the mainland.

Wilson's Promontory contains some spectacular scenery with its mountain peaks, some over 2,000 feet, its deep verdant gullies, its breathtaking coastline of steep granite headlands and sweeping white beaches.

Of the tens of thousands who visit this national park each year most are content to go no further than the places to be reached by road—the Tidal

Over left
Tarra Valley National Park, where a forest of massed tree ferns beneath tall gums is a favourite haunt of the Lyrebird

Over right
Kangaroos at Fraser National Park can be seen bounding across wooded hillsides or feeding in mobs on the grassy flats at evening

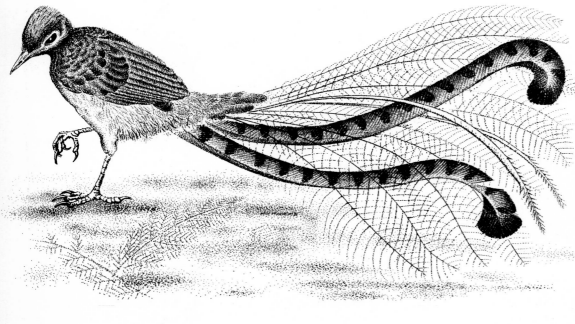

Superb Lyrebird

River camping area, and Norman Beach where swimming, surfing and fishing are the attractions; or nearby Squeaky Beach, Whisky or Picnic beaches. Many climb to the lookout on Mt Oberon (1,968 feet) for views over Norman Bay and southwards across Oberon Bay to the Anser Islands. Short walking tracks lead to Tongue Point and Oberon Bay, and various west-coastal lookout points are popular.

But the park's more adventurous visitors are prepared to tackle the longer walks across to the eastern shore—Sealers Cove, Refuge Cove, and Waterloo Bay—and many do the twenty-seven mile round trip to the lighthouse. While this is often done in a day it's well worthwhile to take two or three days.

Wilson's Promontory has been ravaged by numerous fires, the last major holocaust being in 1951. Timber cutters were active in the area before it became a national park. In early times trees in the Sealer's Cove region attained heights of two hundred feet and were twenty-five feet in circumference; some Lilly Pilly trees (*Eugenia smithii*) were twenty feet in girth.

Though most of the giants are gone, the park still has many attractive wildflowers to show, and considerable bird life—no tourist could help but see the Crimson Rosellas (*Platycercus elegans*), Blue Wrens (*Malurus cyaneus*) and many other birds in the immediate vicinity of the Tidal River camping grounds.

Wilson's Promontory was first suggested as a national park in 1884. Only after a twenty-five year battle was it finally declared a national park in 1909. In recent years the trickle of visitors has grown to a flood as city people have discovered the quality of its coastal and bushland recreation.

It is a tremendous loss to Victoria that, in spite of such early establishment of a large national park, so few others have since been created which, in size at least, deserve the title 'national park'. Most of the parks easily accessible to Melbourne people are so small that their gradual, steady deterioration seems inevitable.

160

VICTORIA

Lyrebird

Those interested in the preservation of the natural, unique Australian scenery and wildlife have made many suggestions for additional national parks, but Victorians still have less national parkland than any other state (0·2 acres per person) and government expenditure upon these parks (14 cents per person in 1966/67) is the lowest in Australia.

TARRA VALLEY NATIONAL PARK
BULGA NATIONAL PARK

A gully of tree-ferns, Beech, Sassafras, Blackwood and other rainforest flora with, high above, the smooth clean straight boles of the tall Mountain Ash rising from the hillsides—this is Tarra Valley, where Lyrebirds are numerous, and the Koala, Platypus, Echidna, Black-tailed Wallaby, possums and gliders are known to live. Ground flora includes numerous ferns, herbs and orchids—ninety flowering plant species and thirty-six ferns grow here. One hundred and sixty species of fungi and liverworts flourish in the humid forest areas.

Tarra Valley National Park, 130 miles from Melbourne, is very small—315 acres in the valley of the Tarra River, in the Strzelecki Ranges of South Gippsland. It is dedicated to the preservation of flora and fauna native to Gippsland.

Only a few miles away is Bulga National Park, even smaller in area than Tarra. Its ninety-one acres cover part of a stream flowing through a narrow valley, in the green twilight beneath a dense forest canopy. Under the 165 feet long suspension bridge spanning Mack's Creek grow some of the most perfect tree-ferns in Victoria.

Tarra and Bulga are renowned for their massed tree-ferns growing in sheltered abundance. There are two rare species here, the Skirted Treefern, and the Slender Treefern, as well as the common Rough, and Soft Treeferns. Short walking tracks lead to beauty spots in both parks, and along these tracks may be seen such rainforest birds as the Rose Robin (*Petroica rosea*), Pink Robin (*P. rodinogaster*) and through the summer, the Rufous

Fantail (*Rhipidura rufifrons*). Crimson and Eastern Rosellas dart through the trees while the Whipbird's sharp call cracks nearby.

Because these parks are so small there is a real danger that they will eventually be trampled out of existence, or the quality of their lush vegetation ruined by land clearing and settlement about their borders. They are a tiny remnant of the magnificent forests that once covered these ranges—samples of this country as nature made it. With their huge trees, lavish greenery and grand cover of ferns and mosses they are a contrast to the bare, often eroded ridges which now form the greater part of the Strzelecki Ranges.

FRASER NATIONAL PARK

After the rising waters of Eildon Reservoir had inundated the lower slopes of the surrounding hills a tract of land, overlooking the man-made shores, was set aside for public use as Fraser National Park; it is approximately ninety miles north-east of Melbourne.

The park's 7,750 acres cover hill slopes, and rounded hilltops clothed by grass and scattered gums (much of the original vegetation was cleared for farming) or patches of native scrub that now are rapidly spreading. Many new sapling trees are shooting up beneath the old gums and much replanting has been done in treeless parts.

Along Fraser's many miles of indented shoreline the bleached white skeletons of trees are a reminder of the former farmlands now drowned beneath the lake.

At the head of Coller Bay the visitor facilities are situated—camping areas and boat launching ramps. Lake Eildon is very popular with water skiers, yachtsmen and anglers. Fire protection tracks, open to foot traffic, have been constructed throughout the park and lead to excellent vantage points for magnificent panoramic views of the park and Eildon Reservoir.

Many birds, possums, wombats and phascogales inhabit the park. The Grey Kangaroo, however, provides the most exciting wildlife spectacle.

Mallacoota, a national park on a deep inlet of the sea, in south-eastern Victoria.

Below
Wave-cut cliffs and residual spires at Port Campbell. This coast's scenery includes a series of island spires known as the 'Twelve Apostles', natural bridges, blowhole, and gorges

162

One of Victoria's largest and most popular national parks is Wilson's Promontory, a mountainous peninsula where massive granite headlands shelter wide sandy beaches

White-breasted Robin

VICTORIA

On a grassy hillside I counted thirty kangaroos feeding in small groups quite close to weekend campers. As the sun rose above the hill each morning long lines of kangaroos could be seen thudding up the slopes to shady scrub and some summer evenings as many as ninety come to feed on the greener lakeside grass at the head of Coller Bay. It is estimated that there are 300 kangaroos in this national park.

PORT CAMPBELL NATIONAL PARK

On Victoria's southern coast, running from Peterborough almost to Princeton in the east, are many miles of vertical cliffs formed where the high flat coastal plains are being eroded away by the stormy seas of the Southern Ocean. This magnificent coastal scenery is now Port Campbell National Park (1,750 acres).

This is a spectacular area. In places, the vertical-walled headlands have been undercut to form immense archways such as 'London Bridge'; some are completely detached from the main line of cliffs. At another point the pounding sea has battered a tunnel into the base of the cliffs and surges through to an immense blowhole a quarter mile inland. Residual towers of harder rock rise from the sea and stand several hundred feet above the waves, the most famous group is the 'Twelve Apostles'.

One narrow canyon, the Loch Ard Gorge, cut deep into this line of cliffs, bears the name of one of the many ships lost on this coast between 1855 and 1908. Here the *Loch Ard*, a three-masted iron clipper of 1,623 tons, foundered in 1878 with the loss of fifty lives. Looking down from the heights of these cliffs it is not difficult to appreciate the terrible plight of those cast into the waves among sharp rocks and pounding seas at the foot of unscaleable cliffs.

FERN TREE GULLY NATIONAL PARK

This national park is situated on the southern and western slopes of One Tree Hill in the Dandenong Ranges. The deep red-brown soil supports a lush vegetation, the fern gully community. Its most beautiful parts may be seen by following the main walking track which winds beside the creek. In the gully the vegetation forms layers similar to the northern tropical rain-forests.

More than 150 different native flowering plants, ranging in size from giant Manna Gums to tiny Ivy-leaf Violets, grow in this area. Numerous grasses and brightly-coloured pea-flowered plants such as the bush-peas (*Pultanaea*) are common, thirty types of orchids bloom in spring and there are many species of the lily family.

About 100 species of birds have been recorded in this national park. Most visitors come to see the Superb Lyrebird whose calls can be heard from the fern-clad hillside and in the gullies.

Twenty species of native animals live within the park; one of the most common is the Echidna while Black Wallabies, the Platypus, bandicoots, phascogales and possums can also be found.

MT ECCLES NATIONAL PARK

Victoria's smallest national park (84 acres), situated 200 miles west of Melbourne, is of geological interest as it features an impressive volcanic crater and crater lakes. Mt Eccles is a mound of scoria rising 588 feet above sea level. The scrub-covered land to the west and south is not suitable for agriculture because of the rough stony surface of the old lava flow. Also of interest is the lava cave so different from limestone caves at Buchan and Jenolan.

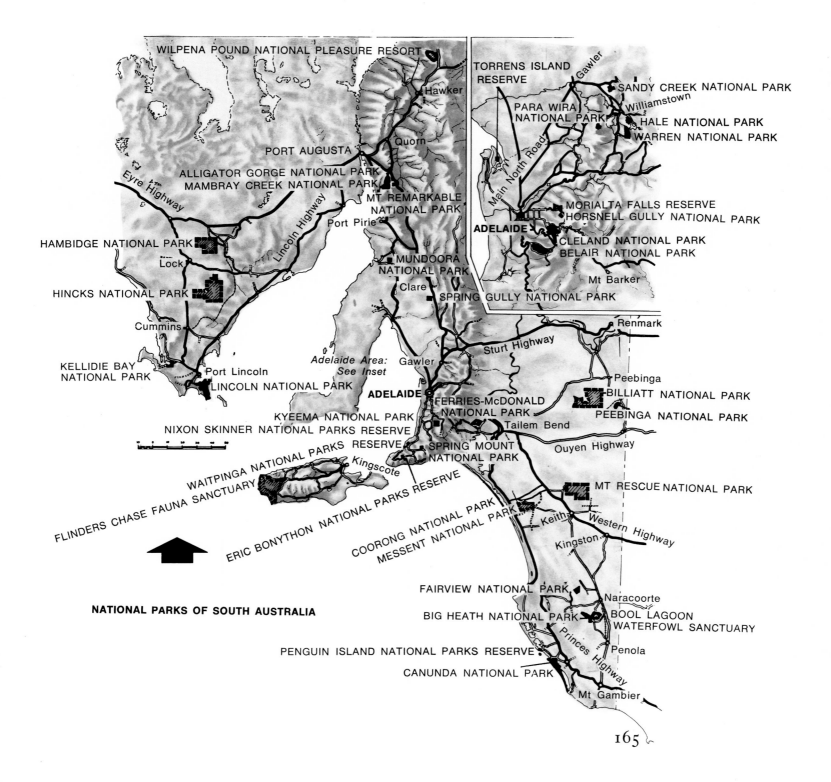

WILPENA POUND NATIONAL PLEASURE RESORT

TORRENS ISLAND
RESERVE

Gawler

Hawker

SANDY CREEK NATIONAL PARK

Williamstown

PARA WIRA
NATIONAL PARK

HALE NATIONAL PARK
WARREN NATIONAL PARK

Quorn

PORT AUGUSTA

ALLIGATOR GORGE NATIONAL PARK
MAMBRAY CREEK NATIONAL PARK

Eyre Highway

MORIALTA FALLS RESERVE
HORSNELL GULLY NATIONAL PARK

MT REMARKABLE
NATIONAL PARK

Main North Road

ADELAIDE

Port Pirie

Lincoln Highway

CLELAND NATIONAL PARK
BELAIR NATIONAL PARK

HAMBIDGE NATIONAL PARK

Lock

MUNDOORA
NATIONAL PARK

Mt Barker

Clare

HINCKS NATIONAL PARK

SPRING GULLY NATIONAL PARK

Renmark

Cummins

Sturt Highway

Peebinga

KELLIDIE BAY
NATIONAL PARK

Adelaide Area:
See Inset

Gawler

Port Lincoln

LINCOLN NATIONAL PARK

ADELAIDE

BILLIATT NATIONAL PARK

FERRIES-McDONALD
NATIONAL PARK

KYEEMA NATIONAL PARK

PEEBINGA NATIONAL PARK

NIXON SKINNER NATIONAL PARKS RESERVE

Tailem Bend

RESERVE

Ouyen Highway

SPRING MOUNT
NATIONAL PARK

WAITPINGA NATIONAL PARKS RESERVE

Kingscote

MT RESCUE NATIONAL PARK

FLINDERS CHASE FAUNA SANCTUARY

ERIC BONYTHON NATIONAL PARKS RESERVE

Keith

Western Highway

COORONG NATIONAL PARK
MESSENT NATIONAL PARK

Kingston

FAIRVIEW NATIONAL PARK

Naracoorte

NATIONAL PARKS OF SOUTH AUSTRALIA

BIG HEATH NATIONAL PARK

BOOL LAGOON
WATERFOWL SANCTUARY

Princes Highway

Penola

PENGUIN ISLAND NATIONAL PARKS RESERVE

CANUNDA NATIONAL PARK

Mt Gambier

165

Left
A hunting Egret stalks in the shallows of a swamp; a great many places used by our water birds have been drained or polluted

Below
White-faced Herons, ducks and other water birds, live in Big Heath, Messent, Fairview, Kinchega and The Lakes national parks

Right
Brightly plumaged Rainbow Lorikeets (Trichoglossus moluccanus) are often conspicuous in the forest trees of Belair National Park

Eastern Yellow Robin

WYPERFELD NATIONAL PARK

Situated in the Victorian Mallee, 280 miles north-west from Melbourne, is Wyperfeld National Park (139,760 acres), Victoria's largest national park. It is a region of sand dunes and interesting desert wildlife.

Wyperfeld lies on the final extremities of the Wimmera River system. Outlet Creek from Lake Albacutya follows a tortuous course among sand dunes, forming numerous dry lakes through the centre of the park. Only on rare occasions do these lakes hold much water, but at these times water birds arrive in great numbers.

The dominant vegetation is small drought resistant eucalypts with multiple stems rising from each large, knotted ligno-tuber. The many small inland eucalypts which take this form are known collectively by their aboriginal name, 'mallee'. One of the commonest here is the Yellow Mallee, (*Eucalyptus incrassata*) which extends westwards into South Australia.

With the little mallee gums are patches of Scrub Cypress Pine (*Callitris verucosa*), tea-trees (*Leptospermum*), and banksias, while the ground beneath has clumps of prickly Porcupine Grass (*Triodia*), or shrubs often prolific in flower—species of *Acacia, Cassia, Eremophila, Prosanthera* and *Calytrix*.

Early spring brings a burst of colour from the mallee lands as the annuals carpet the ground—the Papery Sunray (*Helipterum corymbiflorum*), Orange Immortelle (*Waitzia accuminata*) and Poached Egg Daisy (*Myriocephalus stuartii*).

Wyperfeld National Park was dedicated for the purpose of preserving the unique mallee flora and wildlife, fast disappearing from many other places, and particularly to protect a truly unique bird of Australia. This bird, the Lowan, or Mallee Fowl (*Leipoa ocellata*), is one of the 'incubator birds' which lay their eggs in specially prepared mounds of rotting vegetation and rely upon the combined heat of decomposition and sun to hatch young.

The Lowan cannot survive where the mallee scrub has been cleared or where sheep graze, and it takes as long as fourteen years to breed again in an area devastated by fire, due no doubt to the resultant scarcity of leaf and twig litter with which to construct the necessary large incubator mound.

Altogether, more than 180 species of birds have been recorded for Wyperfeld National Park; it is the wealth of dry-country birdlife which makes this park a 'must' for any serious naturalist.

At Wyperfeld may be seen the Emu, many Wedge-tailed Eagles, Purple-crowned Lorikeets in large numbers when the mallees are in blossom, Red-backed Parrots, Mulga, Blue-winged and Elegant Parrots, and Budgerigars. Red-backed Kingfishers are often present, and Rainbow Birds throughout the summer. In scrub-pine groves the Red-capped Robin is often to be seen, while the Crested Bellbird has a preference for the mallee parts.

LITTLE DESERT NATIONAL PARK
BILLIATT NATIONAL PARK
MT RESCUE NATIONAL PARK
HINCKS NATIONAL PARK
HAMBIDGE NATIONAL PARK
LINCOLN NATIONAL PARK

Across southern Australia there are other national parks in mallee country, some of quite large size. In Victoria there is the new Little Desert National Park; South Australia has Billiatt National Park (90,874 acres), Mt Rescue (70,149 acres), and Messent (28,000 acres) in its eastern mallee region. On Eyre Peninsula are Hincks National Park (163,315 acres), Hambidge (93,865 acres) and, with coastal scenery of considerable attraction as well as sand-hills and dense mallee scrub, the Lincoln National Park (35,521 acres) at the south-eastern tip of that peninsula.

KINCHEGA NATIONAL PARK

From its headwaters in the snows of the Australian Alps the Murray River flows westwards, twisting and turning a thousand miles across the plains to its junction with the Darling, before turning south to the sea.

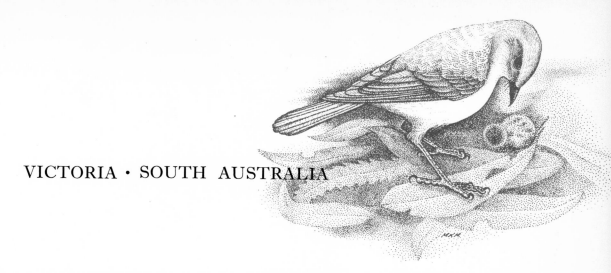

Western Yellow Robin

When these western rivers run high their waters spread out over the countryside filling lakes and marshes, where water birds from half the continent congregate. Huge nesting colonies, such as on the Macquarie Marshes, are one of the wonders of inland Australia.

On the lower reaches of the Darling, surrounded by grey plains and red sand ridges are the Menindee overflow lakes, which abound with waterfowl. These large lakes, together with a section of the Darling River, are the main feature of the Kinchega National Park (87,000 acres) situated seventy-five miles east from Broken Hill. Formerly a sheep station, this area is now being allowed to return to its original state of semi-arid vegetation.

This is the first national park to be dedicated in all the vast western division of New South Wales —made possible by the material support of North Broken Hill Ltd., Broken Hill South Ltd. and Conzinc Riotinto Ltd., representing a valuable service to Australian wildlife conservation.

HATTAH LAKES NATIONAL PARK
In north-western Victoria the Hattah Lakes National Park features lakes, billabongs and large areas of virgin mallee country. A two-thousand acre portion of this park contains five small lakes which are filled by the Murray's periodic flooding. Their native names, Hattah, Arawak, Bulla, Marramook and Nip Nip are a reminder of the vanished tribes of the Kulkyne area—some of the old trees still show symmetrical scars left by Aboriginal canoe and coolamon makers many years ago.

Along the watercourses and river flats plant species include River Red Gums (*Eucalyptus camaldulensis*), Black Box (*E. largiflorens*), Native Pine (*Callitris columellaris*) and Buloke (*Casuarina luehmanni*). By far the largest section of this park's 44,000 acres is mallee scrub.

Though both Kinchega and Hattah Lakes support fauna unique to Australia—Red Kangaroo, Black-faced Kangaroo, possums, Echidna, Emu and Mallee Fowl—interest centres upon the bird life and almost every bird group is represented.

On the waters of the lakes may be seen, depending upon seasonal conditions, numerous Black Swans (*Cygnus atratus*), Pelicans (*Pelecanus conspicillatus*), Maned Geese (*Chenonetta jubata*), Black Duck (*Anas superciliosa*), Mountain Duck (*Casarca tadornoides*), Chestnut Teal (*Anas castanea*), Pink-eared Duck (*Malacorhynchus membranaceus*) and many other duck species.

Around the margins of lakes and swamps, stalking in the shallows, can be found White Egrets (*Egretta alba*), White-faced and White-necked Herons (*Ardea novae-hollandiae* and *A. pacifica*), Royal and Yellow-billed Spoonbills (*Platalea regia* and *flavipes*), White Ibis (*Threskiornis molucca*), and Straw-necked Ibis (*T. spinicollis*). On occasions a White-breasted Sea-eagle (*Haliaeetus leucogaster*), Swamp Harrier (*Circus approximans*), Spotted Harrier (*C. assimilis*) or more often a Grey Goshawk (*Accipiter novae-hollandiae*) or Wedgetail Eagle (*Aquila audax*) can be observed in the distance.

The big River Red Gums, with their numerous hollow branches, are the nesting and roosting places for countless Galahs (*Kakatoe roseicapilla*) and White Cockatoos (*K. galerita*), Pink Cockatoos (*K. leadbeateri*), Regent Parrots (*Polytelis anthopeplus*), Ringneck Parrots (*Barnardius barnardii*) and Mulga Parrots (*Psephotus varius*).

MESSENT NATIONAL PARK
Messent National Park (28,000 acres) near the long inlet known as the Coorong and westward of Keith, contains lake, swamp and sedge habitats where water-birds gather, as well as sandplain, sand hill, mallee and heathlands; it is a wildlife sanctuary rather than a tourist attraction.

In South Australia there are several large national parks containing lakes, swamps, or extensive areas subject to periodic flooding; all are magnificent waterfowl sanctuaries, becoming increasingly vital as other swamplands are drained for agricultural use.

170

SOUTH AUSTRALIA

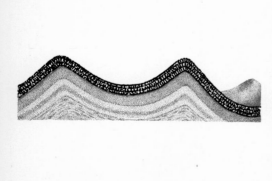

BIG HEATH NATIONAL PARK

Southwards, near Naracoorte, is the Big Heath National Park (5,809 acres) situated adjacent to Bool Lagoon, a large water-bird sanctuary. Much of Big Heath is regularly flooded, and huge congregations of birds can be seen at times; on occasions Bool Lagoon has a hundred or more Brolgas (*Grus rubicunda*) on its wide expanses of waterlogged flats.

WILPENA POUND 'NATIONAL PARK'

A huge, rock-rimmed amphitheatre which dominates the northern Flinders Ranges, Wilpena Pound is one of the most spectacular of possible future additions to the national parks of South Australia—at present it is a 'National Pleasure Resort' of 10,000 acres. The Pound is an immense elevated basin covering about thirty-two square miles and encircled by sheer cliffs. Massive river gums grow along the creeks and lower areas while native pines cover the higher parts.

Within the Pound, tracks lead to high cliff-top peaks, while its massive walls dominate the surrounding landscape. One morning at dawn I climbed from our valley campsite to a hill overlooking the wide Bunyeroo Valley. Away across countless small rounded, pine-clad hills and intersecting dry watercourses rose high rock walls—a jagged horizon where the moon's descent preceded by minutes the first faint flush of light on the ramparts of Wilpena. Quite suddenly the blue-and-grey of sky and stone and pine-studded hills was transformed by the touch of sunlight on the peaks. For a few moments the walls of the Pound glowed between shadowed valley and dawn sky, as the ochre and rust-red rock strata of high cliffs, along the four-thousand foot bluffs, caught the first rays of sun. Soon, tinged with the haze of distance, these far walls of Wilpena acquired a delicate magenta tint that became even more blue as the sun lifted from the eastern horizon. Late afternoon would see these same steep slopes lost in blue shadow, only the purple cast of sunlit

ridges and peaks hinting of the raw-rock colours of the range.

Nearer, low rounded hills and folded ridges across the broad valley's lower slopes now caught the sun, their cold, grey, pre-dawn monotones giving way to golden and rich-brown hues where the first brightness touched dry grass and bare earth; minutes later the bright yellow-green of the topmost foliage of the river red-gums was added to the colour spectrum of the awakening Flinders as the lifting sun broke the gloom of innumerable gullies and tree-lined watercourses.

Sunlight on foliage signalled the end of morning quiet. Small but noisy flocks of dazzling white Corellas rising from the shadows, pink and grey Galahs, in twos and threes and in small flocks, noisily winging their way from creekside gums to open plains. Small flocks of Budgerigars rushing through the trees, conspicuous in swift flight and sharp sound. Among the gums vociferous honey-eaters search for nectar, or for insects on flowers and foliage. An occasional Brown Tree-creeper may be seen spiralling up massive grey-white trunks and branches.

Almost everywhere there seems to echo the cheerful, ticking trill of the Red-capped Robin, a dry-country bird that is common through the Flinders. Common too are Ring-necked Parrots, of rich green plumage, with bright yellow collars and intense blue on wings and tail. In the far distance a majestic Wedgetail Eagle on rigid wings rides the lifting wind above a ridge—a bird to match the grandeur of this wild landscape.

Giant River Red Gums, along the watercourses, provide nesting places for the parrots and cockatoos, and homes for Brushtail Possums which are the commonest marsupial found here.

The rugged Flinders hide a small colony of Yellow-footed Rock Wallabies, which have so far managed to escape the complete extermination which has been the fate of some of Australia's most attractive marsupials in other, less mountainous parts. Possibly this wild terrain will ensure their survival. More often seen are Red Kangaroos, feeding at evening in the valleys where grassed clearings meet pine-clad slopes.

My visit to Wilpena Pound included the Easter holiday period. Tourist buses, and cars (many towing caravans) followed the narrow roads and tracks to well-known places of interest in seeming endless succession; tents large and small appeared under the spreading limbs of the river gums on grassy flats. Everywhere along the way were people from the southern cities. Yet a few hundred yards, a quarter mile at most, from any roadway there remained the seclusion of the bush, the apparently unchanging face of this ancient continent.

ALLIGATOR GORGE NATIONAL PARK
MAMBRAY CREEK NATIONAL PARK

The Flinders Ranges are steeped in history of man's efforts to conquer the arid inland. Today the road north of Wilmington—through Quorn to Hawker and on to Wilpena—runs through a barren, eroded landscape where the ruins of deserted homesteads at Willochra, Kanyaka, Arkaba, and of abandoned towns like Gordon seem more common than occupied farms or thriving townships.

Through the long dry summer months, dust blankets this landscape as the winds sweep away what remains of its good soil. Erosion has carved hideous gullies across its barren, treeless paddocks. First this land was grazed, and bared of much of its low vegetation by sheep. Then came a succession of favourable seasons—the plains were cleared of their few trees, stripped of their protective mulga scrub and grew magnificent crops for a few years.

But soon the exceptional years of bountiful rains had passed, and conspicuous is the ruin that followed the return of normal semi-arid conditions—a desert in the making, a grim warning against the clearing of the drought-resistant scrub which covers and protects the fringes of Australia's arid heart.

Just how devastating has been the work of man upon this land in the short space of time since its first settlers arrived (and it is but a moment in the history of the making of this ancient continent) can be seen when its farmlands are compared with any of the few remaining protected, and relatively undamaged, areas. Among these are the national parks at Alligator Gorge, Mambray Creek and Mt Magnificent.

Alligator Gorge is a narrow, crimson-walled slash through the rounded hills. Walk down through the gorge and it deepens, the walls close in, overhanging and almost like a tunnel in places, then, further downstream, becoming a close-walled, vertical crevice. Above, the sky's blue is cut to a narrow strip between overhanging red-rock ledges, from which pines lean out to form a silhouette tracery against the light.

Native Cypress Pines set the character of Alligator Gorge. Almost every vista through the gorge is through a tracery of slender, dark-foliaged pines, while the massive sugar gums, some wedged in crevices of naked rock, lift white branches and bright greenery against the gorge's fiery stone. Standing along the rim of the gorge, gnarled grey or black against the sky's brightness, and often almost devoid of leaves, the Cypress Pines seem to create an ancient, timeless landscape.

On these scrub-clad hills wallabies are common; small birds are in the undergrowth, and often the bright red-and-yellow of Adelaide Rosellas can be seen winging swiftly between the tall gums to feed among the Casuarina trees.

Joining Alligator Creek's south-western boundary is the Mambray Creek National Park, of 6,650 acres. This area covers rough, forested ranges, and is a sanctuary for Yellow-footed Rock Wallabies, while the creek itself provides a popular picnic place beneath big old River Red Gums.

BELAIR NATIONAL PARK

Belair National Park in the Mt Lofty Ranges overlooking Adelaide in South Australia, contains a considerable area which is undisturbed natural bushland. The remainder, where many exotic

trees were planted long ago, includes recreation areas and visitor facilities.

It is a popular picnic resort and its sporting facilities include a golf course, tennis courts and eight ovals. These were all established many years ago; today it would not be desirable to clear away the natural vegetation for sporting facilities which can be placed elsewhere.

Within Belair is the old Government House, built in 1860. Together with its gardens, the historic building has been preserved as a museum and contains a collection of items dating from the State's early pioneering days.

At least half of Belair's 2,058 acres remains natural bushland—a delightful place for people to see wildflowers and birdlife close to a big city. The bush is most attractive in spring when many species of wildflowers appear; while all year round the flowers of the gums attract honeyeaters and lorikeets, particularly the brilliantly-coloured Rainbow Lorikeets (*Trichoglossus moluccanus*), Purple-crowned Lorikeets (*Glossopsitta porphyrocephala*) and Musk Lorikeets (*G. concinna*).

PARA WIRA NATIONAL PARK
Further north in these ranges is the Para Wira National Park where rocky gorges are inhabited by Black-faced Kangaroos. A portion of the park, the Humbug Scrub, is reserved solely for wildlife. Other parts have sporting facilities.

CLELAND NATIONAL PARK
Also in the Mt Lofty Ranges is the Cleland National Park, stretching from the foothills nearby to the Mt Lofty summit. A display area of native fauna is being developed here.

Left
Gnarled Casuarinas *on the heights of Alligator Gorge National Park, South Australia, frame distant views of the Southern Flinders Ranges*
Right
Trees set the character of Alligator Gorge's red-walled chasm

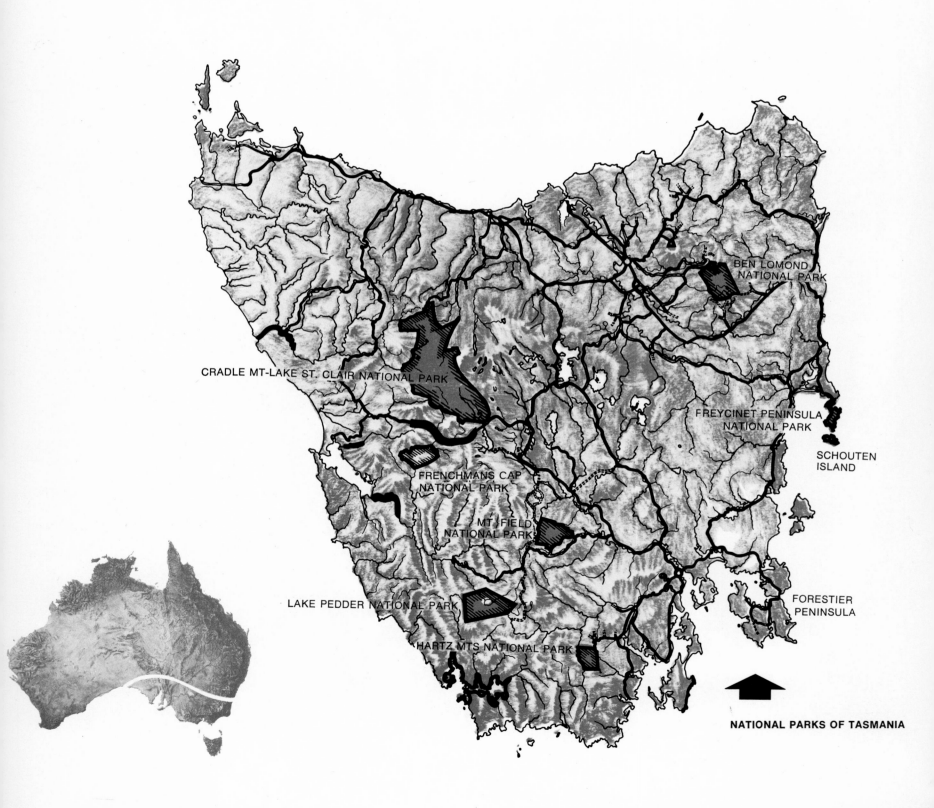

CRADLE MT-LAKE ST. CLAIR NATIONAL PARK

BEN LOMOND
NATIONAL PARK

FREYCINET PENINSULA
NATIONAL PARK

SCHOUTEN
ISLAND

FRENCHMANS CAP
NATIONAL PARK

MT. FIELD
NATIONAL PARK

LAKE PEDDER NATIONAL PARK

FORESTIER
PENINSULA

HARTZ MTS NATIONAL PARK

NATIONAL PARKS OF TASMANIA

TASMANIA

TASMAN PENINSULA RESERVES

A policy of development and restoration has been
carried out by the Scenery Preservation Board in
order to restore and preserve some of the historic
buildings on the Tasman Peninsula.

Port Arthur is historically famous and naturally
beautiful. Situated on a picturesque bay, its stone
buildings stand among green lawns and English
trees. It served as a convict settlement from 1830
to 1877. Soon after its abandonment many of its
old buildings were sold for demolition and bush
fires destroyed others.

Today, thousands of tourists visit this interesting and beautiful place. The most important
buildings still standing at Port Arthur are the
Penitentiary, the Church, the Model Prison, the
Hospital and the Guard House—all grim
reminders of those early convict days. The Lunatic
Asylum is now used as the Tasman Council
chambers and the Commandant's house is now a
private home.

Ruins of other settlements in the area are still
to be seen. The Coalmines Scenic Reserve is a
popular place and many of its ruins are undergoing
restoration. Other places of historical interest are
the Saltwater Creek agricultural centre and the
timber mills at Premaydena and Koonya.

The extremely rugged coastline of this
south-eastern corner has superb scenic beauty,
particularly near Eaglehawk Neck.

HARTZ MOUNTAINS NATIONAL PARK

South-west from Hobart, reached via Huonville
and Geeveston, is the Hartz Mountains National
Park (22,300 acres), a glacier-carved remnant of
an old plateau surface, with peaks still rising to
4,113 feet. It is snow-capped for most of the year,
and has several high-altitude lakes of great beauty,
the highest being Hartz Lake.

A road from Geeveston through the Arve
Valley winds up to the high plateau level, ending
not far below the summit in an area of interesting
alpine vegetation; from this point tracks branch

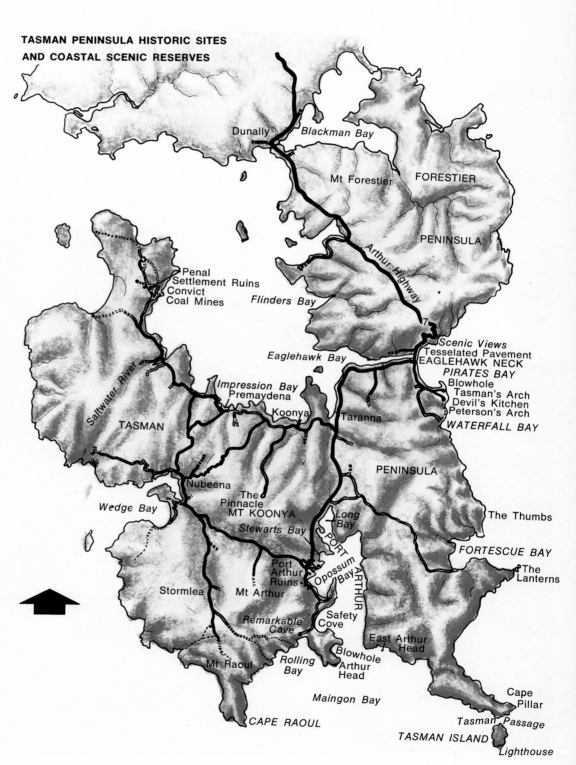

TASMAN PENINSULA HISTORIC SITES
AND COASTAL SCENIC RESERVES

Dunally   Blackman Bay

Mt Forestier   FORESTIER

PENINSULA

Arthur Highway

Penal
Settlement Ruins
Convict
Coal Mines   Flinders Bay

Saltwater River

Eaglehawk Bay

Scenic Views
Tesselated Pavement
EAGLEHAWK NECK
PIRATES BAY
Blowhole
Tasman's Arch
Devil's Kitchen
Peterson's Arch
WATERFALL BAY

Impression Bay
Premaydena

Koonya   Taranna

TASMAN

PENINSULA

Nubeena

The
Pinnacle
MT KOONYA

Wedge Bay   Stewarts Bay   Long
Bay

The Thumbs

Port
Arthur
Ruins   Opossum
Bay

FORTESCUE BAY

The
Lanterns

Stormlea   Mt Arthur

Safety
Cove

Remarkable
Cave

East Arthur
Head

Mt Raoul   Rolling
Bay   Blowhole
Arthur
Head

Cape
Pillar

Maingon Bay

CAPE RAOUL   Tasman Passage

TASMAN ISLAND

Lighthouse

Left
Beech forest, Cradle Mountain, cathedral-like in its soft subdued light, open aisles between mossy treetrunk columns, and floor carpeted with mosses and ferns

Right
Russel Falls, in the Mount Field National Park, Tasmania

Below
Hartz Mountains National Park, southern Tasmania, where clear glacial lakes are set among peaks capped with snow for many months

178

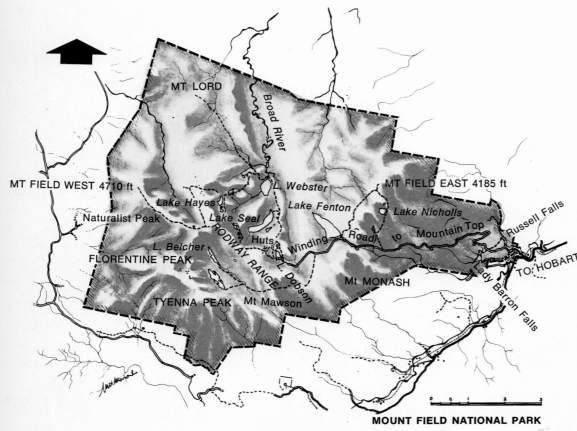

MT LORD

Broad River

MT FIELD WEST 4710 ft

L. Webster

MT FIELD EAST 4185 ft

Naturalist Peak

Lake Hayes

Lake Fenton

Lake Nicholls

Russell Falls

Lake Seal

RODWAY RANGE

Huts

Winding

Road

to

Mountain Top

L. Belcher

FLORENTINE PEAK

L. Dobson

TO HOBART

Mt MONASH

Lady Barron Falls

TYENNA PEAK

Mt Mawson

MOUNT FIELD NATIONAL PARK

The higher parts carry alpine vegetation, the lower slopes, wet sclerophyll forest.

MT FIELD NATIONAL PARK

Tasmania's fourth-largest national park and one of its best known is Mt Field. Covering 40,000 acres of mountain plateau, this park is easily accessible, located fifty-two miles from Hobart and twenty-six miles west of New Norfolk, overlooking the wide Derwent River valley.

The heights of this dolerite plateau (where the tallest summit is Mt Field West, 4,711 feet) receive heavy snowfalls between July and October, when a ski tow operates on the slopes of Mt Mawson. The area attracts winter sports enthusiasts and development of the snowfields and access to them is being carried out. In summer bush walkers make good use of the numerous tracks.

Many beautiful lakes and tarns, formed during the ice age thirty thousand years ago, today are features of many of Tasmania's national parks—Dove Lake, Crater Lake, Lake St. Clair, and on the high glaciated plateau of Mt Field National Park, Lake Dobson (altitude of 3,382 feet), Lake Fenton (3,300 feet) and lakes Seal, Belton and Webster at slightly lower levels.

In many places, streams tumble down the steep plateau slopes over falls set in lush fern-gully surroundings. Best known are the Russell Falls, a ten minute walk from the entrance to Mt Field. This series of symmetrical cascades tumble 120 feet in two sheer drops into a cool, damp, shaded gorge of high mossy banks and tall Soft Tree Ferns (*Dicksonia antarctica*).

Along the many short walking tracks near Russell Falls the paths almost become tunnels beneath tree-ferns, through dense undergrowth and around huge mossy logs of fallen giant trees. Here enormous Mountain Ash (*Eucalyptus regnans*) soar up to 280 feet in height.

In a newsprint forest adjoining Mt Field National Park some of the world's tallest trees grow (if not already felled), the largest of which has (or had) an estimated age of 385 years, and a

out several miles to the summit, to Hartz Lake, and to Lake Osborne.

From the mountain top, views can be had of the surrounding rugged terrain, particularly into the wild south-west of the state, and to the distant coast. The lower slopes carry magnificent temperate rainforests and wet sclerophyll forests containing fern gullies and stands of large eucalypts.

BEN LOMOND NATIONAL PARK

Another mountain national park, in the only really high region of north-eastern Tasmania, is Ben Lomond. This is a wide, flat-topped dolerite plateau, with several points, Legge's Tor (5,160 feet) and Stack's Bluff, rising above five thousand feet.

Ben Lomond National Park is popular as a winter ski resort, being easily accessible by road.

height of 323 feet. This is exceeded only by a few of the tallest of Californian Redwoods; taller Tasmanian trees have already been destroyed.

Although Mt Field is one of Tasmania's best-known national parks, and a tourist attraction of ever-increasing value to that state, it has not been safe from those who would destroy anything for money—quoting the late Professor A. J. Marshall, from his book *The Great Extermination*:

'In 1950, despite public protests, the boundaries of the Mt Field National Park in Tasmania were altered so that its finest stand of Mountain Ash could be sold for conversion into paper pulp. A special bill was put through Parliament to achieve this spectacular piece of vandalism.'

On the forested slopes of Mt Field much of the unique Tasmanian marsupial and bird life is still abundant. Through dense undergrowth, particularly in the vicinity of streams, occasionally one may see the pads worn by the Tasmanian Devil (*Sarcophilus harrisii*) in its nightly hunting for frogs, snakes, lizards, small mammals, or just about anything it can scavenge in the bush.

Tasmania has 230 species of birds, or about ⅓ the number on the mainland. However, fourteen species are to be found only on this island, and at various times some are to be seen at Mt Field, including the Tasmanian Native Hen (*Tribonyx mortierii*) Yellow Wattle-bird (*Anthochaera paradoxa*), Dusky Robin (*Petroica vittata*) and Green Rosella (*Platycercus caledonicus*).

FRENCHMAN'S CAP NATIONAL PARK

Jutting above the rugged south-western horizon, and visible from a few high points on the Lyell Highway westward from Derwent Bridge, is the distinctive mountain peak known as Frenchman's Cap (4,739 feet), the main feature of the 25,000 acre Frenchman's Cap National Park. Even from the Lyell Highway, fifteen miles away, the south-eastern cliffs of the mountain are clearly visible. This remote park contains spectacular mountain scenery and broad deep valleys of small lakes or tarns.

Although its north-western side is a rounded slope, becoming less steep towards the summit and not difficult to climb, its south-eastern face is an enormous cliff; on the crest is a conspicuous white patch of quartzite. It has been said that the cliffs of Frenchman's Cap compare with those of the Italian Dolomites for sheer height and unbroken vertical drop. Certainly they present one of the hardest rock climbs to be found in Australia, with some thirteen hundred feet of vertical quartzite made all the more difficult by smooth areas and overhangs; it has been climbed on very few occasions.

During the Pleistocene Epoch valley glaciers gouged awe-inspiring cirques (large amphitheatre-like basins with steep or vertical walls) from many of Tasmania's mountains; Frenchman's Cap is one of the most spectacular of all the cirque-cut massifs.

The only access to this national park is a seventeen-mile walk across seemingly endless peat marshes and water channels: signposts on the Lyell Highway mark the beginning of the track.

CRADLE MOUNTAIN–LAKE ST CLAIR NATIONAL PARK

Tasmania is an isle of mountains. More than anywhere else this is expressed within the huge Cradle Mountain–Lake St Clair National Park. In this region is Australia's most spectacular mountain scenery—a wild confusion of mountain ranges which are snow-capped most of the year, jagged horizons, and serrated ridge-top sky-lines. There are white peaks thrusting upwards thousands of feet into clear blue skies, or at other times, glimpses of dark mountain rock revealed through mist and cloud.

Never to be forgotten are its glacier-carved, rock-walled lakes which on still days reflect this mountain scenery, the innumerable limpid-surfaced tarns ringed by bleached pines; or the ancient Beech forests where shafts of sunlight, breaking through the green canopy, illuminate

Over
Tasmania's Cradle Mountain and picturesque Lake Dove are easily accessible at the northern end of the huge, almost roadless Cradle Mt–Lake St Clair National Park

FREYCINET PENINSULA

181

CRADLE MOUNTAIN — LAKE ST. CLAIR

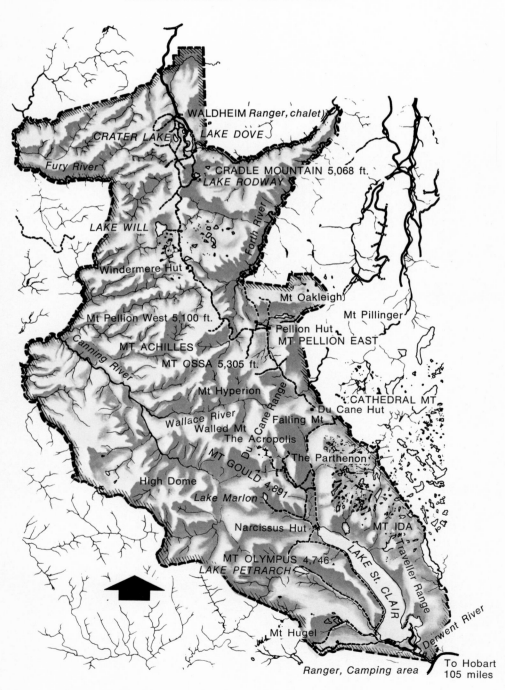

mossy roots, soft rotting green logs, massed ferns and coloured fungi of elfin form.

This is a world of crystal-clear water, in pools on the soggy button-grass plains, in rivulets, cascades and waterfalls, ice-cold from the melting snows, rushing down to lakes and river gorges. Water in distant lakes gleaming like burnished silver—and in rain, mists, low clouds and snow-storms that at any time of the year may sweep suddenly across to blot out the mountain landscape for days or weeks at a time.

For many years only explorers, trappers and prospectors ventured into the region, with a few bushwalkers visiting the more accessible peaks. Among them were men whose far vision and love of these mountains led to the creation of a permanent reserve and wildlife sanctuary, first proposed in 1920, and later enlarged to its present 336,000 acres.

Waldheim, the Cradle Mountain chalet, was built in 1912 by Gustav Weindorfer, an Austrian who was for many years the chalet's genial host, a close student of nature, and a source of inspiration towards the creation of Cradle Mountain Reserve.

The national park measures forty miles from north to south, with an average width of fifteen miles. Its line of high peaks, extending north to south, is the watershed in which rise many of Tasmania's rivers. Roads wind up to Waldheim from the island's north-coastal plains, and also to Lake St Clair from the park's southern boundary.

The intervening region is accessible only to walkers. The fifty mile track is usually traversed in five days though longer may be needed for deviations to points of interest or because of bad weather. A stormproof hut marks the end of each day's stage.

The Cradle Mountain area at the northern end of the park is a region of rough open moorland and windswept heaths, broken by deep, bare-walled gorges and forested valleys in which lie numerous lakes and countless small tarns of great beauty. The whole wild scene is dominated by the high serrated peak of Cradle Mountain and the massive column of Barn Bluff.

This area, like the southern part of Lake St Clair, can be seen by the average visitor who may not wish to tackle long walks.

Following the track southwards, the first day's destination is the hut at Lake Windermere, just over eleven miles along the well defined Overland Track.

Climbing from Waldheim to the plateau overlooking Dove Lake and Crater Lake, then skirting the base of Cradle Mountain's precipitous peak (5,069 feet), the track then follows a great long ridge (Cradle Cirque), towards Barn Bluff (5,114 feet). Far down to the right is Fury Gorge, and soon many small lakes and tarns are visible ahead.

From these heights the track falls away sharply to Waterfall Valley, below Barn Bluff, then through open country over a spur, and down to beautiful Lake Windermere and its comfortable hut.

From Windermere the second day (10½ miles) leads to Pellion Hut, and right into the heart of the mountain country, with magnificent views down to the Forth River's gorge; ahead are the high crags of Mt Oakleigh (4,100 feet).

By the end of the second day's walking we are in Pellion country, a vast amphitheatre, of plains encircled by walls of mountain peaks—Pellion West (5,100 feet), Pellion East (4,760 feet), Achilles (5,000 feet), Thetis (5,000 feet), Ossa (5,305 feet) and Oakleigh (4,100 feet). From Pellion Hut, in the centre of these plains, the peaks can be climbed, with marked routes leading to some summits; another track leads steeply downwards into the gorge of the Forth River where forest and river scenery are magnificent.

The third day on the Overland Track is seven miles through forest and scrub, rising steadily to cross Pellion Gap at an altitude of 3,650 feet. Nearby summits, at approximately the centre of the park, afford some wonderful panoramic views. From here the track drops away through open country, crossing Kia Ora Creek near one of its

many beautiful cascades, before climbing again to the Du Cane Hut set below the sheer cliffs of Castle Crag, with the immense columns and spires of Cathedral Mountain just across the valley.

South-westwards is the Du Cane Range, a ragged chain of mountains with many points exceeding five thousand feet: Falling Mountain (5,000 feet), Mt Gould (4,891 feet), and the Guardians (4,700 feet).

From these peaks the Narcissus River flows into Lake St Clair, 2,419 feet above sea level, 720 feet deep, eight miles long and more than a mile across, set between Mt Olympus (4,746 feet) and Mt Ida.

The Overland Track now follows the Narcissus, eleven miles between the high ranges to either side, until Narcissus hut is reached, at the head of Lake St Clair. The final eleven miles around the shores of the lake are through a magnificent beech forest overlooking the lake waters.

On this walk through the park some thirty species of birds may be seen, with others to be found in the vicinity of Lake St Clair. The marsupials are mostly nocturnal, but at Waldheim and Lake St Clair camping grounds a number of Rufous Wallabies (*Thylogale billardierii*) and Bennett's Wallabies (*Wallabia rufogrisea*), both very thickly furred, and found only in Tasmania, will certainly be seen.

The long overland track is rough, and the huts primitive; all food and other items must be carried. Normally hiking here should be confined to the period October to May, and it is unwise to venture any distance between June and September; hiking alone here has proved fatal. Those intending long hikes should seek the rangers' advice, as snow may render sections of the track impassable.

Centre l to r
Cliffs along south-east Bruny Island, off Tasmania's southern coast, are a scenic-coast reserve

Headlands and cliffs of historic Tasman Peninsula; away across Maingon Bay, Cape Pillar and the tip of Tasman Island mark the peninsula's southernmost point

Freycinet Peninsula's coastline of hills, headlands, sheltered bays and beaches is dominated by The Hazards, a line of jagged hills with peaks of huge granite boulders

Below l to r
Lake Pedder, south-west Tasmania; this valley is to be flooded, destroying the lake and the unique scenery of its encircling white beach

The cliff-walled mountain known as Frenchman's Cap, situated amid magnificent scenery in wild south-western Tasmania, is accessible only to hikers

Deep, glacier-carved Lake St Clair is ten miles long, and surrounded by Tasmania's highest mountains; the distant peak is Mt Ida

Right
The ruins of the church, Port Arthur. Built of stone and with tower and spire, it was calculated to hold twelve hundred people on the ground floor

PARK FACTS AND TRAVELLER'S GUIDE

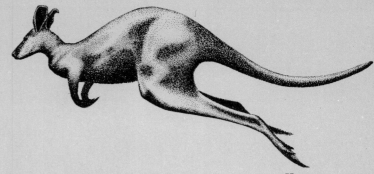

Kangaroo

Among Australia's national parks and wildlife sanctuaries there is diversity not only of geological features, climate and fauna, but also diversity in name, management and security.

Some states (Queensland, New South Wales, South Australia, Victoria and Tasmania) have the greater part by far, of their protected lands as national parks, and a relatively small part in sanctuaries or nature reserves. Yet some of these national parks are, in effect, wholly wildlife sanctuaries and flora reserves. They are not tourist attractions, and no visitor facilities are provided; some are in remote localities, without road access suitable for conventional vehicles, and the terrain is often difficult, even dangerous. There is no intention of attracting visitors to these national parks—they exist to provide a home for the unique Australian fauna and flora. One such park is Queensland's Simpson Desert National Park, and also, South Australia's Elliott Price Wilderness National Park, Simpson Desert, and some of its large mallee area parks.

On the other hand, in Western Australia, the Northern Territory and the Australian Capital Territory, by far the greater part of protected natural environment is in the form of flora and fauna reserves and wildlife sanctuaries, and a much smaller area in national parks. Yet some of these reserves and sanctuaries have features which attract visitors, and their tourist potential is promoted—they would perhaps be better named as national parks. These include Tidbinbilla near Canberra, Palm Valley in Central Australia, and the Dale's Gorge area in the Hamersley Ranges of Western Australia (where it is expected a large new national park will soon be created).

But whether they are national parks, wildlife sanctuaries, fauna or flora reserves, scenic or nature reserves, the preservation of the natural environment and the wildlife is the primary objective throughout Australia, and all native birds, mammals, reptiles and plant life are fully protected by law.

As a rule, the national parks provide for public enjoyment of scenery and natural bushland while at the same time trying to protect the vegetation and the wildlife. People—the thousands of tourists who already visit some parks—wandering unrestrained, will in time destroy much of the natural beauty which they would come to see. This is the dilemma of national parks management: to provide for the visitors who are attracted to the parks in ever-increasing numbers, yet at the same time to prevent the gradual deterioration of the irreplaceable natural assets of wilderness landscape, flora and, fauna.

THE LEGISLATION, AIMS AND CONTROL OF AUSTRALIAN PARKS AND SANCTUARIES

QUEENSLAND

National Parks   The parks of Queensland are under the control of the Department of Forestry, and are reserved (as a matter of Government policy upheld by legislation) in perpetuity as areas of scenic, scientific, historic and recreational interest. It is intended that they remain untouched and unspoiled in all essential respects, to be administered as natural havens and habitat for native animals and birds. Once a national park has been proclaimed, it may be alienated only by act of parliament.

Under the *Forestry Act* it is stated that—
The cardinal principle to be observed in the management of National Parks shall be the permanent preservation to the greatest possible extent, of their natural condition . . .'

The policy followed by the Department of Forestry is in accordance with these principles and interferes as little as possible with natural values within the parks. Specifically, the Department emphasises that on national parks there is no marketing of timber, no gathering or destruction of native flora, no hunting of wild animals, no introduction of any plant or animal not indigenous to the particular locality, and no attempt to adorn nature by landscaping or artificial' gardening or construction.

Under a *1968 Amendment* to the *Forestry Act* all scenic areas (under 1,000 acres) became known as national parks. This amendment also provided for specialized management of areas for special purposes. A part, or the whole of any park can be declared a primitive area, a recreation and primitive area, a recreation area, a scientific area or an historic area. In the case of a primitive area, there shall be no roads, buildings or lookouts. A scientific area must be maintained so as to preserve it as a sample of the natural environment of the national park concerned.

Queensland's policy has been to keep roads out of national parks as far as possible; this will greatly assist in preserving their natural attractive qualities, and interferes least with the wildlife. Public roads provide access to the perimeter, and in places pass through a national park, but for the most part access to the most attractive features of Queensland's parks is by good graded walking tracks, many quite short, others long enough to constitute a worthwhile hike. In the larger national parks great areas are inaccessible to all but experienced bushwalkers. This has the great advantage of preserving the maximum area as unspoiled wilderness necessary for the survival of many plants and animals, allowing for undisturbed scientific study of the ecology of bush or jungle, and providing a challenge for those who would rather a rough cross-country trek where the going is tough but rewarding.

Improvement work on tracks and visitor facilities is carried out by resident overseers and forestry workmen, directed and supervised by the National Parks Rangers.

Every effort is now being made to preserve a complete sample of Queensland's major natural environments, with new parks being sought to fill gaps in the present coverage.

Permits are required for camping or fishing in national parks, and will be given by a forests officer; generally there is no difficulty regarding camping permits, and no charge is made for the use of any facilities and improvements on the parks. National parks officers patrol many of the more frequented parks to enforce conservation laws (wildlife and plants being fully protected) and are always willing to assist visitors to obtain the greatest benefit from their visit.

Sanctuaries   In addition to its national parks, Queensland has several sanctuaries, the main ones being under trusteeship of the Department of Primary Industries. This department is interested in increasing the number of its Crown land sanctuaries, which would be maintained as 'large natural areas strictly for fauna undisturbed by other activities including recreation.' All state forests are deemed to be fauna sanctuaries, as are national parks and some private areas.

Shores   The coasts below high water mark are under protection of the Department of Harbours and Marine, with complete protection of marine life in certain areas, and prohibition of taking coral in other parts.

NEW SOUTH WALES

National Parks   The *National Parks and Wildlife Act*, which came into force in October 1967, provides for the establishment and control of national parks, nature reserves, and for other aspects of fauna control, by the National Parks and Wildlife Service. Most of the larger parks and nature reserves are now being administered under this legislation, although some still remain under the control of trusts, local authorities and the Lands Department.

The Minister for Lands may dedicate or reserve crown lands for public purposes, including public recreation and preservation of fauna and flora. Any revocation of national park or nature reserve lands must have the approval of both Houses of Parliament.

Generally, the larger areas are called 'national parks' (defined as 'spacious areas containing outstanding scenery or natural features') while the smaller areas are 'state parks'. The smallest national park is about 15,000 acres, the largest state park 5,230 acres. In park management, it is the intention to maintain by far the largest part of each park in wilderness condition, and specific segments have been zoned as 'wilderness areas!'

Rangers (and, at some parks, visitor information centres) provide a park interpretation service, assist visitors, and enforce conservation laws under which all fauna and flora is protected.

Fauna Reserves   New South Wales nature reserves are for the protection and propogation of fauna, and the scientific study of fauna and flora. They are generally primitive or natural areas, in recognition of the fact that wild creatures often can be preserved only by saving the natural habitat. It has long been the policy to establish a system of nature reserves representative of the state's variety of natural environments.

Resident warden-rangers are stationed at some of the nature reserves, others are inspected from time to time by field officers of the National Parks and Wildlife Service; honorary rangers are also appointed.

In New South Wales, entrance fees are charged at some national parks, and entry to some nature reserves is by permit only.

VICTORIA

National Parks   In Victoria the national parks are under control of a National Parks Authority, with the Premier of Victoria having ministerial responsibility for the National Parks Act.

The Authority is required to preserve the natural qualities of the parks, to encourage and direct public use of the parks, and to provide essential park facilities. National parks are created by Act of Parliament, and presumably can be revoked only by Parliament.

The purpose of the national parks, and the administrative aim of the Authority, is 'to protect and preserve indigenous plant and animal wildlife and features of special scenic, scientific or historical interest in national parks; to maintain the existing environment of national parks', and also to 'provide for the education and enjoyment of visitors to national parks and to encourage and control such visitors'.

The National Park Authority is required, as far as possible, to 'maintain every national park in its natural condition'. It is also the Authority's policy to encourage the maximum public use of the parks consistent with the basic conservation ideals.

Rangers are resident at, or near, the most popular parks to assist the public and to enforce conservation laws. A fee is charged for entry to some of the parks.

Wildlife Reserves   Victoria's wildlife reserves are under the control of the Fisheries and Wildlife Department; they are permanent reserves which can be alienated only by Act of Parliament.

The purpose of the faunal reserves is the conservation of wildlife and habitat for scientific study. There are also game refuges and game reserves, for the conservation of game species (duck) for hunting.

Forest Parks   The Forests Commission of Victoria can declare forest lands to be parks, scenic reserves, roadside reserves, alpine reserves and others. There are more than seventy such areas, including five forest parks. These reserves can be revoked at any time by the Forests Commission.

NORTHERN TERRITORY
National Parks   The national parks and many reserves are under the control of the Northern Territory Reserves Board, with curators (rangers) at some parks to assist visitors and maintain facilities. Under *Crown Lands Ordinance*, the areas reserved are set aside for various public purposes including 'the recreation and amusement of the public, the protection and conservation of wildlife, the conservation of native flora, national parks or gardens, and the preservation or protection of places of historic interest.' These reserves may be revoked by the Governor General upon recommendation of the Administrator, if approval is given by the Legislative Council.

There is also a *National Parks and Gardens Ordinance* by which lands can be placed under control of the Northern Territory Reserves Board to be used as places 'for the recreation or amusement of the public, a national park, a monument, a botanical garden, a zoological garden, a reserve or sanctuary for the protection of flora or fauna or any similar purpose.'

To date most attention has been given to acquiring accessible areas of obvious tourist interest, but the Reserves Board is now trying to obtain larger, more remote areas for conservation of wildlife. The Commonwealth Government's response to the Board's request for large new park areas has been most disappointing; the Board's plans for new parks, such as a large Northern Area National Park in western Arnhem Land, have been continually frustrated. It is the Minister for Territories who must give final approval for new parks, and his past attitude seems to show the Commonwealth Government's disinterest in national parks, even though the tourist industry is the greatest single money earner for the Northern Territory.

An entrance fee is charged at some parks and reserves.

Wildlife Sanctuaries   There are five Northern Territory sanctuary areas; these are, in addition, reserves for the use of Aborigines, and all other Aboriginal reserves are 'protected areas'. Only authorized persons may enter these sanctuaries, and the taking of animals, including birds, fish and reptiles, is prohibited. Fauna sanctuaries are administered by the Chief Inspector of Wildlife and are patrolled by wildlife officers; in addition there are honorary rangers, which include the police force.

WESTERN AUSTRALIA
The national parks and flora-and-fauna reserves of Western Australia are Crown land reserves, and are classified as class 'A', 'B', or 'C'. A class 'A' reserve has the greatest security, as it can be revoked only by Act of Parliament; if vested in such body as the National Parks Board, or the Wildlife Authority, these reserves are even less likely to be alienated. If a class 'B' reserve is cancelled, the reasons for doing so must be stated to both Houses of Parliament.

The greatest areas of land reserved for conservation of flora and fauna are unfortunately of 'C' classification, and are relatively easily cancelled by the Department of Lands. However, it has been a long-standing policy of this Department to resist requests for cancellation of these reserves, and comparatively few have been lost. Many are vested, and this increases their security. A huge area of land is protected in these class 'C' reserves, well over four million acres (this is in addition to class 'A' reserves) and it is to be hoped that all the class 'C' reserves which are important for tourist, conservation or scientific purposes will be upgraded to class 'A'. A weakness of W.A. legislation is that mining and oil drilling is allowed even in class 'A' reserves.

The Minister for Lands has stated that in new agricultural sub-divisions ten per cent of the land would be set aside for fauna and flora conservation, and that this is to include good quality land.

National Parks   are usually class 'A' reserves vested in the National Parks Board of Western Australia, but occasionally, in the past, in other boards. The National Parks Board endeavours to preserve the landscape, flora and fauna, and features of special interest in the parks under its control, and to provide basic facilities needed by visitors. Some parks have resident rangers, others are visited by a mobile ranger—who travels as far south-eastwards as Cape Le Grand, near Esperance, and to Cape Range in the north-west, and even to Geikie in the Kimberleys. There are also honorary rangers.

Flora and Fauna Reserves   Almost a hundred reserves totalling more than two million acres are vested in the Wildlife Authority; in addition the Authority is responsible for the control of all reserves which are fauna sanctuaries, an additional 135 reserves of approximately 2,200,000 acres. While the Authority defines broad policy and planning, the day-to-day administration and research is by the Department of Fisheries and Fauna.

The aims of the Wildlife Authority include preservation in perpetuity of representative sections of the environment, management of areas containing rare and endangered species, and control of multiple use areas so that human activities do not endanger wildlife.

Native Flora Protection   On all Crown lands, state forests, public reserves and along roadsides in the south-west and Eucla land divisions of Western Australia the picking of wildflowers is prohibited; certain species are protected throughout the state.

SOUTH AUSTRALIA
National Parks   These are controlled by the National Parks Commission, and include many areas that, prior to 1966, were called wildlife reserves. Many of the largest national parks therefore are not of great tourist interest, though of vital importance in the preservation of samples of the natural environment and its fauna. The revocation of a national park requires a resolution of both houses of parliament.

The National Parks Commission is required, as far as practicable, to 'maintain and preserve the indigenous fauna and the natural features of the national parks for the use and enjoyment of the people of the state.' Large areas are national parks, small areas are known as national parks reserves. Mining is excluded from the national parks.

Some parks have resident staff, others are patrolled by field officers.

Fauna Reserves   Most of the fauna reserves are small offshore islands; there are also game reserves, fauna sanctuaries, and prohibited areas. Private land is sometime declared a fauna reserve or sanctuary upon the owner's request.

National Pleasure Resorts   This system of public reserves is declining in importance, some of the resorts having been handed over to the National Parks Commission. However, South Australia's best-known geological feature, Wilpena Pound, is still a national pleasure resort. Such resorts are under the control of the Director of the Immigration, Publicity and Tourist Department, who is directed to attend to the 'care, control, management and preservation of lands vested in his department, and the protection and preservation of native animals and plants.' It would be better, however, that areas as important as Wilpena Pound become national parks, to be maintained according to scientific principles by the officers of the National Parks Commission. Grazing of stock is now allowed in several of the national pleasure resorts.

Fauna and Flora Reserves   Flinders Chase, on Kangaroo Island, is the only such reserve created under the *Fauna and Flora Reserve Act*; it is, however, a very large and important conservation area. Control is by the Flora and Fauna Board of S.A., which has introduced many species of native fauna. A small staff is employed at the Chase to maintain paths and facilities.

TASMANIA
National Parks   Tasmania's parks have been acquired, developed and controlled under the *Scenery Preservation Act*. The first major change in many years has now been initiated with an Act to repeal the Scenery Preservation Act and make 'fresh provision for the preservation and management of lands of scenic, historical, or scientific interest, and of Aboriginal relics and other objects of historical interest.'

The *National Parks and Conservation Bill 1968* establishes a National Parks and Conservation Board. The reserves will continue to be known as national parks, scenic reserves, historic sites, etc., and other titles may be prescribed. Adequate protection seems to have been given against mining upon such reserves, and they cannot be revoked unless such action has been approved by both Houses of Parliament.

Until the introduction of this new legislation, Tasmania's national parks, scenic reserves, coastal reserves and historic sites were controlled by the Scenery Preservation Board, which provided facilities such as camping-caravan grounds, huts in mountain parks, renovated historic sites and kept rangers at the more popular parks and reserves.

Sanctuaries   The most important, and secure of Tasmanian sanctuaries are those on Crown land and controlled by the Animals and Birds Protection Board. A sanctuary may be revoked only by resolution passed by both Houses of Parliament.

The sanctuaries have been selected for their habitat value for fauna, and all animals and birds are fully protected by law. There are also 'faunal districts' (including a 1,600,000 acre area in south-west Tasmania), 'habitat reserves', and a 'national fauna reserve' on Maria Island. Fauna is not taken from sanctuaries except for scientific purposes.

COMPARISONS: AUSTRALIA   U.S.A.   EUROPE   AFRICA

How do Australia's national parks compare with the great national parks of the world—those of the United States, Canada, Africa, Europe and the U.S.S.R.? Can Australian park areas be compared even with the national parks established in the 'emerging nations' of Africa and Asia?

It is in the United States that the national parks concept is most highly developed. There has been tremendous public and political support; a magnificent system of national parks is the result. Among the United States parks are:

Yellowstone, 3,472 square miles in area
Mt McKinley National Park, 3,030 square miles
Everglades National Park, Florida, 2,100 square miles
Waterton-Glacier, partly in the United States and
    partly in Canada, 1,786 square miles
Olympic National Park, 1,400 square miles
Sequoia–Kings Canyon, 1,314 square miles
Yosemite National Park, 1,200 square miles
Grand Canyon, 1,100 square miles
Big Bend National Park, Texas, 1,100 square miles.

In Canada, the Banff National Park covers an area of 2,564 square miles. In Europe, small Sweden has set aside 2,105 square miles as the Sarek, Padjelanta and Stora Sjofallet national parks. The Soviet Union has over sixty major conservation areas, some of enormous size—for instance, the Kronotzk Sanctuary in Kamchatka has an area of 3,725 square miles; these regions are used extensively for scientific research on such practical problems as the rational use of animal and plant resources.

Nearer home, New Zealand's Fiordland National Park is a magnificent 4,514 square miles in extent, and even Malaya has 1,760 square miles in its King George V National Park.

Africa is famed for its immense national parks—who has not heard of the Kruger National Park? This covers 7,340 square miles and is a tremendous tourist attraction with nearly a quarter of a million visitors annually. Other major national parks of Africa are:

Serengeti National Park, in Tanzania, 5,600 square
    miles
Tsavo National Park, 8,034 square miles
Ruaha, in Tanzania, established in 1964, 5,000 square
    miles
Wankie, in Rhodesia, 5,000 square miles
Kafue National Park and Luangua Valley Game
    Reserve, Zambia, together 8,000 square miles.

These national parks have been established or maintained by the new African governments, demonstrating foresight and responsibility far in advance of the prevailing government attitude in some Australian states.

For comparison, the major Australian national parks and sanctuaries:

Tanami Desert Sanctuary, N. T., 14,490 square miles;
    (it is worth noting, however, that this is some of
    the most barren desert country in Australia)
Kosciusko National Park, N.S.W., 2,065 square miles
Simpson Desert National Park, Qld., 1,950 square
    miles
Murganella Sanctuary, N.T., 1,050 square miles
Cobourg Peninsula Sanctuary, N.T., 740 square miles
Kalbarri National Park, W.A., 559 square miles
Cradle Mt–Lake St Clair National Park, Tas., 528
    square miles
Ayers Rock–Mt Olga National Park, N.T., 518 square
    miles
Stirling Range National Park, W.A., 443 square miles
Blue Mountains National Park, N.S.W., 379 square
    miles
Hincks National Park, S.A., 255 square miles
Wyperfeld National Park, Vic., 216 square miles
Mt Windsor Tableland National Park, Qld., 208
    square miles
Eungella National Park, Qld., 190 square miles
Wilson's Promontory National Park, Vic., 160 square
    miles.

THE EAST

Lyrebird

NAME OF PARK	LOCALITY ACCESS	TOPOGRAPHY VEGETATION TYPES	FEATURES OF INTEREST	ACTIVITIES ACCOMMODATION SEASON TO VISIT
BARANGARY STATE PARK (N.S.W.) 1,970 acres	SE. New South Wales, W of Kiama, and six m. S of Robertson. 91 m. from Sydney via Highway 1, then Highway 23.	Rough, dissected sandstone heights. Dry eucalypt forest, more luxuriant vegetation in gorges.	Main attraction Belmore Falls, where Burrawong Creek drops from high sandstone tops into gorge. Tracks lead to lookouts; extensive views of Kangaroo Valley.	Scenic viewing, photography, bushwalking, observing spring wildflowers, birdlife. Picnic area at falls. Accommodation, caravan and camping areas at nearby towns, and Bundanoon Park. (Information: Superintendent, Fitzroy Falls, Phone 270). Any season.
BARRINGTON TOPS NATIONAL PARK (N.S.W.) 34,500 acres	NE. New South Wales, 60 m. NW. of Newcastle, 170 m. from Sydney. Access from Gloucester and Scone. *See* map p. 20.	Mountain knoll rising to 3,000 ft. Rainforest, Antarctic Beech forest, Snow Gum plain.	Tremendous views from Carey's Peak. (Track from Barrington House). Antarctic Beech trees, rainforest vegetation and associated birdlife.	Trout fishing, bushwalking and general sightseeing. Observing birdlife and fauna. Camping. Photography. Guesthouse outside park boundary, bush camping within the park. Hotel, caravan and camping ground at Gloucester; hotels, motels at Scone on New England Highway; caravan-camping, hotels at Dungog. Any season.
BARREN GROUNDS NATURE RESERVE (N.S.W.) 4,390 acres	S coastal New South Wales, via Kiama, Jamberoo, on heights above Jamberoo Valley.	A 'hanging swamp' plateau, 2,100 ft above sea level, ringed by cliffs; undulating and flat land on heights. Situated on SE. spur of Illawarra Range. Open heathlands, open eucalypt forest, swamp-heath, mallee eucalypts, wet sclerophyll forest, and some rainforest.	Superb views Illawarra coast from encircling wall of steep sandstone cliffs. Profusion of sandstone heath wildflowers. Fine stands of rain-forest below cliffs. Diversity of bird and animal life. Rare species include Eastern Bristle-bird, and Ground Parrot. Wildlife sanctuary and study area, rather than just a tourist attraction.	Camping and caravan area at Visitor Centre. Accommodation at Jamberoo, Kiama. (Lodge at Barren Grounds is reserved for study groups, etc.) Any season; spring months best for wildflowers.
BAUPLE MOUNTAIN NATIONAL PARK (QLD.) 640 acres	Between Gympie and Maryborough. Reached by Bruce Highway. 140 m. from Brisbane, 26 m. from Maryborough.	Densely-timbered portion of a mountain chain, elevation 1,500 ft.	Mountain named by Aborigines after the Bopple nut (*Macrozamia ternifolia*) common here. Hoop Pines prominent on skyline. A conspicuous wildflower is the orange flowered *Cassia sylvestris*.	Sightseeing, observing birds, wildflowers. Gympie or Maryborough. Any season.
BLUE MOUNTAINS NATIONAL PARK (N.S.W.) 244,986 acres	40 m. W of Sydney, off Great Western Highway; main area centred on Grose River Valley. Views down into park from Katoomba. *See* map p. 20.	High, deeply dissected sandstone plateau. Dry sclerophyll forest on heights, wet sclerophyll on lower slopes, gorges.	Spectacular scenery where Grose River has cut 2,500 ft through colourful sandstones, shales and coal measures. Many waterfalls, fern glens. Tall Blue Gums in Grose Valley. Distinctive wildflowers on sandstone plateau heights.	Motor touring to lookout points. Bushwalking. Photography. Bush camping only, in park. Caravan and camping parks at Hazelbrook, Lawson, Katoomba, Blackheath. Hotels, guest houses at all Blue Mountain towns. Any season; spring months for most wildflowers.
BOUDDI NATURAL PARK (N.S.W.) 1,200 acres	Coastline and surrounding lands between Kilcare and McMasters Beach near Gosford. Entrance from Scenic Road.	Coastal hills, cliffs at Maitland Bay. Heathlands, eucalypt forest.	Attractive coastal scenery. Heights covered with veteran Red Gums. Magnificent wildflower display Bombi Moors area in spring.	Scenic viewing, photography, trail-walking. Caravan and camping parks, hotels at Gosford. Any season; spring for best wildflower displays.
BOUDDI STATE PARK (N.S.W.) 1,366 acres	Coastal New South Wales, 65 m. N of Sydney, 10 m. along Scenic Highway from Gosford.	Sandstone slopes, heights. Coastal heaths, subtropical rainforest.	Panoramic views of rugged coastline, sandstone cliffs, wave-cut platforms. Nature trail, passing through various vegetation zones—coastal heaths (with great variety of wildflowers) to sub-tropical rain-forest. Variety of birdlife and small marsupials.	Scenic viewing, photography. Observing spring wildflower displays, birdlife. Swimming, surfing, picnicking. Motels and camping areas outside park boundary. Spring months for wildflowers, otherwise any season.
BRISBANE WATERS NATIONAL PARK (N.S.W.) 16,500 acres	40 m. N of Sydney, near Gosford. *See* map p. 20.	Rough, dissected sandstone plateau, eucalypt (dry, sclerophyll) forest, some sub-tropical rainforest.	Panoramic vistas from 300 ft cliffs rising vertically from sea-filled Hawkesbury River Valley. Displays of Waratah and Christmas Bells (November–December): Aboriginal rock engravings.	Nature walks, bushwalking. Observing birdlife, wildflowers, photography, picnicking. No accommodation in park. Caravan park, hotels, at Gosford. July–December for wildflowers.
BUNDANOON STATE PARK (N.S.W.) 3,330 acres	SE. New South Wales between Goulburn and Sydney, E of Bundanoon, on Bundanoon Creek.	Sandstone into which the Bundanoon Creek has become entrenched. Eucalypt forests.	Trails and vista points overlook rugged gorge of Bundanoon Creek, other trails lead to gorge floor. Sandstone tops produce fine array of wildflowers.	Sightseeing, walking trails, bushwalking. Photography of landscape, wildflowers. Picnic grounds. Camping and caravan area (enquiries to the Superintendent, Fitzroy Falls, phone Fitzroy Falls 270). Hotels, motels in Bundanoon. Any season, spring months best for wildflowers.
BUNYA MOUNTAINS NATIONAL PARK (QLD.) 24,024 acres	S Queensland 60 m. NW. from Toowoomba via Bowenville, Yamsion and Horse Creek. Alternate route 25 m. SW. from Nanango or Kingaroy. *See* map p. 37.	Part of Great Divide: Mt Kiangarow (3,725 ft), Mt Mowbullan (3,610 ft). Bunya Pine forest, rainforest, open hardwood forest.	Extensive views from cliffs; huge Bunya Pines. Spectacular cascades and waterfalls; grass plains; Aboriginal associations.	Sightseeing; 15 m. of walking tracks. Picnicking at Koonawarra, Dandabah, Cherry Plain, Bambanjie, Wescott. Caravan and camping area at Dandabah. Resident overseer on main road ½ m. distant. Any season; September–November for rainforest orchids and other wildflowers.

NAME OF PARK	LOCALITY ACCESS	TOPOGRAPHY VEGETATION TYPES	FEATURES OF INTEREST	ACTIVITIES ACCOMMODATION SEASON TO VISIT
BURLEIGH HEADS NATIONAL PARK (QLD.) 58 acres	S from Brisbane via Pacific Highway to Gold Coast; 10 m. from Southport, 9 m. from Tweed Heads. *See* map p. 37.	Headland rising to 275 ft; outcrops of columnar basalt, heavily timbered with rainforest and open forest.	Views over coast, beaches, and to Moreton Bay islands, walking tracks, Aboriginal feasting grounds. Indigenous colony of Koalas. Brush Turkeys, lorikeets, wallabies. Nearby, at Burleigh Heads, is the Fleay Fauna Reserve, one of Australia's finest collections of native animals. Birds of the area best seen at Currumbin Bird Sanctuary, between Burleigh Heads and Coolangatta.	Scenic viewing, swimming, bush walking, photography, observing birdlife, Koalas. Camping and caravan grounds at Burleigh Heads; caravan parks, motels, etc. at all Gold Coast towns. Any season.
BURRUM RIVER NATIONAL PARK (QLD.) 1,410 acres	S Queensland, close to Burrum Heads at mouth of Burrum River, 27 m. from Maryborough.	Coastal banksia country fronting Burrum River, including lagoons and marshes.	Wildflowers, honeyeaters, wading and swamp birds. Valuable sanctuary for birdlife.	Observing birds, wildflowers. At Burrum Heads. Any season.
CARNARVON NATIONAL PARK (QLD.) 66,480 acres	Inland S Queensland, on Great Dividing Range about 60 m. NW. of Injune, 250 m. inland from Bundaberg. From Brisbane, 477 m. via Roma (318 m. bitumen); 60 m. to Injune on Carnarvon Highway, then 73 m. to Carnarvon Creek turnoff, and another 26 m. to park entrance. Also from Springsure, about 110 m. *See* map p. 44.	Rugged sandstone ranges 3,500 ft high, deeply dissected by Carnarvon Gorge and tributary canyons. High cliffs and palms, tree ferns in gorges.	Mt Percy (3,500 ft); Carnarvon Gorge is 20 m. chasm, 50 to 400 yds wide, vertical cliffs up to 600 ft high. Many side gorges, in places 200 ft deep, 6 ft wide. Many caves: Cathedral Cave (overhanging wall) 270 ft long, 70 ft deep, 100 ft high—Aboriginal 'art galleries' (rock carvings, stencils). Panoramic view from Battleship Spur. Platypus in deep pools. The sculptured white cliffs of Carnarvon Range were discovered in 1844 by explorer Ludwig Leichhardt. He named it Ruined Castle Valley.	Hiking up gorge is only way to see this impressive scenery; a 5 m. walk into gorge necessary to see best of gorge, and Cathedral Cave paintings. Superb photographic opportunities; observing birds, wildflowers in spring. Camping and caravan grounds at gorge entrance (resident overseer); new tourist chalet near park. (Enquire Qld Govt Tourist Bureau.) Early spring months (wildflowers), late autumn, winter.
COALSTOUN LAKES NATIONAL PARK (QLD.) 65 acres	S Queensland, 14 m. SW. of Biggenden (54 m. W of Maryborough).	Volcanic craters, drier-type rainforest.	Craters fringed with pumice; interesting rainforest. Ban Ban Springs at Coalstoun Lakes–Gayndah–Goomeri road junction; Aboriginal name 'Minberrie' meant 'ever-flowing spring'.	Sightseeing, geological interest. Hotel at Coalstoun Lakes township. Any season.
CUNNINGHAM'S GAP NATIONAL PARK (QLD.) 7,470 acres	S Queensland, 70 m. W from Brisbane via Cunningham Highway; 30 m. from Warwick and 67 m. from Toowoomba. *See* map p. 37.	A pass in the Great Dividing Range. The Gap is a deep saddle between Mt Cordeaux (4,100 ft) and Mt Mitchell (3,751 ft). Dense rainforest in Gap vicinity, open forest at higher levels.	Panoramas over mountains and plains, rainforest trees, ferns, arboreal orchids, palm groves, cliffs, Box Forest walk. Bower-birds, Brush Turkey, Lyrebird, Koalas.	Walking through lush forests, to summits (14 m. of graded tracks). Photography. Four picnic grounds with tables, fireplaces. Camping and caravan area at western entrance to park. Resident overseer. Any season.
DHARUG NATIONAL PARK (N.S.W.) 29,040 acres	On N side of Hawkesbury River near Wiseman's Ferry, 46 m. N of Sydney.	A rugged dissected sandstone plateau, eucalypt (dry sclerophyll) forest.	Named after an Aboriginal tribe of the area, Dharug is important for great wealth of rock engravings, some possibly up to 8,000 years old. Remains of convict-built Great North Road. Sandstone-country wildflowers.	Bushwalking, photography, observing birdlife, wildflowers. Bush camping only in park. Hotel at Wiseman's Ferry. Hotels, caravan parks in northern Sydney suburbs. Any season; spring months for wildflowers.
DORRIGO STATE PARK (N.S.W.) 3,870 acres (Enlargement planned).	NE. New South Wales, on highway two m. E of Dorrigo, 360 m. N of Sydney. *See* map p. 20.	Slopes of the Dorrigo Mountain (plateau); deep, gorge-like valley of Little North Arm of Bellinger River. Sub-tropical rainforest and eucalypt (wet sclerophyll) forest. Giant buttressed trees, palms, ferns, orchids.	Views from 'The Glade' over densely forested valley. Walks along tracks through sub-tropical rainforest. Beautiful waterfalls. Rich variety of marsupial and birdlife; rainforest birds, include Regent Bowerbird, Pitta, Spine-tailed Logrunner.	Scenic viewing, walks on nature trails through rainforest, birdwatching. Rugged bushwalking to bottom of valley. Picnic and barbecue facilities. Small camping and caravan area at 'The Glade'. Accommodation at Dorrigo. Ranger. Region of summer rainfall. Most orchids, flame trees, flower in spring.
FASSIFERN VALLEY (Mt Edwards, Mt Greville, Mt Moon) NATIONAL PARKS (QLD.)	Boonah (55 m. SW. of Brisbane) to Mt Edwards is 13 m. via Charlwood. Mt Greville National Park is 6 m. from Cunningham Highway via Mt Edwards village. From Boonah to Mt Moon, 15 m.	Reynolds Creek Gorge between Mt Edwards (2,079 ft) and Little Mt Edwards is the central feature of Mt Edwards National Park (820 acres) and is site of the Moogerah Dam; picturesque creek below dam, Hoop Pines along spurs.	Boating facilities on Lake Moogerah. (Moogerah is Aboriginal word for thunder). Mt Greville (2,522 ft) is cone shaped, deeply fissured, partly wooded. Palms in narrow gorges (park area 320 acres). Mt Moon (2,577 ft) is a sparsely timbered dome and carries fine show of wildflowers in spring, summer (park area 295 acres).	Bushwalking. Boating, water ski-ing on Lake Moogerah. Observing wildflowers. Bush camping, or local towns for caravan-camping parks, hotels. Any season.
GIBRALTAR RANGE NATIONAL PARK (N.S.W.) 38,000 acres	NE. New South Wales, midway between Glen Innes and Grafton on Gwydir Highway, 450 m. N of Sydney. *See* map p. 20.	Granite plateau (3,000 ft) with heaths, swamps, eucalypt forests. Steep slopes (the eastern escarpment of the New England plateau) with sub-tropical rainforest.	High vista points, from Gwydir Highway and other lookouts. Waterfalls, gorges. Heathlands rich in wildflowers, Christmas Bells on swamps November–December, Waratahs in October–November. Flame Trees in rainforest, November. Abundant birdlife, including rare Rufous Scrub-bird. Platypus in mountain streams.	Bushwalking, rock-climbing, observing wildflower displays (easily seen along highway), birdwatching, photography, picnicking, swimming. No accommodation in park. Picnic grounds at Mulligan's Hut (swimming pool in river) and along Gwydir Highway. Ranger. September–December for wildflowers, otherwise any season. Winter nights can be very cold. Summer rainfall.
GIRRAWEEN NATIONAL PARK (QLD.) 12,603 acres	Close to New South Wales border on New England Highway. From Brisbane, via Warwick, Stanthorpe to Wyberba, then 4 m. E to Bald Rock Creek. *See* map p. 37.	Granite boulders, tors and mountains superimposed upon plateau S of Darling Downs.	Rugged granite peaks: Castle Rock 4,072 ft, Mt Norman 4,156 ft. Extensive views from summits. Rock pools, clear mountain rivers. Outstanding wildflower displays. Numerous birds. Wombats, possums.	Very popular with bushwalking, hiking parties. Rock-climbing on granite outcrops. Swimming in river pools. Observing wildflowers, birds. Camping-caravan area, picnic grounds. Resident overseer. September–November for wildflower displays. Otherwise, any season.

NAME OF PARK	LOCALITY ACCESS	TOPOGRAPHY VEGETATION TYPES	FEATURES OF INTEREST	ACTIVITIES ACCOMMODATION SEASON TO VISIT
GLASSHOUSE MOUNTAINS NATIONAL PARKS (QLD.)	Near coast N of Brisbane; via Bruce Highway to Glasshouse Mountains township, then by gravel roads to each park area. *See map p. 37.*	A group of nine massive volcanic trachyte pillars, four of the most prominent being national parks: Coonowrin (280 acres), Beerwah (320 acres), Ngungun (120 acres), Tibrogargon (720 acres).	Mt Beerwah (1,823 ft) is the highest. Names are of Aboriginal origin. Peaks are conspicuous landmarks, rising abruptly from coastal plain.	Touring, sightseeing, rock-climbing. Wide variety of wildflowers in spring. No facilities. Accommodation, caravan parks at coastal resorts, e.g. Caloundra. Any season.
HEATHCOTE STATE PARK (N.S.W.) 3,900 acres	S coastal New South Wales, 20 m. S of Sydney on W side of Princes Highway.	Rough sandstone country, steep forested gullies and heath-covered areas.	Heathcote Creek is a main attraction, bordered by marked walking tracks. Excellent wildflower displays, many species of birds.	Nature trail walks, bushwalking. Bush picnicking and camping. Photography of natural landscape, flora and fauna. No accommodation in park, available in southern Sydney suburbs. Any season. Spring months for wildflowers.
JOWARRA NATIONAL PARK (QLD.) 132 acres	Coastal Queensland 58 m. N of Brisbane, on Bruce Highway 6 m. from Landsborough.	Mooloolah River, rainforest.	Scenic walk along Mooloolah River through rainforest and palm groves. Native name 'Jowarra' means rain tree country.	Sightseeing, short walks, observing birdlife. Bush camping. Hotel accommodation at coastal towns. Any season.
KANANGRA–BOYD NATIONAL PARK (N.S.W.) 90,000 acres	Blue Mountains, W of Sydney. 15 m. from Jenolan Caves, and 130 m. by Highway 32 from Sydney.	Deeply dissected sandstone plateau, dry sclerophyll forest with wet sclerophyll (big gums, ferns) on lower slopes.	Massive cliffs, enormous canyons, gorges, undeveloped limestone caves, waterfalls and crystal clear streams; a magnificent wilderness landscape region.	Bush walks, scenic views from the tremendous heights of the Kanangra Walls. Landscape, colour photography. Trout-fishing. Observing birds and wildflowers. Guest house at Jenolan Caves, otherwise bush camping in the park. Information; Natural Park and Wildlife Service, 187 Kent St., Sydney, 2000. Any season.
KONDALILLA NATIONAL PARK (QLD.) 184 acres	S Queensland, 80 m. from Brisbane Bruce Highway via Palmwoods and Montville; or via Nambour and Mapleton.	On Blackall Range; Kondalilla Falls situated on tributary of Obi Creek, dropping 200 ft in series of cascades to valley of rainforest and piccabeen palms.	Waterfalls; views from top of falls across forest and ranges; Bunya Pines, many birds, marsupials including a few Koalas; habitat of lung fish (*Ceratodus*).	Sightseeing and photography along the 2½ m. of walking tracks; observing birdlife; swimming in deep creek pool. Picnic grounds. Guest houses at Montville, or coastal resorts. Any time of year.
KU-RING-GAI CHASE NATIONAL PARK (N.S.W.) 35,040 acres	15 m. N of Sydney between Pacific Highway and Pittwater. *See map p. 20.*	A dissected sandstone plateau, tidal inlets of Broken Bay. Forests predominantly eucalypt (dry sclerophyll) with sub-tropical rainforest patches on gully shales.	The plateau (with many vista points) falls steeply to flooded valleys of Cowan and Pittwater, creating outstanding scenery. Sheltered waters for boating. Profusion of wildflowers in spring. Aboriginal engravings.	Boating, swimming, fishing, bushwalking. Picnic areas. Visitor Information Centre near Bobbin Head offers slide viewings, photographic displays, brochures, maps, books. Camping in certain areas. Rangers. Caravan parks, hotels, motels in nearby Sydney suburbs. July to November for wildflowers, otherwise any season.
LAMINGTON NATIONAL PARK (QLD.) 48,510 acres	From Brisbane 70 m. via Pacific Highway, Gaven Way, Nerang and Beechmont to Binna Burra. Also from Brisbane 65 m. via Mt Lindesay Highway, Tamborine, Canungra, Beechmont. To O'Reilly's from Brisbane 75 m. via Mt Lindesay Highway, Tamborine, Canungra. *See map p. 37.*	Mountainous plateau, 3,000 ft to 3,925 ft, along the McPherson Range, falling away in cliffs, gorges, at southern border. Tropical rainforest.	Panoramas over NE. New South Wales, views of cliffs, green foothills. More than 500 waterfalls. Magnificent rainforest with tree ferns, orchids, flowering trees. Jungle birds: Brush Turkey, Satin and Regent Bowerbirds. Albert Lyrebird, Rufous Scrub-bird.	Ninety miles of walking tracks lead to views, waterfalls, Antarctic Beeches etc. Half-day, full-day or longer hikes. Landrover excursions. Photography of scenery, flora and fauna. Birdwatching along tracks. O'Reilly's Guest House and Binna Burra Lodge—both situated in park, booking advisable in holiday periods. Picnic grounds with toilets, shelters, fireplace. The rainforest is at its best after summer rains, otherwise any season.
LIMPINWOOD NATURE RESERVE (N.S.W.) Approx. 5,500 acres	Situated at head of Tweed River near Limpinwood, in Murwillumbah district.	On the 3,000 ft plateau of the McPherson Range, joining the southern border of Lamington National Park. Vehicular access even to perimeter of reserve is very difficult, and long climb on foot is needed to reach the plateau and reserve.	This is said to be the best remaining piece of rainforest left undamaged in New South Wales, and the difficulty of access should protect it until fully supervised. Has many of the attractions of adjoining Lamington National Park, and probably the same richness of rainforest wildlife, orchids, ferns.	Because of access difficulty, Limpinwood is mainly of interest to scientists, naturalists, bushwalkers. Bush camping, otherwise hotels and caravan parks at local towns. District Honorary Ranger at Eungella via Murwillumbah. Any season; heavy summer rainfall.
MINNAMURRA FALLS RESERVE (N.S.W.)	SE. New South Wales, W of Kiama; access from the Jamberoo-Robertson Rd.	A gorge cut into sandstone by the Minnamurra River rushing down from the 2,000 ft tablelands of Barren Grounds and Budderoo. Rainforest in the gorge.	Main feature is the plunging descent of the river into a black, spray-filled gorge where constant moisture has given rise to a small patch of interesting rainforest.	Scenic sightseeing, following nature trails where the features of the region are fully explained. At Kiama: Caravan and camping grounds, hotels, motels, cabins. Ranger at Minnamurra. Any season.
MOOLOOLAH RIVER NATIONAL PARK (QLD.) 1,670 acres	3 m. off Bruce Highway between Sippy Creek and Mountain Creek, about 60 m. N of Brisbane. *See map p. 37.*	Part of the coastal plain, frontage to Mooloolah River.	Excellent wildflower habitat. Picnic site on the higher ground.	Wildflower studies, observing birdlife. Bush camping. Caravan parks, hotels, motels at nearby coastal towns. Any season.
MORTON NATIONAL PARK (N.S.W.) 45,380 acres	100 m. S of Sydney, on Moss Vale–Nowra Road. *See map p. 20.*	Dissected sandstone plateau. Eucalypt (wet and dry sclerophyll types) forest, sub-tropical rainforest.	A great gulf in the sandstone plateau, with Fitzroy Falls at its head. Gorge, mesa, cliff and waterfall scenery. Vistas from above falls reach to distant Kangaroo River, Shoalhaven Cliffs. Bird and animal life abundant in forested valley depths.	Walking on marked trails to points of interest. Photography. Observing wildlife. Picnicking. Rugged bushwalking. Camping at Fitzroy Falls. Caravan parks, hotels, etc. at Moss Vale, Nowra, Kiama. Any season.
MUOGAMARRA SANCTUARY (N.S.W.) 3,000 acres	Entrance from Pacific Highway near Cowan. Comprises major part of country W of Highway between Cowan and Hawkesbury River.	Rough, dissected sandstone plateau, dry sclerophyll forest.	Aboriginal rock carvings. Birds, marsupials and wildflowers similar to those of Ku-ring-gai.	Bushwalking, observing birdlife, wildflowers. No accommodation at sanctuary. Any season.

NAME OF PARK	LOCALITY ACCESS	TOPOGRAPHY VEGETATION TYPES	FEATURES OF INTEREST	ACTIVITIES ACCOMMODATION SEASON TO VISIT
MT BARNEY NATIONAL PARK (QLD.) 12,980 acres	SE. Queensland, near Rathdowney. *See* map p. 37.	A prominent peak of the McPherson Range overlooking Mt Lindesay Highway near New South Wales border.	Views over ranges from the summit (4,439 ft), rugged bushwalking, climbing.	Favourite rendezvous of bushwalkers, rock climbers. Bush camping. Any season.
MT COUGAL NATIONAL PARK (QLD.) 900 acres	MacPherson Range, SE. Queensland. 77 m. from Brisbane by Pacific Highway, to West Burleigh via Gold Coast, then by Tallebudgera Creek Rd.	Mt Cougal (2,347 ft) is a double-peaked eminence of the mountain chain. Dense rainforest.	Magnificent specimens of rainforest trees such as Brush Box, Scented Satinwood, Mango Bark, White Beech. Views from heights. Clear, cold permanent mountain streams and cascades.	Exhilarating climbs up steep spurs to rainforest, cascades, views; an attraction for climbers, bushwalkers, scouts. Cross-country walkers can proceed on up old Tallebudgera Creek Road to Springbrook. Camping only, no facilities. Any season.
MT KAPUTAR NATIONAL PARK (N.S.W.) 35,200 acres	N New South Wales, 346 m. from Sydney, 30 m. NE. of Narrabri. *See* map p. 20.	The eroded remnants of volcanos active in the tertiary period; vegetation mainly dry type of eucalypt forest.	Mt Kaputar, a peak on the edge of a once large volcano, rises to 4,000 ft above the plains. Slopes of volcanic debris clothed with open forest woodland. Views from summits. Falls and ferns at Dawson's Springs.	Scenic viewing, bushwalking, rock climbing, photography, picnicking. Cabins and camping grounds at Dawson's Springs. (Information: The Secretary, Mt Kaputar National Park Trust, 14 Balonne St., Narrabri). Ranger. Any season.
MT LINDESAY (QLD.) 600 acres	SE. Queensland, near Rathdowney.	A prominent landmark overlooking Mt Lindesay Highway on New South Wales border.	Views from heights, rugged bushwalking.	Favoured by bushwalkers, rock climbers. Bush camping. Any season.
MT MAROON–MT MAY (QLD.) 3,630 acres	SE. Queensland, near Mt Lindesay Highway and Rathdowney.	Mt Maroon (3,166 ft) is the most northerly of a group of mountains forming a buttress of the McPherson Range W of the headwaters of Logan River.	Interesting feature is Mt Barney Creek gorge, with almost vertical walls, at the reserve's SE. corner.	A favourite rendezvous of bushwalkers, rock climbers. Bush camping. Any season.
MT NEBO and MT GLORIOUS (QLD.) 2,845 acres	Near Brisbane. Scenic road from Brisbane to Maiala (Mt Glorious) 28 m., via Boombana (20 m.) and Manorina (23 m.). *See* map p. 37.	On D'Aguilar Range. Forested, including patches of rainforest.	Four areas: Maiala National Park at Mt Glorious—tracks through forest, ferns, palms, to waterfall; Jolly's Lookout, extensive views to Glasshouse Mountains; Boombana, patches of rainforest, palm groves; Manorina Park with track up Mt Nebo Lookout, cabbage palms.	Sightseeing; walking; within easy reach of Brisbane for family picnicking; observing birdlife—Satin and Regent Bower-birds, Paradise Rifle-bird, Bell-miner. No accommodation in park. Any season.
MT WALSH NATIONAL PARK (QLD.) 7,380 acres	S Queensland, via Maryborough, then 54 m. W to Biggenden, another 5 m. to Mt Walsh.	The rugged northern abutment of Bluff Range. Forested gullies, Hoop Pine on ridges.	Mt Walsh (2,116 ft), The Bluff (3,134 ft), and plateau area.	Bushwalking—the peak may be climbed from the north without difficulty. Hotel at Biggenden. Spring months for wildflowers. Autumn, winter.
MT WARNING STATE PARK (N.S.W.) 5,230 acres	Far NE. New South Wales near Queensland border, 10 m. W of Murwillumbah, 530 m. from Sydney.	A volcanic spire rising from rugged, rainforest-covered hills.	Magnificent views in all directions (to the sea to the east) from the summit, which is reached by a graded walking track. Rainforest vegetation, birdlife.	Bushwalking, sightseeing, photography, observing rainforest bird and animal life. Camping only. Caravan and camping ground, motel, hotels at Murwillumbah. Any season.
MUNGHORN GAP NATURE RESERVE (N.S.W.) 7050 acres	On the Main Dividing Range between Mudgee and Wollar on the Muswellbrook Road. Road passes through reserve.	Flat sandstone country with xeromorphic flora, containing many species of special interest to naturalists.	Under conditions of well preserved natural environment bird and animal life is abundant.	Principally for conservation of wildlife which could not survive if all areas of natural vegetation in the district were destroyed, or gradually degraded. Observation of indigenous flora, birdlife. Caravan and camping park, hotels, motels at Mudgee. Any season.
NEW ENGLAND NATIONAL PARK (N.S.W.) 56,785 acres	NE. New South Wales, 45 m. E of Armidale, 320 m. from Sydney. *See* map p. 20.	The eastern precipice of the New England Plateau. Great altitude range within park: vegetation sequence from sub-alpine on heights, to sub-tropical on low slopes.	Magnificent views from Point Lookout (5,000 ft) to the distant coast and ocean. Snow Gums, Antarctic Beeches, wildflowers on heights; dense sub-tropical rainforest, with Red Cedar trees, in rugged valleys below.	Scenic viewing, nature walks, trails to park features, rugged bushwalking, photography. Lodge, cabins, camping facilities in park (enquiries to the Secretary, New England National Park Trust, P.O. Box 402, Armidale, N.S.W. 2350). Summer, 5,000 ft heights pleasantly cooler; winter, snow and extreme cold may be encountered at 5,000 ft, but good for walking at lower elevations.
NOOSA NATIONAL PARK (QLD.) 792 acres	Near Noosa township, on coast 110 m. N from Brisbane, 42 m. SE. of Gympie. *See* map p. 37.	Open forest on coastal sand hills, rainforest on creeks; rocky headlands and sheltered beaches.	Ocean beaches, rugged headlands, hill-top views of landscape, seascape. Rainforest with Hoop-pine, Kauri Pine, palms, pandanas. Prolific wildflower displays on sandy, open-forest areas.	Sightseeing (roads and tracks), fishing, swimming, observing wildflower and birdlife. Caravan and camping parks, motels, hotels, chalet at Noosa township. Extensive picnic grounds in park. Wildflower displays: September to November. Water sports, fishing, most of the year.
NUMINBAH NATIONAL PARK (Natural Bridge) (QLD) 477 acres	SE. Queensland, Nerang River Valley, between Lamington and Springbrook parks, 70 m. S from Brisbane via Nerang; 27 m. from Gold Coast via Murwillumbah. *See* map p. 37.	River valley between escarpments of Beechmont and Springbrook Ranges.	Natural Bridge, Cave Creek Falls, high rainforest, impressive views of escarpments and waterfalls, prolific birdlife.	Sightseeing, birdwatching (over 100 species can be seen in a day), walking (¾ mile circuit track), picnicking (tables, etc.). Guest house at Numinbah township. Any season, falls best after summer rainy season.
QUEEN MARY FALLS (KILLARNEY) NATIONAL PARK (QLD.) 327 acres	On the Great Dividing Range 30 m. SE. of Warwick. From Brisbane by Cunningham Highway to Warwick, then gravel road to park; or New England Highway via Legume, 118 m. *See* map p. 37.	Mountainous (2,800 ft) area at head of Spring Creek, a tributary of Condamine River. Hardwood forest, rainforest in river gorge.	Queen Mary Falls (132 ft) is major scenic feature. Dagg's Falls (120 ft) can be seen from approach road. Panoramic views from Spring Creek cliffs and from Blackfellow's Knob. Rainforest trees, birds, rock wallabies.	General touring, sightseeing, bushland recreation, walking, photography. Picnicking at parking area: fireplaces, tables, water supply. Hotel at Killarney, 8 m. from park. Caravan-camping areas, hotels at Warwick. Any season.

NAME OF PARK	LOCALITY ACCESS	TOPOGRAPHY VEGETATION TYPES	FEATURES OF INTEREST	ACTIVITIES ACCOMMODATION SEASON TO VISIT
RAVENSBOURNE NATIONAL PARK (QLD.) 247 acres	S Queensland; by Brisbane Valley Highway, 83 m. via Esk; from Toowoomba, 28 m. via Hampton.	Slopes of Great Dividing Range, elevation 2,200 ft, luxuriant rainforest, dense groves of piccabeen palms.	Scenic drive on approach from Esk through forests, fine specimens of Blackbutt, Tallow-wood, Sydney Blue Gum. Palm groves, ferntree groves, cave in Helidon sandstone. Variety of birds. Picnic facilities.	General sightseeing, relaxation, picnicking. Walking tracks to palm groves (1½ m.) and through rainforest (1 m.). No accommodation; nearest at Crows Nest (16 m.). Any season.
ROBINSON GORGE NATIONAL PARK (QLD.) 11,400 acres	Inland S Queensland, on Dawson River watershed, 50 m. NW. of Taroom. *See map p. 44.*	On the Robinson Creek (Dawson River headwater tributary) which rises in the Expedition Range, flows for 8 m. between rugged sandstone cliffs of Robinson Gorge. Sparsely timbered.	Cliffs rising to 300 ft, gorge varying in width from a few chains to a quarter mile. Starkvale Creek gorge, joining the Robinson Gorge, is a sandstone crevice narrowing to a few feet in width, but rising to heights upwards of 300 ft. Fine panorama from Shepherd's Peak to the Battery, Mt Surprise, Mt Cannonvale, Great Dividing Range. In vicinity of Robinson and Starkvale creeks are dense stands of Whip-stick Wattle. Wildflowers include *leptospermum, boronia, hovea*.	Scenic views, photography, observing wild-flowers and other flora. Camping only, no facilities. Early spring months, late autumn, winter.
ROYAL NATIONAL PARK (N.S.W.) 36,729 acres	20 m. S of Sydney, entrance from Princes Highway; also by train to station in park. *See map p. 20.*	Sandstone plateau, dissected by gorges of creeks and river. Coastal cliffs, beaches, lagoons, tidal estuary of Hacking River. Heaths, eucalypt forests, sub-tropical rainforest in gullies.	Fine beaches sheltered by high headlands, boating facilities, sheltered waters of Port Hacking. Wildflower displays in spring on heathlands. Lush jungle vegetation along river drive, good variety of birds.	Boating, surfing, walking, photography of scenery, wildflowers. Guesthouse and camping area. Many picnic grounds. Spring months for wildflowers.
SALVATOR ROSA NATIONAL PARK (QLD.) 48,320 acres	Inland S Queensland, on Great Dividing Range, at head of Nogoa River, 7 m. off Tamba–Springsure Road, 70 m. from Tambo, 90 m. from Springsure. *See map p. 44.*	Eastern slopes of Great Divide. High sandstone ridges—Mt Salvator, Spyglass Peak. Salvator Rosa valley, Lake Salvator.	Named Salvator Rosa by Sir Thomas Mitchell because of peaks resemblance to alpine scenery painted by Italian artist of that name. Has turreted escarpments; Mitchell and Belinda springs clear fresh water.	Rough walking, exploring of rough but beautiful sandstone country. Camping, no facilities. Nearest town Tambo, 70 m. Early spring, late autumn, winter months.
SIR EDWARD HALLSTROM NATURE RESERVE (N.S.W.) 3,200 acres	N of Sydney, between Berowa and Cowan (on Pacific Highway).	Hawkesbury sandstone country, overlooking Berowra Creek (a tributary of the Hawkesbury).	Established for conservation and research into Koala breeding under simulated natural conditions. Several hundred Koala food trees planted.	Visitor facilities: enquire before entering reserve (Ranger, phone 610 1246, or P.O. Cowan 2252). Facilities are to be prepared for those interested in undertaking specialized scientific studies. No accommodation on reserve. Any season.
SOUTHERN BARRIER REEF ISLAND PARKS (QLD.)	About 45 m. NE. of Gladstone, on Great Barrier Reef almost on Tropic of Capricorn. Twice weekly launch service from Gladstone to Heron Island. *See map p. 44.*	Low sand and coral debris islands surrounded by extensive reefs. Casuarina, pisonia, pandanus vegetation.	Islands (Capricorn and Bunker groups)—Heron Island, Lady Musgrave Island, Fairfax Island, Hoskyn Island. Extensive coral reefs, rich reef and marine life. Seabirds—sea eagles, mutton-birds (shearwaters) cormorants, herons, terns.	Reef exploration, swimming, cruises to other islands, observing marine and birdlife. Heron Island tourist resort, tropical-styled cabins. (Enquire Queensland Tourist Bureau). April to November or December.
SPRINGBROOK (Gwongorella and Warrie National Parks) (QLD.)	From Brisbane by Pacific Highway via Mudgeeraba or via Numinbah State Forest, 75 m. from Southport via Rerang, 29 m. From Surfers Paradise via Mudgeeraba, 27 m. From Burleigh Heads via Mudgeeraba, 24 m. *See map p. 37.*	Plateau, spurs, gorges of McPherson Range, elevation 3,000 ft. Luxuriant rainforest.	Scenery featuring cliffs and crags, waterfalls, cascades, forest gorges. Rainforest trees, fern glades, palm groves, orchids, Waratahs. Lyrebirds, Whipbirds, pittas. Natural arboretum at Gwongorella.	Sightseeing at waterfalls, cascades reached via short tracks. Observing jungle birds, flowers. Photography. Picnicking at Purling Brook, Tallanbana, Turramurra, Goomoolahra. Camping—picnic areas with shelter sheds, tables, creek water, toilets. Forestry Department Overseer. Guest house, motel nearby. Any season, waterfalls and rainforest best after summer rains. Wildflowers September–November.
SYDNEY HARBOUR (Proposed National Park) (N.S.W.) about 1,350 acres	On North Head, South Head, Middle Head, Dobroyd Head surrounding entrance to Sydney Harbour.	Magnificent coastal scenery, cliffs and sandstone heights. Potentially a wonderful leisure recreational area for Sydney people, would preserve the beauty of the harbour. Many birds, wildflowers.		At present most of this attractive coastal land is occupied by the army and used for a few minor defence and training installations. In April, 1969 the New South Wales Government released plans to make the area a 1,350 acre National Park which would benefit the people of crowded Sydney. At time of writing (April, 1969) the Commonwealth Government is refusing to make the land available to the Australian people. The area's defence value is negligible. The public can now drive to the spectacular tip of North Head, but along the road flanked by forbidden territory. An area on Dobroyd Head, with scenic road, is open to the public, and also the small Parkhill Reserve.
TAMBORINE MOUNTAIN PARKS (QLD.)	From Brisbane by Pacific Highway via Beenleigh, or via Kingston and Waterford, or by Mt Lindesay Highway via Tamborine, 54 m. Access also from Gold Coast via Pacific Highway, Oxenford, 28 m. *See map p. 37.*	A high, small plateau, edged with cliffs, on the Darlington Range, a spur of McPherson Range.	A number of small park areas: Cedar Creek falls; Joalah (rainforest, falls, creek walk), The Knoll (creek walk through rainforest, cascades, falls); Witches Falls; Macrozamia Grove; McDonald Park (high rainforest); Palm Grove (Piccabeen Palms).	Sightseeing, touring, short walks, photography, bird-watching. Hotel and guest house accommodation at Tamborine, near park. Picnic ground facilities at the Knoll, Witches Falls, Palm Grove, McDonald Park, Joalah, Cedar Creek. Wildflowers September–November.

NAME OF PARK	LOCALITY ACCESS	TOPOGRAPHY VEGETATION TYPES	FEATURES OF INTEREST	ACTIVITIES ACCOMMODATION SEASON TO VISIT
WARRUMBUNGLE NATIONAL PARK (N.S.W.) 15,800 acres	Northern inland New South Wales, 20 m. W of Coonabarabran, 300 m. from Sydney. *See* map p. 20. 33.	Eroded remnants of volcanoes active in tertiary period. Dry sclerophyll forest.	Spectacular scenery resulting from erosion of ancient volcanoes, the solidified lava resisting erosion to form towering spires, walls, particularly a 300 ft high wall only a few feet thick known as the 'breadknife'. Wildflowers in spring months; birds both of inland plains and of east coast.	Bushwalking, rock climbing, scenic viewing (excellent tracks to vantage points), bird and wildflower study, colour photography. Cabins, caravan park, camping areas within the park. (Information: the Secretary, Warrumbungle National Park Trust, P.O. Box 269, Coonabarabran, N.S.W. 2857). Ranger. Spring for wildflowers, otherwise winter, autumn. Summer rather hot, dry.
WOODY ISLAND NATIONAL PARK (QLD.) 1,750 acres	Hervey Bay, 28 m. NE. of Maryborough. Reached by launch from Urangan, 3 m.	Rocky headlands, sandy beaches. Well timbered with hardwood, scattered rainforest.	Nesting place of numerous birds.	Walking, bird-watching, swimming, fishing. (Fresh water on island is in very limited supply). Hotel at Urangan, other accommodation at nearby resorts. Any season.

SMALL PARKS, NATURE RESERVES, SANCTUARY AREAS

NAME, LOCATION	FEATURES OF INTEREST
Bare I., off La Perouse, on N shore of Botany Bay (N.S.W.). 3 acres.	Named by Captain Cook in 1770. Fort built on island in 1885 to repel possible attack by Russian Pacific Fleet. Museum in old fort. Frequent demonstration firings of old cannons. Information: phone 668-9923.
Barrier Reef I., Capricorn, Bunker Groups, off Gladstone (Qld.).	Heron Island (30 acres); Hoskyn Island (20 acres); Fairfax Island (40 acres); Lady Musgrave Island (50 acres).
Bird I. Nature Reserve (N.S.W.). About 18 acres, off central coast near Budgewoi.	Nesting place of sea birds.
Black Ash Nature Reserve (N.S.W.). 220 acres, N of Nowra, W of Berry.	Close to Devil's Glen reserve, but on exposed sandstone tops. Almost entirely surrounded by cliffs. Vegetation of Black Ash or Coastal Ash. Swamp heathlands in depressions.
Blue Lake National Park (Qld.). 1,100 acres.	On North Stradbroke I., near Brisbane.
Blue Mountains (N.S.W.). Sites reservations total 11,000 acres.	Many small beauty spots of the mountains have been reserved: areas including cliff tops, 'glens', waterfalls, numerous small walks. Because areas are small, character tends to be changed by development.
Boondezbah I. Nature Reserve (N.S.W.). About 20 acres. Off entrance to Port Stephens.	Nesting place of sea birds.
Boorganna Nature Reserve (N.S.W.). 906 acres. On Comboyne Plateau, 200 m. N of Sydney, near Wingham.	Wet sclerophyll and brush country at 2,000 ft elevation. Rich in fauna, including Brush Turkey, Lyrebirds, fruit pigeons. Platypus in creek. Visitor centre, nature trail, at Rawson's Falls.
Bowraville Nature Reserve (N.S.W.). 144 acres. Alongside roadway between Bowraville and Bellingen, N coast N.S.W.	To preserve a sample of impressive rainforest and wet sclerophyll forest of heavily timbered headwaters of Bowra River. Koalas in this district. Walking tracks.
Burrinjuck Dam Park (N.S.W.). 125 acres.	At Burrinjuck Dam via Murrumbidgee, near Yass.
Captain Cook's Landing Place (Historic Site). At tip of Kurnell Peninsula, 25 m. from Sydney (N.S.W.). 800 acres.	Dedicated in 1899 to preserve site of landing of Cook on E coast of Australia in 1770. Visitor centre, museum telling story of Cook, historic pathway past historic monuments.
Castle Tower National Park (Qld.). 3,830 acres.	About 20 m. S of Gladstone, 5 m. W of Iveragh, near lower reaches of Boyne River.
Coalstoun Lakes National Park (Qld.). 65 acres.	NE. of Coalstoun Lakes township, E of Gayndah, SW. of Biggenden.
Coloured Sands National Park (Qld.). 1,141 acres.	Colourful sand dune formation just N of Noosa, SE. Queensland.
Cook I. Nature Reserve (N.S.W.). About 10 acres off extreme N New South Wales coast just S of Tweed Heads.	Island is rookery for Crested Tern and Wedge-tailed Shearwater. Landing on island is difficult.
Coolbaggie Nature Reserve. Near Eumungerie, Dubbo district (N.S.W.).	Area of mallee scrub alongside Goonoo State Forest at head of Coolbaggie Creek.
Curumbenya Nature Reserve (N.S.W.). W New South Wales, 10 m. N of Parkes, on road to Wellington.	Steep, rugged ridges where Curumbenya and Crokers Ranges intersect. Excellent example of open dry sclerophyll forest and heathland. Trees are Stringy Bark, Snappy Gum, Cypress Pine, grevilleas, grass-trees. Permanent water in Coobang Creek. Various birds, wallabies, wallaroos, kangaroos, possums.
Devil's Glen Nature Reserve (N.S.W.). 100 acres. N of Nowra, W of Berry, S coastal N.S.W. Access difficult.	Reserve area almost entirely surrounded by vertical cliffs. Dense cover of sub-tropical rainforest, such as once covered Robertson Plateau. Important sanctuary for fauna of region.
Dularcha National Park (Qld.). 342 acres.	Between Landsborough and Mooloolah, crossing main north–south railway.
Fairlie's Knob National Park (Qld.). 100 acres.	Range summit, about 16 m. due E of Biggenden, and about 30 m. W of Maryborough.
Five Islands Nature Reserve (N.S.W.). Total area about 66 acres; situated off Port Kembla.	Well-known breeding place for Crested Tern, Silver Gull, Wedge-tailed Shearwater, Little Penguin.
Frazer National Park (N.S.W.). 2,000 acres. Entered from Pacific Highway S of Elizabeth Bay turnoff.	Coastline and surrounds, between Catherine Hill Bay and Lake Munmorah.
Garrawarra Park (N.S.W.). 1,500 acres.	Coastline and some surrounding lands, S of Royal National Park to about Lilyvale. Similar to parts of Royal National.
Glenbawn Dam National Park (N.S.W.). 345 acres. Near Scone.	Glenbawn Dam.

NAME, LOCATION	FEATURES OF INTEREST
Gurumbi Nature Reserve (N.S.W.). 375 acres. Lies between St George's Basin and Nowra–Jervis Bay Road.	Contains small hanging swamp draining into attractive creek passing through open forest. Name Gurumbi from Aboriginal word meaning 'white gum tree', referring to the many Scribbly Gums in area.
Hill End Historical Site (N.S.W.). 52 m. N of Bathurst, 180 m. from Sydney.	Site of first profitable gold workings (1851). Townsite in 1872 had 28 hotels. Site features neat cottages built in mining days. Royal Hotel in use since 1872. Evidence of gold-digging activities.
Hole Gulf Nature Reserve (N.S.W.). 1,800 acres. On edge of New England Tableland, 25 m. NE. of Walcha on Oxley Highway.	Region typical of broken eastern escarpment. Sub-tropical rainforest in gullies, remainder of sclerophyll forest. Isolated nature of reserve—its forests and wildlife are undamaged, contain full range of species.
Isla Gorge National Park (Qld.). 10,650 acres. Approx. 150 m. inland from Bundaberg, about 15 m. SW. of Theodore.	Deep sandstone gorge on tributary of Dawson River. Mixed tropical woodland vegetation. Somewhat similar to other sandstone gorges (Robinson, Carnarvon) further inland.
Islands, Keppel Bay (Qld.).	North Keppel I. (1,454 acres); Pelican I. (20 acres); Divided I. (20 acres); Corroboree I. (50 acres); Sloping I. (20 acres); Miall I. (100 acres); Middle I. (160 acres); Halfway I. (20 acres); Humpy I. (160 acres).
John Gould Nature Reserve (N.S.W.). About 60 acres. Covers Cabbage Tree I., off Port Stephens, N of Newcastle.	Only known nesting place of White-winged (or Gould) Petrel, which nest on ground. Island sides steep, landing difficult except in calm weather. Partly covered with rainforest.
Keepit Dam Park (N.S.W.). 40 acres.	At Keepit Dam on Namoi River near Gunnedah.
Lane Cove National Park, on Lane Cove River (N.S.W.). 830 acres. Entrances from Ryde, Chatswood.	Upper reaches of Lane Cove River. Hawkesbury sandstone country. Flora-fauna similar to Royal, Ku-ring-gai. Recreational usage.
La Perouse Monuments (N.S.W.). (Historic Site). La Perouse 9 m. from Sydney. 19 acres.	French navigator La Perouse anchored off this point in 1788 two days after arrival of first fleet. Monuments, watch tower built 1820 to prevent rum smuggling.
Lion I. Nature Reserve (N.S.W.). Island discovered by Governor Phillip in 1788, at entrance of Broken Bay, immediately N of Sydney.	One of only two known nesting places in N.S.W. of the Sooty Shearwater; nearest breeding place to Sydney of Wedge-tailed Shearwater. Little Penguins nest on island. Members of Royal Australian Ornithologist's Union have been studying migration, breeding, rate of growth of Shearwaters on this island.
Little Broughton I. Nature Reserve (N.S.W.) 90 acres. Just N of Newcastle.	The eastern head of Broughton I., separated by narrow channel from main island. Breeding place for many sea birds.
Moolabanya National Park (Qld.). 224 acres. SE. Qld.	Small reserve almost joining SW. part of Lamington National Park.
Moon I. Nature Reserve (N.S.W.). About 2½ acres. Near Swansea, mid N.S.W. coast.	In the entrance to Lake Macquarie. Recorded nesting place of colonies of Silver Gull, Black-backed Gull, Crested Tern, Little Penguin, Wedge-tailed Shearwater, Sooty Oyster-Catcher.
Mount Seaview Nature Reserve (N.S.W.). Nearest town is Yarras, on Oxley Highway between Walcha and Wauchope.	Close to Mt Seaview. 480 acres of sub-tropical rainforest reserved for scientific purposes. Many birds, including several bower-bird species, fruit pigeons, lyrebirds.
Narrandera Nature Reserve (N.S.W.). 180 acres. Close to town of Narrandera (Originally town common).	Sample of River Red Gum riverine woodland environment. Many species of parrots.
Nature Reserves off N New South Wales coast. SW. Solitary I., 8 acres; Split Solitary I., 9 acres; Julian Rocks.	Nesting places of sea birds.
North Rock Nature Reserve (N.S.W.). About 11 acres. Off Red Rock, near Woolgoola, N coast.	A rookery for Silver Gulls.
Quanda Nature Reserve (N.S.W.). 1,061 acres. Near Nyngan and Nymagee, W New South Wales.	Mallee country. A reserve for the purpose of conservation of wildlife of the semi-arid interior.
Res. No. 2155. Parish of Tiffin (Qld.). 5,200 acres.	On Moreton I., E of Brisbane.
Rocky Creek National Park (Qld.). 157 acres.	S Queensland, about 15 m. S of Cunningham's Gap and E of Emu Vale.
Round Hill Nature Reserve (N.S.W.). 12,980 acres. Situated between Euabalong and Mt Hope, W of Condobolin, W New South Wales.	Semi-arid mallee lands, a reserve for Mallee Fowl and other mallee fauna. Areas heavily grazed by sheep, support few Mallee Fowl, as insufficient food left for these birds.
Rowley's Creek Gulf Nature Reserve (N.S.W.). 4,100 acres, about 15 m. E of Walcha (Oxley Highway).	An entrenched valley on edge of New England Tableland, at head of Rowley's Creek, a tributary of Apsley River, which joins Macleay River. Patches wet eucalypt and rainforest. Good views over valley from cliff rim.
Small Park, Monto Forestry district (Qld.).	Auburn River (in Parish of Delembra) 961 acres.
Small Parks, Parish of Hewittville (near Yeppoon) (Qld.).	Double Head, 28 acres; Rosslyn Head, 100 acres; Bluff Point, 122 acres; Mulambin, 20 acres.
The Basin Nature Reserve (N.S.W.). In north between Armidale and Bundarra; turnoff 34 m. from Armidale.	Where granites of New England Tableland drop to NW. slopes, Georges Creek has carved out a large meander. On the ridge running into the creek's loop there is about 2,600 acres of dry sclerophyll forest (Cypress Pine, Iron Bark association) inhabited by Wallaroos, Grey Kangaroos, Gliders.
The Palms National Park (Qld.). 30 acres.	Situated Parish of Cooyer, SE. of Bunya Mountains.
Tuckers Creek National Park (Qld.). 133 acres.	Situated N of Nambour, between Bruce Highway, fronting railway.
Tucki Nature Reserve (N.S.W.). Tuck-Tuckurimba district south of Lismore.	A Koala preservation project, involving the planting of Koala food trees by school, Rotary Club, townspeople.
Un-named park, reserve No. 629 (Qld.). 584 acres.	SE. of Bunya Mountains, between Crow's Nest and Esk.
Un-named park, reserve No. 836 (Qld.). 3,360 acres.	On Great Dividing Range NNE. 10 m. from Cunningham's Gap National Park, similar topography, vegetation.
Vaucluse House (Historic Site) (N.S.W.). At Vaucluse, 6 m. from Sydney. 19 acres.	Example of mediaeval gothic architecture, built 1829. Property originally purchased 1803. Features include furniture of better homes of the period (piano, four-poster beds).
Warrah Sanctuary (N.S.W.). Near Woy Woy. 1,000 acres.	N shore of Hawkesbury River and adjacent lands between Pearl Beach and Patonga.

SOME BIRDS OF EASTERN NATIONAL PARKS

(Southern Queensland to Kosciusko)

Glossy Ibis (*Plegadis falcinellus*); swamps and grasslands.
Plumed Tree-duck (*Dendrocygna eytoni*); lakes and swamps.
Little Eagle (*Hieraaëtus morphnoides*); inland plains and open forest.
Black-shouldered Kite (*Elanus notatus*); open and light-timbered forest.
Collared Sparrowhawk (*Accipiter cirrocephalus*); open forest.
Grey Goshawk (*Accipiter novae-hollandiae*); forests.
Peregrine Falcon (*Falco peregrinus*); forests and mountains.
Little Falcon (*Falco longipennis*); forests, timbered ranges.
Kestrel (*Falco cenchroides*); open forest, paddocks and plains.
Brush Turkey (*Alectura lathami*); rainforests and scrubs.
King Quail (*Excalfactoria chinensis*); swampy grasslands, nomadic.
Brolga (*Grus rubicunda*); plains and swamps.
Jacana (*Irediparra gallinacea*); lagoons and swamps.
Wonga Pigeon (*Leucosarcia melanoleuca*); rainforest.
Green-winged Pigeon (*Chalcophaps chrysachlora*); rainforest.
Rainbow Lorikeet (*Trichoglossus moluccanus*); eucalypt forests.
Scaly-breasted Lorikeet (*Trichoglossus chloralepidotus*); open forest.
Glossy Black Cockatoo (*Calyptorhynchus lathami*); forests.
Pink, or Major Mitchell Cockatoo (*Kakatoë leadbeateri*); mallee and semi-arid areas.
Sulphur-crested Cockatoo (*Kakatoë galerita*); forests.
Galah (*Kakatoë roseicapilla*); open forests and plains.
Cockatiel (*Leptolophus hollandicus*); inland plains and scrubs.
Superb Parrot (*Polytelis swainsoni*); open forest and grasslands.
King Parrot (*Aprosmictus scapularis*); dense forests.
Paradise Parrot (*Psephotus pulcherrimus*); grasslands.
Regent Parrot (*Polytelis anthopeplus*); mallee and open forest.
Yellow Rosella (*Platycercus flaveolus*); grassland and open forest.
Eastern Rosella (*Platycercus eximius*); open forest.
Red-backed Parrot (*Psephotus haematonotus*); grasslands.
Blue bonnet (*Psephotus narethae*); grasslands and open scrub.
Turquoise Parrot (*Neophema pulchella*); grasslands and open forest.
Scarlet-chested Parrot (*Neophema splendida*); dry interior, rare.
Brush Cuckoo (*Cacomantis variolosus*); rainforest.
Masked Owl (*Tyto novae-hollandiae*); forest.
Boobook Owl (*Ninox boobook*); forests.
Spotted Owl (*Ninox novae-zeelandiae*); dense forests.
Azure Kingfisher (*Alcyone azurea*); fresh and saltwater streams.
Mangrove Kingfisher (*Halcyon chloris*); mangroves.
Sacred Kingfisher (*Halcyon sanctus*); forests.
Forest Kingfisher (*Halcyon macleayi*); woodlands and forests.
Rainbow Bird (*Merops ornatus*); coastal forests to inland plains.
Dollar-bird (*Eurystomus orientalis*); forests and jungle.
Buff-breasted Pitta (*Pitta versicolor*); rainforest.

Prince Albert Lyrebird (*Menura alberti*); rainforest.
Rufous Scrub-bird (*Atrichornis rufescens*); rainforest.
Southern Figbird (*Sphecatheres vieilloti*); jungle and open forest.
Pied Currawong (*Strepera graculina*); forests.
Regent Bower-bird (*Sericulus chrysocephalus*); rainforests.
Satin Bower-bird (*Ptilonorhynchus violaceus*); rainforests.
Spotted Bower-bird (*Chlamydera maculata*); inland scrub.
Green Catbird (*Ailuraedus crassirostris*); rainforest.
Brown Tree-creeper (*Climacteris picumnus*); open forest.
White-headed Sittella (*Neositta leucocephala*); open forest.
Chestnut-crowned Babbler (*Pomatostomus ruficeps*); inland scrub.
Cinnamon Quail-thrush (*Cinclosoma cinnamomeum*); arid, stony country.
Rufous Songlark (*Cinclorhamphus mathewsi*); open areas.
Tailor-bird (*Cisticola exilis*); swampy areas.
Tawny Grass-bird (*Megalurus timoriensis*); reedbeds.
Red-backed Wren (*Malurus melanocephalus*); creekside grasses and undergrowth.
Chestnut-tailed Heath-wren (*Hylacola pyrrhopygia*); heaths.
Inland Thornbill (*Acanthiza albiventris*); thickets and low scrub.
Shy Ground-wren (*Hylacola cauta*); mallee scrub.
Rock-warbler (*Origma solitaria*); ravines and hillsides near streams.
Red-capped Robin (*Petroica goodenovii*); inland forest, scrub.
Hooded Robin (*Petroica cucullata*); forest and scrub.
Northern Yellow Robin (*Eopsaltria chrysorrhoa*); rainforest.
Rufous Fantail (*Rhipidura rufifrons*); rainforest.
Golden Whistler (*Pachycephala pectoralis*); jungle and forest.
Olive Whistler (*Pachycephala olivacea*); rainforest.
Rufous Whistler (*Pachycephala rufiventris*); open forest.
Restless Flycatcher (*Seisura inquieta*); open forest.
Black-faced Wood-swallow (*Artamus cincereus*); open country.
Painted Honeyeater (*Grantiella picta*); forests.
Yellow-plumed Honeyeater (*Meliphaga ornata*); mallee.
Blue-faced Honeyeater (*Entomyzon eyanotis*); open forest.
Scarlet Honeyeater (*Myzomela sanguinolenta*); flowering trees, nomadic.
Regent Honeyeater (*Zanthomiza phrygia*); nomadic.
Lewin Honeyeater (*Meliphaga lewini*); rainforests.
New Holland Honeyeater (*Meliornis novae-hollandiae*); coastal heathlands.
Noisy Friar-bird (*Philemon corniculatus*); nomadic.
Eastern Shrike-tit (*Falcunculus frontatus*); open forest.
Eastern Whip-bird (*Psophodes olivaceus*); rainforest and thickets.
Beautiful Firetail (*Zonaeginthus bellus*); heath and low scrub.
Chestnut-breasted Finch (*Lonchura castaneothorax*); reedbeds and grasslands.
Plum-headed Finch (*Aidemosyne modesta*); open country.

SOME FURRED ANIMALS OF EASTERN PARKS AND SANCTUARIES

Platypus (*Ornithorhynchus anatinus*); active early and late in the day; coastal streams.
Spiny Anteater (*Tachyglossus aculeatus*); diurnal; widespread, rainforest to semi-desert.
Yellow-footed Marsupial Mouse (*Antechinus flavipes*); nocturnal; widespread in forests.
Dusky Marsupial Mouse (*A. swainsonii*); nocturnal; undergrowth near streams of highlands.
Pigmy Marsupial Mouse (*A. maculatus*); nocturnal; north-coastal jungles.
Mouse-like Sminthopsis (*Sminthopsis murina*); nocturnal; very widespread.
White-footed Sminthopsis (*S. leucopus*); nocturnal; terrestrial, insectivorous.
Brush-tailed Phascogale (*Phascogale tapoatafa*); nocturnal; widespread, active hunter in treetops.
Eastern Native Cat (*Dasyurus viverrinus*); nocturnal, cat-like carnivore, forests, trees.
Tiger Cat (*Dasyurops maculatus*); nocturnal carnivore; heavy forests, mountainous areas.
Long-nosed Bandicoot (*Perameles nasuta*); nocturnal, coastal forests, insectivorous.
Wombat (*Phascolomis mitchelli*); nocturnal; forests of coastal mountains.
Feathertail Glider (*Acrobates pygmaeus*); nocturnal; forests and flowering trees.
Sugar Glider (*Petaurus breviceps*); nocturnal; forests and open bushland, common.
Squirrel Glider (*P. norfolcensis*); a larger version of Sugar Glider; coastal ranges.
Yellow-bellied Glider (*P. australis*); nocturnal; coastal forests.
Greater Glider (*Schoinobates volans*); largest flying phalanger; inhabits coastal highlands.
Brush-tailed Possum (*Trichosaurus vulpeca*); commonest of possums; forests and open bush.
Short-eared Brushtail (*T. caninus*); rainforest along Great Divide.
Common Ringtail Possum (*Pseudocheirus peregrinus*); rainforest, eucalypt forest and woodlands.

Rufous Ringtail (*P. rubidus*); copper-red colour; only on Bunya Mts. Qld.
Koala (*Phascolarctos cinereus*); active at night; dry sclerophyll forest or woodland.
Rufous Rat-Kangaroo (*Aepyprymnus rufescens*); coastal regions, open woodlands.
Potoroo (*Potorous tridactylus*); nocturnal; rainforest and wet sclerophyll forest.
Brush-tailed Rock-Wallaby (*Petrogale penicillata*); mainly nocturnal; mountainous, dry forests.
Red-legged Pademelon (*Thylogale stigmatica*); coastal forests in dense vegetation.
Red-necked Pademelon (*T. thetis*); scrubs of north-east N.S.W. and southern Qld.
Swamp, or Black-tailed Wallaby (*Wallabia bicolor*); large species; jungle and wet forests.
Whiptail, or Pretty-face Wallaby (*W. parryi*); diurnal; open woodlands and dry forest.
Black-striped Wallaby (*W. dorsalis*); dry sclerophyll forest and woodlands.
Parma Wallaby (*W. parma*); very rare; jungle and eucalypt forest.
Agile, or Sandy Wallaby (*W. agilis*); open woodland, most common in far north.
Red-necked Wallaby (*W. rufogrisea*); large, common; usually in dry eucalypt forest.
Wallaroo, or Euro (*Macropus robustus*); very large, heavy species; widespread in rocky ranges.
Grey Kangaroo (*M. major*); dry sclerophyll forest and open woodlands.
Dingo (*Canis antarticus*); may be found in any wild bush areas.
Grey-headed Flying Fox (*Pteropus poliocephalus*); nocturnal; coastal forests, jungles.
Little Reddish Fruit-Bat (*P. scapulatus*); widespread species; largely blossom-feeding.
Queensland Tube-nosed Bat (*Nyctimene robinsoni*); east-coast Qld., northern N.S.W.
Eastern Water-Rat (*Hydromys chrysogaster*); widespread in eastern rivers.

Koala

Emu

THE CENTRE

NAME OF PARK	LOCALITY ACCESS	TOPOGRAPHY VEGETATION TYPES	FEATURES OF INTEREST	ACTIVITIES ACCOMMODATION SEASON TO VISIT
ALICE SPRINGS TELEGRAPH STATION HISTORIC SITE (N.T.) 1,096 acres	On Stuart Highway 2 m. N of Alice Springs. *See* map p. 61.	The thousand-acre tract surrounding these historic buildings has a topography of scattered granite boulders somewhat similar to those of Devil's Marbles area. Part of Todd River passes through this area.	Old Telegraph Station buildings, main link in telegraph line to Darwin, established 1872. Buildings being restored as museum of those times. Also a fauna park with native animals on display.	Sightseeing, photography, picnicking. Accommodation close by in Alice Springs: Hotels, motels, numerous guest houses. Cabins for rent. Four caravan and camping parks. May to November.
AYERS ROCK—MT OLGA NATIONAL PARK (N.T.) 311,680 acres	276 m. SW. of Alice Springs via Erldunda, on Stuart Highway. This road is a rough dirt track, impassable after moderate rains. A sign at the turnoff from Stuart Highway advises if it is open. Air service from Alice Springs. Airstrip for light aircraft at Ayers Rock. Dirt road 20 m. W to Mt Olga. *See* map p. 61.	Undulating or flat country, red sandhills, clay flats. Mulga (*Acacia*) scrub, Desert Oaks (*Casuarina*). Massive conglomerate residuals at Ayers Rock, Olgas.	Ayers Rock, famed as huge 'monolith' 5½ m. circumference, 1,100 ft high, appears to change colour as touched by different light of morning, mid-day, sunset. Caves feature Aboriginal paintings and tell stories of native mythology. Permanent waterhole at Maggie Springs. Olgas comprise 26 huge, smooth, vividly coloured domes separated by deep narrow chasms; highest rises to 1,800 ft. Vivid wildflowers after rain.	Scenic touring, climbing on Ayers Rock and domes of Olgas. Visit caves. Walks through canyons of Olgas. Colour photography. Observing wildflowers, desert birds, which are numerous in good seasons. Near Rock: hotel-motel, motel, three chalets. Caravan and camping area. Rangers. June to October; July to September for wildflowers.
DEVIL'S MARBLES SCENIC RESERVE (N.T.) 4,519 acres	Central Northern Territory, on Stuart Highway, about 250 m. N from Alice Springs, 60 m. S of Tennant Creek. *See* map p. 96.	Undulating plains with residual granite tors, low bare granite outcrops. Very sparse mulga scrub, scattered low ground cover, occasional small gums.	Huge rounded red granite boulders, piled one upon another as if scattered carelessly by a giant hand. In some places the cavities beneath the house-sized boulders are large caverns.	Sightseeing, colour photography. Tennant Creek: two hotels, camping ground. May to October.
ELLERY CREEK GORGE NATIONAL PARK (N.T.) 4,366 acres	W Macdonnell Ranges, about 50 m. W of Alice Springs. *See* map p. 61.	Jagged ranges, cut by a tributary flowing S to Finke River. Severe folding in the rock strata of gorge. Many river gums, shrubs along river, very sparse on hills.	Colourful small gorge, with lush green, white trunked river gums contrasting against dark red rock walls. Usually a large pool in gorge.	Scenic viewing, colour photography. Attractive shady picnic-parking area. At Alice Springs: hotels, motels, caravan parks. June to October.
ELLIOTT PRICE WILDERNESS NATIONAL PARK (S.A.) Approx. 160,000 acres	Far N South Australia, on S shores of Lake Eyre North. Access limited and difficult. Trucks and light aircraft used by scientific expeditions. *See* map p. 64.	Hummocky sand dunes and limestone plains, dry salt lake and saltpans. Desert vegetation including some sparse mulga.	A region of interesting geology. Considerable amount of wildlife, depending upon the nature of the season. Birds prolific at times: Orange Chats, Crimson Chats, Blue-and-white Wrens, White-backed Swallows. Red Kangaroos. A region of scientific interest, for the creatures which have adapted to dry salt lake environment.	Geology scientific expeditions. Wildlife observation. Hotel at William Creek.
EMILY and JESSIE GAP SCENIC RESERVES (N.T.) 1,718 acres	In Macdonnell Ranges, 7 m. SE. of Alice Springs, along dirt roads. *See* map p. 61.	A jagged ridge of the Macdonnell Ranges, cut by tributaries flowing S to Todd River. Sparse vegetation on rocky ridge, large gums along river.	Two gaps (short gorges), Emily Gap nearest to Alice Springs, Jessie Gap a short distance E. Some Aboriginal paintings, very symbolic type, typical of region.	Scenic touring, short walks through gaps. Colour photography. At Alice Springs: hotels, motels, caravan parks. No facilities at reserves. June to October. Wildflowers best July to September.
GLEN HELEN NATIONAL PARK (N.T.) 954 acres	W Macdonnell Ranges, 81 m. W of Alice Springs, along dirt road. *See* map p. 61.	A jagged red-rock ridge of the ranges, river gorge.	Strongly coloured cliffs, reflected in clear, still pools of Finke River; white-trunked Ghost Gums.	Scenic sightseeing, magnificent colour photography opportunities, painting. Observing birdlife. Alice Springs, otherwise bush camping. June to October.
GREEN VALLEY SCENIC RESERVE (N.T.) 1,239 acres	E Macdonnell Ranges, 54 m. E of Alice Springs via Corroborree Rock, Ross River. Dirt road.	Rugged ranges, gums along watercourses.	Wide gorge with greenery of Ghost gums, scrub, strongly coloured rock walls, pools after good winter rains.	Sightseeing, colour photography. Picnicking. Limited tourist accommodation in self-contained cabins at Ross River (7 m.), otherwise Alice Springs. June to October.
KING'S CANYON (Proposed National Park) (N.T.) 14,720 acres (Acquisition proceeding)	Central Australia, in George Gill Range, by road 231 m. WSW. of Alice Springs, via Henbury, Wallara Ranch. Or from Ayers Rock, via Angas Downs, Wallara Ranch. 4-wheel-drive last 60 m. *See* map p. 61.	Rough red sandstone ranges. Sparse vegetation on heights, Mulga and desert oak on red plains, with many flowering annuals after good rains. Large gums along watercourses.	A canyon ringed by smooth-walled, red cliffs several hundred feet high. Dense growth of vegetation (white-trunked gums, wildflower shrubs) along canyon floor. Pools after rains. Above cliffs is an area where rock is fantastically eroded by the wind into caves, sculptured shapes. Many wildflowers to be seen along way if good rains have previously fallen.	Sightseeing, walking and climbing in gorge. Colour photography. Observing wildflowers, desert birdlife. Motel and caravan-camping ground at Wallara Ranch. July–September for wildflowers after good rains, otherwise June–October.
ORMISTON GORGE AND POUND NATIONAL PARK (N.T.) 19,520 acres	W Macdonnell Ranges, 72 m. W of Alice Springs. *See* map p. 61.	A gorge on a tributary of the Finke River, near Mt Sonder. Ghost gums, river gums along the river, elsewhere sparse mulga scrub, porcupine grass.	One of central Australia's most spectacular canyons, lower cliffs of deep purple-reds, white bars of rock in the river bed, higher walls of red and ochre. On the west, above the gorge, a cliff rising to tremendous heights. Through the gorge is Ormiston Pound, a basin-like valley surrounded by rocky ranges, peaks.	Scenic sightseeing, rugged walking through gorge and pound. Unequalled opportunities for colour photography. Camping area below gorge, but few facilities. Alice Springs has nearest hotels, motels and caravan parks. June to October.

NAME OF PARK	LOCALITY ACCESS	TOPOGRAPHY VEGETATION TYPES	FEATURES OF INTEREST	ACTIVITIES ACCOMMODATION SEASON TO VISIT
PALM VALLEY FAUNA AND FLORA RESERVE (N.T.) 113,000 acres	W Macdonnells, from Alice Springs via Hermannsburg (76 m. W), then 12 m. S. Last 5 or 6 m. along sandy river bed, 4-wheel-drive essential. See map p. 61.	A long twisting gorge where Finke River has cut between James and Krichauff Ranges for about 100 m. Many tributary gorges. Gums, relic palms along river bed.	Reserve takes name from *Livistona mariae* palms. Palm Valley of tourists is on a tributary of main gorge, where palms are most numerous. Many high, spectacular red-rock cliffs. Long stretch of water down-river at Boggy Hole. Valley discovered 1872 by explorer Ernest Giles. Considerable variety of wildlife.	Sightseeing, colour photography. For the more adventurous, a long rewarding walk (up to 30 m.) down the Finke's gorge towards Boggy Hole. Some accommodation for bus tour visitors, otherwise bush camping, or at Alice Springs. June to October.
SERPENTINE GORGE NATIONAL PARK 2,400 acres	W Macdonnell Ranges, about 60 m. W of Alice Springs. See map p. 61.	Jagged ranges, with very sparse vegetation on heights. Mulga scrub on flats, gums along watercourses.	Colourful small gorge, containing a pool of water if sufficient winter rains.	Sightseeing, colour photography. At Alice Springs. June to October.
SIMPSON DESERT NATIONAL PARKS (QLD. and S.A.) Queensland: 1,250,000 acres. S.A.: 1,718,800 acres	Qld.: SW. corner, joining N.T. and S.A. borders. Access via Birdsville, parks eastern boundary being about 20 m. W of that town. S.A.: joins Qld. park, access from Birdsville track difficult, 4-wheel-drive required. See map p. 64.	Mostly sandhill desert. Sand-ridges up to 100 ft high running unbroken full length of park, SE. to NW., possibly 100 m. long 300 yards to ½ mile apart. Vegetation of sparse grass, low scrub, some trees on eastern fringe.	A valuable wildlife sanctuary, and not without scenic grandeur. Lush growth follows occasional rains, desert becomes a profusion of wildflowers, great influx of birds. Protects desert animals whose habitat elsewhere has been destroyed by cattle and sheep: hopping mice, marsupial mice, Rabbit-eared Bandicoot. Prolific birdlife after rain—Orange Chats, Crimson Chats. Sand dunes of this waterless region have proved great barrier to east-west crossings. Should be entered only by well-equipped parties. It is possible to explore more easily the fringe country, west of Birdsville and along the Alice Springs–S.A. railway.	Observing desert life. Camping, but must be well-equipped. This can be very attractive country if winter rains penetrate. Best season usually July–September. Summers dangerously hot and dry.
SIMPSON'S GAP NATIONAL PARK (N.T.) 640 acres	W Macdonnell Range, 14 m. W of Alice Springs. See map p. 61.	A gap in the rough rock ridges of the ranges. Flats between ranges carry scattered Ghost Gums, shrubs.	Permanent waterhole and attractive scenery in the Chewing Range. Good display of flowering annuals after winter rains. (N.T. Nat. Parks Board has tried to have whole station of 75,520 acres made a national park, it being too small to be a profitable cattle run. The area would be stocked with many native animals, and would be great tourist attraction for Alice Springs. But the Commonwealth Government has not been interested.)	Accommodation: Alice Springs. June to October.
STANDLEY CHASM, (Proposed National Park) (N.T.) 2,400 acres	W Macdonnell Ranges, 32 m. W from Alice Springs. See map p. 61.	Rugged range with sparse vegetation, gums along creek beds.	A very deep, vertical-walled crevice, into which sun penetrates for a very short time to light the 200 ft high walls a fiery red. Proposed as a national park, but this opposed by Northern Territory Director of Welfare.	Sightseeing, colour photography, picnicking. At Alice Springs. June to October.
TANAMI DESERT WILDLIFE SANCTUARY (N.T.) 9,300,000 acres	Desert of N central Australia, 200 m. NW. of Alice Springs. Access by track from Alice Springs to Halls Creek, W.A., a route now taken by some tourist buses. See map p. 96.	Flat or undulating country, mainly covered with harsh spinifex, scattered shrubs and stunted trees. Low rocky ridges, shallow dry watercourses.	This vast reserve was set aside to conserve central Australian wildlife; its harsh spinifex had no grazing value. Contains about 7 species of Kangaroos, Wallabies. Hare-wallaby and Rabbit-eared Bandicoot survive here, though rare or extinct in most other places. Numerous desert birds, such as the Rufous-crowned Emu-wren. The area has many reptiles. Wildflowers appear when rains penetrate this far inland.	June to October. Visitors need to be well equipped, make enquiries about prevailing conditions, advise police of route.
TREPHINA GORGE NATIONAL PARK (N.T.) 4,378 acres	E Macdonnell Ranges, 46 m. E from Alice Springs. See map p. 61.	A jagged ridge of the ranges, very sparse vegetation on heights, many large eucalypts along the river bed.	A large gorge cut by a tributary of the Todd River. Dark red cliffs, rising several hundred feet in places, white-trunked ghost gums, with lush green foliage, attractive contrast of light and colour, against dark gorge walls.	Scenic sightseeing; walking up sandy river bed through gorge. Colour photography. Picnicking. Alice Springs: hotels, motels, caravan parks. No facilities at Trephina Gorge. June to October.

NATURE RESERVES

NAME, LOCATION	FEATURES OF INTEREST
Corroboree Rock Scenic Reserve (N.T.) 18 acres.	A remarkable wall-like ridge, composed of dolerite beds tipped by past earth movements to stand on edge. Rectangular joint planes broke the dolerite into great blocks. At one point where the wall is only one layer thick a block has fallen out to leave a 'window'. The site is said to have been important to the Aborigines.
Heavitree Gap Police Station (N.T.) 1 acre. Situated at Heavitree Gap, Alice Springs.	Historic building of first settlement times; now being restored to show its original features.
Henbury Meteorites Reserve (N.T.) 40 acres. Situated approx. 8 m. W of Stuart Highway, the turnoff (to White Horse Gap and Wallara Ranch also) being 3 m. S of Henbury, which is 72 m. S of Alice Springs.	Meteor craters comprising three large craters close together, also ten smaller ones.
Other Reserves Administered by the N.T. Reserves Board.	Attack Creek Memorial (2r 7p), Central Mt Stuart Memorial (2r 7½p), John Flynn's Grave, (3r 13p), John Flynn's Memorial Monument (1 acre), Kintore Caves Reserve (1,046 acres).

SOME BIRDS OF 'THE CENTRE'

Emu (*Dromaius novae-hollandiae*); plains and open forest.
Wedgetail Eagle (*Aquila audax*); inland plains, forests, ranges.
Square-tailed Kite (*Lophoictinia isura*); inland plains and watercourses.
Black-breasted Buzzard (*Hamirosta melanosterna*); inland plains.
Grey Falcon (*Falco hypoleucus*); plains and inland ranges.
Little Quail (*Turnix velox*); in coveys on open plains.
Red-kneed Dotterel (*Erythrogonys cinctus*); margins of rivers and lagoons.
Banded Stilt (*Cladorhynchus leucocephalus*); swamps, tidal flats, salt lakes.
White-headed Stilt (*Himantopus leucocephalus*); shallow lakes and swamps.
Plumed Pigeon (*Lophophaps plumifera*); stony spinifex country.
Western Plumed Pigeon (*Lophophaps ferruginea*); rocky, spinifex.
Rose-throated Parrot (*Polytelis alexandrae*); grasslands and spinifex.
Port Lincoln Parrot (*Barnardius zonarius*); watercourse gums, scrublands.
Naretha Parrot (*Psephotus narethae*); scrub on Western Nullarbor.
Scarlet-chested Parrot (*Neophema splendida*); plains and low scrub. Rare.
Budgerigar (*Melopsittacus undulatus*); open country with occasional trees.
Night Parrot (*Geopsittacus occidentalis*); spinifex, samphire, or sandstone ranges. Rare.
Black-eared Cuckoo (*Misocalius oseulans*); scattered through interior. Rare.
Cave Owl (*Tyto novae-hollandiae troughtoni*); caves of the Nullarbor.
Crow (*Corvus cecilae*); ranges and inland scrub.
Little Crow (*Corvus bennetti*); inland scrubs.
Mudlark (*Grallina cyanoleuca*); open areas, usually near water.
Grey Butcher-bird (*Cracticus torquatus*); open forest and scrub.
White-browed Tree-creeper (*Climacteris affinis*); scrub-lands.
White-browed Babbler (*Pomatostomus superciliosus*); scrub and open forest.
Nullarbor Quail-thrush (*Cinclosoma alisteri*); open plains and low scrub.
Spinifex Bird (*Eremiornis carteri*); spinifex and low scrub.
Rusty Field-wren (*Calamanthus isabellinus*); heath and low scrub.
Western Grass-wren (*Amytornis textilis*); saltbush, spinifex, low scrub.

Dusky Grass-wren (*Amytornis purnelli*); porcupine-grass on ranges.
Turquoise Wren (*Malurus callainus*); low scrub, gorges of ranges.
Purple-backed Wren (*Malurus assimilis*); low inland scrub.
Whitlock Thornbill (*Acanthiza whitlocki*); Nullarbor Plains.
Robust Thornbill (*Acanthiza robustirostris*); mulga scrubs.
Samphire Thornbill (*Acanthiza iredalei*); low bushes and samphire flats.
Yellow Weebill (*Smicrornis flavescens*); foliage of river gums and mallee.
Western Whiteface (*Aphelocephala castaneiventris*); open scrub-lands.
Chestnut-breasted Whiteface (*Aphelocephala pectoralis*); open scrub-lands.
Rufous Grass-wren (*Amytornis whitei*); spinifex.
Eyrean Grass-wren (*Amytornis goyderi*); cane grass near Lake Eyre.
Willie Wagtail (*Rhipidura leucophrys*); open country, usually near water.
Masked Wood-swallow (*Artamus personatus*); open forest and scrub.
Little Wood-swallow (*Artamus minor*); open country and ranges.
White-fronted Honeyeater (*Gliciphila albifrons*); low scrubs and dry heaths.
Grey Honeyeater (*Lacustroica whitei*); mulga.
Singing Honeyeater (*Meliphaga virescens*); scrub and open forest.
Grey-headed Honeyeater (*Meliphaga keartlandi*); stunted eucalypts and scrub.
Yellow-fronted Honeyeater (*Meliphaga plumula*); mallee and other eucalypts.
Yellow-throated Miner (*Myzantha flavigula*); open forest and scrub.
Crested Bellbird (*Oreoica gutturalis*); open forest, mallee and mulga.
Wedgebill (*Sphenostoma cristatum*); mulga scrub.
Crimson Chat (*Epthianura tricolor*); open plains with low bushes.
Orange Chat (*Epthianura aurifrons*); samphire flats.
Desert Chat (Gibber-bird) (*Ashbyia lovensis*); stony 'gibber' plains.
Mistletoe Bird (*Dicaeum hirundinaceum*); eucalypts, such as river gums.
Painted Finch (*Emblema picta*); spinifex and grasslands.
Zebra Finch (*Taeniopygia guttata*); grasslands and scrub.

SOME FURRED ANIMALS OF CENTRAL AUSTRALIAN PARKS

Spiny Anteater (*Tachyglossus aculeatus*); active in daylight; scrub and rocky areas.
Flat-headed Marsupial Mouse (*Planigale ingrami*); is smallest marsupial; savannah woodland, grassland.
Southern Planigale (*P. tenuirostris*); nocturnal, insectivorous; western Qld., N.S.W.
Fat-tailed Marsupial Mouse (*Sminthopsis crassicaudata*); insectivorous; savannah woodland.
Large Desert Sminthopsis (*S. macrura*); scrublands, sandhills, porcupine grass.
Stripe-headed Sminthopsis (*S. larapinta*); burrowing; north-central Australia.
Hairy-footed Sminthopsis (*S. hirtipes*); in region of N.T.–S.A. border.
Jerboa Marsupial Mouse (*Antechinomys spenceri*); desert grassland, spinifex, saltbush.
Eastern Jerboa (*A. laniger*); a smaller species, insectivorous, nocturnal.
Red-tailed Phascogale or Wambenger (*Phascogale calura*); nocturnal; solitary hunter in treetops.
Crest-tailed Marsupial Mouse (*Dasycercus cristicaudata*); central N.T., W.A. stony and spinifex deserts.
Western Crest-tail Marsupial Mouse (*D. blythi*); a carnivore; Great Sandy Desert, W.A.
Byrne's Marsupial Mouse (*D. byrnei*); a small carnivore of western Qld., Simpson Desert.
Fat-tailed Phascogale (*Pseudantechinus macdonnellensis*); stony deserts of north-west and N.T.
Western Native Cat (*Dasurinus geoffroyi*); western interior, formerly in N.S.W., Qld., S.A., N.T.
Rusty Numbat or Banded Anteater (*Myrmecobius fasciatus rufus*); Everard Ranges, S.A.
Marsupial Mole (*Notoryctes typhlops*); rarely seen; burrows in sand-ridge deserts.
North-west Marsupial Mole (*N. caurinus*); Great Sandy Desert, north-west Australia.
Desert Bandicoot (*Parameles eremiana*); nocturnal; southern N.T., sandhills, scrub plains.
Bilby, or Rabbit-eared Bandicoot (*Thylacomys lagotis*); interior W.A., Simpson Desert.
Lesser Bilby (*T. minor*); nocturnal; Lake Eyre–Simpson Desert, burrowing.

Pig-footed Bandicoot (*Chaeropus ecaudatus*); possibly extinct; interior W.A., S.A., southern N.T.
Hairy-nosed Wombat (*Lasiorhinus latifrons*); Nullarbor, in warrens under limestone.
Brush-tailed Possum (*Trichosaurus vulpeca*); in hollows of trees along watercourses.
Brush-tailed Rat-kangaroo (*Bettongia penicillata*); nocturnal, rare; western Tanami area.
Leseur's P.at-kangaroo (*B. leseur*); rare; far interior W.A., N.T., S.A., in burrows.
Desert Rat-kangaroo (*Caloprymnus campestris*); Simpson Desert, Qld., S.A., sandridges and stony plains.
Brown Hare-wallaby (*Lagorchestes conspicillatus*); Macdonnell Ranges, N.T.
Bridled Nail-tailed Wallaby (*Onychogalea fraenata*); rare; western plains, scrub, Qld., N.S.W.
Crescent Nail-tailed Wallaby (*O. lunata*); rare; southern N.T. and W.A., north-west S.A.
Yellow-footed Rock-Wallaby (*Petrogale xanthopus*); Flinders Ranges, south-west Qld., in ranges.
Brush-tailed Rock-Wallaby (*P. lateralis*); Macdonnell Ranges, and north-west W.A.
Wallaroo, or Euro (*Macropus robustus*); rocky ranges, interior of Qld., N.S.W., S.A., N.T., W.A.
Red Kangaroo (*M. rufus*); largest kangaroo, found on all inland shrub and grass plains.
Grey Kangaroo (*M. maior*); western Qld. and N.S.W., open woodlands.
Dingo (*Canis antarctica*); throughout this region.
Mitchell's Hopping-Mouse (*Notomys mitchelli*); a rodent, nocturnal, burrowing.
Long-tailed Hopping-Mouse (*N. longicaudatus*); from interior of W.A. to western N.S.W.
Short-tailed Hopping-Mouse (*N. amplus*); rarely recorded; vicinity of N.T.–S.A. border.
Northern Hopping-Mouse (*N. alexis*); wide distribution: Tanami to interior W.A., Qld., S.A.
Neck-pouched Hopping-Mouse (*Ascopharynx cervinus*); sandy country, S.A. and central Aust.

THE FAR NORTH

Bustard or Plains Turkey

NAME OF PARK	LOCALITY ACCESS	TOPOGRAPHY VEGETATION TYPES	FEATURES OF INTEREST	ACTIVITIES ACCOMMODATION SEASON TO VISIT
BARRON FALLS NATIONAL PARK (QLD.) 7,000 acres	19 m. from Cairns. Spectacular railway journey from Cairns to Kuranda up the Barron Gorge. Approach also by Kuranda Highway. *See* map p. 104.	Waterfall on the Barron River, drops 800 ft into Barron Gorge.	Unfortunately the falls are worth seeing only during the wet season when great volumes of water still plunge into the huge gorge. The Tinaroo Dam holds back the Barron River waters for irrigation purposes, and at the falls most of the normal flow is diverted for hydroelectric power generation.	Photography, views of majestic Barron Gorge. Cairns (hotels, motels, caravan parks); Kuranda, near head of falls (hotels). To see the falls at their best, the wet season January–March.
BELLENDEN-KER NATIONAL PARK (QLD.) 80,140 acres	Mt Bartle Frere may be approached from E, via Babinda on Bruce Highway, 18 m. N of Innisfail; from W, branch off Bruce Highway at Gordonvale, travel on Gillies Highway past Lake Eacham, through Peeramon, then continue on Peeramon–Boonjie Road. Either way, roads terminate some miles from foot of mountain. *See* map p. 104.	The Bellenden-Ker Range, culminating in Mt Bartle Frere (5,275 ft), highest mountain in Queensland. Upland tropical rainforest vegetation.	Magnificent tropical rainforest, which varies in character from lowest levels to mountain top heights. Principally a sanctuary for Queensland's rainforest birds, marsupials. Some species found usually only at high altitudes—Golden Bowerbird, Green Possum, Tree Kangaroo, Lemur-like Possum.	Scenic viewing: the jungle-clad mountain is a conspicuous backdrop to the landscape between Innisfail and Cairns, and from points on Atherton Tableland, Gillies Highway. Bushwalking, climbing to summit. Photography. Accommodation at Innisfail (hotels, motels, caravan parks); Cairns (hotels, motels, caravan parks); Atherton (hotels, caravan parks); at all towns on main highway. April to November. Summers hot, wet, very humid.
BRAMPTON ISLAND NATIONAL PARK (QLD.) 1,280 acres	722 m. from Brisbane via Bruce Highway to Mackay the mainland port for Brampton. Brampton I. 20 m. NE. of Mackay: frequent launch services or charter air services. *See* map p. 120.	One of the Cumberland Group in Whitsunday Passage. Mountainous. Vegetation of Hoop Pine scrub on headlands and hillsides, with some rainforest species, eucalypts in places.	A number of white, sandy beaches. Coconut Palm groves. Coral reefs. Lookout point on Brampton Peak. Wildlife includes megapode birds and other birds. Boats available for hire, including glass-bottom type for reef viewing. Well developed resort.	Reef exploration, swimming, walking (6 m. of tracks to scenic features). Short launch cruises included in resort tariff. Evening entertainment organized at tourist resort. Tennis courts. Hotel with lodge units. (Also shop, bank, other services on island.) May to November.
BROOKING GORGE (Proposed National Park) (W.A.) Proposal by Australian Academy of Science Committee on National Park and Nature Reserves W.A.	Kimberleys, far N of W.A., 10 m. from Fitzroy Crossing, on Brooking Station. As this is private property, permission, directions, should be sought. Gorge not well known even to Fitzroy Crossing people (1968). Rough dirt track. *See* map p. 88.	Limestone ranges similar to those at Geikie Gorge. Dense growth of eucalypts, Leichardt Pine, Pandanus, fig, and other trees along watercourse. Range tops barren.	A long, narrow gorge eroded by Brooking Creek at SE. extremity of the Oscar Range. Large pool of permanent water. Abundant wildlife. Brooking Station is maintained by its owners as a wildlife sanctuary, and shooting is prohibited. Many Brolgas, Bustards can be seen on the broad savannah plains of the station en route to the gorge.	Hotel at Fitzroy Crossing. May to November. Summer hot, wet, area subject to flooding, roads impassable.
CHILLAGOE and MUNGANA CAVES NATIONAL PARKS (QLD.) 4,732 acres in nine separate areas	N Queensland, about 150 m. W of Cairns, via Mareeba and Dimbulah. Gravel road last 30 m. *See* map p. 104.	Rugged castle-like limestone outcrops many square miles in extent. Caves are in and below these limestone 'towers' and 'castles'.	Royal Arch Caves, Donor and Tower of London Caves, Jubilee and Piano Caves, Cathedral Cave, Eclipse Cave, Ryan Imperial Cave, Markham Cave, Royal Archway Cave, Geck Cave, Spring Cave. Some caves of great size—Royal Arch 170 ft long, 100 ft wide, 40 ft high. Some caves well decorated with stalactite and stalagmites in colours from pure white to light and dark brown, green in one cave (no artificial coloured lighting). Aboriginal paintings in some shallow caves.	Touring caves. Several hotels, camping grounds at Chillagoe. Caravans best left at Atherton, Cairns or Mareeba (caravan parks). Overseer at Chillagoe. Guided tours of caves can be arranged every day of week except Tuesday and Saturday, 9 a.m. or 1.30 p.m., Dirt road to Chillagoe often closed during wet season.
COBOURG PENINSULA SANCTUARY (N.T.) 505,600 acres	Northernmost point of Northern Territory, a large peninsula. Access by air or sea only— enquiries to Chief Inspector of Wildlife, N.T. Administration, Darwin: N.T. 5790. *See* map p. 96.	Peninsula with rather low hills, cliffs along northern shores. Savannah woodland and tropical monsoon forest, mangrove swamps along southern coast.	The northernmost part of Australia other than the top of Cape York Peninsula, Cobourg experiences a tropical monsoonal climate, 50–60 in. rainfall. Was an Aboriginal reserve prior to 1961. Balinese cattle (Bantangs) run wild on peninsula. Many interesting tropical birds, marsupials. A refuge for wildlife, not a tourist attraction at present. Historical: Victoria Settlement, Port Essington, on Cobourg Peninsula. (1838–49).	Wildlife observation. Photography. Nearest town Darwin, about 100 m. Resident Ranger at Cobourg. May to October.
CONWAY NATIONAL PARK (QLD.) 48,060 acres	From Brisbane, via Bruce Highway to Proserpine, then E via Airlie Beach to Shute Harbour, which is surrounded by the hills of the park. *See* map p. 120.	Coastal ranges with tropical rainforest (including lowland rainforest) and mixed coastal woodland.	Rugged ranges (to 1,850 ft), densely forested, dropping steeply to island-studded sea. Forms western side of picturesque Long Island Sound, and encloses Shute Harbour and its islands. Gateway	Sightseeing, cruises by launch along coast, to islands, outer barrier reef. Fishing, photography, bird observing. Small camping area in park near Shute Harbour. Tourist resorts on islands. Caravan parks and other accommodation at Airlie Beach (14 m.

NAME OF PARK	LOCALITY ACCESS	TOPOGRAPHY VEGETATION TYPES	FEATURES OF INTEREST	ACTIVITIES ACCOMMODATION SEASON TO VISIT
			to the Whitsunday Island group (more than 100 islands). Views from coastal hills (some lower points accessible by road). Many birds, of rainforest and mangrove habitats.	E of Proserpine). April to November.
CRYSTAL CREEK (Mt Spec) NATIONAL PARK (QLD.) 17,850 acres	Tropical N Queensland. Follow Bruce Highway 42 m. N of Townsville, turn off W 13 m. to township of Paluma, and park. *See* map p. 104.	Centred upon Crystal Creek, and including heights of Mt Spec (3,150 ft). Upland tropical rainforest and hardwood forest.	Magnificent panoramic views from heights, to coast, offshore islands, canefields. Cool, bracing air on summit. Interesting rainforest. Walking tracks beside creek, through bush and rainforest.	Park is a feature of scenic drives by car and tourist coach from Townsville. Sightseeing, walking. Picnic grounds at 'The Loop'. Camping only, at park; accommodation at Paluma, ½ m. from park, or at Townsville, Ingham. May to November.
DAMPIER LAND (Proposed National Park) (W.A.) About 300,000 acres. Proposal by Aust. Academy of Science, control being sought by W.A. National Parks Board (1968 annual report).	Kimberley region, far NW. Western Australia, between Broome and Beagle Bay. Approx. 40 to 60 m. due N of Broome. Access difficult.	Rather flat, sandy. 'Pindan' vegetation, of tall grasses under compact *Acacia* scrub, scattered Bloodwood trees.	Required principally as a fauna-flora sanctuary, a typical sample of Kimberley littoral savannah land. Wildlife of region not well known, but known to include Nail-tailed Wallaby, Sandy or Agile Wallaby, and Rabbit-eared Bandicoot which is now very rare over most of Australia.	Observing interesting fauna and flora. At Broome (hotels, guest house, caravan and camping park). Winter months. Summer hot, wet, roads impassable.
DRYSDALE RIVER AREA (Proposed National Park) (W.A.) About 1,000,000 acres. Proposal by Aust. Academy of Science Committee on National Parks and Nature Reserves (W.A.). W.A. National Parks Board seeking park in this area (1968 annual report).	Kimberley region, far N Western Australia, on Drysdale River, W to Carson River (14°35' to 15°17' S, 126°32' to 127°12' E.). Access extremely difficult, nearest town Wyndham 100 m., no roads.	Very rugged sandstone country, also basalt hills, flats, isolated red-soil, black-soil pockets. Savannah woodlands.	Most spectacular feature is the Morgan Falls, a series of falls, one 80 ft high, one 200 ft, many smaller falls. Native paintings in waterworn caverns. Perpendicular-walled sandstone gorge below falls, with multi-coloured walls, below which creek is a blue ribbon fringed with tall white gums, Cajuputs, pandanus. In places gorges are 300 ft deep. Area scientifically valuable because it is undamaged by cattle or buffaloes which have caused great ecological upset in N.T., will eventually be valuable as tourist attraction. C.S.I.R.O. report states region unsuitable for cattle industry.	Scenic viewing. Photography. Wyndham, 100 m. May to October. Summers very hot, wet, with most roads impassable.
DRYSDALE RIVER SANCTUARY (N.T.) 544,900 acres	NW. Northern Territory, W of mouth of Daly River. 82 m. S of Darwin turn off Stuart Highway onto unsealed road 75 m. to Daly River station, is nearest approach.	Coastal lowlands, swamps. Tropical tussock grasslands, tropical layered forest.	A sanctuary for tropical wildlife. Entry to Northern Territory sanctuaries restricted to authorised persons. Enquiries to Chief Inspector of Wildlife, Animal Industry and Agricultural Branch of Northern Territory Administration, Darwin.	No accommodation at sanctuary. Nearest town Adelaide River, 85 m. (hotel, camping sites). Inaccessible during 'the wet'.
DUNK ISLAND NATIONAL PARK (QLD.) 1,805 acres	In N Qld. 3 m. off coast opposite Tully, and 120 m. N of Townsville. Access by light aircraft from Tully, Innisfail, Townsville, Cairns. Regular launch service from Clump Point Jetty, E of Tully. *See* map p. 104.	Luxuriant rainforest, also open forest. Coastline on seaward side rough. Sandy beaches on mainland side. Picnic facilities for day visitors.	One of least spoiled of reef resorts. Golden beaches, exquisite coral gardens, fine palm trees. Coastal scenery. Named by Cook. Once had large Aboriginal population. Some caves of interior have paintings. Many turtles visit island November–December. More than 90 species of birds recorded.	Swimming, fishing, reef exploration. Observing birdlife. Walking: 5½ m. formed tracks to points of interest. Cruises and fishing trips by launch may be arranged. On island, outside park area. Hotel with suites and family units. (Enquire Queensland Tourist Bureau). May to November.
EDITH FALLS NATIONAL PARK (N.T.) 402 acres	On Stuart Highway about 35 m. N of Katherine. Just north of where highway crosses Edith River, turn E, follow rough dirt road about 18 m. *See* map p. 96.	The western escarpment of West Arnhem Land highlands, where Edith River drops to lower plains to join the Daly River. Lush vegetation along river gorge.	A series of beautiful small waterfalls and clear deep, pandanus-fringed pools which shelter fresh-water crocodiles. Aboriginal paintings.	Sightseeing, walking, photography, swimming, picnicing. At Katherine. Caravan parks at Low-level reserve, and in town, also hotels. May to October.
EUNGELLA NATIONAL PARK (QLD.) 122,600 acres	50 m. W of Mackay, on the Clarke Range. Easy access by good road along Pioneer River valley, via Finch Hatton, Dalrymple Heights; or by train to Netherdale 44 m., then by road 5 m. *See* map p.120.	Extremely rugged ranges, including heights of Mt Dalrymple (4,190 ft), Mt William (4,082 ft), Mt David (3,900 ft). Highland tropical rainforest, tropical woodland.	Dense vine jungles, palm groves. Magnificent views over Pioneer Valley from the Sky Window, Bevan's Lookout, The Summit, Dalrymple Heights. Falls in Finch Hatton Gorge. Huge rainforest trees, tropical ferns, flowers. Prolific birdlife, animals including Platypus in Broken River. Eungella means 'land of cloud'.	Scenic viewing along roads and from high lookouts. Walking on good tracks through rainforest. Observing birds, vegetation. Photography. Picnicking. No accommodation in park. Caravan, camping, picnic area at Broken River. Hotel at Dalrymple Heights adjoining park. Caravan park at Finch Hatton, at foot of range (road up range very steep for caravan towing). Forestry Department Overseer. May to November.
GEIKIE GORGE NATIONAL PARK (W.A.) 7,750 acres	Kimberleys, far N of Western Australia, just 10 m. off main Darwin-to-Perth road about half-way between Halls Creek and Derby. Turn-off to gorge is at Fitzroy Crossing township. *See* map p. 88.	Exposed Devonian reef limestone at junction of Oscar and Geikie ranges. Eucalypts, pandanus along river, hills barren.	A wide gorge cut by the Fitzroy, one of the major northern rivers. Coloured cliffs, honeycombed by caves at water level, drop to the water. Permanent water along river in gorge throughout dry season: freshwater crocodiles (protected), barrumundi. Though 200 m. from sea, gorge contains sawfish, stingrays.	Sightseeing, best by rowing boat up gorge, otherwise on foot from gorge entrance. Colour photography. Camping at gorge entrance (Picnic areas, barbecue fireplaces), hotel at Fitzroy Crossing. Honorary rangers resident Brooking Station near gorge. May to November. Summer hot, wet—gorge and river crossing flooded, roads impassable.
GREEN ISLAND NATIONAL PARK (QLD.) Island 32 acres, park portion 17 acres	Far N Queensland, about 18 m. NE. of Cairns, on the Great Barrier Reef. Daily launch service from Cairns.	A true coral cay, rising but a few feet above high tide level, and surrounded by reefs. Dense tree cover of *Pandanus*, casuarinas, White Cedar.	Extensive reefs with colourful corals, bright reef fish. Inspection by glass-bottom boats, underwater observatory. Reef life can be seen in Marineland aquariums; films and slides at Reef Theatre. Many sea birds on reefs, shores, forest.	Reef exploration, swimming, (spearfishing not permitted), walking (tracks around and across island). Evening entertainments. Coral Cay Hotel (suites, individual lodges). April–November. Launch access may be curtailed at times during summer cyclone season.

NAME OF PARK	LOCALITY ACCESS	TOPOGRAPHY VEGETATION TYPES	FEATURES OF INTEREST	ACTIVITIES ACCOMMODATION SEASON TO VISIT
HINCHINBROOK ISLAND NATIONAL PARK (QLD.) 97,232 acres	N Queensland, about midway between Townsville and Innisfail. No direct transport, but arrangements can be made for launch access from Orpheus Island, or to disembark from cruises from Townsville past island. *See* map p. 104.	Mountainous, extremely rugged ranges (Mt Bowen 3,650 ft). Tropical rainforest, coastal woodlands. Extensive mangroves swamp. Hinchinbrook Channel on mainland side.	The largest of Queensland island national parks; 22 m. long, 10 to 15 m. wide. Mountain, jungle and waterfall scenery; coastline with numerous small coves. Separated from mainland by beautiful Hinchinbrook Channel. Island mountain scenery (and waterfalls after heavy rain) visible from Bruce Highway.	Exploration of magnificent coast by boat. Extremely rugged bushwalking into the largely unexplored, trackless, mountainous interior of island. Fishing. No settlement or accommodation on island, no facilities. Bush camping only, fresh water at Zoe Bay, on eastern side of island. At 'The Haven' is fresh creek, sandy beach, picnic area. May to November.
HOOK ISLAND NATIONAL PARK (QLD.) 12,800 acres	N Queensland coast, E of Proserpine, and immediately S of Hayman Island tourist resort. May be visited from resorts on other islands. *See* map p. 120.	A large, mountainous island. Highest point Hook Peak, 1,478 ft. Tropical rainforest and mixed coastal woodland.	Rugged rock coasts broken by beaches. Several deep, sheltered inlets: Nara Inlet, Maona Inlet. Coral reefs on parts of coast.	Launches cruising the waterways of the Whitsunday group, its beaches, reef. Its rough, jungle-clad interior is largely unexplored, a challenge to adventurous bushwalkers. A sanctuary for wildlife. Accommodation on other island resorts. May to November.
JOURAMA FALLS NATIONAL PARK (QLD.) 2,360 acres	N Queensland, just W of Bruce Highway, about 22 m. S of Ingham (enquire from Ingham Forestry Office). Last 2 or 3 m. on foot. *See* map p. 104.	Rough hills just north of Mt Spec (Seaview Range). Vegetation of tropical woodland type, some rainforest species in gullies.	Jourama Falls, a series of waterfalls and cascades dropping over salmon-coloured rock amid lush greenery, creek flowing among huge, water-smoothed boulders.	Bushwalking to scenic points of falls. Photography. Accommodation at Ingham: hotels, motels, caravan parks. May to November (falls best after summer rains).
KATHERINE GORGE NATIONAL PARK (N.T.) 56,069 acres	On Katherine River 22 m. E from town of Katherine, which is on the Stuart Highway. 220 m. S of Darwin. *See* map p. 96.	Rugged ranges of the SW. part of the Arnhem Land plateau. Vegetation of tropical woodland, orange-flowered *Euc. miniata* common.	Katherine Gorge is one of the most attractive, grandly proportioned river canyons in Australia. Its beauty results principally from the fact that for most of its length it is filled wall to wall with deep water, so that the coloured cliffs, sky, are reflected in its depths. Wildlife abundant, including freshwater crocodiles, rock wallabies, bowerbirds, parrots. Aboriginal paintings.	Touring gorge by boat: guided tours which, depending upon distance gorge is explored, may take an hour, half-day, day, or several days. Colour photography. Walking: several tracks follow cliff-tops from camping area. Horseback rides. Caravan-camping area in park at gorge mouth; hotels, motels, caravan park at Katherine. May to November.
LAKE BARRINE NATIONAL PARK (QLD.) 1,213 acres	On Atherton Tableland, N Queensland, 38 m. from Cairns by Gillies Highway, which passes through the park.	A deep lake within a crater formed by explosive volcanic eruption. It is at altitude 2,400 ft on the tableland, and surrounded by tropical rainforest.	The crater lake has an average depth of 360 ft, surface area of 256 acres. Abundant birdlife— occasional cassowary seen on roads, tracks. Rifle-bird, Brush Turkey, Whipbird and Tooth-Billed Bowerbird comparatively common.	Walking: four miles of tracks, encircling the lake, passing huge twin Kauri Pines. Swimming. Bird observing, photography. Overnight accommodation, refreshments at lodge beside lake. Also hotels, caravan parks at Cairns, Atherton, Millaa Millaa. April–November.
LAKE EACHAM NATIONAL PARK (QLD.) 1,200 acres	On Atherton Tableland, N Queensland, 47 m. from Cairns via Gillies Highway, and 4 m. from Yungaburra.	An old volcanic crater formed by an explosive eruption. It is at an altitude of 2,450 ft on the tableland, and is surrounded by tropical rainforest.	Lake which now occupies crater is 131 acres in area, has average depth of 480 ft. Sides, of volcanic debris clad in dense rainforest, ferns, drop very steeply to deep blue water. Birdwatchers' paradise—rainforest birds, Rifle-bird, Tooth-billed Bowerbird. Turtle sanctuary.	Walking—main track encircles lake, others lead to Goddard Falls, Vision Falls, Wishing Well. Observing birdlife. Swimming, boating facilities. Picnic grounds, barbecue facilities with outdoor lighting. Kiosk. Caravan parks, hotels at Atherton, Cairns, Millaa Millaa. April to November.
LINDEMAN ISLAND NATIONAL PARK (QLD.) 1,767 acres	42 m. NE. of Mackay which is 722 m. from Brisbane. Direct air service from Mackay, daily except Sunday. Regular launch services from Mackay and Shute Harbour.	Principally an elevated plateau. Mt Oldfield (700 ft). Vegetation mainly open forest (Bloodwood, Ironbark, Poplar Gum, Blue Gum), some tea-tree.	Rough rocky shores broken by beaches. 8 m. of graded walking tracks to scenic features including Coconut Bay, Boat Port, and Mt Oldfield from where 72 other islands can be seen. Main beach at S end.	Launch cruising, coral viewing. Launches available for big-game fishing. Swimming and other water sports. Walking, photography of islands seascape. Tourist accommodation on island. Enquire Queensland Tourist Bureau. May to November.
LONG ISLAND NATIONAL PARK (QLD.) 2,066 acres	SW. side of Whitsunday Passage, off Shute Harbour, about 120 m. E of Proserpine. Access by launch from Shute Harbour.	High, rugged. Luxuriantly forested with dense vine jungle, dotted with Hoop Pine.	Rugged, rocky coastline, broken by good beaches at many points. Separated from mainland (Conway National Park), by the very beautiful Long Island Sound.	Reef exploration, fishing, swimming, bushwalking, photography. Island launch cruises (half-day or full-day). Water ski-ing. Tennis. Two tourist resorts: Happy Bay, hotel suites, cabins. Palm Bay, lodge, cabins. May to November.
MAGNETIC ISLAND NATIONAL PARK (QLD.) 6,260 acres	5 m. from Townsville across Cleveland Bay (Townsville 979 m. N of Brisbane via Bruce Highway). Several launch services daily from Townsville to island. *See* map p. 104.	Mountainous, thickly wooded island. Park covers the central steep, rugged areas. Walking tracks to high points (Sphinx Lookout 1,085 ft, Mt Cook 1,682 ft).	Attractive coastal scenery, rugged, boulder-strewn headlands, high crags. Bays between the headlands, some with coral reefs. Island's name given by Cook in 1770 because he thought island had magnetic ore which affected his compass. Koala colony.	Swimming and other water sports. Reef exploration. Sightseeing around island. Bushwalking. Photography. Island has golf course, bowling green, tennis courts. On island but outside park area: hotels, guest houses, holiday flats. May to November.
MILLSTREAM FALLS NATIONAL PARK (QLD.) 910 acres	N Queensland, reached from Atherton Tableland via Ravenshoe, turn-off into falls 4 m. W of Ravenshoe on road to Mt Garnet. *See* map p. 104.	Towards headwaters of Herbert River, W slopes of Atherton Tableland. Open eucalypt forest.	The falls, though only 60 ft high, are 200 ft wide, and said to be widest in Queensland. Carry a good flow of water all the year, and always quite spectacular. ¾ mile away are the Little Millstream falls (approached from the Tully Falls road on outskirts of Ravenshoe) where a track leads to a swimming pool at the base of the falls; here platypuses have often been seen.	Swimming, walking, picnicking. Photography. Picnic area above main falls, with shed, tables, fireplace. Accommodation at Atherton, Millaa Millaa. Any season. Falls best in March, April, May, after wet season. Summer very hot, wet, humid.

NAME OF PARK	LOCALITY ACCESS	TOPOGRAPHY VEGETATION TYPES	FEATURES OF INTEREST	ACTIVITIES ACCOMMODATION SEASON TO VISIT
MURGANELLA SANCTUARY (N.T.) 72,000 acres	Far N Northern Territory, centred upon Murganella Creek, and located between Cobourg Peninsula and Oenpelli Mission. Access very difficult, no roads. *See map p. 96.*	Low Hills, rising towards south-east. Tropical layered forest, mangroves.	A sanctuary for tropical wildlife. Entry to Northern Territory sanctuaries restricted to authorised persons. Enquiries to Chief Inspector of Wildlife, Animal Industry and Agricultural Branch of Northern Territory Administration, Darwin.	No accommodation. Inaccessible during 'the wet'.
MT ELLIOTT NATIONAL PARK (QLD.) 63,245 acres	N Queensland, between Ayr and Townsville, off Bruce Highway. *See map p. 104.*	Coastal tropical woodland, some upland rainforest.	Rough, high hills. Principally a wildlife sanctuary, rock wallabies and other marsupials, birds.	Rough bushwalking, bird observing. Townsville: many hotels, motels, guest houses. Caravan park. May to November.
MT HYPIPAMEE (THE CRATER) NATIONAL PARK (QLD.) 900 acres	On the Atherton Tableland, N Queensland, about 15 m. S of Atherton and 1½ m. off the Atherton–Ravenshoe highway. *See map p. 104.*	A 'geological oddity' of uncertain origin. It is said not to be of volcanic origin as it has granite sides; no other explanation of its origin. Set in rainforest.	From railed lookout one can gaze down into the crater's depths, 185 ft to dark water, which is 285 ft deep. Shaft measures 200 by 160 ft at water level. Headwaters of Barron River nearby.	Sightseeing at crater, small waterfalls along the Barron River. Walking tracks beneath giant trees carrying huge Staghorns on branches. Picnic–barbecue area on river at Dinner Falls. At Atherton (hotels, caravan parks) or Millaa Millaa (hotels, good caravan park). Very hot, wet, humid from December to April.
MT WINDSOR TABLELAND NATIONAL PARK (QLD.) 139,500 acres	Far N coastal Queensland, about 15 m. inland from coast, to the NW. of Mossman. Access only to fringe areas such as Mossman Gorge, 3 m. from Mossman. *See map p. 104.*	Eastern slopes of the northernmost elevated plateau of the Great Dividing Range. Upland tropical rainforest and tropical woodland. Approximate northern limit of main rainforest area of Queensland.	Magnificent wilderness region: majestic scenic features of Upper Daintree and Adeline Creek Gorges, Adeline Creek Falls. Plateau at elevation 3,500 ft with peaks over 4,000 ft. Wealth of tropical bird and marsupial life.	Sightseeing at such places as are accessible. Rugged bushwalking. Camping only, in park. Motel at Mossman, caravan-camping grounds at Newell, 4 m. from Mossman. May to November, summer being the cyclone season, hot, wet, very humid.
NORTHERN AREA Also called ARNHEM LAND (Proposed National Park) (N.T.) Initially 1,185 sq. mls. Proposed by Northern Territory Reserves Board, but so far blocked by Commonwealth Govt.	W edge of Arnhem Land plateau, adjoining W border of Arnhem Land Aboriginal Reserve. Access via the Jim Jim settlement. *See map p. 96.*	Extremely rugged ranges, blacksoil plains in northern parts towards Alligator Rivers.	Many scenic features, including the Jim Jim falls. Aboriginal cave paintings. Rich in wildlife. The initial proposal by Northern Territory Reserves Board was for a park of 1,185 sq. miles. This was not approved by Commonwealth Minister for Territories, or Northern Territory Administration. It was rejected on the grounds that the area 'might be needed for buffalo leases'. The Board has applied for ever-smaller areas in this region, but 'every effort to acquire suitable areas has met with opposition and frustration'. It would appear that the Commonwealth Government is not interested in preserving the unique features of the region, nor in developing its tourist attractions.	
ORPHEUS ISLAND NATIONAL PARK (QLD.) 3,380 acres	One of islands of Palm Group, 22 m. E of Ingham. Access by road from Ingham 18 m. to Dungeness then by launch to island. Also weekly launch from Townsville, or by air from Townsville.	Rocky, hilly, sparsely vegetated, mainly with eucalypt species including the broad-leaved Poplar Gum.	Excellent sandy beach facing Hazard Point; tourist resort established here.	Swimming and other water sports. Walking. Fishing. At island tourist resort. Enquire Queensland Government Tourist Bureau. May to November.
PALMERSTON NATIONAL PARK (QLD.) 6,315 acres	Situated along the Innisfail–Millaa Millaa section of the Palmerston Highway, beginning 20 m. W of Innisfail, ending 9 m. E of Millaa Millaa. *See map p.104.*	Hilly pass climbing beside the Johnstone River to the heights of the Atherton Tableland. Tropical rainforest.	This scenic journey through magnificent rainforest is unsurpassed for beauty in Australia. Vantage points along highway give views into depths of Johnstone River Gorge. Walking tracks at intervals along highway lead to waterfalls in lush jungle setting. Picnic facilities at Crawfords Lookout, explorer Kennedy's Tree, Goolagan Creek, Henrietta Creek.	Touring along highway through park. (Road is narrow, very winding, in places is almost a tunnel through the jungle; much of its beauty would be destroyed by excessive widening or straightening). Walking, to falls, etc., 4 m. of tracks. Birdwatching: Cassowaries can at times be seen on highway verges. No accommodation in park. Hotels, motels, caravan parks at Innisfail; good caravan park, also hotel at Millaa Millaa. Overseer, resident Henrietta Creek. May to November. Summers hot, wet, humid.
PRINCE REGENT RIVER RESERVE (W.A.) 1,565,000 acres The establishment of this reserve was first proposed by the Australian Academy of Science in 1962).	Kimberley region, far north of Western Australia on the Prince Regent River, from the coast inland towards Mt Hann. Access extremely difficult by land. Probably only practical access is by pearling lugger or other boat from Derby, the nearest town, about 170 m. to the S. *See map p. 88.*	Extremely rugged sandstone country around the Prince Regent River. Tropical woodland.	The enormous, precipitous gorge of the Prince Regent is one of the most spectacular in W.A. The river rises between Mt Hann (2,547 ft) and Mt Agnes (2,300 ft) and descends to sea level within the short distance of 25 to 30 m. through a majestic gorge. Area has highest rainfall in tropical Western Australia, vegetation consequently very rich. Fauna of region not well known, but known to include very rare Scaly-tailed Possum, various rock wallabies, gliders. Enormous number of rock carvings and paintings, mostly of the strange Wandjina type, found only in the Kimberleys.	May to October. Summer dominated by cyclonic rains, very hot, wet, humid.

NAME OF PARK	LOCALITY ACCESS	TOPOGRAPHY VEGETATION TYPES	FEATURES OF INTEREST	ACTIVITIES ACCOMMODATION SEASON TO VISIT
SOUTH MOLLE ISLAND NATIONAL PARK (QLD.) 1,016 acres	Part of Whitsunday Group, about 20 m. E of Proserpine. Tourist resort, regular launch service from Shute Harbour, or helicopter service from Proserpine to island.	Ranges of undulating hills 500–600 ft high. Grassy with patches of scrub and forest.	Fine panoramic views of island-studded waterways from Mt Jeffreys and Spion Kop. (7 m. of tracks to scenic features). Fine beaches on northern and western shores. Coral reefs, reef fish.	Swimming, reef exploration (weekly cruise to outer reefs), launches for charter, speedboats for ski-ing. Short golf course, bowling green, tennis courts. Accommodation at tourist resort. (Telephone, P.O. bank facilities). Enquire Queensland Tourist Bureau. May to November.
THORNTON PEAK NATIONAL PARK (QLD.) 5,760 acres	Far N Queensland, N of Mossman, between Daintree River and Bloomfield River. *See* map p. 104.	Mountainous ranges of the N end of the Great Divide. Rainforest vegetation.	A high peak with scenic potential (access at present difficult). Valuable as a sanctuary for the magnificent bird and marsupial life of the north Queensland jungles.	Bushwalking, exploration, for the tough and adventurous. Nearest settlement at Daintree about 5 m. to the S of Thornton Peak National Park. Unit accommodation at Ellis Beach. Motel, caravan and camping park at Mossman. May to October or November. Very hot, wet, humid in summer.
TUNNEL CREEK NATIONAL PARK (W.A.) (A national park reserve vested in the Shire of West Kimberley).	Kimberley region, far NW. Australia, about 90 m. E of Derby, in Napier Range E of Windjana Gorge. Obtain detailed directions in Derby. Rough dirt roads, unsuitable for caravans.	Napier Range is a jagged wall of limestone formed as a reef. Through this range Tunnel Creek has eroded a large tunnel, an unusual physiographic feature of interest to geologists, and of scenic interest.	Tunnel ½ mile long, right under range, contains permanent water, freshwater crocodiles, many flying foxes. Broken in middle by collapsed section leading to top of range. Historic interest: hiding place of outlawed Aboriginal Pigeon during uprising, about 1894–1900.	Wading through tunnel; small crocodiles not dangerous. Scenic viewing. Bush camping only. Nearest supplies, facilities at Derby. Winter dry season. Roads impassable during summer cyclone season.
TULLY FALLS NATIONAL PARK (QLD.) 1,240 acres	N Queensland, 15 m. from Ravenshoe, S of Atherton Tableland, and W of Tully. Access via Ravenshoe, good bitumen road. *See* map p. 104.	Rugged mountain country, luxuriant rainforest.	The falls, 900 ft high, were among the most magnificent in Australia, but water has now been diverted above falls for generation of hydro-electric power. It is possibly still worth visiting for the rugged grandeur of the gorge.	Walking track leads to a pool above falls, and to bottom of gorge. Platforms provide scenic views at vantage points. There are picnic tables, shelter shed, fireplace, running water. No accommodation at park. Hotels, caravan parks at Atherton, Millaa Millaa. April to November.
WALLAMAN FALLS NATIONAL PARK (QLD.) 1,280 acres	N Queensland, near Ingham. From Ingham, westwards, about 30 m. over Lannercost Range Road. *See* map p. 104.	Mountainous country overlooking the Herbert River Valley; falls on a tributary of the Herbert River, rising on heights of Mt Fox. Tropical woodland above falls, dense rainforest on slopes, in gullies.	A tremendous gorge, over 100 ft deep, with vertical walls. Probably highest clear-drop fall in Australia (910 ft). Dense rainforest below falls. Lookout points on rim of gorge.	Scenic sightseeing, photography. Picnic areas above falls. Accommodation at Ingham (hotels, motels, caravan parks). Falls best after wet season, otherwise between May and November.
WHITSUNDAY ISLAND NATIONAL PARK (QLD.) 27,000 acres	Located on Whitsunday Passage off N Queensland coast via Proserpine, Shute Harbour. No regular transport, but visited by many island cruise launches operating from Shute Harbour or Mackay. Launches cruising among the Whitsunday group of islands often disembark tourists on beach. *See* map p. 120.	A high, rocky island; a peak of a chain of mountains submerged by rising sea level. Tropical rainforest and mixed coastal woodland.	Magnificent scenery: rugged mountain slopes, peaks (Whitsunday Peak highest, 1,438 ft), dense jungle. Presents a most attractive view from waterways. Hill Inlet, and Whitehaven Bay with fine white beaches, are attractions on eastern side. Cid Harbour on western shores is favourite anchorage for cruising parties. Whitsunday Passage was navigated and named by Captain Cook in 1770.	Swimming, reef exploration. Great area of unspoiled wilderness land for bushwalkers. Observing birdlife. Photography. No settlement or accommodation on island; fresh water for campers, visitors at old sawmill site, at Cid Harbour. May to November.
WINDJANA GORGE (Proposed National Park) (W.A.) Proposed by Aust. Academy of Science, now under National Parks Board consideration.	Kimberley region, far N of Western Australia, about 80 m. E of Derby. Proceed initially along Gibb River beef road in direction of King Leopold Ranges, then follow Lennard River to gorge. Enquire in Derby. *See* map p. 88.	Jagged ranges of Devonian limestone, formed as a barrier reef 300 million years ago. Blacksoil plains with savannah woodland.	Some of most beautiful scenery in Western Australia, unique in whole of Australia, a narrow canyon cut by Lennard River. Vertical cliffs of dark limestone, 100 to 300 ft high. Pools, surrounded by greenery of trees, shrubs, along 3 mile gorge. Grottos and caves in walls, cave paintings. Historical interest—Aboriginal uprising of 1894, police outpost ruins nearby.	Sightseeing, photography in gorge. Walking along river banks through gorge. Fishing—barramundi. Bush camping only, no facilities, supplies. Nearest town Derby (hotel, caravan park) about 80 m. by rough dirt tracks. May to November. Cyclonic rains December–March flood rivers, render most roads impassable.
WOOLWONGA WILDLIFE SANCTUARY (N.T.) 193,680 acres	On lower reaches of Alligator River, NW. Arnhem Land. Access from Darwin via Humpty Doo, Mt Bundy, then by rough dirt track to Jim Jim. Another track from Jim Jim to Pine Creek. 4-wheel-drive helpful. *See* map p. 96.	Extensive swamps and lagoons, paperbark trees, at junction of South Alligator River, Jim Jim Creek, Deaf Adder Creek.	A waterfowl sanctuary, breeding grounds for Magpie Geese, Jabiru, Green Pygmy Geese, Sea-eagles, and many other birds.	Bird observing, exploring huge areas of swamp and lagoon by boat. Camping and limited accommodation at Jim Jim Store. May to October. Rivers flooded, roads impassable during summer cyclone season.

NAME, LOCATION	FEATURES OF INTEREST
Barnard Group I. National Parks (NE. Qld.). Approx. 15 m. SE. of Innisfail.	Hutchinson I. (48 acres); Jessie I. (16 acres); Stephens I. (60 acres); Sisters I. (12 acres).
Berry Springs Recreation Reserve (N.T.) 628 acres. 40 m. S from Darwin.	Excellent swimming, interesting bush country. Popular for camping; visitor facilities being developed.
Broadwater Creek Falls National Park (N Qld.). 1,280 acres. About 23 m. NW. of Ingham.	On a tributary of Herbert River.
Brook Group I. National Parks (N Qld.).	North I. (160 acres); Tween I. (16 acres); Middle I. (40 acres).
Cape Hillsborough and Wedge I. National Park (N Qld.). 1,695 acres.	Coastal hills, shores, small island. Between Ball Bay and Sand Bay. Caves, bushwalking, fishing, swimming. Extensive picnic and camping area.
Clump Mountain National Park (N Qld.). 745 acres. 1 m. N of Clump Point Jetty, near Bingil Bay, NE. of Tully.	Tropical rainforest, lookouts to islands.
Daly River Recreation Reserve (N.T.) 148 acres. Access road (approx. 60 m.) W from Stuart Highway, turnoff being about 90 m. S of Darwin.	On the Daly River Crossing; a very popular camping, swimming spot.
Eubenagee Swamp National Park (N Qld.). 3,050 acres, 10 m. NW. of Innisfail.	A nature sanctuary area which contains ti-tree swamps, sedges, open lily pools (Reserve created 1969).
Family Group I. National Park (N Qld.).	Wheeler I. (76 acres); Coombe I. (120 acres); Smith I. (24 acres); Bowden I. (24 acres); Hudson I. (50 acres).
Flinders Group I. National Park. 7,320 acres. Far north-east Queensland. About 120 m. N of Cooktown.	Flinders I., Stanly I., Blackwood I., Denham I., Maclear I. A group off coast between Princess Charlotte Bay and Bathurst Bay.
Fogg Dam Bird Sanctuary. Access by bitumen road to Humpty Doo (22 m. E of Stuart Highway) then short, good gravel road to dam.	Huge flocks of water birds. (Campers note: hordes of mosquitoes after dark.)
Garrawalt Falls (N Qld.). 1,280 acres. Approx. 28 m. straight line distance NW. of Ingham.	On a tributary of Herbert River.
Gloucester I. National Park (Qld.). 6,080 acres. About 15 m. E of Bowen.	One of the offshore islands, similar to those of Whitsunday group, hilly, forested.
Goold I. National Park (N Qld.). 2,050 acres. Approx. 5 m. N of Hinchinbrook I.	In Rockingham Bay.
Gordonvale National Park (NE. Qld.). 233 acres. On Gillies Highway, about 3 m. from Gordonvale.	On northern banks of Mulgrave River.
Herbert River Falls National Park (N Qld.). 830 acres.	On Herbert River, about 8 m. SSE. of Cashmere (approx. 45 m. due W of Rockingham Bay).
Herkes Creek Falls National Park (N Qld.). 1,280 acres. Approx. 36 m. straight line distance NW. of Ingham.	On a tributary of Herbert River.
High I. National Park (NE. Qld.). 170 acres.	About 3 m. off coast approx. half-way between Innisfail and Cairns.
Hope I. National Park (N Qld.). 430 acres.	About 25 m. SE. of Cooktown, about 6 m. off coast.
Howard Springs Recreation Reserve (N.T.) 700 acres. Situated several miles E of Stuart Highway 20 m. S from Darwin, bitumen road.	An attractive swimming pool in jungle setting. Caravan park with good facilities, supplies available.
Shaw I. (4,100 acres); Thomas I. (1,000 acres); Blacksmith and Ladysmith I. (1,200 acres); Goldsmith I. (1,600 acres); Linne I. (1,000 acres); Scawfell I. (2,560 acres); Curlew, Bluff, Hirst, Wallace, Treble, Dinner I. (1,750 acres); Prudhoe I. (1,280 acres); Carlisle I. (1,280 acres); North East I. (760 acres); West Hill I. (983 acres); Double Cone I. (100 acres); Armit I. (320 acres); Silversmith I. (125 acres); Blackcombe I. (22 acres); Pentecost I. (260 acres); Maher I. (260 acres); Mansell I. (390 acres); Keyser I. (260 acres); Gumbrell I. (260 acres); Pine I. (200 acres); No. 1 Repulse Group (260 acres); No. 3 Repulse Group (100 acres); Border I. (960 acres); Arkhurst I. (20 acres); Langford I. (5 acres); Bird I. (4 acres); Black I. (25 acres); Shute, Tancred and Repari I. (55 acres); North Molle I. (640 acres); Mid Molle, Planton and Denham I. (82 acres); Henning I. (100 acres); Saddleback I. (112 acres); Cid I. (960 acres); Baynhan, Gaibirra, Volskow, Comston and Triangle I. (360 acres); Deloraine, Dumbell and Esk I. (220 acres); Perseverance, Dungarra I. and Surprise Rock (112 acres); Seaforth I. (50 acres); Anchorsmith I. (20 acres); Anvil I. (8 acres); Hammer I. (225 acres); Locksmith I. (24 acres); Bellows I. (9 acres); Pincer I. (9 acres); Tinsmith I. (200 acres); Ingot I. (75 acres); Allonby I. (90 acres); Renou I. (40 acres); Minister I. (260 acres); Beverlac I. (64 acres); Hull I. (65 acres); Still I. (20 acres); Henderson I. (130 acres); Noel I. (320 acres); Digby I. (380 acres); Keelan I. (65 acres); Penn I. (12 acres); Newry I. (165 acres); Cockemouth I. (640 acres); Wigton I. (640 acres); Calder I. (500 acres); Aspatria I. (260 acres); Outer Newry I. (144 acres); Mausoleum I. (16 acres); Penrith I. (400 acres); Bushy I. (5 acres); Acacia I. (50 acres); Rabbit I. (860 acres).	Island national parks of the central Queensland coast from Bowen south to Broad Sound. These islands are the peaks and summits of coastal ranges submerged by rising ocean. Many are fringed by coral, but are not true coral cays formed wholly by corals. Most are hilly, and more or less forested. These island-studded seas, and rugged coastline of the Conway Range, form probably the most spectacularly beautiful part of the eastern coast. Tourist resorts are established on some islands. December to April is the cyclone season, weather hot, very humid, insect pests prevalent, also sea-wasps, stonefish, Portuguese Man-O-War more common. Whether exploring coral reefs around these islands or on the outer barrier reefs, take care not to damage reef life; replace any rocks overturned. Very low tides are best for coral viewing; lowest daylight tides coincide with new and full moons.
Katherine Low Level Reserve (N.T.) 40 acres. Several miles to Darwin side of Katherine township, where Stuart Highway crosses the Katherine River.	An attractive swimming, caravan-camping area.
Lizard I. National Park (N Qld.). 2,500 acres.	About 150 m. N of Cairns, 20 m. NNE. of Cape Flattery, well out towards the Great Barrier Reef. Nearest port Cooktown, about 50 m.
Mataranka Pool Reserve (N.T.) 10 acres. 64 m. S of Katherine, 5 m. E of Stuart Highway.	Warm springs, pool and picturesque palm forest. Accommodation at nearby Mataranka Homestead or at hotel on highway. Elsey Memorial Cemetry is 11 m. S on highway.
Mission Beach–Hull River National Park (N Qld.). 1,350 acres. (Created 1969). E of Tully.	Lowland rainforest, palm forest, ti-tree forest and tropical woodland savannah.
Mt Aberdeen National Park (N Qld.). 4,120 acres.	Situated about 25 m. inland from Bowen, almost midway, just N of Bowen–Collinsville Road.
Mt Burrumbuck National Park (N Qld.). 2,360 acres.	Approx. 25 m. SE. of Townsville, W of the mouth of the Haughton River, almost to Bruce Highway.
Mt Jukes National Park (N Qld.). 566 acres.	About 20 m. NW. of Mackay, between Bruce Highway and Sand Bay. Coastal ranges.
Mt Mandurana National Park (N Qld.). 255 acres.	Situated about 10 m. NW. of Mackay, just N of Bruce Highway. Coastal hills.
Mt Maria National Park (NE. Qld.). 800 acres.	On the coast NW. of Innisfail, on southern shores of Ella Bay. Rainforest on coastal ranges.

NAME, LOCATION	FEATURES OF INTEREST
Sixteen Mile Caves (N.T.) 640 acres. Situated just W of Stuart Highway 16 m. S of Katherine, but the short access track is extremely rocky.	Enquire parks rangers, Katherine regarding entry, as gate may be locked to prevent vandalism in caves, which are not exceptionally attractive. Large colony of Orange Horseshoe Bats in cave.
Snapper I. National Park (NE. Qld.). 138 acres.	3 m. E of mouth of Daintree River.
Swan's Lagoon Fauna Sanctuary. 19,300 acres. On lower reaches of Burdekin River, S of Ayr, Clare.	Waterbird sanctuary under trusteeship of Queensland Dept. of Primary Industries. Feeding, breeding grounds for many water and swamp birds—Brolgas, Jabiru, egrets, herons, waterfowl.
Small island national parks in the Whitsunday Group, approx. 30 m. W of Proserpine (Qld.). Total area 2,990 acres.	Nunga, Teague, Gungwiya, Yerumbinna, Hazlewood, Lupton, Nicolson, Workington, Wirrainbeia, Jreby, Harold, Sillago, Edward, Buddibuddi and Yiumdilla Islands. These are small islands around Whitsunday I., not coral cays but summits of drowned ranges. Most are hilly, more or less forested. Fringing coral reefs.
South I. National Park (Qld.). 4,000 acres. About 80 m. SE. from Mackay.	The southernmost large island of the Northumberland Group. An offshore-type island, hilly, forested.
Southwood National Park. 17,500 acres. At Southwood bordering the Moonie Highway.	A sample tract of the brigalow-scrub country that is now rapidly being destroyed elsewhere for agriculture.
Sword Creek Falls National Park (N Qld.). 1,280 acres.	On a tributary of the Herbert River, approx. 33 m. straight-line distance NW. of Ingham.
Three Islands and Two Islands National Parks. 136 acres. Far NE. Qld.	Three Islands: about 8 m. ESE. of Cape Flattery. Two Islands: about 12 m. SE. of Cape Flattery.
Townsville Common. Borders airfield, a few miles NW. of town.	A few acres of swampy flats between highway and sea, flooded during summer rains. Favoured by Brolgas, which congregate huge flocks and may easily be watched. Many other northern water birds.
Turtle Group I. National Park. 225 acres. Far NE. Qld.	About 20 m. NW. of Cape Flattery, 50 m. due N of Cooktown.
Un-named park, reserve No. 255 Atherton district (N Qld.).	About 6 m. SE. of Ravenshoe.
Un-named park reserve No. 645. 13,800 acres.	Situated in Parish of Pitt, Ingham Forestry Sub-district.
Un-named park, reserve No. 686. 2,760 acres.	Very near northern borders of the big Eungella National Park, just S of Yalboroo on Bruce Highway about 40 m. NW. of Mackay.
Yamanie Falls National Park (N Qld.). 1,280 acres. Approx. 38 m. straight-line distance NW. of Ingham.	On a tributary of the Herbert River.

SOME BIRDS OF FAR NORTHERN NATIONAL PARKS

(Cape York to the Kimberleys)

Cassowary (*Casuarius casuarius*); Cape York rainforest.
Jabiru (*Xenorhynchus asiaticus*); swamps and lagoons.
Green Pygmy Goose (*Nettapus pulchellus*); swamps and mangroves.
Pied, or Magpie Goose (*Anseranas semipalmata*); swamps and mangroves.
White-breasted Sea Eagle (*Haliaeetus leucogaster*); coast and rivers.
Crested Hawk (*Aviceda subcristata*); forests, and riverbank trees.
Red Goshawk (*Erythrotriorchis radiatus*); open forests.
Jungle Fowl (*Megapodius freycinet*); rainforest.
White-quilled Rock Pigeon (*Petrophassa albipennis*); spinifex sandstone.
Chestnut-quilled Rock Pigeon (*Petrophassa rufipennis*); sandstone hills.
Rose-crowned Pigeon (*Ptilinopus ewingi*); coastal rainforest.
Wompoo Pigeon (*Megaloprepia magnifica*); rainforest.
Torres Strait Pigeon (*Myristicivora spilorrhoa*); rainforest.
Northern Rosella; (*Platycercus venustus*); open forests.
Red-collared Lorikeet (*Trichoglossus rubritorquis*); open forests.
Cloncurry Parrot (*Barnardius macgillivrayi*); grassland and river trees.
Crimson-winged Parrot (*Aprosmictus erythropterus*); open forest and river trees.
Varied Lorikeet (*Psitteuteles versicolor*); open forests, riverbank trees.
Red-browed Fig Parrot (*Opopsitta macleayana*); rainforest.
Great Palm Cockatoo (*Probosciger aterrimus*); jungle and open forest.
Electus, or Red-sided Parrot (*Lorius pectoralis*); rainforest.
Hooded Parrot (*Psephotus dissimilis*); open forest and spinifex.
Golden-shouldered Parrot (*Psephotus chrysopterygius*); open forest.
Northern Boobook (*Ninox ocellata*); jungle and open forest.
Rufous Owl (*Ninox rufa*); open forest.
Papuan Frogmouth (*Podargus papuensis*); jungle and open forest.
Little Kingfisher (*Alcyone pusilla*); rainforest and mangroves.
Yellow-billed Kingfisher (*Suma torotoro*); jungle and open forest.
White-tailed Kingfisher (*Tanysiptera sylvia*); rainforest.
Blue-breasted Pitta (*Pitta mackloti*); rainforest.
Papuan Cuckoo-shrike (*Coracina papuensis*); open forest and mangroves.
Spangled Drongo (*Chibia bracteata*); jungle and open forest.
Yellow Oriole (*Oriolus flavocinctus*); open forest.
Olive-backed Oriole (*Oriolus sagittatus*); jungle and open forest.
Shining Starling (*Aplonis metallica*); rainforest.

Yellow Fig-bird (*Sphecotheres flaviventris*); forests.
Golden Bower-bird (*Prionodura newtoniana*); rainforests above 3,000 ft.
Tooth-billed Cat (or Bower) Bird (*Scenopaeetes dentirostris*); rainforest.
Prince Albert Rifle-bird (*Ptiloris magnificus*); rainforest.
Queen Victoria Rifle-bird (*Ptiloris victoriae*); rainforest.
Manucode (*Phonygammus keraudreni*); rainforest.
Black-headed Log-runner (*Orthonyx spaldingi*); rainforest.
Northern Scrub-robin (*Drymodes superciliaris*); rainforest.
Purple-backed Wren (*Malurus assimilis*); low scrub and spinifex.
Lovely Wren (*Malurus asabilis*); low scrub and spinifex.
Lilac-crowned Wren (*Malurus coronatus*); cane-grass and pandanus.
Fern-wren (*Oreoscopus gutturalis*); rainforest.
Lemon-breasted Flycatcher (*Micraeca flavigaster*); forests.
Little Yellow Robin (*Eopsaltria kempi*); in and near rainforests.
Pale Yellow Robin (*Eopsaltria capito*); rainforest.
Buff-sided Robin (*Paecilodryas cerviniventris*); rainforest and mangroves.
Pearly Flycatcher (*Monarcha frater*); jungle and open forest.
Spectacled Flycatcher (*Monarcha trivirgata*); rainforest.
Brown-tailed Flycatcher (*Micraeca brunneicauda*); open forest and mangrove.
Leaden Flycatcher (*Myiagra rubecula*); coastal forests.
Broad-billed Flycatcher (*Myiagra ruficollis*); mangroves.
Pied Flycatcher (*Arses kaupi*); rainforest.
Frill-necked Flycatcher (*Arses lorealis*); rainforest.
Golden-backed Honeyeater (*Melithreptus laetior*); open woodland.
Red-headed Honeyeater (*Myzomela erythrocephala*); mangrove and forest.
Yellow-breasted Sunbird (*Cyrtostomus frenatus*); rainforest fringes and clearings.
Black-headed Pardalote (*Pardalotus melanocephalus*); woodland and riverbanks.
Red-browed Pardalote (*Pardalotus rubricatus*); woodland and riverbanks.
Crimson Finch (*Neachmia phaeton*); grasslands and pandanus.
Gouldian Finch (*Chlaebia gouldiae*); grasslands and spinifex.
Painted Finch (*Emblema picta*); grasslands and spinifex.
Masked Finch (*Paephila personata*); grasslands.
Pictorella Finch (*Heteramunia pectoralis*); grasslands.
Yellow-tailed Finch (*Lonchura flaviprymna*); cane-grass swamps.
Long-tailed Finch (*Peophila acuticauda*); grasslands.

Platypus (*Ornithorhynchus anatinus*); coastal streams of north-east Qld.
Spiny Anteater (*Tachyglossus aculeatus*); jungle of ranges and drier plains.
Harney's Marsupial-Mouse (*Antechinus bilarney*); recorded western Arnhem Land.
Pygmy Marsupial Mouse (*A. maculatus*); smallest of genus; north-east and Groote Eylandt.
Fawn Marsupial Mouse (*A. bellus*); 'top end' of N.T., nocturnal and insectivorous.
Flat-headed Marsupial Mouse (*Planigale ingrami*); smallest of all marsupials.
Large Desert Sminthopsis (*Sminthopsis macrura*); recorded from Kimberleys, W.A.
Stripe-headed Sminthopsis (*S. larapinta*); nocturnal, insectivorous; N.T., north Qld.
White-footed Sminthopsis (*S. leucopus*); vicinity of Cooktown, Qld.
Stripe-faced Sminthopsis (*S. rufigenis*); east coast of Cape York, also New Guinea.
Brush-tailed Phascogale (*Phascogale tapoatafa*); woodlands, 'top end' of N.T., Kimberleys.
Northern Native Cat (*Satanellus hallucatus*); Kimberleys Ra. of W.A., Darwin area, Cape York.
Tiger Cat (*Dasyurops maculatus*); rainforests, timbered ranges of north-east Qld.
Long-nosed Bandicoot (*Parameles nasuta*); east-coastal forests, feeds on insect larvae.
Rufescent Bandicoot (*Echimypera rufescens*); McIlwraith Range, near Coen, Cape York.
Short-nosed Bandicoot (*Isoodon obesulus*); forests, woodlands, Cape York, and Kimberleys of W.A.
Brindled Bandicoot (*I. macrourus*); a larger species; top end of N.T., and east coast.
Queensland Pygmy-Possum (*Cercartetus caudatus*); head-plus-body 4 inches; Atherton, Qld.
Feathertail Glider (*Acrobates pygmaeus*); fringed tail resembles Emu feather; east coast.
Sugar Glider (*Petaurus breviceps*); forests, woodlands from Kimberley to east coast.
Yellow-bellied Glider (*P. australis*); near Cairns, mountainous sclerophyll forest.
Striped Possum (*Dactylopsila trivirgata*); squirrel-like, black-striped, north-east Qld.
Spotted Cuscus (*Phalanger maculatus*); large, slow, prehensile tail; forests, Cape York.
Grey Cuscus (*P. orientalis*); grey, unspotted; McIlwraith Ra., Cape York, Qld., also N.G.
Scaly-tailed Possum (*Wyulda squamicaudata*); bare, prehensile tail, Kimberley Ra., W.A.
Brush-tailed Possum (*Trichosaurus vulpeca*); Kimberley Ra. to east coast, coppery variety at Atherton Qld.
Common Ringtail (*Pseudocheirus peregrinus*); forests of Cape York and east coast.
Herbert River Ringtail (*P. herbertensis*); very dark brown, pure white under, Atherton district.
Striped, or Green Ringtail (*P. archeri*); grey-green fur, rainforests of Atherton–Cairns.
Rock-haunting Ringtail (*P. dahli*); rocky ranges of western Arnhem Land, N.T.
Lemur-like Ringtail (*Hemibelideus lemuroides*); in dense rainforests of Atherton Tableland.
Greater Glider (*Schoinobates minor*); a smaller form of the Greater Glider (*S. volans*), north-east forests.
Koala (*Phascolarctos cinereus*); east-coast sclerophyll forests southwards of Townsville.
Musk Rat-kangaroo (*Hypsiprymnodon moschatus*); a link between possums and kangaroos; Cape York.

Brush-tailed Rat-kangaroo (*Bettongia penicillata*); once very widespread, now Cairns area.
Rufous Rat-kangaroo (*Aepyprymnus rufescens*); open woodlands, forests, north-east coast.
Spectacled Hare-Wallaby (*Lagorchestes conspicillatus*); Kimberley Ra., Arnhem Land, Townsville area, Qld.
Queensland Rock-Wallaby (*Petrogale inornata*); north Qld. from Coen to Mackay, and inland.
Black-flanked Rock-Wallaby (*P. lateralis*); Derby area, west Kimberley Ra., W.A.
Roper River Rock-Wallaby (*P. wilkinsi*); yellow shoulder mark; Roper River area, N.T.
Short-eared Rock-Wallaby (*P. brachyotis*); Kimberley Ra., W.A., and Darwin district, N.T.
Little Rock-Wallaby (*Peradorcas concinna*); smallest rock-wallaby, Kimberley Ra., and Arnhem Land.
Northern, or Sandy Nail-tailed Wallaby (*Onychogalea unguifer*); from Broome to Normanton.
Lumholtz's Tree-kangaroo (*Dendrolagus lumholtzi*); mountainous rainforest, Cairns area, Qld.
Dusky Tree-kangaroo (*D. bennettianus*); mountainous rainforest, Daintree to Cooktown, north Qld.
Red-legged Pademelon (*Thylogale stigmatica*); thick vegetation, forests of Cape York, Cairns.
Swamp Wallaby (*Wallabia bicolor*); nocturnal, common; rainforest and sclerophyll forest, north-east coast.
Whiptail, or Pretty-face Wallaby (*W. parryi*); diurnal; woodland and forest, north-east coast.
Agile Wallaby (*W. agilis*); coastal northern Australia through Kimberley Ra., N.T., north-east Qld.
Wallaroo, or Euro (*Macropus robustus*); heavily built; Kimberley Ra., N.T. and Qld.
Red Kangaroo (*M. rufus*); inland plains of north, and gulf country.
Grey Kangaroo (*M. Major*); dry sclerophyll forest and open woodland, inland and north-east Qld.
Dingo (*Canis antarctica*); widespread through north and inland.
Cape York Hopping-Mouse (*Notomys aquilo*); a pale-coloured species found only on Cape York.
Little Reddish Fruit-bat (*Pteropus scapulatus*); around the entire coastal belt of the north.
Gould's Fruit-bat (*Pteropus gouldii*); coastal north, from Broome to Maryborough.
Spectacled Fruit-bat (*P. conspicillatus*); coastal north Qld., from Cardwell to Cape York.
Spinal-winged Fruit-bat (*Dobsonia magna*); fruit diet; in caves, Cape York and New Guinea.
Queensland Tube-nosed Bat (*Nyctimene robinsonii*); coastal Qld., Cape York southwards.
Papuan Tube-nosed Bat (*N. papuensis*); a small species; Cape York, N.G. and islands.
Northern Blossom-bat (*Odontonycteris lagochilus*); Cape York to Derby, along the coast.

Cassowary

Cuscus

THE WEST

Yellow-winged Honeyeater at Kangaroo-paw

NAME OF PARK	LOCALITY ACCESS	TOPOGRAPHY VEGETATION TYPES	FEATURES OF INTEREST	ACTIVITIES ACCOMMODATION SEASON TO VISIT
ALBANY COASTAL NATIONAL PARK (W.A.) Reserves 'A' 24258, 9,043 acres; and 'A' 27107, about 4,000 acres	S coast of Western Australia, a few miles SW. of Albany. Bitumen road to Frenchman's Bay. Part on Mt Taylor, E of Oyster Harbour, access via Nannerup Beach.	Undulating coastal hills SW. of Albany; cliffs along ocean. Stunted scrub, taller trees in sheltered valleys.	Magnificent coastal scenery of high cliffs, sweeping beaches between high rocky headlands. Coastal features include The Gap, Blowhole, Natural Bridge, Jimmy Newell's Harbour, Bald Head, Frenchman's Bay. Stunted, windswept coastal vegetation rich in wildflowers particularly banksias, W.A. Christmas Tree in summer. Honeyeating birds, Honey Possum.	Scenic drives along good road to coastal features. Colour photography. Excellent fishing including big game fishing for tuna and marlin. Swimming. Boating in King George Sound. Albany: 6 hotels, 4 motels, 3 caravan parks, many guest houses, holiday flats. A very pleasant, mild summer climate November to May. Wildflowers September to January.
BARLEE RANGE NATIONAL PARK (W.A.) New flora and fauna reserve No. 26808, about 300,000 acres. Western Australia National Parks Board now seeking control, park establishment not yet finalized.	NW. Western Australia, in Barlee Range, on Tropic of Capricorn about 150 m. E of coast. Final approach to range very difficult, no roads, no tracks, entry must be on foot.	Very rugged ranges. *Triodia* steppe vegetation on hilltops, with few small shrubs. Eucalypts in valleys, with *Melaleuca, Acacia* and *Eremophila* shrubs.	An area of spectacular scenery with steep-sided gorges, deep permanent pools. Would have tourist potential when access road, proper range supervision can be provided. Wildlife includes rock wallabies, Euros. Many desert shrubs bear attractive flowers.	Rough bush camping only; all supplies must be carried in. Winter, early spring months. Summer dangerously hot, dry.
BARROW ISLAND FAUNA-FLORA RESERVE (W.A.) 50,000 acres	Off NW. coast of Western Australia, about 65 m. N of Onslow (890 m. N of Perth) and 200 m. N of Tropic of Capricorn.	Barrow Island, one of oldest, most important reserves off Western Australian coast, was set aside as Class A Reserve for protection of fauna and flora in 1908. It is about 18 m. long, 5 to 8 m. wide, of low red sandhills, highest only 270 ft, has a desolate appearance. Mangroves on some beaches, low *Acacia* scrub, extensive spinifex.	It is most mammal-rich Western Australian island. 6 species of mammals: Spectacled Hare-wallaby (*Lagorchestes conspicillatus*), Rock Wallaby (*Petrogale lateralis*), Barrow Island Bandicoot (*Isoodon obesulus barrowensis*). Crest-tailed Marsupial mouse (*Dasycercus cristicauda*), Barrow Island Native Mouse (*Thetomys ferculinis*), Barrow Island Kangaroo (*Macropus robustus isabellinus*). Also a distinctive form of the White-winged Wren. Most of these are distinctly different to their mainland relatives, and still plentiful in spite of oil drilling operations.	Flora and fauna observation. Onslow: hotel, caravan park.
BEEDELUP NATIONAL PARK (W.A.) 3,350 acres	Extreme SW. corner of Western Australia, about 10 m. W of forestry town of Pemberton, on Pemberton–Nannup road.	Hills, undulating or occasionally steep, with wet sclerophyll forest.	Beedelup Falls, two cascades with total drop of 350 ft. Lush forest greenery, including Karri trees.	Motor touring, sightseeing, walking on good tracks, observing wildflowers and south-western birdlife. Photography. Pemberton: Hotel, guest house. Manjimup: Hotel, motels, caravan park. September–October for wildflowers. Summer pleasantly mild.
BERNIER AND DORRE ISLANDS RESERVE (W.A.) 26,000 acres	Central W coast of Western Australia, on W side of Shark Bay, and about 30 m. W of Carnarvon (611 m. N of Perth).	Both islands are Class A reserves for preservation of flora and fauna, of great biological interest in providing a comparison with adjacent mainland, and nearby Dirk Hartog Island, where sheep have caused serious deterioration of natural vegetation making country more desert-like.	Important sanctuary for the Banded Hare-wallaby (*Lagostrophus fasciatus*) and a rat-kangaroo the Boodie (*Bettongia lesueruri*), both probably extinct on mainland. The islands are now only place in world where these marsupials survive. Also on islands is Western Hare-wallaby (*Lagorchestres hirsutus*) and the Bandicoot (*Parameles bougainvillei*), both now very rare on mainland. Islands were first visited by Dampier; French Baudin expedition of 1802 first described their fauna. Still important for scientific study.	Scientific studies of fauna and flora. Carnarvon: 4 hotels, 2 motels, guest house, caravan and camping parks.
BIG BROOK NATIONAL PARK (W.A.) 300 acres	Extreme SW. corner of Western Australia, adjacent to the forestry town of Pemberton, 211 m. S of Perth via South-Western Highway.	Hill slopes, with dense forest including tall Karri trees.	Karri forest, lush forest under-growth with good wildflower displays in spring months. Tracks and trails.	Scenic drives, walking, photography, picnicking Pemberton: 1 hotel, guest house. September, October for wildflowers. Summer pleasantly mild.
BREMER RANGE (Proposed National Park) (W.A.) Now flora and fauna reserve No. 27623. Recommended area 576,000 acres.	SE. Western Australia, approx. 70 m. SW. of Norseman, 90 m. NW. of Esperance. Access by the Norseman–Lake King Rd., passing through centre of area.	S end of proposed park area largely occupied by salt lake systems of Lake Tay, Lake Sharpe. Peak Charles (2,160 ft) highest point. Bremer Range at NW. part is a low rock ridge. Vegetation similar to that seen around Norseman.	First recommended by Australian Academy of Science in 1962 as a national park. Control sought by Western Australia National Parks Board (1968 Annual Report) but has not been finalized. This national park area has been selected as representative of halophytic botanical associations of widespread salt lake system of Western Australia, and is on boundary of central Australian flora.	Bush camping only. Extremely dry area lacking in fresh water. Autumn, winter, spring months.

NAME OF PARK	LOCALITY ACCESS	TOPOGRAPHY VEGETATION TYPES	FEATURES OF INTEREST	ACTIVITIES ACCOMMODATION SEASON TO VISIT
BROCKMAN FOREST NATIONAL PARK (W.A.) 120 acres	Extreme SW. corner of Western Australia. Near Warren River bridge, a few miles S of forestry town of Pemberton.	Hill slopes, creeks. Wet sclerophyll type forest.	Magnificent tall Karri trees, lush forest vegetation, good wildflower displays in spring.	Scenic sightseeing, photography. Pemberton: hotel, guest house. Manjimup: hotels, motels, caravan park. September–October for wildflowers. Pleasantly mild summers.
CAPE ARID NATIONAL PARK (W.A.) 642,000 acres At present flora and fauna reserve No. 24047; title change to 'national park' expected.	S coast of Western Australia, about 100 m. E of Esperance, between Israelite Bay and Cape Le Grand.	Granite headlands, sandplains. Reserve is of great botanical importance because it contains the flora examined by botanist Robert Brown who accompanied Matthew Flinders on his voyage of exploration in 1801, is basis of early work in Western Australia, i.e. reserve is *type locality* for many wildflower species. Cape Arid has very many wildflower species, some being magnificent in flower, and found only on these granite headlands.	Marsupial, birdlife probably similar to Cape Le Grand, e.g. Honey Possum. Botanical interest of area.	Bush camping only. It has been recommended that a small portion eventually be set aside for public recreation and camping. Esperance is nearest town for accommodation, supplies. October to May, both for wildflowers and for pleasant weather.
CAPE LE GRAND NATIONAL PARK (W.A.) 39,500 acres	S coast of Western Australia on Cape Le Grand E of Esperance Bay. Access road from Esperance, 20 m. E, fairly rough. *See map* p. 00.	Granite hills and headlands, vegetation of stunted eucalypts, low coastal scrub.	Rugged coastal scenery, with attractive sandy coves between high granite headlands. Many wildflowers through spring and summer. Marsupials include rock wallabies, Honey Possum.	Good fishing, swimming. Observing wildflowers, birdlife. Picnic facilities at Cape Le Grand and Lucky Bay. Esperance: hotels, motel, holiday cottages for rent, two caravan parks. September to May.
CAPE RANGE NATIONAL PARK (W.A.) 33,171 acres	On North-West Cape, Western Australian coast 100 m. N of Tropic of Capricorn. Access by Highway One via Carnarvon to Minilya. Then 243 m. to Cape. A few miles N of Learmonth, Shot Hole Canyon Rd, Charles Knife Rd., lead to park.	Rocky ranges dissected by gorges. White-trunked gums, shrubs on range top, spinifex on gorge slopes, ridges (Sclerophyll shrub savannah).	Scenery of extremely rugged, cliff-walled gorges; views E over Exmouth Gulf, W over Indian Ocean. A few miles N is giant U.S. Naval radio station. Site of Australia's first oil strike.	Scenic sightseeing, photography, bird observing. Good fishing on coast. Accommodation at Exmouth: hotel, two caravan–camping grounds. May to September. Hot, arid region (10″ annual rainfall). Most attractive a month or two after a cyclonic rainstorm.
DRYANDRA STATE FOREST (S.F. 51) (W.A.) Serves as vital sanctuary for beautiful Banded Anteater or Numbat.	SW. Western Australia, a few miles WNW. of Narrogin, and NE. of Williams.	Gently undulating land, carrying very attractive forest of white-trunked Wandoo gums. (*E. redunca* and *E. accedens*), Sheoak (*Casuarina*), *Acacia* and *Dryandra* bushes.	Serves as a wildlife sanctuary in a region almost entirely given over to wheat farming; a last sample of undamaged Wandoo forest, and its fauna. Chiefly of importance for its considerable Numbat population, also Mallee Fowl. The Numbat is already extinct in most other places it once inhabited; Dryandra is therefore one of the last strongholds of this most attractive marsupial. The Australian Academy of Science has recommended that 'should the State Forest No. 51 or portions of it and the adjacent State Forest No. 53 no longer be required for purposes of forestry they should be set aside for the preservation of flora and fauna.' Dryandra contains a large plantation of West Australian ornamental flowering trees, easily found not far from the Forests Office. The Forestry Department has taken much care to maintain the forest as a sanctuary for its unique wildlife; it has so far been more a sanctuary than most fauna reserves.	Wildlife observation. Narrogin: hotel, motel, caravan and camping park. Any season.
FITZGERALD RIVER FLORA AND FAUNA RESERVE (W.A.) 604,000 acres. Reserve No. 24048 soon to be given national park status.	S coast of Western Australia, about 150 m. W of Esperance, about 140 m. E of Albany. Reserve touches Ravensthorpe–Jerramungup Road. Access usually via Ravensthorpe, Hopetoun to E end of Barren Range.	Coastal ranges, Fitzgerald River and tributaries. Extensive sandplains. Low coastal scrub, heaths, stunted eucalypts, mallee, many species of *Banksia*.	Magnificent coastal scenery where the Fitzgerald River cuts through Barren Range near Middle Mt Barren (1,500 ft) right on coast. Views from range overlooking coast. Reserve was established in 1954 because of exceptional richness of flora—a magnificent wildflower area in spring and summer. 25 species found nowhere else. Many honeyeating birds. Honey Possum.	Scenic sightseeing, good fishing. Bushwalks to hilltop viewpoints, wildflower walks. Swimming in summer months. No accommodation or visitor facilities at park. Caravan parks, hotels at Albany and Esperance, possibly at Hopetoun. September–April for wildflowers, otherwise any season.
HAMERSLEY RANGES NATIONAL PARK (W.A.) At present flora and fauna reserve No. 24438, 74,000 acres to become a national park 'in the near future'.	Dale's Gorge and new park about 40 m. SE. of Wittenoom 181 m. SW. of Roebourne on North West Coastal Highway, 116 m. W of Roy Hill on Great Northern Highway.	Extremely rugged ranges reaching 200 m. west to east. Mt Bruce (4,024 ft) and Mt Meharry are highest in Western Australia. Harsh Porcupine Grass, occasional Ghost Gums, and hardy shrubs.	Region of spectacular gorges, cut into iron-rich, dark red rock. Small waterfalls dropping to gorge depths, pools, lush vegetation. New park will include Mt Bruce, Dales Gorge. Other scenic spectacles are Yampire Gorge, Fortescue Falls, Wittenoom Gorge.	Scenic sightseeing, colour photography. At Wittenoom: hotel, caravan park. Winter, early spring months. Extremely hot, dry October to May.

NAME OF PARK	LOCALITY ACCESS	TOPOGRAPHY VEGETATION TYPES	FEATURES OF INTEREST	ACTIVITIES ACCOMMODATION SEASON TO VISIT
HOUTMAN ABROLHOS ISLANDS RESERVE (W.A.) Total area unknown. West Wallabi Island 1,500 acres; East Wallabi 930 acres	Islands off Western Australia mid-west coast, 30 m. W and NW. of Geraldton. (312 road m. N of Perth). Launch excursions to islands can be arranged at Geraldton.	Small, low islands, remnants of coastal dunes inundated by rising sea level. Highest 40 ft above sea level. Only East Wallabi Island has trees, most have low scrub, fringe of mangroves. Three groups: Wallabi Group, Easter Group, Southern Group; also, isolated North Island.	Abrolhos discovered by Dutch mariners, many ships wrecked. Dutch ship *Batavia* 1629, with crew mutiny and massacre of survivors, on Abrolhos. *Zeewyck* wrecked 1727, others more recently. Islands very important as main breeding places for sea birds on western coast. Abrolhos Tammar Wallaby found only on these islands (used illegally, at times, as cray bait).	Waters are clear, with extensive reefs, luxuriant coral growth, abundant marine life giving great potential for underwater reef exploring, spearfishing, fishing. At Geraldton: hotels, guest houses, holiday flats, cottages for rent, 3 caravan parks. Birds, July–November. Winter climate warm enough for water sports; summers very hot, especially on mainland.
JOHN FORREST NATIONAL PARK (W.A.) 3,648 acres	On edge of Darling Range escarpment 16 m. E from Perth. Great Eastern Highway forms S boundary of park.	Undulating hills of Darling Range top, falling westwards to Perth coastal plains. Eucalypt forest, Jarrah, Marri, Wandoo, Banksia.	Views over coastal plains, with buildings of Perth on horizon. Many wildflowers in low scrub beneath trees: Pink (Swan River) Myrtle, Pink Calytrix, Pimelea, Blue Leschenaultia, dark-blue Hovea, Red-and-Green Kangaroo Paws. Beds of cultivated wildflowers, with name plates. Park named after W.A. explorer and statesman, Lord Forrest.	Walking along tracks. Short, guided wildflower tours in spring. Sightseeing from lookouts, at small falls. Swimming, pool in creek. Picnicking. No accommodation at park. Many hotels, motels, caravan parks in Perth and suburbs. Rangers. July to October for most Darling Range wildflowers, otherwise any season.
KALAMUNDA NATIONAL PARK (W.A.) 919 acres	Darling Ranges about 17 m. E of Perth, just E of Kalamunda, touching Kalamunda–Mundaring Weir road.	Undulating hills along Darling Range top, jarrah forest vegetation.	Open forest of Jarrah, Marri, Wandoo and banksias, low ground scrub, many wildflowers: Red-and-green Kangaroo Paws, Pink (Swan River) Myrtle, Pink Calytrix, Blue Leschenaultia, Hovea.	Bush and wildflower walks; observing south-western birds. (Park will be left almost entirely in its natural state.) No accommodation in park. Ranger based John Forrest Park. Hotels, motels, caravan parks in Perth and suburbs. July to October for most wildflowers. Bush least attractive January to May.
KALBARRI NATIONAL PARK (W.A.) 358,000 acres	Western Australian coast, 415 road m. N of Perth, 103 m. N of Geraldton. Turn W from Highway One at Ajana, (N of Northampton) then W through park to Kalbarri township. *See* map p. 129.	Elevated sandstone plains, meandering Murchison River deeply incised into coloured rock. Colourful coastal cliffs. Undulating sandplains, sand heath flora, gums in river gorge.	The huge gorge of the Murchison River, about 50 m. long, 500 ft deep, cut through multicoloured rock. Hawk's Head Lookout, Ross Graham Lookout accessible by road. The Loop area suitable only 4-wheel-drive. Sandplains surrounding gorge very rich in wildflowers, can be seen along roads. Park to be extended to include magnificent Red Bluff coast, but Western Australian Liberal Government slow in finalizing this, though area has great tourist potential.	Sightseeing, colour photography. Fishing along Kalbarri coast. Swimming, boating in Murchison estuary. Wildflower studies. At Kalbarri township: several caravan parks, hotel, flats and cottages. Most wildflowers August to November, but some outstanding species flowering December, May. Summer months very hot, suitable only for beach activities.
LAKE BARKER (Proposed National Park) (W.A.) 516,420 acres. At present this is flora and fauna reserve No. 24049; change to national park planned.	Central-southern Western Australia, about 30 m. SE. of Southern Cross. Access at present limited, 4-wheel-drive may be necessary.	Flora is of interest, being borderline between South-west floral province, and the Eremean (Centralian). Some plants found only in this area. Good wildflowers early spring.	Has historical interest, one of earliest significant gold discoveries in this area, 1887. Area will be of additional interest as a good example of appearance of vegetation of Goldfields and eastern agricultural areas before extensive timber-cutting for mines, or clearing for farming. Marsupial and birdlife not well known. This reserve or national park will preserve a significant sample of wilderness land, flora, fauna, of scientific interest. Also a place for the adventurous bush explorer, naturalist.	Flora observation. Bush walking. At Southern Cross: hotels, motels, caravan park. August to October.
LAKE MAGENTA FLORA AND FAUNA RESERVE (W.A.) 232,700 acres (Reserve A 25113).	Southern Western Australia. From Perth, via Wagin, Lake Grace, then S from Newdegate or E from Pingrup. Such tracks as exist may require 4-wheel-drive.	Salt lake, heath and mallee vegetation. Extensive dry lake has gypsum dunes, lake floor of crystalline gypsum, clay and salts. Mallees include *Eucalyptus spathulate*, *E. astringens*.	Reserve is fine example of sclerophyllous woodland typical of arid inland southern Western Australia. It is a stronghold of mallee bird species disappearing in other parts as land is cleared. Marsupials known to include Honey Possum, Red-tailed Phascogale. Reserve will also serve as yardstick against which to measure changes brought about by man in farming of adjacent low-rainfall areas. It is a Class A reserve for preservation of flora and fauna, vested in Fauna Protection Advisory Committee of Western Australia.	Observation of birdlife, marsupials. Bush camping. Spring or autumn months.
LESMURDIE FALLS NATIONAL PARK (W.A.) 81 acres	Darling Range near Perth. Access by Albany Highway, Welshpool Road, Hales Road, Anderson Road to falls. Also from Welshpool Road via Lesmurdie Road, Falls Road to top of falls.	W edge of Darling Range. Open forest of Wandoo, Marri, Jarrah gums, low scrub undergrowth.	Waterfall, views overlooking Perth and suburbs. Good spring wildflower displays. Picnic facilities. Walking tracks.	Touring and scenic sightseeing, photography. Observing Western Australian wildflowers, western birds. Picnicking. Accommodation, caravan parks in Perth and suburbs. July to November for wildflowers, otherwise any season.

NAME OF PARK	LOCALITY ACCESS	TOPOGRAPHY VEGETATION TYPES	FEATURES OF INTEREST	ACTIVITIES ACCOMMODATION SEASON TO VISIT
MT MANYPEAKS FLORA AND FAUNA RESERVE (W.A.) about 5,000 acres	S coast of Western Australia. Proceed to Mt Manypeaks township (25 m. E of Albany) where Mt Manypeaks is visible on right. Gravel roads lead near foot of range, or to coast at Cheyne Beach. Rough track to Waychinicup inlet. *See* map p. 144.	Rugged granite range falling steeply to seas of Two People Bay. Sandplains, with low heaths, wildflowers.	A reserve created 1967 for protection of the only known population of the small carnivorous marsupial 'Dibbler', rediscovered here after 83 years. However, the Mt Manypeaks range has national park potential. The coastal scenery on the ocean side of the range is magnificent, particularly from the heights of Mt Manypeaks (1,885 ft) which falls very steeply in great bare granite headlands to the ocean. Very beautiful scenery at the estuary of Waychinicup River, which cuts through range. Good fishing, swimming. Excellent wildflowers on coastal heaths through spring, summer.	Scenic viewing of coast. Fishing, swimming. Wildflower observation. Photography. Camping at Cheyne Beach (small fishing settlement) otherwise at Albany (many hotels, motels, caravan parks). Spring, summer, autumn.
NAMBUNG NATIONAL PARK (W.A.) 39,991 acres	Near the coast about 120 m. N of Perth, just S of Jurien Bay. Road access to Jurien Bay via Gingin or Moora, but access to park very limited, at present requires 4-wheel-drive.	Coastal limestone belt, sandplains, heathlands with scattered banksia and stunted gum trees, low mallee thickets.	Most outstanding scenic feature is the 'Pinnacles' desert, where wind erosion has exposed tall limestone spires, which rise in hundreds like giant tombstones from sands almost bare of vegetation. Other parts rich in wildflowers, some unique to this area. (Until access and supervision are improved, Western Australian National Parks Board not encouraging visitors).	No accommodation. Spring months for wildflowers, otherwise any season.
NEERABUP NATIONAL PARK (W.A.) 2,785 acres	SW. Western Australia, about 22 m. N of Perth along W sides of Perth–Yanchep road.	Flat or slightly undulating sandplain, open forest of gums, banksias, with scrub understory.	Wildflowers, Western Australia's prime tourist attraction, grow profusely in this park which is to be maintained in its natural state. Note: this park currently endangered: National Parks Board making 'every effort to oppose granting of mineral licences for quarrying of limestone and building stone in this park.' From the outcome it will be seen whether Western Australia Liberal Government is genuinely concerned for tourist industry or conservation in that state.	Wildflower observation, photography. At Yanchep: lodge, guest house, hotel, caravan park; or at Perth and suburbs. July to November for best wildflower displays.
PORONGORUP RANGE NATIONAL PARK (W.A.) 5,531 acres	Southernmost Western Australia. 25 m. N of Albany by Borden road. From Perth, by Albany Highway to Mt Barker (225 m.) then E 10–15 m. *See* map p.133.	Steep granite hills, with Karri forest on slopes.	High hills with magnificent tall trees, Karri forest wildflowers. Enormous granite boulders, bare granite domes, sculptured rocks, on summits. Castle Rock, Devil's Slide. Views to S coast, and N to jagged peaks of Stirling Range National Park.	Motor touring (scenic roadways around ranges, into Bolganup Dam), sightseeing, photography. Walking, climbing on easy tracks to summits. Observing wildflowers, birds. Albany: 6 hotels, 4 motels, 3 caravan and camping parks; Mt Barker: hotel, caravan park. Any season; September to October best for wildflowers. Summers mild.
ROTTNEST ISLAND RESERVE (W.A.) 3,962 acres. Declared a public reserve and wildlife sanctuary in 1917.	Off W coast of Western Australia, 12 m. NW. of Fremantle. Regular launch services from Fremantle, air service from Perth Airport.	Formerly a high point on sand dunes, Rottnest became an island when rising seas flooded intervening lowlands. Vegetation has been changed by man, much of original tree cover being lost. *Melaleuca* and *Callitris* pine scrub now main vegetation.	Historical interest: occupied by colony's first settlers 1830, was later prison for Aboriginal offenders. Old buildings still standing were erected 1840–1860, for penal settlement use, and have survived relatively undamaged. Island has good beaches, fishing, is a major holiday centre. Of particular interest is the large and flourishing colony of Quokkas (*Setonix brachyarus*), rat-kangaroos, for which the island was named 'rats nest'. Island serves Western Australian University as natural laboratory; should be zoned for greater wildlife protection.	Swimming, fishing. Fauna observation. Island has hotel, hostel, cottages and bungalows, campsites. Most pleasant October to May.
SERPENTINE NATIONAL PARK (W.A.) 1,571 acres	About 32 m. S of Perth, via Armadale (18 m.), South-Western Highway to Serpentine township, then E several miles to park.	W escarpment of Darling Range. Vegetation open forest (Wandoo, Marri, Jarrah) with dense low undergrowth.	Waterfall dropping about 50 ft to large, very deep pool. Good wildflowers on surrounding hill slopes July–November. Views over coastal plain from heights. Nearby large Serpentine Dam (cultivated wildflowers) worth visiting (access via Jarrahdale).	Scenic sightseeing, swimming. Walking along Serpentine River above falls. Picnicking, facilities provided. Hotels, caravan parks in Perth, suburbs. Any season.
SOUTH-WEST CAVES (YALLINGUP CAVES AND MARGARET RIVER) At present a collection of small reserves for caves, flora and fauna, public recreation. Western Australian National Parks Board hopes to unify these as a caves national park.	Extreme SW. corner of Western Australia, via Bunbury, Busselton (148 m. S of Perth). Southernmost caves at Augusta (204 m. S). Good roads.	Limestone overlying granite, making low coastal hills. Extensive areas of magnificent Karri forest, very tall trees, lush undergrowth. Also Jarrah, Marri forest. Good beaches along coast.	About 120 caves have been discovered in the 60 m. stretch of coastal limestone, many only partly explored. Great beauty of stalactite, stalagmite decorations, exquisitely coloured calcite, argonite, calcium carbonate formations. Four caves open to public inspection are at least equal to any others in Australia. Jewel Cave, Augusta. Main cavern 91 yards long, 50 yards wide, ceiling 95 ft high. Clear pools, variety of formations, effective lighting. Lake Cave,	Busselton: hotels, motels, 4 caravan parks. Dunsborough: cottages, camping. Yallingup: hotel. Margaret River: hotel. Augusta: hotel, guest house, flats, cottages, caravan park. Any season for caves, September–October, wildflowers, summer for beach activities.

NAME OF PARK	LOCALITY ACCESS	TOPOGRAPHY VEGETATION TYPES	FEATURES OF INTEREST	ACTIVITIES ACCOMMODATION SEASON TO VISIT
			entered through huge 'crater' of collapsed cave in which grow Karri trees, ferns, masses of coloured stalactites reflected in waters of underground lake. Mammoth Cave, immense vaulted chambers. Fossilized marsupial bones of species extinct in Western Australia, such as Tasmanian Tiger, Koala. Yallingup Cave, many chambers, colourful formations.	
STIRLING RANGE NATIONAL PARK (W.A.) 285,874 acres	Near S coast Western Australia, about 55 m. N of Albany via Porongorups; about 210 m. S of Perth by Albany Highway, via Cranbrook. See map p. 141.	Very steep, jagged line of peaks of sedimentary rock, rising above flat plains. Dry sclerophyll forest, dense low scrub, low mallee, heaths.	Magnificent scenery of pointed peaks, mountain top cliffs, often cloud-capped. Extensive views over flat plains from heights. Rough tracks up Bluff Knoll (3,640 ft), Mt Toolbrunup (3,450 ft). Stirling Range Scenic road through length of park, from Chester Pass to Redgum Pass. Road up to foothill of Bluff Knoll—good views. Outstanding region for wildflowers, many found in no other place.	Scenic motor touring, spectacular climbing, bushwalking. Photography, observing wildflowers, birds. Rock climbing on eastern peaks. Picnicking, facility areas at Bluff Knoll, Redgum Spring, Moingup Spring, near Toolbrunup, and along scenic drive. Albany: 6 hotels, 4 motels, 3 camping and caravan parks. Mount Barker: hotel, caravan park. Most pleasant weather September to November. April–May. Wildflowers September to November.
TUTANNING (EAST PINGELLY) RESERVE (W.A.) 3,260 acres	Due east of Pingelly (103 m. SE. of Perth) about 10–15 m. along road to Bullaring, or access from Pingelly–Wickepin road.	Granite rock and sandplain country, laterite breakaways. Savannah woodland, abundant ground flora.	An important wildlife research centre, and wildlife sanctuary. Has a great diversity of flora, with many magnificent wildflowers, owing to diversity of soils. Very rich in mammals which once inhabited other parts of the Western Australian wheatbelt—Woilies, Grey Kangaroos, Tammar Wallabies, Quendas, Wambengers, Numbats, Echidnas.	Flora and fauna observation. Wildflower photography. Hotels at Pingelly. Any season; spring for wildflowers. Summers often hot, dry.
TWILIGHT COVE (Proposed National Park) (W.A.) 1,263,100 acres At present flora and fauna reserves No. 24047 and 27632. Change to national park planned.	Along Great Australian Bight, S of Eyre Highway, Eyre to Israelite Bay. Track from Cocklebiddy (270 m. E of Norseman) to coast.	Coastal cliffs of Great Australian Bight, ocean beaches and sandplains in vicinity of Eyre and Israelite Bay. Inland to Eyre Highway in vicinity of Cocklebiddy Tank, dry-country bushland, sandplain and coastal flora.	High cliffs along Bight. Area is of historical interest, being traversed by Eyre in exploration of coastline between west and south Australia. A small part of park would be selected as public recreation area, remainder set aside for preservation of flora and fauna. First recommended by the Australian Academy of Science in 1962, as a national park of 1,263,100 acres. Control sought by Western Australian National Parks Board (1968 Annual Report) but has not been finalized.	Flora and fauna observation. Bush camping. Motel on Eyre Highway at Cocklebiddy. Any time of year.
TWO PEOPLE BAY FLORA AND FAUNA RESERVE (W.A.) 11,460 acres	S coast of Western Australia, about 15 m. E of Albany. Limited access. 4-wheel-drive useful on final tracks.	High coastal granite peak of Mt Gardner, with bare rock slopes, gullies of dense mallee scrub. Coastal flats, sandy, swampy in places.	Set aside to protect the rare Noisy Scrub Bird and other rare fauna. Also Honey Possum, many honeyeating birds, coastal wildflowers. Discovery of Noisy Scrub Bird, long thought extinct, created world-wide interest. Western Australian Government showed great foresight in cancelling planned townsite to establish this reserve.	Wildlife, bird and wildflower observation. At Albany: hotels, motels, caravan parks. September to January for wildflowers.
VASSE ROAD BRIDGE NATIONAL PARK (W.A.) 520 acres	Extreme SW. corner of Western Australia, near forestry town of Pemberton (211 m. S of Perth, on South-West highway).	Hill slopes, creeks. Wet sclerophyll forest.	Tall Karri forest, lush undergrowth with wildflowers in spring.	Scenic sightseeing, photography. Pemberton: hotel, motel. Manjimup: hotels, motels, caravan park. September, October for wildflowers. Pleasantly mild summer.
WALPOLE-NORNALUP NATIONAL PARK (W.A.) 32,229 acres	S coast of Western Australia. 70 m. W of Albany; also from Bunbury via Manjimup on South-West Highway. See map p. 140.	Coastal hills with Karri forest; coastal sandplains with heaths, scrub, stunted eucalypts.	Magnificent stands of Karri, Red Tingle, Jarrah, Marri, Casuarina, with lush undergrowth of Karri Wattle, Umbrella Plant, Crowea, Tree Kangaroo-paws. Views of Nornalup and Walpole inlets from Knoll Drive. Rest Point Drive, Hilltop Road Scenic Lookout gives views over Frankland River, Southern Ocean, Casuarina Isles. Short drives to Circular Pool, Mt Frankland, Valley of Giants, Petrified Forest. Wildlife includes Black Swans, Pelicans.	Sightseeing, fishing, swimming. Yachting, boating and water ski-ing facilities. Bush walking, observing birds, wildflowers. Colour photography. Walpole: hotel, guest house, caravan and camping grounds. Nornalup: guest house, holiday cottages. September to October for most wildflowers, some species midsummer. Summer for swimming, yachting, fishing. Summers mild.
WALYUNGA NATIONAL PARK (W.A.) 4,000 acres	SW. of Western Australia. Access by Great Northern Highway, turning off (towards ranges) between 22 and 23 m. posts, then E 3 to 4 m.	Hills of Darling Range, along upstream part of Swan River. Open eucalypt forest with low underscrub.	Attractive upper reaches of Swan River, Walyunga Pool, Long Pool. Former Aboriginal campsite, largest known site within 50 m. of Perth and of considerable anthropological interest (Aboriginal stone artefacts are protected, and must not be removed from the area). Darling Range wildflowers.	Sightseeing, picnicking (facilities provided). Swimming in river pools. Bushwalking. Observing birdlife. No caravan or camping facilities. Accommodation, caravan parks in Perth and suburbs. July to November for wildflowers, otherwise any season.

NAME OF PARK	LOCALITY ACCESS	TOPOGRAPHY VEGETATION TYPES	FEATURES OF INTEREST	ACTIVITIES ACCOMMODATION SEASON TO VISIT
WARREN NATIONAL PARK (W.A.) 3,350 acres	Extreme SW. corner of Western Australia, adjacent to forestry town of Pemberton which is 211 m. S of Perth via South-Western Highway.	Undulating hills, densely vegetated with wet sclerophyll forest (Karri, *Eucalyptus diversicolor*).	Enormous trees rising to 250 ft or more, and well over 100 ft to first branch, bark an attractive salmon-tinted white. Lush undergrowth. Nearby is Gloucester tree, with forestry lookout on top, 200 ft above ground.	Sightseeing, motor touring. Photography. Observing wildflowers. Pemberton: hotel, guest house. Manjimup: hotel, motels, caravan park. September to October for wildflowers. Pleasantly mild summers.
WAVE ROCK RESERVES (W.A.) Total area 12,975 acres Flora and Fauna Reserves A 21253, 27175 and 26661.	Central SW. Western Australia, adjacent to township of Hyden, 217 m. WSW. of Perth via Brookton, Corrigin, Kondinin.	Massive bare outcrops of granite rock. Mallee eucalypt vegetation.	Unusual rock formation, known as Wave Rock, is main tourist attraction. An overhang, some 50 ft high, has the appearance of a breaking wave, being vertically streaked by water stains of grey, ochre, red.	Motor touring, photography. A 50 m. road circuit from Hyden leads to other rock formations such as Bates Cave (Aboriginal paintings), The Humps, King Rocks, Gnamma Hole. Hyden: hotel, caravan and camping area. Any season, but midsummer hot and dry.
YANCHEP NATIONAL PARK AND CAVES RESERVE (W.A.) 6,840 acres	SW. Western Australia. From Perth, proceed N by Wanneroo Road, parallel to coast, for 32 m. This road leads into the park.	Coastal limestone and sandy plains, Tuart forest, Marri gums, dense undergrowth of many wildflower species. Coastal lakes.	Yanchep is famous for its limestone caves (guided tours), its spring wildflower displays. Red-and-green Kangaroo-paws, W.A. floral emblem, common in park. Display of Koalas and other native animals. Beds of cultivated wildflowers. Very attractive scenery around Loch McNess, a lake with densely vegetated shores, many little islands. Black swans and other birds on lake.	Cave tours (details Western Australian Tourist Bureau); Launch trips daily on Loch McNess; hiking, bush and wildflower walks. Conducted tours of wildflower plots in spring. Golf course, tennis courts, swimming pool. Surfing and fishing at beach 4 m. W. Lodge, guest house, hotel in park. Caravan–camping grounds at beach, also at Perth and suburbs. July to October for most wildflowers, otherwise any season.
YALGORUP NATIONAL PARK (W.A.) 7,684 acres (A new park, 1968)	SW. of Western Australia, about 80 m. S of Perth, W of the Old Coast Road between Mandurah and Bunbury. Limited access at present.	Sandy coastal areas, dunes with heaths, thickets. Tuart forest, with understorey of Banksias and acacias. Paperbarks and Flooded Gums in swampy parts.	Borders Lakes Clifton and Preston, which in summer are covered with water-birds; swampy area at south of Preston probably breeding area for ducks. One observer recorded 100 species of birds for this area. At one time on Lake Clifton, about 1,370 birds of 16 species, including 265 Black Swans, were counted. Area very rich in wildflowers in season. Historical interest in old farms by Old Coast Road. Some are more than 100 years old; one barn in area loopholed for defence against attack by natives. Good beaches along coast. Presence of such numbers of birds, other features within a few hours drive from Perth is potential tourist attraction, but of the 30,000 acre area recommended by Australian Academy of Science, W.A. Government has granted only 7,684 acres.	Birdlife observation. Wildflowers. Viewing historical farms. Mandurah: hotels, caravan parks, cottages and flats. Bunbury: hotels, caravan parks, guest houses, holiday cottages. July to December for wildflowers; summer for water sports at beach resorts.

SMALL PARKS, NATURE RESERVES

NAME, LOCATION	FEATURES OF INTEREST
Bald I. Reserve. 2,000 acres. S coast of W.A., 15 m. E of Two People Bay and about 30 m. E of Albany.	A high, hilly granite island, densely vegetated in parts with Tea-tree forest, stunted Mallee eucalypts. Marsupial population yet undamaged by man, includes Quokka (*Setonix brachyurus*)—a type of rat-kangaroo—and also bandicoots.
Blackwood River National Park. 3,394 acres. Extreme SW. corner of W.A. Situated on the eastern banks of the lower reaches of the Blackwood River, about 10 m. NE. of Augusta. Access from Brockman Highway.	Probably paperbark and blackboy flats, Marri forest in parts. Wildflowers such as swamp bottlebrush, tree kangaroo-paw. No facilities, limited access.
Dampier Archipelago. NW. W.A., off coast NW. of Roebourne.	Offshore islands are valuable wildlife sanctuaries, often undamaged by grazing of sheep, cattle, rabbits and wildlife unharmed by cats, foxes. W.A. National Parks Board seeking control over these islands.
Dumbleyung Lake Fauna Reserve 26664. 10,360 acres. About 160 m. SE. from Perth.	Entire area is lake and shores. A water-bird sanctuary situated between Wagin and Dumbleyung.
Esperance Flora and Fauna Reserves, S coast W.A., almost whole of coastline for 35 m. W of Esperance, and up to about 5 m. inland, in reserves 27888, 26885, 24486, with a total area of 54,081 acres. Eastwards, between Esperance and Cape Le Grand National Park, are reserves 23825 and 26893, combined area, 6,320 acres.	Preserving coastal scenery and wildflowers west and east of port of Esperance. These wildflower reserves are particularly valuable now that huge areas are being cleared for agriculture in this region.
Flora and Fauna Reserve 'A' 23756. 1,930 acres. SW. W.A. on SW. shores of Harvey Estuary, about 60 m. S of Perth.	Coastal plain swamplands, lakes, paperbark flats, important for feeding and breeding of waterfowl, and essential in preserving population of wild ducks in Western Australia. Access via Mandurah or Pinjarrah and Coolup.
Flora and Fauna Reserves 24491, 24450, 24229. Total area 76,644 acres. Central W-coastal W.A. 140 m. N of Perth.	Outstanding wildflower country easily accessible to all tourists. Proceed via North-west Coastal Highway to Watheroo (141 m. N of Perth), then W about 5 m. Road passes through southern part of reserves. Many banksias, including orange *Banksia prionotes*. Brilliant verticordias, leschenaultias, eucalypts, kangaroo-paws.
Flora and Fauna Reserve No. 24496. 174,450 acres. W coast of W.A. Begins 110 m. N of Perth, extends 65 m. along coast except for 5 m. gap. May become a national park soon.	Coastal limestone country, containing caves in places, some with fossils of mammals now extinct in the area. Includes rugged country at Cockleshell Gully. This part of reserve carries very distinctive endemic flora and at least five plants found nowhere else in the world. Most parts require 4-wheel-drive. Access by track N from Jurien Bay, or from Three Springs via Eneabba, or S from Dongara.

NAME, LOCATION	FEATURES OF INTEREST
Flora and Fauna Reserves No. 24618 and 25210. 9,179 acres. Central W-coast of W.A.	Sandplains with many banksias bearing huge orange or yellow flowers, flowering mallee eucalypts, and small flowering shrubs. Access via Coorow (174 m. N of Perth on Highway 1) then 5 m. W to reserve 24618, or 15 m. SW. to reserve 25210.
Flora and Fauna Reserves 'A' 25134, 'A' 25135, 'A' 25136, 27481. Total area 9,282 acres. SW. W.A.	On the Coblinine River Flats, shallow lakes, swamps NE. of Katanning, S of Dumbleyung.
Flora and Fauna Reserve No. 26647. 9,365 acres. Central W-coastal W.A. about 25 m. WSW. of Jurien Bay.	Sandplain country with many wildflowers, such as *Eucalyptus rhodantha* (huge crimson flowers), *Verticordia grandis*, many banksias. Proceed via Gingin or Moore via Dandaragan to Badgingarra, then about 4 m. to reserve on left of road to Jurien Bay.
Flora and Fauna Reserves 27283 and 26259. Total area 10,083 acres. 50 m. E of Wubin.	On western shores of the extensive dry salt lake system of Lake Moore. Mallee and mulga country, some tall trees. Many good wildflowers July to September.
Flora and Fauna Reserves 28462 (area 26,030 acres) and 28558 (area 5,260 acres). W-coastal W.A. about 60 m. N of Perth.	Sandplain country with magnificent wildflowers: many large-flowered banksias, masses of tall golden *Verticordia nitens*, golden kangaroo-paws, W.A. Christmas tree. December a good month, September, October and November. Access from Perth via Gingin (52 m.) then along Dandaragan Road, 20–25 m. Reserve 28462 is on plains W side of road. Reserve 28558 is about 5 m. N of Moore River then about 10 m. W.
Flora and Fauna Reserves 28497. 180 m. due E of coast at Kalbarri, and 80 m. NW. of Mt Magnet.	Arid mulga-scrublands, dry-country fauna.
Kalbarri Flora and Fauna Reserve, No. 12996. 3,000 acres. Access, accommodation as for Kalbarri National Park.	The estuary of the Murchison River, immediately N of Kalbarri township and W of Kalbarri National Park. Attractive coastal scenery, outstanding wildflowers, boating, fishing, swimming in river estuary.
Lake Disappointment. Proposed national park of approx. 1,230 sq. m. On Tropic of Capricorn 560 m. inland from W coast; nearest settlement, Jiggalong Mission.	Sandy desert country, extremely inhospitable, but in places has great scenic grandeur, and is of biological importance. Includes section of historic Canning Stock Route. Gibber plains, sand dunes. Waterholes important to Aborigines; rock paintings. Country too barren for agricultural or pastoral use, but contains desert fauna, flora.
Ludlow Tuart Forest. Extreme SW. of W.A. along both sides of highway between Capel and Busselton. About 5,000 acres. (At present part of State Forest Nos. 1 and 2.)	The finest remaining example of south-western Tuart forest, ancient specimens up to 120 ft tall. Forests policy has aimed at perpetuation of prime forest and preservation of scenic value of highway strip; trees felled for safety reasons only. This should be made a Scenic Highway (like Tasmania's Scenic Roads); Aust. Academy of Science recommends 5 chain strip along highway be made a national park.
Millstream National Park, NW. W.A., on Fortescue River, Millstream Station. 1,090 acres.	Long, deep river pool, surrounded by lush greenery of trees, undergrowth. Gathering place for birdlife in dry seasons. Access from Roebourne–Wittenoom Road.
Mt Manypeaks Flora and Fauna Reserves, S coast of W.A.	Reserve 26385 (2,490 acres) about 5 m. N of Mt Manypeaks Township, and Reserve 27157 (1,075 acres) about 7 m. E of Mt Manypeaks township. Wildflowers September–December.
Narrogin District Flora–Fauna Reserves; Reserves 'A' 15266 (154 acres), 27286 (1,425 acres), Toolibin Lake, 9617 (500 acres), Lake Wallabing 'A' 14398 (292 acres), Nomans Lake 26785 (437 acres), 26787 (257 acres), 26786 (710 acres), 26788 (2,387 acres), 26790 (858 acres), 26789 (2,641 acres) and 9508 (1,931 acres).	A chain of small lakes, paperbark swamps, between Highbury and East Wickepin, being headwaters of the Arthur River. These are feeding and breeding grounds for many water birds, including Spoonbills and Plumed Egrets. Some of these reserves are open to duck shooters each year. This has on occasions caused heavy mortality among nesting Egrets and other birds, due to indiscriminate shooting, and noise causing young Egrets fluttering from nests to be drowned in the swamps.
Northern Nullarbor Area proposed National Nature Reserve. 5,552,000 acres. S of W.A. (Proposal by Aust. Academy of Science.)	Southern part typical flat limestone country of Nullarbor. Northwards is grassland, with *Acacia* scrub, Bluebush. Further north, hilly land, Acacia species. Northernmost is belt of sand, with eucalypts, shell lakes. Eastwards are dunes, with spinifex, mallee. Purpose: to preserve flora, unique fauna such as the Marsupial Mole of the desert sand dunes.
Ongerup–Pingrup Area Flora and Fauna Reserves.	No. 28324, 20 m. NE. of Ongerup, 2,494 acres. No. 24589, between Pingrup and Ongerup, 3,700 acres.
Queen Victoria Spring proposed National Nature Reserve. 618,750 acres. Situated about 140 m. ENE. of Kalgoorlie. (Proposal by Aust. Academy of Science.)	The spring is a soak in patch of grassland surrounded by sand dune desert, mulga and *Triodia* steppe lands. Spring was discovered in 1875 by explorer Ernest Giles, who named it after Queen Victoria. It is a watering place at times for a great multitude of desert birdlife.
Recherche Archipelago Reserve, area unknown. S-coast of W.A., at W end of Great Aust. Bight near Esperance.	Altogether 109 small islands, varying in size from rocks of less than 1 acre to islands up to 3 m. long. Most are steep-sided, hilly, making boat landings difficult. Marsupials of great scientific interest; include a rock wallaby, a bandicoot, and the Tammar Wallaby. 240 species plants so far recorded, some confined to one island. It is planned to make the reserve a national park.
Scenic Road National Park Reserve, Mt Manypeaks—Green Range, S coast W.A. Reserve 'A' 26650, area 3,160 acres.	A roadside strip beginning 6 m. E of Mt Manypeaks township (25 m. E of Albany) and extending about 20 m. along the main bitumen road towards Jerramungup. Good displays of wildflowers September–April, including various kangaroo paws, banksias, Christmas Tree.
Sir James Mitchell National Park. 2,717 acres. Extreme SW. of W.A.	Situated along the South-coast highway between Manjimup and Walpole, beginning 19 m. S of Manjimup at Quininup Mill and extending about 30 m. along road. From Albany, park begins about 30 m. NW. of Walpole. A scenic road of the type well known in Tasmania. Others could well be established in Western Australia.
Stirling Range area Flora and Fauna Reserves, S W.A. Reserve 'A' 25812 (373 acres), 'A' 26160 (2,509 acres), 'A' 26161 (7,944 acres), 26162 (881 acres), 25194 (1,091 acres), 'A' 25386 (814 acres), and 26688 (2,179 acres).	7 small reserves preserving samples of country rich in wildflowers, adjacent to, or close by the Stirling Range National Park.
Tree Society's Wildflower Reserve (No. 26663). 17,033 acres. About 30 m. SE. of Geraldton (312 m. N of Perth).	Outstanding wildflower country, with great variety of spectacular species best seen July–December. Access route by Highway 1 towards Geraldton to Mingenew, another 12 m. on Highway to Strawberry, turn N, then NW. about 20 m. From Geraldton, via Walkaway, then E about 20 m.
Toodyay Forest. About 84,000 acres (at present State Forest No. 61). S of W.A., near town of Toodyay, 53 m. ENE. of Perth.	Recommended (by Aust. Academy of Science) as fauna and flora reserve when relinquished by Forests Dept. Contains Wandoo forest, very rich in western wildflowers, and sheltering large number of birds, marsupials. A wildlife sanctuary of great importance.

NAME, LOCATION	FEATURES OF INTEREST
W.A. Historical Sites.	
The Round House, Fremantle	Built 1831, State's oldest public building.
Old Mill, South Perth.	At S end of Narrows Bridge, restored as historical showpiece. Open 1 p.m. to 5 p.m.
Old Court House	Built 1836 (Now the Arbitration Court).
Toodyay Old Gaol	1860's Restored by Toodyay Shire Council and Tourist Development Authority; historical museum.
Strawberry Hill Farm, Albany	Built 1836.
The Deanery, Perth	About 1860.
Perth Town Hall.	Built 1870.
West Pingelly Flora and Fauna Reserve (No. 20610). 9,990 acres. SW. W.A. about 70 m. SE. of Perth, (by Brookton Highway) turning S 13 m. W of Brookton.	A magnificent mass of exposed granite rock and its associated flora. Alongside Boyagin Rock there is a small, pleasant picnic area, on edge of main reserve. Flora, fauna similar to that described for Tuttanning and Dryandra. Access also via Pingelly, Dattening.
Wolf Creek Meteor Crater, geological reserve. (Proposed by Aust. Academy of Science.) Approx. 5 sq. m., location 19°12′S, 127°51′E.	One of largest craters known on the earth's surface. Has attracted world-wide interest, and was featured in a nation-wide television programme in America ('CBS Presents') as a typical example of a crater resembling those on moon.

SOME BIRDS OF WESTERN NATIONAL PARKS

Emu (*Dromaius novae-hollandiae*); plains and open forests.
Nankeen Night Heron (*Nycticorax caledonicus*); streams and swamps.
Mangrove Bittern (*Butorides striata*); muddy foreshores.
Red Mangrove Bittern (*Butorides rogersi*); coastal area, Onslow district.
Black Swan (*Cygnus atratus*); lakes, rivers and swamps.
Whistling Eagle (*Haliastur sphenurus*); plains and open forest.
Fork-tailed Kite (*Milvus migrans*); inland plains.
Letter-wing Kite (*Elanus scriptus*); open and lightly-timbered land.
Brown Goshawk (*Accipiter fasciatus*); forests.
Spotted Harrier (*Circus assimilis*); swamps and reedbeds.
Brown Hawk (*Falco berigora*); open country.
Banded Rail (*Hypotaenidia philippensis*); swampy areas.
Black-tailed Native Hen (*Tribonyx ventralis*); swamps and reedbeds.
Western Swamphen (*Porphyrio bellus*); lakes and streams.
Bustard (*Ardeotis australis*); inland plains.
Red-capped Dotterel (*Charadrius alexandrinus*); beaches, lakes.
Black-fronted Dotterel (*Charadrius melanops*); river banks.
Crested Pigeon (*Ocyphaps lophotes*); inland scrubs.
Flock Pigeon (*Histriophaps histrionica*); plains.
Western Plumed Pigeon (*Lophophaps ferruginea*); rocky and spinifex.
Red-tailed Black Cockatoo (*Calyptorhynchus banksi*); forests.
Mulga Parrot (*Psephotus varius*); open forest and dry scrub.
Bourke Parrot (*Neophema bourki*); mulga scrubs.
Long-billed Corella (*Kakatoë tenuirostris*); inland plains.
Western Rosella (*Platycercus icterotis*); open forest.
Twenty-eight Parrot (*Barnardius semitorquatus*); open forest.
Red-capped Parrot (*Purpureicephalus spurius*); south-west forests.
Elegant Grass Parrot (*Neophema elegans*); plains and grasslands.
Rock Parrot (*Neophema petrophila*); islands and south coast.
Swamp Parrot (*Pezoporus wallicus*); swampy heathlands.
Tawny Frogmouth (*Podargus strigoides*); forests.
Owlet Nightjar (*Aegotheles cristata*); forests.
Mangrove Kingfisher (*Halcyon chloris*); mangrove swamps.
Red-backed Kingfisher (*Halcyon pyrrhopygius*); dry interior.
Blue-winged Kookaburra (*Dacelo leachi*); open forests, and mangroves.
Ground Cuckoo-shrike (*Pteropodocys maxima*); mallee and mulga.
Noisy Scrub-bird (*Atrichornis clamosus*); low coastal thickets.

White-backed Swallow (*Cheramoeca leucosterna*); inland areas.
Western Magpie (*Gymnorhina dorsalis*); open forest.
Rufous Tree-creeper (*Climacteris rufa*); open forest.
Western Bower-bird (*Chlamydera guttata*); open forest and scrub.
Black-capped Sittella (*Neositta pileata*); open forest.
Western Thrush (*Colluricincla rufiventris*); open forest.
Chestnut-breasted Quail-thrush (*Cinclosoma castaneothorax*); mulga and mallee.
Spinifex Bird (*Eremiornis carteri*); spinifex and low scrub.
Southern Scrub-robin (*Drymodes brunneopygia*); mulga and mallee.
Black-and-white Wren (*Malurus leucopterus*); Dirk Hartog and Barrow I.
Banded Wren (*Malurus splendens*); forests and coastal thickets.
Blue-and-white Wren (*Malurus cyanotus*); saltbush and bluebush flats.
Variegated Wren (*Malurus lamberti*); heathlands, undergrowth, low scrub.
Red-winged Wren (*Malurus elegans*); forest undergrowth and heathlands.
Southern Emu-wren (*Stipiturus malachurus*); swampy heathlands.
Rufous-crowned Emu-wren (*Stipiturus ruficeps*); spinifex.
Redthroat (*Pyrrholaemus brunneus*); stunted scrub.
Western Grass-wren (*Amytornis textilis*); saltbush and spinifex.
Western Warbler (*Gerygone fusca*); open forest.
Spotted Scrub-wren (*Sericornis maculatus*); dense undergrowth.
Rufous Bristle-bird (*Dasyornis broadbenti*); low scrub.
Bristle-bird (*Dasyornis longirostris*); swampy heaths and scrubs.
Mangrove Robin (*Peneoenanthe pulverulentius*); mangroves.
Scarlet Robin (*Petroica multicolor*); forests.
Red-capped Robin (*Petroica goodenovii*); inland forests and scrub.
Western Yellow Robin (*Eopsaltria griseogularis*); forests.
White-breasted Robin (*Eopsaltria georgiana*); forests.
Gilbert Whistler (*Pachycephala inornata*); inland forest and scrub.
Pied Honeyeater (*Certhionyx variegatus*); heaths and scrublands.
Spiny-cheeked Honeyeater (*Acanthagenys rufogularis*); open forest and scrub.
Western Spinebill (*Acanthorhynchus superciliosus*); banksia and eucalypt forest.
Tawny-crowned Honeyeater (*Gliciphila melanops*); heath and low scrub.
Crested Bellbird (*Oreoica gutturalis*); open forest and scrublands.
Black-throated Whipbird (*Psophodes nigrogularis*); mallee.
Yellow-tailed Pardalote (*Pardalotus xanthopygus*); inland dry scrub.
Western Silvereye (*Zosterops gouldi*); forests and gardens.
Red-eared Firetail Finch (*Zonaeginthus oculatus*); forest and heathlands.

SOME FURRED ANIMALS OF THE WESTERN PARKS AND RESERVES

Spiny Anteater (*Tachyglossus aculeatus*); diurnal; widespread, many habitats.
Yellow-footed Marsupial Mouse (*Antechinus flavipes*); nocturnal; widespread in forests.
A north-west Marsupial Mouse (*A. rosamondae*); a russet-coloured species, named 1964.
Fat-tailed Marsupial Mouse (*Sminthopsis crassicaudata*); insectivorous; savannah woodland.
Mouse-like Sminthopsis (*S. murina*); nocturnal, insectivorous; widespread.
Long-tailed Sminthopsis (*S. longicaudata*); tail twice length of head plus body, Pilbara.
Jerboa Marsupial Mouse (*Antechinomys spenceri*); interior of W.A., desert-like areas.
Brush-tailed Phascogale (*Phascogale tapoatafa*); forests, nocturnal hunter in treetops.
Red-tailed Phascogale or Wambenger (*P. calura*); nocturnal hunter; forests and woodlands.
Western Crest-tailed Marsupial-Mouse (*Dasycercus blythi*); north-west W.A., fattened tail.
Fat-tailed Phascogale (*Pseudantechinus macdonnellensis*); stony desert, interior, and on Barrow I.
Dibbler, or Freckled Marsupial Mouse (*Antechinus apicalis*); rare; small carnivore.
Northern Native Cat (*Satanellus hallucatus*); nocturnal; rocky terrain, north-west W.A.
Western Native Cat (*Dasurinus geoffroyi*); southern W.A. forests and scrublands.
Numbat, or Banded Anteater (*Myrmecobius fasciatus*); diurnal; south-west, in wandoo forest.
Western Barred-Bandicoot (*Perameles bougainvillei*); rather indistinct bands on rump.
Short-nosed Bandicoot (*Isoodon obesulus*); south-west forests, digs for insect larvae.
Barrow Island Bandicoot (*I. barrowensis*); black bands on rump, only on Barrow I., W.A.
Bilby, or Rabbit-eared Bandicoot (*Thylacomys lagotis*); now rare; inland-southern W.A.
Pig-footed Bandicoot (*Chaeropus ecaudatus*); once an inhabitant of inland south-west W.A.
Honey Possum (*Tarsipes spenserae*); a specialised nectar feeder; confined to south-coast W.A.
Western Pygmy Possum (*Cercartetus concinnus*); insect and nectar-eating, south-west forests.
Brush-tailed Possum (*Trichosaurus vulpeca*); feeds on leaves, buds, shoots, forests and open woodlands.

Western Ringtail Possum (*Pseudocheirus occidentalis*); extreme south-west, in forests.
Gilbert's Potoroo (*Potorous gilberti*); extremely rare; south-coast W.A., forests and scrub.
Broad-faced Potoroo (*Potorous platyops*); possibly extinct; coastal scrub and forest, southern W.A.
Brush-tailed Rat-kangaroo or Woilie (*Bettongia penicillata*); south-west, dry sclerophyll forest.
Lesueur's Rat-kangaroo (*B. lesueur*); Bernier, Dorre, Dirk Hartog Is., and extreme south-west.
Western Hare-wallaby (*Lagorchestes hirsutus*); inland southern W.A., Bernier and Dorre I.
Spectacled Hare-wallaby (*L. conspicillatus*); Barrow I., north-west W.A.
Banded Hare-wallaby (*Lagostrophus fasciatus*); Bernier and Dorre I. fauna reserves and extreme south.
Crescent Nail-tailed Wallaby (*Onychogalea lunata*); very rare; extreme south-west.
Black-flanked Rock-wallaby (*Petrogale lateralis*); northwards from Perth to Derby.
North-west Rock-Wallaby (*P. rothschildi*); confined to Roebourne–Port Hedland area
Quokka (*Setonix brachyurus*); once plentiful on mainland, now common only on Rottnest and Bald I.
Tammar, or Dama Wallaby (*Wallabia eugenii*); south-west W.A., and on Houtmann Abrolhos.
Brush, or Black-gloved Wallaby (*W. irma*); south-west W.A. in dry sclerophyll forests.
Wallaroo, or Euro (*Macropus robustus*); in rocky ranges of north-west and inland.
Red Kangaroo (*M. rufus*); north-west and interior, in open grassland and scrub plains.
Grey Kangaroo (*M. major*); reasonably common; south-western forests and woodlands.
Dingo (*Canis antarcticus*); scattered throughout inland and northern parts.
Western Swamp-rat (*Rattus fuscipes*); south-coastal W.A., coastal forests and swamps.
Abrolhos Rat (*Rattus glauerti*); on East Wallabi I., Abrolhos group.
Sooty Water-rat (*Hydromys fuliginosus*); western rivers and streams.

THE SOUTH

Cape Barren Goose

NAME OF PARK	LOCALITY ACCESS	TOPOGRAPHY VEGETATION TYPES	FEATURES OF INTEREST	ACTIVITIES ACCOMMODATION SEASON TO VISIT
ALFRED NATIONAL PARK (VIC.) 5,406 acres	SE. Victoria, straddles Princes Highway 300 m. E of Melbourne, between Mt Drummer and Karlo Creek.	Tree-covered, mountainous terrain, one of most southerly occurrences of sub-tropical rainforest ('Jungle').	Outstanding scenery along Princes Highway. Epiphytic orchids, many ferns and vines.	Highway sightseeing on jungle verges. Bushwalking in wilderness forests. Picnic facilities at Governor's Bend on highway. Ranger at Mallacoota. Motel and camping park at Cann River. Visit at any season.
ALLIGATOR GORGE NATIONAL PARK (S.A.) 9,466 acres	Lower Flinders Ranges. From Adelaide on Highway 83 via Clare, Gladstone, Wilmington. Last few m. very steep; leave caravans at Wilmington. *See* map p. 165.	Rugged heights of the southern Flinders Ranges, deep valleys and gorges.	Main feature is a narrow, red-walled chasm known as Alligator Gorge. Yellow-footed Rock Wallabies, Euros, Adelaide Rosellas.	Sightseeing, colour photography. Observing birdlife, wildflowers. No overnight accommodation; caravan park at Wilmington. Ranger based at Wilmington. Winter, spring (for wildflowers), autumn.
BAW BAW ALPINE RESERVE (VIC.) (Forests Commission) 13,000 acres	From Melbourne by Princes Highway to Robin Hood or Warragul, then N about 25 m. to Noojee, and E via Vesper, Tanjil Bren. Special transport available over snow in winter.	Mountain summit and high plains, altitude up to 5,127 ft.	Preserves a large area of interesting alpine scenery, vegetation, with wildflower displays in summer, extensive snowfields in winter.	Sightseeing, skiing in winter months (rope tows operate). Moe: hotels, motel, caravan and camping park. Visit in winter for snow, otherwise any season.
BELAIR NATIONAL PARK (S.A.) 2,058 acres	Mt Lofty Range, 8 m. S of Adelaide via Unley Road. *See* map p.165.	Hills, valleys, some parts deeply dissected, 800 to 1,600 ft above sea level. Savannah woodlands, with many attractive, tall, white-trunked gums.	Generally an attractive bushland landscape, tall trees and native bush. Wildflower displays in spring. Wildlife enclosures, sporting facilities. Old Govt. House museum.	Most used as weekend recreation by Adelaide residents, picnics, etc. Tracks for bird and wildflower observation. Tennis, golf. Caravan park, all facilities. Rangers, and headquarters of National Park Commission of South Australia. All seasons.
BEN LOMOND NATIONAL PARK (TAS.) 39,615 acres	NE. Tasmania, between Launceston and St Marys.	A high dolerite plateau, alpine vegetation on the heights, wet sclerophyll forests on the slopes. Winter snow. Highest: Legge's Tor (5,160 ft), Stack's Bluff (5,010 ft).	Winter sports on snowfields (partly developed ski resort). Views from heights, overlooking NE. Tasmania. Tasmanian birdlife, flora.	Ski-ing. Bushwalking, sightseeing. Launceston: 38 fully licensed hotels, 4 motels, 10 private hotels, caravan park. Winter months for snow, otherwise spring, summer, autumn.
BIG HEATH NATIONAL PARK (S.A.) 5,809 acres	SE. South Australia, SW. from Naracoorte which is 222 m. from Adelaide. *See* map p. 165.	Sandplain and swamp, limestone rises with pink gum. Heath and mallee-heath.	Big Heath is a sanctuary for waterfowl when flooded by rising waters of Bool Lagoon. Large flocks of Brolgas can be seen in the area at times, and a great many water birds. Also shelters Red-necked Wallabies, Black-tailed Wallabies, Black-faced Grey Kangaroos. A rewarding place for anyone interested in birdlife.	Birdlife observation. No overnight accommodation at park. Naracoorte: 3 hotels, 3 motels, guest house, camping and caravan park; Penola: 1 hotel, 1 motel. Any season.
BILLIATT NATIONAL PARK (S.A.) 90,874 acres	E South Australia, approx. 25 m. W of Victorian border and 30 m. S of Murray River, between townships of Peebinga and Mindarie. *See* map p. 165.	Very sandy: sandplains, sandhills, mallee vegetation.	Principally a wildlife sanctuary, a sample of the original environment, where studies can be made by scientists of the association between land, climate, vegetation and living creatures. Serves also as a comparison by which to measure changes in cleared and farmed areas of similar soils, climate..	Scientific study of environment. Wildlife observation. No accommodation. Winter, spring months.
BULGA NATIONAL PARK (VIC.) 91 acres	S Gippsland, between Yarram on South Gippsland Highway, and Traralgon, on Princes Highway. 120 m. SE. from Melbourne.	In Strzlecki Ranges, sample of original South Gippsland forest and temperate rainforest vegetation.	Tall Mountain Ash trees, magnificent gully of tree ferns, many Superb Lyrebirds and other birdlife.	Sightseeing along short tracks, birdwatching. Colour photography. No camping or accommodation within park. Ranger at weekends and public holidays. Any season.
CANUNDA NATIONAL PARK (S.A.) 22,120 acres	SE. coast of South Australia, W of Mt Gambier and S of Beachport. *See* map p.165.	Coastal cliffs and large dunes. Low coastal vegetation.	Coastal scenery. Aboriginal middens and artefacts. Wildlife includes Rufous Bristle-bird, Orange-bellied Parrot.	General sightseeing, photography. Bird and wildlife observation. No accommodation at park. Millicent: 3 hotels, 2 motels, caravan and camping parks; Mt Gambier: 9 hotels, 8 motels, guest houses, caravan parks. Honorary rangers visit park. Any season.
CHURCHILL NATIONAL PARK (VIC.) 477 acres	20 m. E of Melbourne, 8 m. N of Dandenong. On Scoresby–Rowville Road between Dandenong and Ferntree Gully.	Ranges and open eucalypt forest.	Views from walking tracks of Dandenong and suburbs. Recreational area for family picnics, fireplaces and water.	Outings from city, general weekend relaxation in bushland. Photography, bird watching. No camping or overnight accommodation. Nearby towns, all facilities. Ranger. Spring or autumn usually most pleasant.

NAME OF PARK	LOCALITY ACCESS	TOPOGRAPHY VEGETATION TYPES	FEATURES OF INTEREST	ACTIVITIES ACCOMMODATION SEASON TO VISIT
CLELAND NATIONAL PARK (S.A.) 1,749 acres	Mt Lofty Ranges, from foothills almost up to Mt Lofty summit. From Adelaide via Glen Osmond and Mt Barker Roads. *See* map p. 165.	Steep hills and gullies. Part dry sclerophyll (eucalypt) forest, part old, cleared grazing land.	Native fauna park—large enclosures contain Koalas (some free in bush), kangaroos, wallabies, Emus, Euros, Cape Barren Geese, Black Swans, waterfowl. Peat bog area with relic tree ferns (*Todea barbara*).	Pleasant place for family picnics, bush recreation, and for close, easy look at wildlife. Kiosk. Ranger. No overnight accommodation at park. Adelaide and suburbs, all facilities. Any season.
COCOPARA NATIONAL PARK (N.S.W.) 20,000 acres	Central-southern New South Wales, on Cocopara Ranges, 12 m. N of Griffith. Access from Griffith.	Low, timbered range.	Vista points overlooking Murrumbidgee irrigation area. Interesting ground flora offers shelter for Grey Kangaroos.	Bushwalking, bird and wildflower observation. Picnicking. Griffith: 3 hotels, 3 motels; caravan and camping park at Lake Wynangan. Spring months for wildflowers, or autumn.
COORONG NATIONAL PARK (S.A.) 7,800 acres	Coastal SE. South Australia, on the Younghusband Peninsula between the Coorong and the sea, and across the Coorong from Princes Highway. *See* map p. 165.	Coastal sand dunes and dune vegetation.	Principally a wildlife sanctuary preserving the coastal dunes, flora and fauna. The Rufous Bristlebird is one of its more interesting species.	Wildlife observation. No accommodation or facilities at park. Any season.
CRADLE MOUNTAIN–LAKE ST CLAIR NATIONAL PARK (TAS.) 338,496 acres	Central Tasmanian highlands. Access from N is via Sheffield and Wilmot to Waldheim. From S (i.e. Hobart) approach via Tarraleah Highway and Derwent Bridge to Lake St Clair. *See* map p. 184.	Mountainous, heavy winter snowfalls, many glacial lakes, headwaters of several Tasmanian rivers. Alpine vegetation on heights, temperate rainforest and wet sclerophyll forest.	Unsurpassed mountain scenery—Cradle Mountain (5,069 ft), Barn Bluff (5,114 ft), Mt Ossa (5,305 ft), Lake St Clair, Lake Dove, Crater Lake. Ancient mossy Beech forests, alpine wildflowers, Tasmanian wallabies.	Sightseeing on short (2–5 m.) tracks, or long hikes up to 52 m. Unlimited photographic opportunity. Ski-ing at Cradle Mountain, Mt Rufus. Chalet and cabins at Waldheim, cabins, caravans and camping areas at Lake St Clair. Huts on overland track. Rangers at Waldheim and Lake St Clair. November to March or April, except for winter ski-ing.
FAIRVIEW NATIONAL PARK (S.A.) 2,690 acres	Lower SE. of South Australia, WNW. from Naracoorte, S of Padthaway. *See* map p. 165.	Undulating sandplains and limestone rises, lagoons and swamp.	A wildlife sanctuary, important for waterfowl and waders. Also Emus, Mallee Fowl. Its mammals are known to include South-west Pygmy Possum, Sugar Glider, Eastern Swamp-rat, Red-necked Wallaby and Black-faced Kangaroo.	Wildlife observation. No accommodation at park. Naracoorte: 3 hotels, 3 motels, guest house, camping and caravan park. Any season.
FERNTREE GULLY NATIONAL PARK (VIC.) 927 acres	22 m. E of Melbourne, via Burwood Highway. Also, E from Upper Ferntree Gully Station 1 m. walk. *See* map p. 152.	Hills and gullies of Dandenong Ranges. Forest trees including large gums.	Attractive walks, picnic areas, Lyrebirds and other birdlife. Native flowering plants.	Sightseeing along walking tracks; views over city. Family recreation. Photography. Bird observing. Barbecue facilities, shelters, tables. Ranger. No camping or overnight accommodation. Spring, summer, autumn.
FERRIES–McDONALD NATIONAL PARK (S.A.) 2,085 acres	Lower Murray River area, SE. South Australia, SW. from Murray Bridge.	Sandplain, mallee-broombush scrub.	Principally a wildlife sanctuary, a sample of the natural environment. Mallee Fowls, Black-faced Kangaroos, Scrub Robins.	Wildlife and bird observation. No accommodation provided at park. Murray Bridge: 2 hotels, 4 motels, camping and caravan parks. Winter, spring, autumn.
FLINDERS CHASE FLORA AND FAUNA RESERVE (S.A.) 35,680 acres	W end of Kangaroo Island. Daily air services and twice weekly vehicular ferry service between Kingscote and Port Adelaide or Port Lincoln, then via Playford Highway or South Coast Road. *See* map p.165.	A tilted plateau deeply dissected by watercourses. Northern and western coasts have spectacular cliffs broken by steep valleys and small beaches.	Spectacular coastlines, 'Remarkable Rocks', near Cape du Couedic. Wildlife including Kangaroo Island Kangaroo, Wallabies, pygmy possums, native cats, bandicoots, possums. Meeting place of flora of Western Australia and of Tasmania. Koalas (introduced from Victoria.)	Wildlife and bird observing—island has 120 bird species including Cape Barren Goose. General sightseeing and photography of coastal scenery, flora and fauna. Camping. Otherwise at Kingscote (eastern end of island), American River or Penneshaw. Any season.
FLUTED CAPE–CLOUDY BAY COASTAL RESERVE (TAS.) 600 acres	SE. coast of South Bruny I., between Fluted Cape and Cloudy Bay. Access from Hobart via Channell Highway to Kettering, vehicular ferry to Bruny I., road to Adventure Bay, short walk to Fluted Cape.	High cliffs where hills of South Bruny meet the sea. Highest point Mt Bruny, (1,659 ft). Scenic reserve also at Waterfall Creek.	Magnificent coastal scenery. Historical: Adventure Bay was visited by early navigators Furneaux (1773), Cook (1777), Bligh (1788) and D'Entrecasteaux (1792–93); relics on display at Bligh Museum.	Sightseeing, photography. Camping and caravan area, Adventure Bay, all facilities. Hotel at Alonnah, South Bruny. Any season.
FRASER NATIONAL PARK (VIC.) 7,749 acres	On W shores of Lake Eildon, 90 m. N from Melbourne, via Hume Highway to Seymour then Goulburn Valley Highway to Alexandra, then 7 m. NE. *See* map p. 152.	Hill tops and slopes above the water level of Lake Eildon. Former grazing land being allowed to regenerate.	Attractive lake-side scenery. Many kangaroos, wallabies. Nature trails.	Boating, fishing, water ski-ing. Major holiday resort. Observing wildlife, particularly kangaroos. Good and extensive camping area, supplies available at holiday periods. Ranger at Coller Bay. Summer (water sports) spring (wildflowers, birds) or autumn.
FRENCHMAN'S CAP NATIONAL PARK (TAS.) 25,240 acres	SW. Tasmania, about mid-way between Derwent Bridge and Queenstown, S of Lyell Highway, access only by walking tracks. *See* map p. 176.	High quartzite range and peaks, glaciated landforms. Alpine vegetation on heights, temperate rainforests and eucalypt (wet sclerophyll) forests at lower levels.	Spectacular mountain scenery; tremendous ice-cut cliff-face on SE. side of 4,739 ft peak of Frenchman's Cap mountain.	Bushwalking. Mountain climbing—among most difficult in Australia. No accommodation nor facilities in or near the park. Uninhabited wilderness area. November to March but all seasons for experienced walking–climbing teams.

NAME OF PARK	LOCALITY ACCESS	TOPOGRAPHY VEGETATION TYPES	FEATURES OF INTEREST	ACTIVITIES ACCOMMODATION SEASON TO VISIT
FREYCINET PENINSULA NATIONAL PARK (TAS.) 18,420 acres	E coastal Tasmania, via Tasman Highway, then turning S between Cranbrook and Bicheno; 19 m. from Highway to Coles Bay and park. *See* map p. 181.	A mountainous peninsula with many rough granite peaks up to 2,014 ft. Stunted eucalypt forests, dense low scrub in exposed places.	Magnificent coastal scenery; jagged peaks of 'the Hazards'. Walking tracks to Mt Graham, Mt Freycinet, Mt Amos (a climb) give views of coast, Wineglass Bay, Hazards Beach, Coles Bay.	Yachting, boating, fishing, swimming (in sheltered bays). Short and long walking tracks. Motor touring. Photography. Caravan sites within park at Coles Bay (Ranger); Accommodation and supplies also at Coles Bay township. Any season, summer for water sports.
GLENALADALE NATIONAL PARK (VIC.) 403 acres	SE. Victoria, 180 m. E of Melbourne, via Princes Highway to Sale, Fernbank, then 18 m. N to Glenaladale.	Dry forest of gums, Red Box and Yellow Box trees intersected by deep rainforest gullies. (Severe fire damage in 1965).	Picturesque Mitchell River gorges of pink rock. 'Den of Nargun', a limestone cavern associated with Aboriginal legend.	Sightseeing, photography along tracks to 'Den'. No camping or accommodation at park. Bairnsdale, all facilities. Ranger visits. Any season.
GORDON RIVER RESERVE (TAS.) 6,200 acres	W coast of Tasmania, where Gordon River flows into Macquarie Harbour. Access by boat from Strahan, or 25-mile hikers' track from Queenstown.	The Gordon River here cuts through spectacular mountain country, dense rainforests, between the Elliott and D'Aguilar ranges; the reserve is a long narrow strip containing the lower reaches of river.	Magnificent wilderness scenery unmarked by man's activities; sanctuary for wildlife. Former convict settlement at Macquarie Harbour.	Sightseeing: launch tours up river from Macquarie Harbour, inspecting ruins of penal settlement, Isle of Condemned. Fishing in harbour. Rugged bushwalking. Ocean beach swimming. Camping and caravan parks, hotels, at Strahan. Summer. Very high rainfall makes weather uncertain at most times.
GRAMPIANS WONDERLAND FOREST PARK (VIC.) (No true national park in the Grampians; Forests Commission has made part of its land available to serve as a park.)	W Victoria; 147 m. from Melbourne to Stawell via Western Highway then 14 m. SW. to the tourist centre Hall's Gap.	Stark ridges of upthrust sandstone running north-south for 60 m., with peaks above 3,500 ft.	Magnificent scenery: high ridges with sweeping slopes to one side, perpendicular cliffs to the other, deeply eroded by wind and water. Highest: Mt William (3,829 ft). The heights carry scrubby vegetation and heaths, forests on lower levels. Famed for wildflowers which cover thousands of acres in spring—boronia, ground orchids, wattles—altogether 700 species of flowering plants. Rich in birds. Mobs of kangaroos in Wartook Valley, Koalas at Hall's Gap, Platypus in streams.	Motor touring. Bush walking, rock climbing. Wildflower and bird observing. Scenic and nature photography. Hall's Gap: hotel, guest houses, caravan and camping parks. Camping grounds at Wartook (Forests Commission), Fyan's Lake, McKenzie Creek. September–October (wildflowers) and autumn months.
HAMBIDGE NATIONAL PARK (S.A.) 93,865 acres	Central Eyre Peninsula, approx. 10 m. NE. from Lock. See map p. 165.	Sandridges and sandplains. Vegetation of mallee and heaths.	A major wildlife sanctuary. Many mallee birds and mammals (*see* Hincks National Park) and also Brush-tailed Rat Kangaroo, Blue-Breasted Wren. Principally of interest to amateur naturalists, scientists.	Wildlife observation. No accommodation at park. Spring months.
HARTZ MOUNTAINS NATIONAL PARK (TAS.) 21,300 acres	S Tasmania, from Hobart via Huon Highway to Geeveston, then W about 8 m. into Arve Valley. Road then climbs almost to summit. *See* map p. 176.	High dolerite plateau, glacier-carved. Alpine vegetation on heights, temperate rainforest and wet sclerophyll (magnificent tall gums) forests on slopes.	Mountain scenery, and views into the wilderness of SW. Tasmania. Picturesque lakes on high plateau. Peaks up to 4,113 ft, with snow much of the year.	Bushwalking: short, signposted tracks to lakes, summits; long tracks to Mt Picton (10–15 m.), Arthur Range (20–30 m.) and Federation Peak (15–20 m.) in roughest wilderness country. Hut for weather protection. No amenities nor supplies at park. Huonville: hotel; Geeveston: 1 hotel, camping ground, moderate facilities; Dover: hotel. November to March.
HATTAH LAKES NATIONAL PARK (VIC.) 44,000 acres	Murray River overflow lakes, NW. Victoria, 300 m. NW. of Melbourne via Ouyen on Calder Highway to Hattah, then on Murray Valley Highway.	Sandy mallee country, and lakes filled by Murray floods.	Many water birds, Mallee Fowl, mallee birds, Red and Grey Kangaroos.	Of great interest to naturalists and birdwatchers. Nature photography. Camping area; no accommodation provided. Ranger. Drinking water scarce. Ouyen: hotel, motel, caravan park. Winter, spring. Summer very hot and dry.
HEALESVILLE SANCTUARY (VIC.) 432 acres	Situated about 40 m. E of Melbourne, and 3 m. from Healesville township. Access as far as the township is via the Maroondah Highway. Electric train service and direct bus service to the township from Melbourne.	The Sanctuary is at the foot of Badger Valley just above its opening into the Yarra Valley, and nestles below the heights of Ben Cairn (3,400 ft) and Donna Buang (4,080 ft). Of the Sanctuary's 432 acres, 380 are natural bushland, with some seven species of eucalypt including the attractive, smooth-barked Manna Gum, a favourite food tree of the Koala.	The best-known feature of the Sanctuary is its fauna park (82 acres) where there are exhibits including a great many birds in large walk-through aviaries. The Lyrebird aviary, filled with dense natural-looking vegetation, is 200 ft long, and there is also a very large Wedgetail Eagle aviary. Other features include a Platypus aquarium, and exhibits of kangaroos, wallabies, water birds and reptiles. Tracks also lead to a natural bushland area. Beyond the fauna park is the larger Coranderrk Bushland, about 380 acres.	Sightseeing, photography, and picnicking. Numerous picnic facilities are located in fauna park and car park areas. At Healesville township: 3 hotels, motel, guest houses, holiday flats, and cottages for rent; 4 caravan and camping areas. Visit at any season, though high rainfall makes fine weather a matter of good fortune in winter.
HELLYER GORGE NATIONAL PARK (TAS.) 1,406 acres	NW. Tasmania, on Waratah Highway between Somerset and Waratah.	The deep, steep-sided valley of the Hellyer River, heavily forested.	Attractive scenery where highway winds down into gorge, crosses river and climbs out on the other side.	Sightseeing, photography. Flora–fauna observing. Picnicking. Camping—picnic area near the river bridge; few facilities. Any season.
HINCKS NATIONAL PARK (S.A.) 163,315 acres	Eyre Peninsula, E from midpoint of road from Lock to Cummins. *See* map p. 165.	Sandplains, stabilised dunes and rocky ranges. Vegetation of Mallee-broombush, Mallee and heath-type association.	A wildlife sanctuary of great value. Many mallee-country birds—Mallee Fowl, Emu—and inland fauna including Pouched Mice (*Sminthopsis*), Hopping Mice, and Black-faced Grey Kangaroo.	Flora and fauna observation. No accommodation at park. Spring months.

NAME OF PARK	LOCALITY ACCESS	TOPOGRAPHY VEGETATION TYPES	FEATURES OF INTEREST	ACTIVITIES ACCOMMODATION SEASON TO VISIT
			Of great interest to naturalists and observers of birds, wildflowers, etc., bushwalkers; of scientific value to ecologists, zoologists, botanists; a vital sanctuary for the flora and fauna as surrounding land is cleared.	
JIP JIP NATIONAL PARK (S.A.) 350 acres	Lower SE. South Australia.	Large granite outcrops, and natural vegetation.	Its name derives from the Aboriginal 'Djipdjip', of unknown meaning. This was part of the territory of the Pataruwutj tribe.	Sightseeing, photography. Birdwatching. No overnight accommodation. Any season.
KELLIDIE BAY NATIONAL PARK (S.A.) 4,321 acres	SW. corner of Eyre Peninsula, approx. 20 m. W of Port Lincoln, at the E inlet of Coffin Bay.	Limestone rises and sandy areas. Black Tea-tree, sheoak, cutting-grass flats.	Coastal scenery. A wildlife sanctuary for many creatures including occasional Cape Barren Geese, Black-faced Grey Kangaroos, Euros.	Sightseeing, fishing, boating, swimming. Port Lincoln: 5 hotels, 4 motels, guest houses, caravan and camping park. Spring, summer, autumn.
KINCHEGA NATIONAL PARK (N.S.W.) 175,000 acres	W bank of Darling River, taking in lakes Cawndilla and Menindee; 75 m. E of Broken Hill, 2 m. SW. of Menindee township.	Overflow lakes of the Darling River. River environment: the Darling and its blacksoil floodplains, large river gums. Lakes: vitally important for waterfowl breeding, nesting. Red sandhills and sandplains: grassland vegetation, acres of wildflowers after rain.	Rich in Aboriginal relics, middens, burial grounds and camp grounds on the claypans. Birdlife: parrots, hawks, eagles among river gums; water birds on lakes, pools; arid-country birds in sandhill environment. Was part of a 2,000,000 acre pastoral property (1870).	Aquatic sports on some lake areas. Otherwise, a rewarding region for anyone interested in dry-country fauna, flora, Aboriginal relics. Camping area at the Menindee lakes. Accommodation, Ranger, at Menindee township. Winter, early spring. Very hot in summer, where water sports are main attraction.
KINGLAKE NATIONAL PARK (VIC.) 14,079 acres	Approx. 40 m. NE. of Melbourne, via Whittlesea, Kinglake West, to Mason's Falls turnoff. Alternatively, via Yarra Glen or Dixon's Creek. *See* map p. 152.	Forested ranges, eucalypt forests. Tall gums.	Views of city from heights, tall timber, waterfalls. Lyrebirds, Wombats and other wildlife.	Bushland hiking, or casual walking along easy tracks. Bird watching. Photography. Family picnics in bush surroundings. No camping or overnight accommodation. Barbecue facilities, etc. near Mason's Falls. Ranger. Spring, summer, autumn.
KOSCIUSKO NATIONAL PARK (N.S.W.) 1,322,000 acres	The Snowy Mountains, Great Dividing Range, SW. from Canberra. *See* map p. 153.	High plateaux with glaciated landforms and extensive winter snowfield. Altitude range within the park is greater than 6,000 ft. Vegetation: Alpine on summits, wet and dry sclerophyll forests, temperate woodlands.	Highest mountains in Australia: Kosciusko (7,314 ft), Ramshead (7,189 ft), Townsend (7,351 ft), Carruthers (7,042 ft), Twynam (7,207 ft). Magnificent views, e.g. from Mt Townsend down to Murray Valley 5,000 ft below. Snow-covered landscape from June to October. Massed wildflowers in summer. Alpine lakes: Lake Cootapatamba at altitude 6,800 ft, Lake Albina (6,340 ft) and Blue Lake (6,160 ft). Primitive area of 100 sq. m. around summit as living museum of Australian flora and fauna.	Winter: Ski-ing, skating (chair lifts, ski lifts, ski instruction at most winter sport centres). Summer: Drift ski-ing, trout fishing, trail riding on horseback, picnicking, bushwalking, motor touring, viewing wildflower displays, photography, birdwatching, golf, ranger-guided nature trail walks, campfire talks at Sawpit Creek. National park cabins and caravan park at Sawpit Creek (Park Headquarters and Visitor Information Centre). Hotels, lodges, chalets, guest houses at Thredbo (4,450 ft), Perisher Valley (5,500 ft), Pipers Gap, Smiggin Holes (5,500 ft), Charlotte Pass (5,740 ft), Wilsons Valley (4,800 ft), Kiandra (4,640 ft), Diggers Creek (5,005 ft). Caravan and camping areas at Adaminaby, Berriedale, Buckanderra, Jindabyne. Winter sports, June to mid-October. Wildflowers, December–January. Fishing, Sept.–April on small lakes, all year round on Lake Eucumbene.
KYEEMA NATIONAL PARK (S.A.) 800 acres	Adelaide Hills, south of Adelaide.	Dense eucalypt scrub, hills.	Interesting birds and wildflowers.	Bushwalking, bird and wildflower observations. Portion to be developed as future recreation area. Buildings under lease by National Fitness Council, until park can be developed for public use. Any season.
THE LAKES NATIONAL PARK (VIC.) 5,238 acres	Gippsland lakes, SE. Victoria. On Spermwhale Head Peninsula between Lakes Victoria and Reeve. Access via Sale, Loch Sport. *See* map p. 152.		Varied and rich birdlife, water birds. Also kangaroos, emus.	Water sports. Bird and wildflower observation. Camping and accommodation at Loch Sport on park's western boundary, no facilities in park. Ranger: weekends, public holidays. Any season.
LINCOLN NATIONAL PARK (S.A.) 35,521 acres	On SE. tip of Eyre Peninsula, SE. from Port Lincoln. *See* map p. 165.	Sandhills and coastal cliffs. Dense mallee scrub with Black Tea-tree, sheoak trees.	Coastal scenery at the northern, south-western and easterly limits of the park is quite spectacular. A sanctuary for White-breasted Sea-eagles, Ospreys, Western Whipbirds.	Sightseeing along the coast, fishing. Port Lincoln: 5 hotels, 4 motels, guest houses, caravan and camping park. Access roads and tracks in the park. Spring, summer, autumn.
LIND NATIONAL PARK (VIC.) 2,882 acres	East Gippsland. On Princes Highway between Orbost and Cann River, 290 m. E from Melbourne.	Mountainous, dense subtropical rainforest, dry eucalypt forests.	Wildflowers: habitat of Gippsland Waratah.	Sightseeing along the highway. Picnicking. Exploring the rainforest vegetation. Observing birdlife and flora. No accommodation or facilities, no camping at park. Nearest accommodation at Cann River: hotel, motel, camping ground. Fireplaces, picnic table, etc. on highway at Bright Light Saddle. Ranger based at Mallacoota. Any season.

NAME OF PARK	LOCALITY ACCESS	TOPOGRAPHY VEGETATION TYPES	FEATURES OF INTEREST	ACTIVITIES ACCOMMODATION SEASON TO VISIT
LITTLE DESERT (VIC.) (Includes former Kiata Lowan Sanctuary)	Central W Victoria; from Melbourne via Western Highway, 225 m. to Kiata, then 5 m. S. *See* map p. 00.	Sandplains and mallee country, mallee eucalypts.	Great variety of sandplain wildflowers and birds, including Mallee Fowl. Of interest to all natural history enthusiasts.	Searching for birds, wildflowers. Nature photography. Camping only; hotel at Kiata, motels at Dimboola and Nhill. Ranger. Spring and autumn.
LYELL HIGHWAY RESERVE (TAS.) 18,000 acres	W highlands of Tasmania. Land each side of Lyell Highway for much of its length between Queenstown and Derwent River.	A rugged, in places mountainous, region with extensive temperate rainforests, and forests of tall eucalypts.	Wilderness mountain and forest scenery of unsurpassed grandeur; glimpses S Frenchman's Gap peak; the beautiful, forested Surprise Valley (through which the road passes) sheltered below the heights of Mt Arrowsmith (2,800 ft).	Motor touring via Lyell Highway the length of the reserve. Photography. Observing birds, wildflowers. Bushwalking. Caravan park at Lake St Clair (National Park); hotels, motels, caravan parks at Queenstown. Summer for best chance of fine weather.
MACQUARIE ISLAND SANCTUARY (TAS.)	900 m. SE. of Tasmania; whole of Macquarie Island.	Narrow island. Mainly plateau area at elevation of 800 ft, rising in places to low rounded spurs and hills of 1,200 to 1,400 ft. Sub-Antarctic flora. No trees but thirty-five plant species are known.	This island is, politically, a part of Tasmania, and as such was proclaimed a sanctuary in 1933. Important station in southern ocean meteorological reading network. Island has important role in the life of sub-Antarctic dwelling species of birds, and other animals, and those which at various times of the year converge upon the Antarctic region. It is a base for A.N.A.R.E. research in conjunction with the C.S.I.R.O. Division of Wildlife Research. Prior to the declaration of the sanctuary the animals of Macquarie, particularly the fur seals, elephant seals and penguins were heavily exploited for their oil. The fauna has recovered remarkably under sanctuary conditions. Important wildlife research.	Access not open to the general public.
MALLACOOTA INLET NATIONAL PARK (VIC.) 11,225 acres	On Mallacoota Inlet, SE. Victoria near N.S.W. border. 326 m. from Melbourne via Princes Highway and Genoa. *See* map p.156.	Drowned river valley, forested shores.	Many attractive views on inlet and sheltered upper branches; rich in wildflowers, many birds.	Boating, fishing, swimming on inlet and wide sandy beaches near the ocean. Bushwalking, birdwatching. No accommodation in park; camping and caravan reserves adjacent to Mallacoota township. Ranger. Spring for wildflowers, summer for water sports, etc.
MAMBRAY CREEK NATIONAL PARK (S.A.) 7,781 acres (Formerly a National Pleasure Resort.)	Adjoins Alligator Gorge; reached from Port Pirie–Port Augusta Road.	High, rugged hills of the southern Flinders Range.	Wide valley between steep hills has many magnificent old River Red Gums (*Eucalyptus camaldulensis*).	A popular picnic site. Wildlife in surrounding bush and hills; Euros, Yellow-footed Rock-Wallabies, parrots and other birdlife, make bushwalking interesting. No overnight accommodation; picnic–barbecue area. Winter, spring, autumn.
MESSENT NATIONAL PARK (S.A.) 28,000 acres	Near the Coorong, central SE. coast of South Australia. *See* map p.165.	Lake, sedge flats, swamps. Higher parts are sandplain and sandhills with mallee-broombush and mallee-heath.	Principally a wildlife sanctuary, important feeding and breeding grounds for waterfowl. Also present are White-breasted Sea-eagles, Mallee Fowl, Wombats, Echidnas, Emus, Black-faced Grey Kangaroos.	Wildlife observation. No accommodation in park. Any season.
MOOTWINGEE HISTORIC SITE (N.S.W.) 1,200 acres	82 m. NE. from Broken Hill.	Low sandstone and conglomerate hills, dissected by streams, and with wind carved hollows, overhangs, caves. Permanent rock waterholes. River Red Gums in creek beds, elsewhere, sparse mulga scrub. (Natural vegetation almost entirely destroyed by sheep).	Aboriginal rock paintings and engravings, artefacts such as spearheads and scrapes (which should not be removed). Burial mounds. Birdlife includes many inland parrots, cockatoos, eagles.	Exploration of site's Aboriginal relics. Observation of dry-country birdlife, and perhaps mammals such as Euro, Yellow-footed Rock Wallaby, Red Kangaroo. Photography: recording Aboriginal art and engravings. Camping area, but water is often scarce. Winter, early spring. Summers very hot and dry.
MORWELL NATIONAL PARK (VIC.) 341 acres	South Gippsland. Reached via Princes Highway and Morwell, or South Gippsland Highway and Boolarra. 10 m. S of Morwell on road from Yinnar to Jumbuk. *See* map p.152.	Timbered slopes of a Gippsland valley, magnificent forests.	Forest scenery—tall Blue Gums and Grey Gums with understorey flora, magnificent fern gully. Rare epiphytic Butterfly Orchid. Many birds.	General sightseeing, bushland relaxation. Bird watching, photography, observation of flora. No accommodation; no camping permitted. No ranger. Summer and autumn.
MT BARROW NATIONAL PARK (TAS.) 1,134 acres	NE. Tasmania, via Tasman Highway for 18 m. then 9 m. to the summit, with a steep zig-zag road for last few miles.	The summit of Mt Barrow, altitude 4,644 ft.	Views overlooking the North Esk and St Patrick river valleys. Winter snow.	Sightseeing, climbing, photography. Winter ski-ing. At Launceston. Any season.
MT BOOTHBY NATIONAL PARK (S.A.) 9,996 acres	Upper SE. South Australia.	Mallee and Pink Gum vegetation.	A sanctuary for mallee country flora and fauna.	No accommodation or facilities at park. Spring for wildflowers.
MT BUFFALO NATIONAL PARK (VIC.) 27,280 acres	The mountains of NE. Victoria; 200 m. from Melbourne on the Ovens Highway, 10 m. W of Bright.	A mountain plateau, part of the Great Dividing Range. Eucalypt forests below 4,500 ft, alpine flora on the 'high plains'—low heaths, peaty areas.	Magnificent alpine scenery, high views from plateau, winter snow.	Snow sports in winter (chair lift), skating on Lake Catani after a heavy freeze. Fishing and boating at Lake Catani in summer. Bushwalking, general sightseeing. Photography. Horse riding, tennis.

NAME OF PARK	LOCALITY ACCESS	TOPOGRAPHY VEGETATION TYPES	FEATURES OF INTEREST	ACTIVITIES ACCOMMODATION SEASON TO VISIT
				Mt Buffalo Chalet, Tatra Inn (Bookings necessary). Camping permitted in summer. Ranger. Winter for ski-ing, skating; late spring and summer for wildflowers, bushwalking, camping.
MT BULLER ALPINE RESERVE (VIC.) (Forests Commission) ,357 acres	Western Victorian Alps. Access by Maroondah Highway, via Alexandra, Merton, Mansfield.	Mountain summit area, with alpine vegetation, wildflowers.	Mountain scenery (Mt Buller reaches 5,911 ft), wildflower displays in summer months, extensive snowfields, with good ski slopes.	Hiking, camping, picnicking, fishing, sight-seeing, winter snow sports. Accommodation at alpine village in park, with lodges and flats. Enquire Forests Commission, Treasury Place, Melbourne 3000. June–August for snow sports, otherwise any season.
MT ECCLES NATIONAL PARK (VIC.) 84 acres	200 m. W of Melbourne; 6 m. W of Macarthur, approx. halfway between Hamilton and Port Fairy.	The crater of an extinct volcano, containing the beautiful little Lake Surprise.	The scenery of the crater and its lake; also, lava flows, caves and collapsed tunnels in the old lava. Flora and fauna.	Sightseeing among the scenery of the extinct volcano (walking tracks). Camping permitted, but no accommodation provided. Ranger. Any season.
MT FIELD NATIONAL PARK (TAS.) 40,058 acres	Overlooking the Derwent Valley, about 25 m. W of New Norfolk.	High plateau with glacier-carved valleys and cirques. Highest peak, Mt Field West (4,721 ft). Alpine vegetation on the heights, wet sclerophyll (tall gums etc.) and temperate rainforest on slopes.	Winter snow sports—region receives heavy snowfalls July to October. Ski huts, ski tow near Mt Mawson. Magnificent views from heights. Waterfalls in tree-fern gorges. Glacial lakes: Lake Dobson, (Altitude 3,450 ft), Lake Fenton and others.	Ski-ing, bushwalking and following tracks to scenic features. Road to plateau (to about 3,500 ft) for sightseeing. Camping, picnicking. Camping and caravan sites in park. All facilities. Kiosk. Hotel close outside park. July–October for snow sports. Summer for touring, walking.
MT REMARKABLE NATIONAL PARK (S.A.) 673 acres	S Flinders Ranges, S of Wilmington on the Clare–Gladstone–Port Augusta Road. The peak is clearly visible from this road.	Southern slopes of Mt Remarkable (3,180 ft). (Northern slopes are a forest reserve). Very steep, with dense scrub.	Fine views from the heights; wildlife includes many Euros.	Bushwalking and sightseeing. No accommodation except at nearby towns. Winter, spring, autumn.
MT RESCUE NATIONAL PARK (S.A.) 70,149 acres	SE. South Australia, approx. 10 m. due N of Keith and E of Tintinara, both of which are on the Western Highway from Melbourne. See map p. 165.	Sandplain and sandhills, Mallee-broombush scrub and mallee-heathlands, Pink Gums.	Principally a wildlife sanctuary, preserving the habitat of the mallee fauna. Its area is sufficient that the original vegetation and fauna population should remain unchanged. Also contains Aboriginal camp sites and burial grounds.	Wildflower observation. No accommodation or amenities at park. Keith: hotel, motel, guest house, camping and caravan park. Spring months, particularly for wildflowers.
MT RICHMOND NATIONAL PARK (VIC.) 1,534 acres	Near coast of SW. Victoria, approx. 250 m. W from Melbourne via Princes Highway, 20 m. W of Portland, off Portland–Nelson–Mt Gambier Road.	Mt Richmond (745 ft). Sandy soils support approx. 450 species of flowering plants.	Scenic views overlooking coastline at Discovery Bay, (road to summit); wildflowers, including some 50 orchid species. Coastal flora and fauna.	Sightseeing, bird and wildflower observing, photography. No camping or accommodation; no amenities yet constructed. Accommodation at Portland. Spring for wildflowers, otherwise any season.
MUNDOORA NATIONAL PARK (S.A.) 1,352 acres	Mid-N South Australia.	Preserves a sample of the northern mallee country and its fauna.	A sanctuary rather than a tourist attraction for mallee flora and fauna.	Principally of interest to ecologists, botanists, naturalists. No accommodation at park. Winter, spring, autumn.
NADGEE NATURE RESERVE (N.S.W.) 9,249 acres	Extreme SE. corner of New South Wales between Disaster Bay and Cape Howe, E of Princes Highway. Joins Victorian border. Access road in from highway, 12 m.	Coastal lowlands and forested hills, lagoons, streams, coastal dunes. Vegetation includes wet and dry sclerophyll forests, heaths, swamp vegetation.	A sanctuary for the wildlife of south-east coast, a valuable asset now that much of the east coast is being destroyed by beach-sands mining, holiday resort sub-divisions. Views over reserve from Tumbledown Mountain (1,100 ft). On moors and heaths of southern part—wallabies, Grey Kangaroos, Wombats, Ground (Swamp) Parrots, and Southern Emu-Wrens. Aboriginal middens at Cape Howe. Bellbird colonies in forested gullies, many wildflowers in spring months.	Walking on tracks through the reserve, camping. Observing birds, animals, wildflowers. Swimming. Camping. A hut is provided for use of supervising rangers, scientific study groups, etc. Spring, autumn. May be closed at times of high fire danger in summer.
PARA WIRA NATIONAL PARK (S.A.) 1,908 acres	Approx. 25 m. NE. of Adelaide, via Main North-East Road. See map p.165.	Ranges, overlooking the rugged South Para gorge. Dry sclerophyll forest.	Principally a recreation reserve, now being developed along lines similar to Belair. More than half will be kept in natural state. Scrub kangaroos, Euros, many birds. Picnic and sports facilities. Kiosk.	Family picnics, sightseeing. Bush walks along tracks. Sports. No overnight accommodation at park. Ranger. Any season.
PEEBINGA NATIONAL PARK (S.A.) 7,775 acres	E South Australia; very near Victorian border, approx. 75 m. S of Murray River, and just W of Peebinga. See map p. 165.	Sandplain, vegetation-stabilized sand dunes. Mallee scrub.	A wildlife sanctuary. Black-faced Grey Kangaroos, Mallee Fowls, and other mallee country birds including Emus, possibly Western (Mallee) Whipbirds, Major Mitchell Cockatoos, Striated Grass-wrens.	Principally of interest to zoologists, botanists, ecologists, naturalists. No accommodation. Spring months.
PIEMAN RIVER RESERVE (TAS.) 8,125 acres	NW. coast; from Waratah Highway turn W, 45 m. via Waratah to Corinna, which is surrounded by the reserve.	Rugged scenery, wild ranges overlooking the lower reaches and estuary of the Pieman River. Dense rainforest.	A spectacularly wild and beautiful region, outstanding scenery, forests, wildlife.	Sightseeing: exploring river by boat from Corinna, or motor touring along the route from Waratah to Corinna. Though not part of reserve, this road shows a variety of west-coast scenery. At Waratah (hotel), Savage River (motel), otherwise camping without facilities. A region of very high rainfall. Summer offers greater chance of fine weather.

NAME OF PARK	LOCALITY ACCESS	TOPOGRAPHY VEGETATION TYPES	FEATURES OF INTEREST	ACTIVITIES ACCOMMODATION SEASON TO VISIT
PORT ARTHUR AND TASMAN PENINSULA RESERVES (TAS.) Approx. total area 1,440 acres	Tasman Peninsula, extreme SE. Tasmania, 63 m. from Hobart. Follow Arthur Highway from Sorell to Port Arthur. *See* map p. 177.	Rugged coastline of towering cliffs, sheltered bays and beaches. Timbered hills, pasture land.	The old townsite and prison buildings at Port Arthur are reserved as an historic site, together with the convict coal mines at Saltwater River. Also on the Tasman Peninsula are the coastal reserves at Tasman Arch and Blowholes, Waterfall Bay, Fossil Island, Eaglehawk Neck, Remarkable Cave, Pt Puer, Stewarts Bay, and Tesselated Pavement.	Sightseeing among the penal settlement ruins (guided tours) and in the Tasman Arch–Blowhole area. Surf beach and game fishing at Eaglehawk Neck–Penzance–Doo Town. Caravan parks and/or camping areas at Port Arthur, Stewarts Bay, Doo Town; Hotels at Eaglehawk Neck, Doo Town. Motel at Port Arthur. Any season; summer gives better chance of fine weather.
PORT CAMPBELL NATIONAL PARK (VIC.) 1,750 acres	SW. coast of Victoria, between Princetown and Peterborough, 180 m. from Melbourne via Great Ocean Road, or 150 m. via Cobden. *See* map p. 152.	A long line of cliffs where high flat plains meet the ocean.	Spectacular coastal scenery—golden cliffs, and wave-cut features including the Arch, London Bridge, Twelve Apostles, Blowhole.	Sightseeing, photography. Motor touring or walking along miles of cliffs (more views seen by walking). Birdwatching—Muttonbirds on islands, birds of coastal heathlands. Port Campbell: hotel, motel, guest houses, camping and caravan reserve all facilities; also at other coastal towns. Ranger. Summer, autumn.
PORT DAVEY COASTAL RESERVE (TAS.) 1,552 acres	SW. coast of Tasmania. Accessible only to hikers. Long track, some 50 m., from Gordon River Road. Easiest access from sea.	A deeply indented harbour, formed by the drowning of valleys by rising sea. Was once thought to be a fiord carved by glaciers, but the glaciers did not reach the sea.	The landlocked arms of the harbour, surrounded by the high, rugged hills and button-grass plains of the undamaged south-west Tasmanian wilderness makes this a region of magnificent scenery, a rewarding place for the adventurous bushwalker; has great photographic potential.	Bushwalking, mountain climbing. Scenic viewing. No accommodation, no supplies or assistance available within 50 m., no roads within this distance. Food, tent, etc. must be carried in. Hiking alone inadvisable. Summer; but all seasons for experienced mountain climbing, bushwalking teams.
ROCKY CAPE NATIONAL PARK (TAS.) 4,000 acres	W north-coast. Bass Highway via Wynyard, Boat Harbour, Detention River, and Rocky Cape township. *See* map p. 00.	A rugged coastline of massive rocky outcrops, jutting into Bass Strait.	Spectacular coastal scenery. Old sea caves 60–70 ft above waves show former higher sea level. Aboriginal kitchen middens on cave floor, rock art. Lighthouse.	Sightseeing, photography. Swimming, surfing, fishing. North-coastal towns; Wynyard: 3 hotels, motel, caravan and holiday cottage park; Boat Harbour: motel, holiday cottages, flats, caravan and camping parks. Any season, summer for water sports.
SCHOUTEN ISLAND COASTAL RESERVE (TAS.) 8,500 acres	Off E coast of Tasmania, near tip of Freycinet Peninsula. (Boat required). *See* map p. 176.	Hills, stunted eucalypt forests and low dense scrub.	Visible from Freycinet National Park. Schouten I. is part of the region's coastal scenery, and a valuable wildlife sanctuary.	Sightseeing, bushwalking. As for Freycinet National Park. Ranger at Coles Bay. Any season.
SHERBROOKE FOREST PARK (VIC.) (Forests Commission).	Dandenong Ranges, approx. 30 m. E from Melbourne. The road from Belgrave to Kallista passes through the forest. *See* map p. 152.	Forested hills of the Dandenongs. Tall slender eucalypts and densely vegetated fern-gullies.	Renowned for its Lyrebirds, some of which have become almost tame. They may be observed at any time of the year, but the elaborate displays, powerful song and skilful mimicry are at their best early on a winter's morning. Walking tracks provide access from roads into tree-fern gullies, and around forested hillsides. Picnic areas.	Bird observation, bushwalking. Picnicking. No accommodation in forest, caravan parks, hotel in nearby towns. Any season; winter for Lyrebird song and display.
SOUTH-WEST NATIONAL PARK (Includes former Lake Pedder Park) (TAS.) 473,500 acres	SW. Tasmania, stretching N from S coast between Port Davey and New River Lagoon to include Lake Pedder. Access from Gordon River Road via long walking tracks leading to Lake Pedder and Port Davey. *See* map p. 176.	Rugged mountains, snow-capped in winter. Swampy button-grass plains, forests. (Somewhat similar country is visible along the Gordon River Road.)	Spectacular mountain scenery—Mt Anne (4,675 ft), Federation Peak (4,010 ft). Lake Pedder has unique white beaches—but will be flooded by Gordon R. dam. One of the most attractive areas, abounding in birdlife, with magnificent scenery, has been omitted from this new park. This is the New River Lagoon, and nearby high walls of Precipitous Bluff, which remain just outside park boundaries, and could have been included.	Long-distance hiking, camping. Superb photographic opportunities. No facilities, shelter or supplies—a region for experienced, well-equipped bushwalkers. November to April.
TARRA VALLEY NATIONAL PARK (VIC.) 315 acres (to be increased by further 200 acres)	South Gippsland, between Traralgon, on Princes Highway, and Yarram, on South Gippsland Highway; 130 m. from Melbourne. *See* map p. 152.	In Strzlecki Ranges, sample of original South Gippsland forest and temperate rainforest vegetation.	Tall Mountain Ash trees, magnificent gully of tree ferns, many Superb Lyrebirds and other birdlife.	Sightseeing along short tracks, birdwatching, photography. No accommodation or camping. Caravan park nearby, outside park. Ranger present weekends, public holidays. Summer, spring, autumn.
TIDBINBILLA FAUNA RESERVE (A.C.T.) 11,500 acres	The upper Tidbinbilla valley, about 25 m. SW. from Canberra via Monaro Highway, Tharwa Road, and Tidbinbilla Road.	The forested eastern slopes of the Tidbinbilla Range (5,100 ft) and the granite rock formations of Gibraltar Peak. Lower parts at altitude 2,500 ft. Part of valley once cleared. Forests—Candlebark, Broad-leaf Peppermint, Ribbon (or Manna) Gum, Narrow-leaf Peppermint, Alpine Ash, Mountain Gum.	Mountains, forests, massive granite boulders such as along the Hanging Rock Trail. Wildlife includes Swamp Wallabies, Grey Kangaroos, Red-necked Wallabies, Wombats, possums and gliders. The many birds include Lyrebirds in the fern gullies. A spacious fauna enclosure has been developed on the cleared lands.	Walking, picnicking, watching birds, or animals in enclosures. Scenic lookout. Picnic and barbecue facilities. No accommodation or camping. Rangers. Any season. Lyrebird calls best in winter.
TOOMS LAKE SANCTUARY (TAS.) 56,000 acres	E coast; access via Midland Highway, Oatlands, then E via York Plains or Andover, past the Fadden Tier (2,144 ft).	Large lake and rough country; eucalypt (dry sclerophyll) forests.	A fauna sanctuary, where most of the eastern Tasmanian wildlife species are represented. The lake supports small populations of ducks and swans. The area is large enough to ensure the survival of the fauna and flora, and is of a rugged nature which renders it unsuitable for agriculture.	Flora and fauna observation. No accommodation or facilities for visitors; roads may be difficult. Any season.

NAME OF PARK	LOCALITY ACCESS	TOPOGRAPHY VEGETATION TYPES	FEATURES OF INTEREST	ACTIVITIES ACCOMMODATION SEASON TO VISIT
TOWER HILL STATE GAME RESERVE (VIC.) 1,580 acres	Between Warrnambool and Port Fairy in the Western District. Here, from a rise on Highway One, can be seen a deep circular valley containing a lake with islands shaped as small conical hills.	Tower Hill is a 'nested caldera' formed when a large volcano collapsed inwards. Within the lake-filled caldera, further volcanic activity formed the cone-shaped islands, which were active vents not many thousands of years ago.	In 1885 this area supported luxuriant vegetation, and a diverse wildlife; within 10 years the vegetation had been burnt out and the bared land heavily grazed. Vegetation is now being regenerated under protection. A Natural History Centre is being constructed, and is to have among its features an exhibition of photographs, posters, with theme of the destruction, and later re-creation of the wildlife habitat at Tower Hill.	Caravan park, other accommodation at Warrnambool, Port Fairy. Any season.
WILLIAM RICKETTS SANCTUARY (VIC.) (Forests Commission) 3½ acres	In the Dandenong Ranges, 2¼ m. N of Olinda, on the Olinda–Mt Dandenong–Kalorama road.	Part of steep, forested slopes of Dandenongs, in setting of greenery.	Clay sculptures by William Ricketts are main feature. Through the spiritual life expressed in his works he has endeavoured to impart his conception of the human's part in wildlife conservation, and the theme 'reverence for life'.	Public may view the sanctuary and its contents. Accommodation, Melbourne and suburbs. Visit at any season.
WILPENA POUND (National Pleasure Resort) (S.A.) (Administered by South Australian Tourist Bureau, but should be given national park status by South Australian Government) 19,900 acres	Central Flinders Range, via Hawker. *See* map p. 165.	A closed synclinal basin; massive sandstone–quartzite strata dip inwards, outward facing walls are huge cliffs and bluffs of reddish and purple tones. St Mary's Peak (3,900 ft).	Spectacular and unique scenery, massive River Red Gums along watercourses, expanses of springtime flowers, dry-country fauna.	Very popular for touring, sightseeing. Walking, climbing, camping. Much favoured by landscape artists and photographers. Wilpena Chalet, in the entrance to the gorge giving access to the pound—cabins, rooms, motel suites, camping and caravan sites. Caravan park also at Hawker. Winter, spring, autumn. Summer hot, and usually very dry and dusty.
WILSON'S PROMONTORY NATIONAL PARK (VIC.) 102,379 acres	Southernmost tip of Australian mainland; 140 m. SE. from Melbourne via South Gippsland Highway. *See* map p. 157.	A hilly, almost mountainous peninsula jutting into Bass Strait. Granite peaks, headlands. Sand dunes, beaches.	Panoramic views and seascapes. Good beaches, camping facilities for holidays. Considerable variety of birds, wildflowers.	Swimming, surfing, esturine and ocean fishing. Bushwalking, camping. Wildlife-wildflower photography and observation, scenic photography. Lodges, available only by advance booking with the Victorian Tourist Bureau; caravan and camping area at Tidal River. Rangers. Spring for wildflowers, summer for swimming, surfing.
WINGAN INLET NATIONAL PARK (VIC.) 4,730 acres	Coast of E Gippsland. 330 m. from Melbourne via Princes Highway, turning S from Highway W of Drummers Saddle. Last 10 m. through virgin forest, road not suitable for caravans.	Inlet, ocean beaches, rainforest vegetation bordering river.	Attractive coastal and inlet scenery. Small fur-seal colony on 'The Skerries' offshore.	Excellent fishing in estuary and sea (walking track to ocean beach). Bushwalking, wildlife observation. Undeveloped camping ground, no other accommodation. Nearest town, Cann River: hotel, motel, camping ground all facilities. Ranger based at Mallacoota. Any season, but spring, summer, autumn usually best.
WYPERFELD NATIONAL PARK (VIC.) 139,760 acres	NW. Victoria; 280 m. from Melbourne. Approach via Rainbow or Hopetoun.	Sandhill and mallee country. 300 plant species, 200 birds so far recorded, including Mallee Fowl. Kangaroos.	Wildflowers in late winter and early spring are a major attraction. The birdlife (many mallee and dry-country species) is of great interest to all naturalists.	Bushwalking (many miles of tracks), bird and wildflower observing. No overnight accommodation. Shelter hut, drinking water, fireplaces, etc., for campers. Ranger based at nearby Yaapeet township. Winter and spring. Summer here is very hot and dry.

Leadbeater's Possum

Tasmanian Tiger

TASMANIA

NAME	LOCATION, FEATURES OF INTEREST
Cave Reserves.	Hastings Caves, S Tasmania (131 acres); Maracoopa Caves, Mole Creek, N Tasmania (146 acres); King Solomon Caves, Mole Creek (500 acres); Baldock Caves, Mole Creek (105 acres); Gunns Plains Caves, Ulverstone (24 acres).
Coastal Reserve, Bicheno.	Lookout Rock (5 acres).
Coastal Reserve, Bruny I.	Cookville–Penguin I. (3 acres).
Coastal Reserves, Tasman Peninsula.	Scenic shores, cliffs, historic coastal areas at Stewarts Bay (4 acres), Pt Puer–Esplanade (58 acres), Pt Puer–Crescent Bay (92 acres), Remarkable Cave–Brown Mountain (150 acres), Eaglehawk Neck and Foreshore (90 acres), Eaglehawk Neck–Taranna (61 acres), Tasman Arch–Blowhole (140 acres), Fossil I. (3 acres), Waterfall Bay (30 acres).
Forest areas, fern gullies and other scenic features of small area.	Thermal Springs, Hastings (19 acres); Waterfall Creek, Bruny I. (60 acres); Notley Gorge, West Tamar (28 acres); Fairy Glade, Western Tiers (97 acres); St Patricks Head, St Marys (370 acres).
Historic sites, buildings, monuments.	Town of Port Arthur (217 acres), Mt Arthur (10 acres), Convict Coal Mines, Saltwater R. (520 acres); Bowen's Monument, Risdon; Bowen Park, Risdon; George III Monument, Southport (25 acres); Tasman Monument, Dunalley (25 acres); D'Entrecasteaux Monument, Gordon; York Town, West Tamar; D'Entrecasteaux Watering Place, Recherche Bay; Settlement I., Macquarie Harbour (15 acres); Isle of Condemned, Macquarie Harbour; Old Gaol and Paddock, Richmond; Entally House (85 acres); Steppes Homestead, Steppes (25 acres); Shot Tower, Taroona (8 acres); Waubadebar's Grave, Bicheno; Toll House, New Norfolk; Bluff Battery Bellerive; Oatland's Mill; 16 Davey St. Hobart, Batchelor's Grave, Hobart.
Moulting Lagoon.	E coast Tasmania. Sanctuary for swans and other waterfowl. Swans annually moult at lagoon.
Scenic Roads—roadside reserves preserving the great natural beauty along several Tasmanian Highways, principally W Tasmania.	Lyell Highway, Western Highlands, along both sides of highway for much of the distance between Derwent Bridge and Queenstown (area 18,000 acres); Zeehan–Renison Bell Scenic Road, West coast (272 acres); St Marys Pass, St Marys (674 acres); Murchison Highway, W coast (1,640 acres).
Coastal Reserves, Forestier Peninsula.	Tesselated Pavement (9 acres), shore platform of exposed Permian Mudstone near Eaglehawk Neck.

SOUTH AUSTRALIA

NAME	LOCATION, FEATURES OF INTEREST
The Knoll National Park Reserve. 4 acres.	Hills overlooking Adelaide, altitude 2,100 ft.
Torrens I. National Park Reserve. 144 acres.	Tidal vegetation, mangroves, sea birds, waders.
Hale National Park. 471 acres.	Steep hills overlooking South Para Reservoir.
Sandy Creek National Park. 258 acres.	Sandy region. Murray Pines, mallee scrub. A wildlife sanctuary.
Mt Magnificent National Park. 221 acres.	A steep hillside near Adelaide, dense natural vegetation, geological interest.
Un-named area of 389 acres.	Adjoining Morialta Falls Reserve.
Nixon Skinner National Park Reserve. 19 acres.	Example of original vegetation of the Myponga–Yankalilla area.
Waitpinga National Park Reserve. 6 acres.	A creek: permanent water, coral ferns.
Eric Bonython National Park Reserve.	Permanent creek, coral ferns, Kangaroo Island boronia.
Spring Mt National Park Reserve. 85 acres.	Steeply undulating country, large Brown Stringybark trees.
Penguin I. National Park Reserve. 5 acres. SE. of S.A.	Breeding grounds for Little Penguins, Crested Terns, Silver Gulls, other sea birds.
Calectasia National Park Reserve. 34 acres.	Preserves rare Blue Tinsel Lily (*Calectasia cyanea*).
Desert Camp National Park Reserve. 93 acres.	Small area of dense arid land vegetation. Kangaroos, birdlife.
Guichen Bay National Park Reserve. 186 acres.	Coastal dunes, dense scrub.
'The Pages' I. 90 acres.	Near Kangaroo I., reserve for nesting sea birds.
Greenly and Anthoney I. Fauna Reserve. Approx. 1 sq. m.	Off Eyre Peninsula; sanctuary for birds and other fauna.
Person I. Fauna Reserve. About 5 sq. m.	Off Eyre Peninsula; sanctuary for birds and other fauna.
Horsnell Gully National Park. 346 acres.	A small bush reserve near the Cleland National Park. Dense scrub, views.
Warren National Park. 847 acres.	Very rugged hill country near South Para reservoir, NE. of Adelaide. Tall timber, dense low undergrowth. Black-faced Grey Kangaroos.

SOUTHERN NEW SOUTH WALES (South of Jervis Bay).

NAME	LOCATION, FEATURES OF INTEREST
Bell Bird Creek Nature Reserve. 132 acres.	Princes Highway between Eden and Pambula. Sub-tropical rainforest, dry sclerophyll forest, Bell-bird colonies.
Bermagui Nature Reserve. 1,500 acres.	5 m. SW. of Bermagui, S-coast N.S.W. Dry and wet sclerophyll forests.
Brush I. Nature Reserve. 115 acres.	Off Murramarang Head, near Kioloa.
Buddigower Nature Reserve. 340 acres.	Buddigower near West Wyalong, N.S.W. Semi-arid mallee, sclerophyll scrub.
Charcoal Tank Nature Reserve. 213 acres.	S of West Wyalong. Arid and layered scrub.
Cudmirrah Nature Reserve. 310 acres.	Between Berrara Creek and Redhead, just S of Sussex Inlet, S coast. Heathlands, swamps, open forest, coastal dunes. Wildflowers. Camping area.
Goonawarra Nature Reserve. 1,080 acres.	12 m. S of Booligal, Lachlan River, near Quondong Stn. Riverine, River Red Gums.
Goura Nature Reserve. 965 acres.	Under Dromedary Mountain, near Tilba. Wet and dry sclerophyll forests.
Illawong Nature Reserve. 125 acres.	Near Broulee, Moruya. Lagoon swampland, water birds.
Narrandera Nature Reserve. 180 acres.	At Narrandera, on Murrumbidgee, N.S.W. Riverine, River Red Gums.
Pulletop Nature Reserve. 358 acres.	Between Griffiths and Rankin Springs. Semi-arid mallee.
Round Hill Nature Reserve. 13,930 acres.	At the junction of roads between Euabalong–Mt Hope, and Mt Hope–Lake Cargelligo. Semi-arid mallee. Low eucalypts forming a discontinuous scrub layer.
Tabletop Nature Reserve. 255 acres.	Near Gerogery. Sclerophyll forest and woodland scrub.
The Rock Nature Reserve. 470 acres.	The Rock, S of Wagga. Dry sclerophyll forest.
Tollgates I. Nature Reserve. 30 acres.	Off Bateman's Bay.

NATURE RESERVES, SANCTUARY AREAS

VICTORIA

NAME, LOCATION	FEATURES OF INTEREST
Arapiles Wildflower Reserve (Vic.) (Forests Commission) 40 acres. Western Victoria, about 20 m. W of Horsham, and near Arapiles Centenary park and picnic grounds reserve.	Beautiful wildflowers in spring. Picnic areas.
Bat's Ridge Faunal Reserve (Vic.) 275 acres. Portland district.	For preservation of bat colonies, and other wildlife.
Ben Cairn Scenic Reserve (Vic.) (Forests Commission) 104 acres. Access via Healesville.	Heights of Ben Cairn (3,400 ft) overlooking the Healesville Sanctuary.
Berringa Flora and Fauna Reserve (Vic.) (Forests Commission) 490 acres. In reserves forest lands about 16 m. SSW. of Ballarat.	Interesting flora and fauna populations.
Bryan's Swamp State Game Reserve (Vic.) 1,600 acres. Near Portland, SE. Victoria.	Water bird habitat; open to duck shooting only during the open season.
Cape Woolamai Faunal Reserve (Vic.) 320 acres.	For protection of Mutton Birds; at SE. corner of Phillip Island.
Chinaman Island Faunal Reserve (Vic.) 150 acres. In Westernport Bay, S Victoria.	For conservation of all wildlife.
Creswick Koala Park (Vic.) 50 acres. Situated near Creswick, about 12 m. N of Ballarat.	For the preservation of a colony of Koalas.
Cumberland Scenic Reserve (Vic.) (Forests Commission) 650 acres.	A scenic and 'tall timber' area in the Marysville district, in forested ranges just north of the headwaters of the Yarra River.
Dickie's Hill Scenic Reserve (Vic.) (Forests Commission). Between Mirboo and Allambee, Gippsland, near upper reaches of the Tarwin River.	Luxuriant forest vegetation.
Dixon's Creek Scenic Reserve (Vic.) (Forests Commission) 23 acres. About 10 m. NNW. of Healesville.	Thickly forested ranges.
Dowd's Morass State Game Reserve (Vic.) 1,990 acres. Near Sale, E Victoria.	For all water birds, with shooting of duck allowed only during open season.
Ewing's Morass State Game Reserve (Vic.) 10,980 acres. On the coast E of Orbost.	A water bird habitat, important for conservation of migratory waterfowl. Shooting of duck allowed only during the open season.
Fairy Dell Scenic Reserve (Vic.) (Forests Commission) 120 acres. A few miles NE. of Bruthen, and about 16 m. ENE. of Bairnsdale.	For preservation of scenery, flora and fauna.
Ferntree Waterfalls Scenic Reserve (Vic.) (Forests Commission) 395 acres. About 10 m. NW. of Beaufort, in SW. Victoria.	Scenic and picnic area.
Goonmirk Rocks Scenic Reserve (Vic.) (Forests Commission) 50 acres. In the forested ranges of eastern Vic., near Bonang, via Orbost and Bonang Highway.	A scenic and botanical reserve.
Jack Smith's Lake State Game Reserve (Vic.) 2,609 acres. Near Woodside, 12 m. E of Yarram, southern Gippsland.	For all water birds; shooting allowed during open season for duck.
Jones Bay State Game Reserve (Vic.) 900 acres. Near Sale, eastern Gippsland.	For waterfowl, duck shooting allowed in open season.
Kalorama Park Scenic Reserve (Vic.) (Forests Commission) 34 acres. In Dandenong Ranges, via Montrose, or Olinda and Mt Dandenong.	Forest slopes.
Kanuka Creek Scenic Reserve (Vic.) (Forests Commission) 250 acres. Just east of Bonang (on Bonang H'way between Orbost and Bombala, N.S.W.).	Forested ranges.

NAME, LOCATION	FEATURES OF INTEREST
Koorangie State Game Reserve (Vic.) 4,460 acres. Near Kerang, via Loddon Valley Highway.	For waterfowl, duck shooting allowed during open season.
Kowat Faunal Reserve (Vic.). Near N.S.W. border, between Bonang and Bombala (N.S.W.).	For preservation of all wildlife, and specifically of wallabies.
Lady Julia Percy I. Faunal Reserve (Vic.) 330 acres. Off Port Fairy, SW. coast.	For protection of sea birds and seals.
Lake Coleman State Game Reserve (Vic.) 2,861 acres. E of Sale, E Gippsland.	For waterfowl; shooting of duck allowed only during open season.
Lake Goldsmith State Game Reserve (Vic.) 2,500 acres. Access by Western Highway to Beaufort, then 9 m. S to lake.	For all waterfowl, shooting allowed only during open game season.
Lake Reeve State Game Reserve (Vic.) 12,000 acres. *See* map p. 000. Lake Reeve is long narrow strip of water behind the Ninety Mile Beach, E Gippsland. Access by Highway One to Sale, then 28 m. E to lake.	A water bird habitat; duck shooting permitted during open season.
Lawrence Rocks Faunal Reserve (Vic.) 20 acres. Located off Portsea, SW. Victoria.	For sea birds, including Gannets.
Lerderderg Gorge Forest Park (Vic.) (Forests Commission) 7,600 acres. Approx. 45 m. NW. of Melbourne, by Western Highway to Bacchus Marsh, then north to the Lerderderg River, and gorge.	Scenic gorge, forest vegetation.
Limestone Creek Scenic Reserve (Vic.) (Forests Commission) 200 acres. E Victoria, near N.S.W. border and Kosciusko National Park. There is a track from Omeo to Jindabyne, but detailed maps should be obtained, and route enquiries made.	Picturesque scenery.
Long Swamp State Game Reserve (Vic.) 5,830 acres. Extreme SW. corner of Vic., access via Highway One to Dartmoor, then south.	For all water birds. Duck shooting allowed in open season.
Major Mitchell's Lagoons (Vic.) (Forests Commission) 369 acres. Access by Murray Valley Highway to junction of Murray and Wakool rivers.	Site is of historical interest.
McDonald Park Scenic Reserve (Vic.) (Forests Commission) 152 acres. Near Ararat, W Victoria.	Preservation of landscape, flora and fauna.
McKenzie River Scenic Reserve (Vic.) (Forests Commission) 889 acres. Situated west of Stawell, via Halls Gap and Wartook.	
McLeod's Morass, State Game Reserve (Vic.) 1,045 acres. SE. of Bairnsdale, E Gippsland.	For all water birds; duck shooting allowed in open season.
Melville Caves Scenic Reserve (Vic.) (Forests Commission) 120 acres. Access route by Calder Highway (H'way 79) to Inglewood, then west 10 m. through Kingower to caves.	Caves, scenic and picnic area.
Mt Alexander Koala Park (Vic.) (Forests Commission) 77 acres. By Calder Highway, to Elphinstone.	For establishment, maintenance of a colony of Koalas.
Mt Beckworth Summit Scenic Reserve (Vic.) (Forests Commission) 185 acres. About 16 m. NW. of Ballarat.	Scenery, flora and fauna preservation.
Mt Buller Road Scenic Reserve (Vic.) (Forests Commission) 270 acres. Route from Melbourne is via Maroondah Highway and Mansfield.	Leading to Mt Buller Alpine Reserve.
Mt Donna Buang Scenic Reserve (Vic.) (Forests Commission) 460 acres. On Mt Donna Buang (4,080 ft), about 45 m. E of Melbourne, road from Healesville to Warburton.	Mt Donna Buang.
Mt Misery Flora and Fauna Reserve (Vic.) (Forests Commission) 410 acres. About 16 m. SSW. of Ballarat, via Newtown, Berringa.	Interesting flora and fauna.
Mt Pilot Scenic Reserve (Vic.) (Forests Commission) 630 acres. By Hume H'way via Wangaratta to Chiltern, then SE. about 5 m.	
Mt Victoria Scenic Reserve (Vic.) (Forests Commission) 320 acres.	Ranges overlooking the upper Yarra, between Healesville and Warburton.
Mud I. Faunal Reserve (Vic.) 1200 acres. Located in Port Phillip Bay.	For sea birds and waders.
Myer's Creek Scenic Reserve (Vic.) (Forests Commission).	Toolangi Forests District.
Myrtle Gully Scenic Reserve (Vic.) (Forests Commission) 106 acres. Access via Healesville, Warburton.	Ranges above upper Yarra River.
Nooramunga Faunal Reserve (Vic.) 24,600 acres.	Comprised of the Corner Inlet islands, between Wilson's Promontroy and Gippsland coast. Reserved for protection of habitat of all wildlife of the islands.
Otway Ranges Scenic Reserves (Vic.) (Forests Commission). Access by Highway One, via Colac, or from Geelong via Colac on the Great Ocean Road.	Kalimna Falls Scenic Reserve (220 acres); Grey River Scenic Reserve (120 acres); Grey River Roadside Reserve (44 acres); Beauchamp's Falls (180 acres); Calder River Scenic Reserve (93 acres); Mait's Rest Scenic Reserve (184 acres); Otway Roadside Reserve (250 acres).
Princess Margaret Rose Caves Scenic Reserve (Vic.) (Forests Commission) 45 acres. SW. Vic. on Lower Glenelg River. Access via Princes Highway, turning S just E of S.A. border.	Limestone caves open to tourists.
Quail I. Faunal Reserve (Vic.) 2,000 acres. Situated in Westernport Bay.	Reserved for all wildlife.
Rocky Range Faunal Reserve (Vic.) 11,000 acres. *See* map p. 000. Access from Buchan to Jindabyne road, or westwards from Bonang, eastern Victoria.	Reserved for protection of all wildlife but especially for rock-wallabies.
Sale Common Game Refuge (Vic.) 760 acres. Near Sale, E Gippsland.	For all water birds, no shooting allowed at any time—a refuge for duck and other birds even during open season.
Seal Rocks Faunal Reserve (Vic.) 7 acres. Located off Phillip Island.	A seal habitat.
The Gap Scenic Reserve (Vic.) (Forests Commission) 430 acres. Access via Orbost, Bonang Highway to Bonang, then W through Tubbut.	Forest vegetation.

NAME LOCATION	FEATURES OF INTEREST
The Stones Faunal Reserve (Vic.) 12,780 acres. *See* map p. 000. Near Macarthur, SW. Victoria.	Basalt, stony rises. Dry sclerophyll forest. Reserved for wildlife generally.
Wathe Faunal Reserve (Vic.) 14,235 acres. Near Lascelles, on North-Western Highway.	To preserve the habitat of the Mallee Fowl and other mallee fauna.
Yellingbo Faunal Reserve (Vic.) 412 acres.	To preserve the habitat of the Helmeted Honeyeater, a bird of very restricted range.

BIRDS OF SOUTHERN NATIONAL PARKS

Crested Grebe (*Podiceps cristatus*); lakes, streams, swamps.
Hoary-headed Grebe (*Podiceps poliocephalus*); lakes and swamps.
Fairy Penguin (*Eudyptula minor*); coast and islands.
Yellow-billed Spoonbill (*Platalea flavipes*); swamps and lakes.
Chestnut-breasted Shelduck (*Casarca tadornoides*); lakes and swamps.
Musk Duck (*Biziura lobata*); lakes and coastal inlets.
Hooded Dotterel (*Charadrius cucullatus*); seashores and coastal lagoons.
Short-tailed Shearwater (*Puffinus tenuirostris*); breeds on southern islands.
Fairy Prion (*Pachyptila turtur*); southern seas and islands.
Sooty Oyster-catcher (*Haematopus unicolor*); rocky shores and reefs.
White-capped Albatross (*Diomedea cauta*); southern seas.
Cape Barren Goose (*Cereopsis novae-hollandiae*); grasslands and swampy fields.
Plumed Egret (*Egretta intermedia*); swamps, lakes and streams.
Collared Sparrowhawk (*Accipiter cirrocephalus*); open forest.
Grey Goshawk (*Accipiter novae-hollandiae*); forests.
Swamp Harrier (*Circus approximans*); swamps and reedbeds.
Swamp Quail (*Synoicus ypsilophorus*); swampy grasslands.
Painted Quail (*Turnix varia*); open forest and heathlands.
Spotted Crake (*Porzana fluminea*); marshes and reeds.
Spotless Crake (*Porzana tabuensis*); swamps and reeds.
Marsh Crake (*Porzana pusilla*); swamps and reeds.
Tasmanian Native Hen (*Tribonyx mortieri*); marshes and reedbeds.
Green Rosella (*Platycercus caledonicus*); forests and clearings.
Orange-breasted Parrot (*Neophema chrysogaster*); grasslands and open forest.
Swift Parrot (*Lathamus discolor*); flowering eucalypts.
Musk Lorikeet (*Glossopsitta concinna*); flowering gums.
Purple-crowned Lorikeet (*Glossopsitta porphyrocephala*); flowering eucalypts.

Little Lorikeet (*Glossopsitta pulsitta*); flowering eucalypts.
Yellow-tailed Black Cockatoo (*Calyptorhynchus funereus*); forests.
Gang Gang Cockatoo (*Callocephalon fimbriatum*); forested ranges.
Crimson Rosella (*Platycercus elegans*); forests and ranges.
Tasmanian Masked Owl (*Tyto castanops*); forests.
Powerful Owl (*Ninox strenua*); mountain forests.
Tawny Frogmouth (*Podargus strigoides*); forests.
Spine-tailed Swift (*Hirundapus caudacutus*); open skies.
Laughing Kookaburra (*Dacelo gigas*); open forest.
Superb Lyrebird (*Menura superba*); dense forest.
Clinking Currawong (*Strepera arguta*); Tasmanian lowlands.
Reed-warbler (*Acrocephalus australis*); reedbeds.
Blue Wren (*Malurus cyaneus*); forests and thickets.
Southern Emu-wren (*Stipiturus malachurus*); swampy heathlands.
Yellow-throated Scrub-wren (*Sericornis lathami*); rainforest.
Pink Robin (*Petroica rodinogaster*); heavily timbered ranges.
Rose Robin (*Petroica rosea*); coastal rainforest.
Southern Yellow Robin (*Eopsaltria australis*); forests.
Grey Fantail (*Rhipidura fuliginosa*); forests.
Rufous Fantail (*Rhipidura rufifrons*); summer visitor, dense forest.
Black-faced Flycatcher (*Monarcha melanopsis*); forests.
Eastern Spinebill (*Acanthorhynchus tenuirostris*); heaths and open forest.
Fuscous Honeyeater (*Meliphaga fusca*); open forest.
Helmeted Honeyeater (*Meliphaga cassidix*); forests.
New Holland Honeyeater (*Meliornis novae-hollandiae*); heathlands.
Bell-miner (*Manorina melanophrys*); forests.
Spotted Pardalote (*Pardalotus punctatus*); foliage, open and heavy forest.

SOME FURRED ANIMALS OF SOUTHERN NATIONAL PARKS AND SANCTUARIES

Platypus (*Ornithorhynchus anatinus*); active early and late in day; coastal streams.
Spiny Anteater (*Tachyglossus aculeatus*); diurnal; widespread.
Tasmanian Spiny Anteater (*T. setosus*); denser, longer fur; found only in Tasmania.
Yellow-footed Marsupial Mouse (*Antechinus flavipes*); widespread; forests.
Dusky Marsupial Mouse (*A. swainsonii*); Victorian and Tasmanian highlands.
Little Tasmanian Marsupial Mouse (*A. minimus*); Tasmania and Bass St. I.
White-footed Sminthopsis (*Sminthopsis leucopus*); terrestrial, nocturnal, insectivorous.
Brush-tailed Phascogale (*Phascogale tapoatafa*); treetop hunter, forests.
Eastern Native Cat (*Dasyurus viverrinus*); nocturnal, forests and woodlands.
Western Native Cat (*Dasurinus geoffroyi*); western S.A., north-west Vic. open woodlands.
Tiger Cat (*Dasyurops maculatus*); powerful carnivore; forested coastal ranges and Tas.
Tasmanian Devil (*Sarcophilus harrisi*); large, powerful; sclerophyll forests, Tasmania.
Tasmanian Wolf (*Thylacinus cynocephalus*); powerful carnivore, possibly extinct; open forest.
Long-nosed Bandicoot (*Parameles nasuta*); nocturnal; south-coast and Tas. forests.
Short-nosed Bandicoot (*Isoodon obesulus*); terrestrial, nocturnal, common; open forest.
Wombat (*Phascolomis mitchelli*); nocturnal; forests of coastal ranges, burrows.
Tasmanian Wombat (*P. ursinus*); powerful, vegetarian; Tasmania and Bass St. I.
Hairy-nosed Wombat (*Lasiorhinus latifrons*); south-western S.A., mallee, open plains.
Pygmy Possum (*Cercartetus nanus*); nocturnal, arboreal; feeds on nectar and insects.
Little Tasmanian Pygmy Possum (*C. lepidus*); very small, head-and-body less than 3 inches.
South-west Pygmy Possum (*C. concinnus*); Eyre Peninsula and southern S.A.
Feathertail Glider (*Acrobates pygmaeus*); southern forests, feeds on nectar and insects.

Sugar Glider (*Petaurus breviceps*); nocturnal flying phalanger; insect, nectar, flower-eating.
Squirrel Glider (*P. norfolcensis*); similar, but larger, south-east Vic. into N.S.W.
Yellow-bellied Glider (*P. australis*); mountainous areas, eucalypt forests.
Greater Glider (*Schoinobates volans*); large, in mountainous eucalypt forests.
Leadbetter's Possum (*Gymnobelideus leadbeateri*); rare, in wet sclerophyll forest, southern Vic.
Brushtail Possum (*Trichosaurus vulpeca*); nocturnal; widespread and common, arboreal.
Ring-tailed Possum (*Pseudocheirus peregrinus*); forests, in hollows, or nest of leaves.
Tasmanian Ringtail (*P. convolutor*); similar, but back of ear all white.
Eastern Victorian Ringtail (*P. victoriae*); differs in that forelimbs are not rufous.
Koala (*Phascolarctos cinereus*); now rare in southern parts, extinct in S.A. but introduced to Kangaroo I.
Potoroo (*Potorous tridactylus*); forests of Cape Otway, Portland and Tas.
Tasmanian Rat-kangaroo (*Bettongia cuniculus*); plains, stony ridges.
Brush-tailed Rock-wallaby (*Petrogale penicillata*); mountainous sclerophyll forest.
Yellow-footed Rock-wallaby (*P. xanthopus*); Flinders and Gawler ranges, S.A.
Tasmanian Pademelon (*Thylogale billardieri*); once also in S.A. and Vic.
Toolach Wallaby (*Wallabia greyi*); possibly extinct, formerly southern S.A.
Red-necked Wallaby (*W. rufogrisea*); forests of southern Vic. and into N.S.W.
Euro or Hill Kangaroo (*Macropus robustus*); inland S.A., and east coastal ranges.
Grey Kangaroo (*Macropus major*); forests and woodlands of the south, and Tas.
Red Kangaroo (*M. rufa*); grasslands and shrub steppes of northern Vic., and S.A.
Mitchell's Hopping-Mouse (*Notomys mitchelli*); a rodent, nocturnal; inland plains.
Grey's Rat (*Rattus greyi*); nocturnal; forests, hiding beneath logs and boulders.

For the *Australia's National Parks* assignment two cameras were used exclusively—a German-made Plaubel Peco monorail, and a Japanese Zenza Bronica.

The Plaubel has been my favourite instrument since 1960; the Bronica was purchased in 1967 as a second camera for this project. These cameras are of two basically different types—the Plaubel is of the old-fashioned studio-camera pattern, with long bellows, swing and tilt movements, but must always be used on a tripod, and its upside-down image must be focussed and composed beneath a dark-cloth before the film holder is attached.

Nevertheless, it can produce photographs impossible for the quick, easy-to-use cameras of more modern type—such as my Bronica.

The Zenza Bronica is a 2¼ square single-lens reflex of the most modern design. It can be used quickly, without a tripod if need be, to capture a moving subject or if time is critically short; its Nikkor lens certainly gives results equal to any other I have used. By means of some home-made contrivances (including some Araldite glue) it is possible for me to use the Bronica camera body attached to the Plaubel monorail camera in place of the latter's film

holder. In this way I have been able to utilize all the Schneider lenses of the Plaubel, especially the 400 mm. lens, with the Bronica, bringing the whole massive assembly to bear upon Brolgas, Wallabies and distant mountain peaks as the opportunity arises.

One colour film has been used almost exclusively for this book, namely Agfacolor CT18, which not only gives an attractive colour rendering by daylight, but also holds its colours faithfully when used with high-speed electronic flash for flight photos of birds.

The photography of Australia's national parks required two years. First visited were the parks of south-western Australia, which I already knew quite well. In September–October, 1967 a journey was made from Perth to the Kimberleys (Geikie Gorge and Windjana) and to the Hamersley Range—altogether about four thousand miles.

April 1968 saw the beginning of the main long tour, to photograph the national parks of South Australia (April–May), North Queensland (June), the 'top end' of the Northern Territory (July–August), Central Australia (August–September), again through north Queensland (September), Southern Queensland (October), New South Wales (November–January), Victoria (February), Tasmania (February), and back to Victorian parks (March–April, 1969). The total distance, 34,000 miles.

This tour of Australia's national parks was done with a Holden HR panel van, complete with a large and well-loaded roof-rack, extra fuel and water drums, and towing a 15-foot Franklin caravan. As the total weight of vehicle, caravan and contents, extra fuel and water was probably not far short of three tons, and the roads of the Nullarbor the far north and the centre often rough, the trouble-free performance of both vehicle and caravan spoke well of their construction.

At a few national parks, where tracks were impassable for conventional vehicles (e.g. 'The Loop' at Kalbarri, and road to Palm Valley) I was able to ride in with the ranger, or borrow or hire a Landrover. Except for these very few occasions where park access is not yet developed (usually 'new' parks) this long look at Australian national parks was done with a vehicle similar to that used by the average tourist; the park landscapes shown here are not beyond his reach.

N. To Wildlife Sanctuaries July/August 1968
Katherine Gorge August 1968.
Chillagoe Caves, May '68
Crater Lakes, May & Sept. 68
Green Island. May 68.
Bellenden-Ker, May '68.
Windjana Gorge 1967
Geikie Gorge Oct. 1967
Brooking Gorge Oct. 1967
Palmerston May '68
Wallaman Falls May '68
Hamersley Range Oct. 1967
Conway May '68
North-west Cape May 1964
Ormiston Gorge Sept. '68.
Devil's Marbles August 1968
Trephina Gorge Sept. '68
Glen Helen Sept. 68
Noosa May '68
Carnarvon Gorge Oct. '68
Glasshouse Mountain May '68.
Palm Valley Sept. 68
Emily & Jessie Gaps Sept. 1968
Ooraminna Sept '68
Bunya Mountain Oct '68
Kalbarri May and August 1967
Aye's Rock & Mt. Olga. Sept. '68.
King's Canyon Sept. 68
Wilpena April '68
Lamington Oct '68.
Gibraltar Range Oct/Dec. '68
Alligator Gorge April '68.
Wybarba May & Oct. '68
Dorrigo Nov '68
New England. Nov '68
Warrumbungle Nov '68.
Bristane Waters Dec '68
Kuringai Chase Dec '68
Dryandra. April 1967
Blue Mountains Dec. 68.
Royal National May 68.
Nornalup Dec '67.
Mt Manypeaks Dec. '67.
Kosiusco Jan '69
Stirlings Dec '67
Belair April '67
Porongorups. Dec '67.
Tasmania Feb–Mar 69

cludes addresses for further information on parks and sanctuaries.

ENERAL, NATIONAL PARKS, AND CONSERVATION OF NATURAL RESOURCES

arrington, R., *Great National Parks of the World*. London, Weidenfeld and Nicholson, 1967.
avenor, S., and Whitlock, D. (Eds.), *Practical Problems of National Parks*. Proceedings of
  a Seminar at the University of New England, 1966; Armidale (N.S.W.), Department
  of University Extension, 1966.
.S.I.R.O., in association with Melbourne University Press, *The Australian Environment*
  (3rd Ed.) Cambridge University Press, 1960.
itter, R., *Vanishing Wild Animals of the World*. London, Midland Bank, in association
  with Kaye and Ward, N.D.
reenway, J. C., *Extinct and Vanishing Birds of the World*. New York, American Committee
  for International Wildlife Protection, 1958.
Marshall, A. J., *The Great Extermination*. Melbourne, Heinemann, 1966; London,
  Panther, (paperback ed.) 1968.
osley, J. G., *National Parks and Equivalent Reserves in Australia*. Canberra, Australian
  Conservation Foundation, 1968.
ational Geographic Society, *America's Wonderlands, The National Parks*. Washington,
  National Geographic Society, 1966.
orter, E., *The Place No One Knew: Glen Canyon on the Colorado*. New Jersey, Sierra Club,
  Totowa, N.D.
orter, E., *In Wilderness is the Preservation of the World*. New Jersey, Sierra Club, N.D.
dall, S. L., *The Quiet Crisis*. New York, Holt, Rinehart and Winston, 1963.

USTRALIA: NATURAL SCIENCES, NATIVE PEOPLES, TRAVEL

erndt, R. M., *Australian Aboriginal Art*. Sydney, Ure Smith, 1964.
lakely, W. F., *A Key to the Eucalypts*. Canberra, Forestry and Timber Bureau, 1955.
lomberry, A. M., *A Guide to Australian Native Plants*. Sydney, Angus and Robertson, 1967.
reeden, S., and Slater, P., *Birds of Australia*. Sydney, Angus and Robertson, 1968.
ayley, N. W., *What Bird is That?* Sydney, Angus and Robertson, 1960.
ogger, H., *Australian Reptiles in Colour*. Sydney, Reed, 1967.
kin, A. P., *The Australian Aborigines*. Sydney, Angus and Robertson, 1954.
rith, H. J., *The Mallee Fowl*. Sydney, Angus and Robertson, 1962.
rith, H. J., *Waterfowl in Australia*. Sydney, Angus and Robertson, 1921.
arris, T. Y., *Wild Flowers of Australia*. Sydney, Angus and Robertson, 1962.
ill, R., *Australian Birds*. Melbourne, Nelson, 1967.
acaranda Pocket Guides, Brisbane, Jacaranda Press.
  Keast, Allen, *Bush Birds*, 1960.
  Marlow, Basil, *Marsupials of Australia*, 1965.
  McMichael, D. F., *Shells of the Australian Sea Shore*, 1962.
  McPhee, D. R., *Snakes and Lizards of Australia*, 1963.
  Oakman, H., *Some Trees of Australia*, 1965.
  Riek, Edgar, *Insects of Australia*, 1963.
  Whitley, Gilbert, *Marine Fishes of Australia*. (2 vols), 1966.
  Whitley, Gilbert, *Native Freshwater Fishes of Australia*, 1964.
east, A., *Australia and the Pacific Islands*. London, Hamish Hamilton, and New York,
  Random House, 1966.
east, A., Crocker, R. L., and Christian, C. S. (Eds), *Biogeography and Ecology in
  Australia*. Uitgeverig Dr W. Junk, 1959.
inghorn, J. R., *The Snakes of Australia*. Sydney, Angus and Robertson, 1964.
aseron, C., *Ancient Australia*. Sydney, Angus and Robertson, 1969.
fe Nature Library, *The Land and Wildlife of Australia*. New York, Time-Life Inc., N.D.
arshall, A. J., *Bower Birds*. New York, Oxford University Press Inc., 1954.
cCarthy, F. D., *Australian Aboriginal Rock Art*. Sydney, Australian Museum, 1967.
orcombe, M. K., *Wild Australia*. Melbourne, Lansdowne, 1966.
eriwinkle Books, Melbourne, Cheshire-Lansdowne.
  Child, J., *Australian Rocks and Minerals*, 1968.
  Child, J., *Australian Insects*, 1968.
  Child, J., *Australian Spiders*, 1968.
  Child, J., *Australian Seashore Life*, 1968.
  Millett, M., *Australian Eucalypts*, 1969.
  Davey, K., *Australian Desert Life*, 1969.
zzey, G., *Animals and Birds in Australia*. Melbourne, Cassell, 1966.
erventy, V., *A Continent in Danger*. London, Andre Deutsch, 1966.
llyard, R. S., *The Insects of Australia and New Zealand*. Sydney, Angus and Robertson,
  1926.
ndale, N. B., and Lindsay, H. A., *Aboriginal Australians*. Brisbane, Jacaranda, 1963.
roughton, E., *Furred Animals of Australia*. Sydney, Angus and Robertson, 9th Ed., 1967.
hite, O., *Guide to Australia*. Melbourne, Heinemann, 1968.

NATIONAL PARKS OF QUEENSLAND

reeden, S., and K., *Animals of Eastern Australia*, 1967.
illett, K., *The Australian Great Barrier Reef*. Sydney, Reed, 1968.
illett, K., and McNeill, F., *The Great Barrier Reef and Adjacent Isles*. Sydney,
  Coral Press, 1959.
room, A., *One Mountain after Another*. Sydney, Angus and Robertson, 1949.
  (For Lamington National Park.)
ippingdale, O. H., and McMichael, D. F., *Queensland and Great Barrier Reef Shells*.
  Brisbane, Jacaranda Press.
 Reilly, B., *Green Mountains*. Smith and Paterson, 1958. (For Lamington National Park.)
arth-Johnson, V., *Wildflowers of the Warm East Coast*. Brisbane, Jacaranda Press, 1967.
ate Public Relations Bureau, *The National Parks of Queensland*. Brisbane, Premier's
  Department, 1964.

To obtain pamphlets, maps, tourist and other information regarding Queensland National
Parks write to:
  1. The Secretary, Dept. of Forestry, 388-400 Ann St., Brisbane, Qld. 4000
  2. The National Parks Association of Queensland, c/- Box 1752 G.P.O. Brisbane, Qld. 4001
  3. The Wildlife Preservation Society of Queensland, c/- Box 2030 G.P.O. Brisbane, Qld. 4001
  4. Queensland Government Tourist Bureau, Anzac Square, Brisbane, Qld. 4000,
     and in other state capital cities.

NATIONAL PARKS OF NEW SOUTH WALES

Geehi Club, *Snowy Mountains Walks*. Cooma (N.S.W.), The Geehi Club.
  (For Kosciusko National Park.)
Periwinkle Books, Melbourne, Cheshire-Lansdowne.
  Child, J., *Trees of the Sydney Region*, 1968.
  Child, J., *Wildflowers of the Sydney Region*, 1968.
  Child, J., *Australian Alpine Life*, 1969.
Scarth-Johnson, Vera, *Wildflowers of New South Wales*. Brisbane, Jacaranda Press, 1968.
Thomas, M. (Ed.), *New England Tablelands: Walking, Caving, Climbing*. Armidale (N.S.W.),
  University of New England Mountaineering Club.

To obtain pamphlets, maps, tourist and other information regarding the national parks
and fauna reserves of New South Wales write to:
  1. The Director, National Parks and Wildlife Service, A.D.C. Bldg.,
     189-193 Kent St., Sydney, N.S.W. 2000
  2. New South Wales Govt. Tourist Bureau, Challis House, 8-10 Martin Place,
     Sydney, N.S.W. 2000, also in Melbourne and Brisbane.
  3. The National Parks Association of New South Wales, Hon. Sec., P.O. Box 94,
     Sutherland, N.S.W. 2232.

NATIONAL PARKS OF VICTORIA

Cochrane, G. R., Fuhrer, B. A., Rotherham, E. R., Willis, J. H., *Flowers and Plants of
  Victoria*. Sydney, A. H. and A. W. Reed, 1968.
Downes, M. C., and Watson, I., *Australian Waterfowl*. Melbourne, Fisheries and
  Wildlife Dept., 1960.
Galbraith, J., *Wildflowers of Victoria*. Croydon, Longmans, 1967.
Hill, R., *The Corner: A Naturalist's Journey Through Victoria*. Melbourne, Lansdowne, 1969.
MacKenzie, M. E., *Shipwrecks*. Melbourne, National Press, 1956. (For Port Campbell
  National Park.)
Massola, A., *Bunjil's Cave*. Myths, Legends and Superstitions of the Aborigines of South-east
  Australia. Melbourne, Lansdowne, 1968.
Smith, L. H., *The Lyrebird*. Melbourne, Lansdowne, 1968.
Wheeler, W. R., *A Handlist of the Birds of Victoria*. Melbourne, Victorian Ornithological
  Research Group, 1967.

To obtain pamphlets, maps, tourist and other information regarding Victorian parks and
wildlife sanctuaries write to:
  1. The Director, National Parks Authority, Treasury Place, Melbourne, Vic. 3002
  2. The Victorian Govt. Tourist Bureau, 272 Collins St., Melbourne, Vic. 3000,
     also in Sydney, Brisbane, Adelaide.
  3. The Fisheries and Wildlife Department, 605 Flinders St., Melbourne, Vic. 3000
  4. Victorian Forests Commission, Treasury Place, Melbourne, Vic. 3002, (forest parks
     information only).
  5. The Victorian National Parks Association, Hon. Sec. J. R. Garnet, 23 Camdon St.,
     Pascoe Vale, Vic. 3044

NATIONAL PARKS OF SOUTH AUSTRALIA

Black, J. M., *The Flora of South Australia*, 1957.
Bonython, C. W., and Daily, B., *National Parks and Reserves in S.A.* Adelaide,
  Royal Geographical Society of Australasia, S.A. Branch.
Condon, H. T., *A Handlist of the Birds of S.A.* Adelaide, South Australian Museum, 1968.
Jones, F. Wood, *The Mammals of South Australia* (3 vols). Adelaide, Govt. Printer, 1923-25.

To obtain pamphlets, maps, tourist and other information regarding the national parks,
national pleasure resorts and wildlife sanctuaries of South Australia write to:
  1. The Director, National Parks Commission, Belair National Park,
     Box 2, Belair P.O., S.A. 5052
  2. South Australian Govt. Tourist Bureau, 18 King William St., Adelaide, S.A. 5001

NATIONAL PARKS OF WESTERN AUSTRALIA

Blackall, W. E., and Grieve, B. J., *How to Know Western Australian Wildflowers* (4 vols).
  Nedlands (W.A.), University of W.A. Press, 1965.
Crawford, I. M., *The Art of the Wandjina*. Melbourne, Oxford University Press, 1968.
  (For national parks of the Kimberleys.)
Erikson, R., *Orchids of the West*. Perth, Patterson and Brokensha, 1951.
Gardner, C. A., *Wildflowers of Western Australia*. Perth, W.A. Newspapers, 1959.
Idriess, I., *Outlaws of the Leopolds*. Sydney, Angus and Robertson, 1952.
  (For story of Aboriginal uprising, Windjana Gorge.)
Main, B., *Between Wodjil and Tor*. Perth, Landfall Press, 1968.
Morcombe, M. K., *Australia's Western Wildflowers*. Perth, Landfall Press, 1968.

Serventy, D. L., and Whittell, H. M., *A Handbook of the Birds of Western Australia.* Perth, Patterson and Brokensha, 1962.

Standing Committee on Conservation, the Royal Society of W.A., *National Parks and Nature Reserves in W.A.* Perth, National Parks Board.

Uren, M., *Sailormen's Ghosts.* Melbourne, Robertson and Mullens, 1940. (For Abrolhos Islands, Kalbarri areas.)

To obtain pamphlets, maps, tourist and other information regarding the national parks, fauna and flora reserves of Western Australia write to:
1. The Managing Secretary, National Parks Board of Western Australia, 664a Murray St., Perth, W.A. 6000
2. Western Australian Govt. Tourist Bureau, 772 Hay St., Perth, W.A. 6000, and in other state capital cities.
3. Dept. of Fisheries and Fauna, 108 Adelaide Tce., Perth, W.A. 6000

NATIONAL PARKS OF TASMANIA

Boss-Walker, I., *Peaks and High Places: Cradle Mountain–Lake St Clair National Park.* Hobart, Scenery Preservation Board, 1964.

Dept. of Lands and Survey, *Atlas of Tasmania.* Hobart, 1963.

Fish, G. J., and Yaxley, M. L., *Behind the Scenery: the Geological Background to Tasmanian Landforms.* Hobart, Tasmanian Education Dept., 1966.

Gilham, M., *Sub-Antarctic Sanctuary.* Sydney, Reed, N.D. (For Macquarie Island.)

Sharland, M. S., *Tasmanian Wildlife.* Cambridge University Press, 1962.

Sharland, M. S., *Tasmanian Birds, How to Identify Them.* Hobart, Oldham, Beddome and Meredith, 1958.

Skemp, J. R., *Tasmania.* London, Macmillan, 1958.

To obtain pamphlets, maps, tourist and other information regarding the national parks and reserves of Tasmania write to:
1. Tasmanian Govt. Tourist Bureau, Cnr. Macquarie and Murray Sts., Hobart, Tas. 7000, also in Melbourne, Sydney, Adelaide, Brisbane.
2. The Animals and Birds Protection Board, 127 Bathurst St., Hobart, Tas. 7000

RESERVES OF AUSTRALIAN CAPITAL TERRITORY

To obtain pamphlets, maps, tourist and other information write to:
1. The Department of the Interior, Canberra, A.C.T.
2. The Manager, Tidbinbilla Fauna and Flora Reserve, A.C.T.
3. The National Parks Associaton of Australian Capital Territory, Hon. Sec., P.O. Box 457, Canberra City, A.C.T. 2601

NATIONAL PARKS AND SANCTUARIES OF THE NORTHERN TERRITORY

Chippendale, T. M., *Wildflowers of Central Australia.* Brisbane, Jacaranda, 1968.

Elkin, A. P., and Berndt, C. and R., *Art in Arnhem Land.* Melbourne, F. W. Cheshire, 195

Finlayson, H. H., *The Red Centre.* Sydney, Angus and Robertson, 1952.

Mountford, C. P., *Brown Men and Red Sand: Wanderings in Wild Australia.* London, Phoenix House Ltd., 1951.

Smith, R., *The Red Centre.* Melbourne, Lansdowne, 1967.

Spillett, P. G., *Victoria, North Australia.* (To be published). (For the early settlement on the Cobourg Peninsula.)

Woolley, D. R., *A Layman's Guide to the Geology of Central Australia.* Published jointly the Alice Springs Tourist Promotion Committee and the N.T. Tourist Board, 1967.

To obtain pamphlets, maps, tourist and other information write to:
1. The Northern Territory Reserves Board, Gap Road, Alice Springs, N.T. 5750
2. Tourist Bureau, Darwin or Alice Springs, N.T.
3. Chief Inspector of Wildlife, Animal Industry and Agriculture, Northern Territory Administration, Darwin, N.T. 5790

AUSTRALIAN CONSERVATION FOUNDATION

Publications relating to preservation of the Australian environment and wildlife are also bei compiled by the Australian Conservatjon Foundation. The Foundation is a non-profit organization dedicated to ensuring that the Australian countryside and its natural resource will not be despoiled by the rising population and industrial pressures. It receives some financial support from the Commonwealth Government. Membership is open to all who are concerned with conservation; by becoming a member you can have the satisfaction of knowing that you are helping safeguard Australia's natural resources for present and future generations. For details write to the Director, Australian Conservation Foundation, National Science Centre, 191 Royal Parade, Parkville, Vic. 3052.

ACKNOWLEDGMENTS

During the long preparation of this book I received a great deal of valuable assistance. To all these people, and to my wife Irene who helped in very man ways, I wish to make known my sincere thanks.

Gwen and Frank Bailey (Manypeaks, W.A.); Rab Bell (Fitzroy Crossing, W.A.); Jim Bravery (Atherton, Qld.); Sue and John Brudenall (Canberra); Norm Clough (Ingham, Qld.); Mr and Mrs Curtis (Canungra, Qld.); John Davey (Armadale, W.A.); Ian Edgar (Ardross, W.A.); Neville Fenton (Dorrigo, N.S.W.); Iris and Wal Fletcher (Kemp's Creek, N.S.W.); Billie Gill (Innisfail, Qld.); Terry Gill (Hobart, Tas.); Doug Gilmour (Atherton, Qld.); Ernie Grinham (Kalbarri, W.A.); Bernie Hyland (Atherton, Qld.); Olive and Frank Jeeves (Melbourne, Vic.); Peter Judd (Gibraltar Ra., N.S.W.); Malc. Lewis (Armadale, W.A.); Rene Marks (Melbourne, Vic.); Jim Mathews (Armadale, W.A.); Betty and Wal McKenzie (Indooroopilly, Qld.); Helen and Tom Milner (Darwin, N.T.); Roly Paine (Gibraltar Ra., N.S.W.); Greg Perry (Atherton, Qld.); Dr W. D. L. Ride (W.A. Museum); Pat and Peter Slater (Innisfail, Qld.); Kev. Sparkes (Mareeba, Qld.); Peter Spillett (Darwin, N.T.); Arthur Stafford (Dorrigo, N.S.W.); Roy Stirling (Atherton, Qld.); Ann and Victor Urban (Alice Springs, N.T.); Elva and Jim Watson (Balwyn, Vic.); Keith Williams (Ipswich, Qld.).

The rangers at national parks around Australia, national parks administrators, and others who in each state have supplied the data from whic the book was compiled.

Robin Smith for photographs on pages 26, 150–1; Keith Gillett for photograph on page 119; Derrick Stone for photograph on page 154.

M.K.M